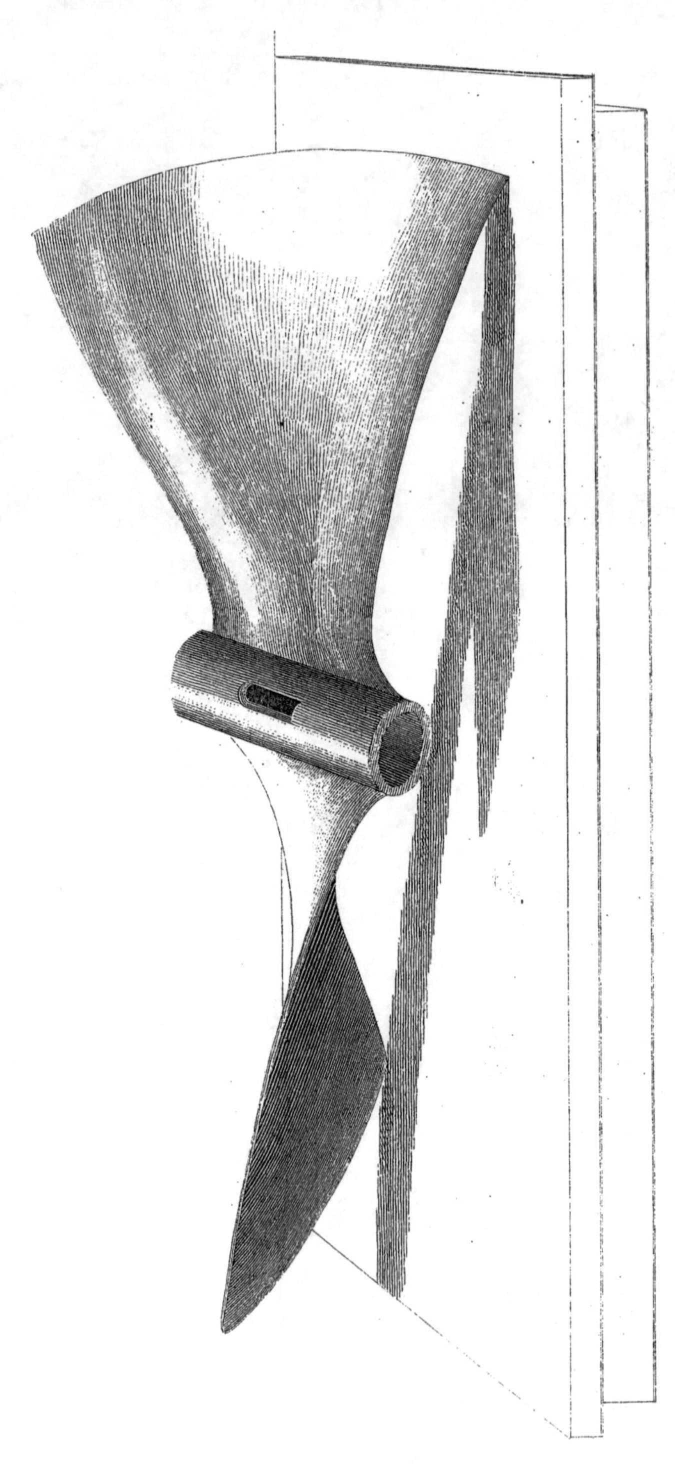

THE

MARINE STEAM-ENGINE.

BY

THOMAS J. MAIN, M.A. F.R.Ast.S.

MATHEMATICAL PROFESSOR AT THE ROYAL NAVAL COLLEGE, PORTSMOUTH

AND

THOMAS BROWN, Assoc. Inst. C.E.

CHIEF ENGINEER, R.N., ATTACHED TO THE R.N. COLLEGE.

FROM THE FOURTH LONDON EDITION.

PHILADELPHIA:

HENRY CAREY BAIRD,

INDUSTRIAL PUBLISHER,

406 WALNUT STREET.

1867.

PREFACE.

THE various publications that have appeared of late years on the Steam-engine render necessary an explanation of the reason for adding one to the list: the authors of the present work feel that they might otherwise lie open to the charge of presumption, considering the eminent talents which have been employed on the subject. The works hitherto published have, while abounding in excellences, been wanting more or less in the kind of information eagerly sought after by those intrusted with the charge of steam-vessels, and which is rarely acquired except through the medium of oral instruction. Some of them, containing little more than a description of the parts of an engine, and of their uses, are simply elementary treatises. Some are chiefly valuable to *manufacturers*, from their containing elaborate details about the dimensions and strength of rods, bars, beams, etc. Some are mainly occupied with criticisms and comparisons of the various kinds of engines or propellers in use at the present day. All are valuable to the several classes of readers to which they are addressed they contain in the aggregate nearly all that can be said on the history and purposes of the Steam-engine: but individually they fail to impart that precise and readily available knowledge which ought to be possessed by every naval officer and by every engineer.

Having experienced, while in the course of instructing others, during many years, the want of a practical work for reference, the authors have been in the habit of supplying the deficiency by manuscripts drawn up for the purpose; and having derived manifest advantage from their use, being moreover encouraged by the advice of their friends, they have been induced to publish them in a carefully arranged form with the object of facilitating thereby the labors of officers studying at the Royal Naval College, and with the hope of being, in some measure, of service to all who may be interested in acquiring steam-knowledge as applied to nautical purposes.

Existing works on steam are generally deficient in maxims for the management of engines in the various circumstances of difficulty and doubt in which steam-vessels, whether of the Navy or the merchant-service, may be placed. These, however, are the ends for which practical men read such works. When at sea they are necessarily thrown on their own resources in every emergency, and therefore a sound rule, framed by experience and previous reflection, is of more value than a scientific investigation. It can matter but little, practically speaking, to the captain or engineers of a steamer, whether side-lever or direct-acting, oscillating or trunk engines are preferable, or whether the paddle or screw have the advantage as an instrument of propulsion: but it does matter very seriously to them, that they should be capable of tracing the imperfect working of an engine to its right cause, and be able to remedy any defect; that they should be skilled in the modes of economizing fuel, on which the efficiency of a steam-vessel mainly depends; and that they should, by a due knowledge of the skilful management of engines, and of the relation of their parts to each other, be able to diminish the inconvenience of a gale of wind, and be prepared against accidents. Impressed with this view, the authors have endeavored to give a practical tendency to their work throughout, without, however, neglecting the considerations which are due to science. While the reader who has not had the advantage of a mathematical education will be able to peruse the work as far as the Miscellaneous Chapter without meeting with an obstacle to its full comprehension, the scientific reader will find in notes, and at the end of the work, the investigations of the rules.

While the authors hope that the work now offered to the public is a step in the right direction, they are conscious of its many deficiencies, arising from its having been compiled in the midst of other business which did not admit of delay. Many of the rules also must be considered as empirical, especially those relating to an action, and are the result of reflection rather than of experience.

NOTE TO THE AMERICAN EDITION.

THE authors having made such extensive revisions and improvements in the present, or fourth edition of "THE MARINE ENGINE," it is deemed important to give the following information for the guidance of those who have purchased their "QUESTIONS ON SUBJECTS CONNECTED WITH THE MARINE STEAM-ENGINE." In the last named volume constant references are made to articles and pages of the present volume. Those references however are to the third edition. The accompanying table gives in one column the numbers of these articles and pages in the third edition, and in another column those in the fourth or present edition. By reference to this table the number of any such article or page as now printed can be had at a glance.

TABLE OF ARTICLES AND PAGES.

	Third Edition.	Fourth Edition.		Third Edition.	Fourth Edition.		Third Edition	Fourth Edition.
Art.	30	36	Art.	129	145	Art.	244	223
"	31	37	"	134	151	"	250	229
"	72	98	"	135	152	"	251	230
"	74	99	"	136	153	"	253	232
"	75	out	"	141	156	"	254	234
"	76	"	"	142	157	"	257	237
"	77	"	"	145	160	"	259	239
"	78	100	"	153	165	"	264	244
"	79	101	"	157	167	"	265	245
"	80	102	"	158	168	"	268	249
"	81	103	"	161	171	"	278	259
"	87	out	"	170	182	"	284	265
"	89	106	"	173	185	"	303	283
"	90	107	"	177	189	"	304	284
"	91	108	"	180	190	"	307	287
"	92	109	"	182	64	"	308	288
"	96	113	"	183	65	"	309	289
"	97	114	"	184	66	"	317	297
"	98	115	"	189	74	"	331	310
"	101	out	"	190	75	"	338	316
"	102	117	"	191	76	"	339	317
"	106	121	"	198	81	"	341	319
"	108	125	"	206	88	"	342	320
"	109	126	"	207	88	"	343	321
"	110	127	"	209	89	"	347	325
"	111	128	"	217	196	"	362	340
"	113	130	"	220	199	"	364	342
"	114	131	"	224	203			
"	115	132	"	228	207	page	298	282
"	119	136	"	230	209	"	300	284
"	121	138	"	231	210	"	304	287
"	124	140	"	237	216	"	307	290
"	126	142	"	240	219	"	309	292

PLATE I.

REFERENCES.

A^1 A^2 Interior of Cylinder.
B B Cylinder-jacket.
C Expansion-valve.
D Interior of Slide-casing.
E E E Slide-casing.
F F Upper and Lower Steam-ports.
G G G Condenser.
H H H H Piston.
I I Piston-rod.
K Foot-valve.
L L Air-pump.
M M Air-pump Bucket.
N N Butterfly-valves.
O Hot Well.
P Air-cone.
Q Delivery-valve
R R Stuffing-box of Cylinder.
S S Stuffing-box Cover.
T T Metallic-Ring (or Packing).
Z Lower Escape-valve.
a Steam-pipe opening into the Jacket.
d Slide-rod.

PLATE II.

REFERENCES.

B B Cylinder.
E E E Slide-casing.
I Piston-rod.
R R Stuffing-box.
S S S Stuffing-box Gland (or Cover).
U U Cylinder Cross-head.
X X Cylinder Side-rods.
Z Lower Escape-valve.
Z^1 Z^2 Side-levers.
1 1 Weigh-shaft, or Bar.
2 Gab-lever.
3 3 Valve-lifter.
4 4 Back-balance.
5 5 D-Slide Cross-head.
6 D-Slide-rod.
g g Fork-head.
p Main Centre.
q q Paddle-shafts.
r r Cranks.
s Connecting-rod.
t t Connecting-rod Brasses.
v v Air-pump Cross-head.
y y Air-pump Side-rods.

CONTENTS.

INTRODUCTORY CHAPTER.

CHAPTER II.

THE BOILER.

CHAPTER III.

THE ENGINE.

CHAPTER IV.

CHAPTER V.

GETTING UP THE STEAM.

CHAPTER VI.

DUTIES TO MACHINERY WHEN UNDER STEAM.

CHAPTER VII.

DUTIES TO MACHINERY DURING AN ACTION, OR AFTER AN ACCIDENT.

CHAPTER VIII.

DUTIES TO ENGINE, ETC., ON ARRIVING IN HARBOR.

CHAPTER IX.

MISCELLANEOUS.

APPENDIX.

MARINE STEAM-ENGINE.

INTRODUCTORY CHAPTER.

1. *Steam.*

STEAM is an elastic fluid generated from water by the application of heat.

2. *Water.*

Water is not a simple substance, but has been discovered to be the result of the chemical union of two gases —oxygen and hydrogen. The experimental chemist proves this in various ways; his most usual method being to take water and separate it into its two components by means of the galvanic battery; or, to take the two gases, mixed together in their proper proportions, and by sending an electric spark through the mixture, he then finds the vessel which formerly contained the gases to be filled with steam, which condenses into water on the inside of the vessel. The gases are in their proper proportions when the volume of hydrogen is double that of oxygen.

3. *Caloric.*

Heat is only known to us by its effects. Theories have been proposed to account for the various phenomena; but as we are concerned only with the effects, it is not our object to enter into them in the present treatise. It will be sufficient for us to state, that the cause of heat, whatever it may be, is called Caloric.

4. *Temperature.*

Temperature is a measure of the intensity of heat in any substance.

5. *Heat and Cold.*

The terms Heat and Cold represent, as is well known, opposite states of any substance as far as regards temperature. It is universally admitted that cold merely expresses the absence of heat.

6. *General Effects of Heat.*

Heat acting on any material substance produces one or more of the following effects, viz.:

Expansion.
Liquefaction (of solids).
Vaporization (of liquids).

And, on the contrary, if heat be abstracted from a substance, it is attended with one or more of the following phenomena:

Contraction.
Solidification (of liquids).
Liquefaction (of gases.)

7. *Expansion.*

As we have just stated, if heat be applied to a body, it is found, as a general law, that it will expand, and that it will contract in cooling; but the rate at which a body or substance expands or contracts depends on its nature; gases universally expand more than fluids, and fluids more than solids.

8. *Expansion of Gases.*

All gases expand at the same rate; thus if the amount by which a given volume of hydrogen gas expands for a given increase of temperature be ascertained, this will also give us the amount by which the same volume of dry steam expands for the same increase of temperature. Another fact has been ascertained, viz., that the gases expand at the same rate at high and at low temperatures. But this is not the case with liquids or solids; for each solid or liquid has its own rate cf expansion, and they all expand more sensibly at a high than at a low temperature (see Table of Dilatations, (C) in the Appendix).

9. *Practical Methods of observing the Expansion of Bodies.*

Let a bar of iron, which exactly fits a metal guage when cold, be heated; and while in that state, let an attempt be made to introduce it again; it will now be found to be too large, from having expanded.

To make the expansion of *liquids* visible, let a glass bulb connected with a fine upright tube be filled with the fluid to be experimented on, and heated; then as the fluid in the bulb becomes hot it will expand, and be partly forced up the tube, along which its motion will become sensible, from the fineness of the bore compared with the bulb.

The effect of heat in expanding *gases* may be observed by partially filling a bladder with air, and then, after having closed it, immersing it in hot water for some minutes. The heat, penetrating the bladder, and acting on the gas, will cause it to make the bladder appear full.

The *difference* in the rates of expansion of two metals may be shown by uniting together two thin strips of different metals, such as copper and steel; then, on the application of heat, since copper expands more than steel, it will be found that the strip will have assumed a curved form, having the copper on the outside and the steel on the inside.

10. *Applications of this Principle.*

It may become applicable in all those cases where metallic substances are required to secure materials together; if they be put on hot, they will contract by cooling, and form a closer union than could be easily effected by manual labor. To this end the wheelwright and mast-maker put on their tires and hoops red-hot; the cranks of the shaft of a steam-engine are put on the shaft while hot, and allowed to contract. Boiler-plates are riveted with red-hot rivets, which, by contracting in length on cooling, bring the two plates of iron closely together.

The unequal expansion of different metals becomes a very useful property at times. As an instance, we may mention the nuts and screws of steam-engines. If they be made entirely of iron, the joint will be equally loose, whether the engine is hot or cold; but if the screw be made of iron, and the nut of brass, the distance between the nut and the head of the screw will be less at a high than at a low temperature. This is particularly observable if the piston be secured to the rod by a brass nut. The difference in the rate of expansion of different metals is likewise applied to the compensation-pendulums of clocks and balance-wheels of chronometers, rods for measuring the base-line in trigonometrical surveys, etc. In many cases, also, accidents would occur if attention were not paid to the expansion of metals: thus in laying pipes for conveying steam or hot water, care is necessary that they do not abut against the walls of the building. Again, pipes for conveying gas or water underground are fitted with expansion joints, that the extremities of the pipes may have a little play throughout the length. The same must also be provided for in large iron constructions, such as iron bridges, sheds, etc. Southwark Bridge is said to rise an inch at the crown in summer; and it has been asserted, that the heat of the sun during a summer's day produces more effect in deflecting the tubular bridge over the Menai Straits than the heaviest train would accomplish. If the iron dampers of chimneys be made flat, and become very hot, they will crack; but if they be curved this will not take place. If hot water be suddenly poured into a thick glass vessel it is apt to split, because the inner part expands before the outer surface is affected. We shall hereafter see how this applies to the fire-bars of steam-boilers.*

11. *The Law of Expansion by Heat not universally true.*

The law of expansion by heat is true, with the following exception: namely, that as hot water cools down from the boiling-point, it contracts till at 40° Fahrenheit; but if it be cooled *below* this point, it begins to expand again; and if it be kept perfectly still, it may be cooled even as much as 20° *below the freezing-point* in a *liquid* state, and the expansion will still proceed. It has also been supposed that clay contracts by heat; but some are of opinion that the contraction of the whole mass arises from the particles coming into closer contact and lessening the air-spaces: moreover it does not again expand when heated a second time.

12. *A beneficial Result arising from the foregoing Anomaly.*

Since 40° is the temperature of maximum density for water, this is approximately the temperature at very great depths, whatever be the *climate* at the surface, because if it were hotter or colder than this it would rise. Therefore, since the ice and the coldest water are lying on the surface in winter-time, they are quickly acted on by the returning heat of the sun, and the equilibrium of temperature is restored; on the other hand, if the general law were not violated, there would be an accumulation of ice every year at the bottom of rivers, etc., which would be unaffected by the summer sun; and after a long interval, it is easy to imagine that the most disastrous consequences would

---

* Sudden contraction will also produce the same effect as sudden expansion. Thus glass plates and dishes are at times broken by putting ices in them.

ensue. See Whewell's *Bridgewater Treatise.* This anomaly, however, is only discoverable in fresh water: for, according to Marcet, sea-water gradually increases in density with the diminution of temperature.

13. *To prove that the general Law of Expansion fails in the foregoing Instance.*

Let two thermometers be made, one containing water and the other containing mercury; they will show the same temperature till they descend to 40°; but if the room in which they are kept cools below 40°, the mercury thermometer will still show the true state of the room; but the one filled with water will *seem,* by its expanding, to exhibit a higher temperature, thereby proving that the water has increased in bulk. Hence it is clear, apart from all other considerations, that water could not be used instead of mercury for a thermometer.

14. *To ascertain the Temperature of any Substance.*

The temperature of very hot bodies is found by an instrument called the Pyrometer, and that of others whose temperature is above the freezing-point of mercury by the mercurial thermometer; while the temperature of very cold substances is ascertained by the alcohol thermometer. The latter instrument is a thermometer filled with alcohol instead of mercury, because alcohol is a substance that has never been solidified by cold.

15. *The Pyrometer.*

The most perfect pyrometer is that invented by Daniell. Its action depends on the difference of expansion by heat between a platinum bar and a tube of well-baked black-lead ware, neither of these being liable to become fused by great heat. The metallic bar is shorter than the tube; and a short plug of earthenware is placed in the mouth of the tube above the platinum bar. It is secured in its place by a small wedge; so that it moves with difficulty when heated, and remains in its new position after the cooling (and consequent contraction) of the metallic bar. The expansion of the platinum bar thus obtained is measured by adapting to the instrument an index, which traverses a circular arc. The degrees marked on this scale are compared with those of the mercurial scale, and the ratio of the two marked, so that its degrees are convertible into those of Fahrenheit.

16. *The Mercurial Thermometer.*

This thermometer consists of a fine glass tube, having a bulb at one extremity filled with mercury, taking care that the tube be of perfectly uniform bore throughout the space traversed by the metal: the bulb is very thin, that the sensitiveness of the instrument may be the greater. It is filled with mercury in the following manner: The end of the tube opposite the bulb being open, the bulb is held over the flame of a spirit-lamp until the air inside is heated and rarefied; the open end is then inverted, and immersed in a cup of mercury that has been previously boiled to deprive it of its air-bubbles. As the air contained in the instrument cools down, it contracts, and the pressure of the atmosphere on the surface of the cup forces the mercury up the tube, and partly fills the bulb. Let now the instrument be placed upright, with the bulb downwards, having a paper funnel tied round the open end of the tube, into which pour some mercury, and let the bulb of the instrument be held again over the lamp; the mercury will boil after a time, and as it rises will carry up with it the small quantity of air remaining in the bulb. As it cools down again, the mercury in the funnel will fill the instrument; and when it has cooled down to the highest temperature it is intended the instrument shall range to, the end must be closed by passing the flame of a blow-pipe over it, which process is termed hermetically sealing it; and the only remaining process is to graduate the tube.

17. *Method of graduating Thermometers.*

It was discovered by Newton that melting snow has invariably the same temperature. If, therefore, the thermometer be plunged in melting snow, and a mark be made on it where the mercury stands, this will be one fixed point for all instruments, and is called the *Freezing-point.* Again, distilled water boils, under *a given atmospheric pressure,* at a certain temperature; let, therefore, the instrument be placed in boiling water when the barometer stands at 30 inches, and let the stationary point of the mercury be observed; this serves for another fixed point, common to all instruments, and is called the *Boiling-point.* The space between these two graduations is divided into a number of equal and arbitrary parts, and the instrument receives different names according to the number of the parts into which it is divided. Thus, if the space be divided into 100 equal parts, and the freezing-point be called 0°, it is called a Centigrade thermometer; if the freezing-point be called 0°, and the boiling-point 80°, it is called Reaumur's thermometer; if, again, the freezing point be called 32°, and the boiling-point 212°, giving 180 equal divisions between these points it is called Fahrenheit's, and is the one commonly used in England. The graduations, in every case, may be continued by equal divisions above the boiling and below the freezing point.*

* *To compare two differently graduated Thermometers.*

Let AD be a thermometer, having two differently graduated scales attached to it; and let A, B be the boiling and freezing points respectively. Suppose the mercury in the thermometer to be standing at some point C. For the left-hand scale, let a°, b°, and x°, be the graduations corresponding to those temperatures; and for the right-hand scale, let c°, d°, y°, be the corresponding graduations.

Now, it is clear that $$\frac{\text{space CB}}{\text{space AB}}=\frac{x^\circ-a^\circ}{b^\circ-a^\circ}$$

and $$\frac{\text{space CB}}{\text{space AB}}=\frac{y^\circ-c^\circ}{d^\circ-c^\circ}$$

$$\therefore \frac{x^\circ-a^\circ}{b^\circ-a^\circ}=\frac{y^\circ-c^\circ}{d^\circ-c^\circ}$$

18. *On the Laws of Cooling of Hot Bodies.*

When hot bodies cool down, the process is said to take place according to one or more of the three following laws: Conduction, Convection, and Radiation. Sometimes one and sometimes more of these are in operation; and if a

---

1. To compare Fahrenheit's and Reaumur's scales.

If the left-hand represents Fahrenheit's and the right-hand Reaumur's we shall have, writing F for x° and R for y°:

$$\frac{F-32}{212-32}=\frac{R-0}{80-0}$$

$$\therefore \quad \frac{F-32}{180}=\frac{R}{80}$$

$$\text{or,} \quad \frac{F-32}{9}=\frac{R}{4}$$

2. To compare Fahrenheit's with the Centigrade.

As before, writing C for y°, we have:

$$\frac{F-32}{212-32}=\frac{C-0}{100-0}$$

$$\text{or,} \quad \frac{F-32}{180}=\frac{C}{100}$$

$$\therefore \quad \frac{F-32}{9}=\frac{C}{5}$$

3. To compare the Centigrade with Reaumur's.

$$\text{Here we have} \quad \frac{C-0}{100-0}=\frac{R-0}{80-0}$$

$$\text{or,} \quad \frac{C}{100}=\frac{R}{80}$$

$$\text{or,} \quad \frac{C}{5}=\frac{R}{4}$$

To convert any number of Degrees in Reaumur's Thermometer to the corresponding number in Fahrenheit's.

If F be the number of degrees in Fahrenheit's scale,
and R . . . . Reaumur's scale,

$$\text{we have, as above} \quad \frac{F-32}{9}=\frac{R}{4}$$

$$\text{or,} \quad F=32+\frac{9}{4}R$$

Hence: multiply the number of degrees according to Reaumur by 9, and divide by 4, and to the result add 32; this will give the corresponding number according to Fahrenheit.

body receive more heat from those substances which surround it than it imparts to them according to these laws, it gets warmer; and, on the contrary, if it imparts more than it receives, it becomes cooler.

19. *On Conduction.*

When heat passes from particle to particle of a solid body, it is said to be *conducted;* thus, if a bar of iron be put into the fire, the heat travels from one end to the other by conduction.

To convert any number of Degrees Centigrade into the corresponding number in Fahrenheit's Scale.

Since, as before, $\frac{F-32}{9}=\frac{C}{5}$ $\therefore$ $F=32+\frac{9}{5}C$

Hence: multiply the number of degrees in the Centigrade scale by 9, and divide by 5, and to the result add 32: this will give the corresponding number according to Fahrenheit.

To convert any number of Degrees in Fahrenheit's Scale into the corresponding Degree by Reaumur.

Since $\frac{F-32}{9}=\frac{R}{4}$ $\therefore$ $R=\frac{4}{9}(F-32)$

Hence: from the number of degrees by Fahrenheit take 32, multiply the difference by 4, and divide by 9: the result is the corresponding number by Reaumur.

To convert any number of Degrees in Fahrenheit's Scale into the corresponding number by the Centigrade Scale.

Since $\frac{F-32}{9}=\frac{C}{5}$ $\therefore$ $C=\frac{5}{9}(F-32)$

Hence: from the number of degrees in Fahrenheit's scale take 32, multiply the difference by 5, and divide by 9; the result is the number in the Centigrade scale.

To convert from Reaumur's Scale to the Centigrade, and vice versâ.

Multiply the number of degrees in Reaumur's scale by 5, and divide by 4; the result is the number of degrees Centigrade.

Or, multiply the number of degrees Centigrade by 4, and divide by 5; the result is the number of degrees Reaumur.

20. *Conducting Power of Substances.*

Many bodies conduct very badly; indeed, gases, and fluids, and earthy substances, scarcely conduct at all. If heat be applied to the upper surface of water, a thermometer at the bottom of the vessel will not be affected by it. As an instance of the bad conducting property of water, we may mention that when steam is first raised in a boiler, the hand may be applied to the lower part, although the temperature of the upper portion of the water is 240° or 250°. Water in the solid state, viz., ice, appears to have the same property; for, according to Dr. Sutherland, "ice and snow conduct heat very slowly. If a piece of fresh-water ice be plunged into water after it has been exposed to a temperature of —20° or —30°, it flies to pieces, in the same way that red-hot glass does when plunged into water; and if water be poured upon ice, the same thing happens, and the crepitating sound is almost loud enough to resemble small explosions."* The non-conducting property of water must be borne in mind in the construction of steam-boilers. Metals are generally good conductors, though there is a sensible difference in their power in this respect. Thus, by Despretz's experiment, the conducting powers of some few substances will be represented by the following table:

Gold	100·	Tin	30·38
Platinum	98·1	Lead	17·96
Silver	97·3	Marble	2·34
Copper	89·82	Porcelain	1·22
Iron	37·41	Brick Earth	1·13
Zinc	36·37		

A knowledge of the difference in the conducting powers of substances is of great utility; for by these means it is possible to keep any material hot or cold, at pleasure, for a considerable time. If the source of heat be *internal*, and

---

* Dr. Sutherland's *Journal of Captain Penny's Voyage in* 1850-51, vol. i. p. 498.

we wish to keep it warm, it must be cased in some *non-*conductor, such as flannel or felt, or swan-down, or the shaggy skin of beasts, which has originally been adapted to the wants of animated beings by the Creator. On these accounts we cover our bodies with woollen clothes in winter, and cotton or linen in summer; steam-cylinders also, and boilers and steam-pipes, are frequently coated with felt or wood, because they are bad conductors. Porous substances are generally bad conductors; and this may probably be the reason a layer of snow is so effective in preserving the temperature of the ground. Earthy matter conducts so badly, that at any sensible depth below the surface of the ground the temperature is nearly uniform; and, in consequence, wine is placed in *underground* cellars. It is supposed by some that the central portion of the earth, to within about twenty miles of the surface, has a temperature greater than that of molten iron, the intense heat of which is prevented from making its escape by the non-conducting properties of the outer crust.

21. *Our Sensations serve but very imperfectly to measure the Temperature of any Substance.*

Good conductors feel hotter or colder than bad conductors of *equal* temperature, according as their temperature is above or below blood-heat, because they are more ready to give out or absorb heat; thus, if a piece of iron and a piece of wood be exposed to the influence of the atmosphere, the iron will *feel* much hotter than the wood when both are exposed to the meridian sun, while it will *appear* to be colder than the wood at midnight.

22. *On Convection.*

Liquids and gases, being bad conductors, transmit heat by convection, which process may be explained as follows: If heat be applied to the *lower* particles of a fluid mass, it will cause them to expand, and therefore their specific gravity becomes less than that of the upper strata; consequently a displacement of the particles ensues, the lighter rise to the surface and are replaced by the heavier ones, which in their turn become heated and are replaced by the others, and so by this process the heat is conveyed throughout the general mass. The same principle applies to gases.

23. *The Advantages to be derived from a Knowledge of the Law of Convection.*

In apparatus for boiling fluids, the fire should be applied as low down as possible; the surface exposed to the fire should be large, and there should be a facility for the heated particles to rise to the surface. This principle also explains the whole theory of ventilation. If we confine air in a close vessel, and apply heat to the lower strata, a continual interchange will take place; but if we make two orifices, one in the lower part of the vessel and another in the upper, the heated air will escape at the higher orifice, and its place be supplied by that which enters at the lower one, and a continual draught be produced through the vessel. Hence it follows that a tall upright shaft produces a violent current of air through a furnace. Yet there are limits to the practical application of this principle, from the cooling of the upper portion of the column, and from the friction of the air against the sides of the shaft. The wind-sails of a ship afford an instance in which the law of convection is made available for ventilation; we may also mention the casing placed round the funnel of a steam-boiler to prevent its burning the deck. There would be no advantage from this casing if the air were confined between it and the funnel; but the top is open, and the casing is pierced with holes below the deck, whereby the warm current of air from the top of the boiler and engine-room enters, and by continually ascending is dissipated in the atmosphere without becoming very hot. The fire-doors of steam-boilers would become red-hot were it not for a similar contrivance. At the back of the fire-door is a plate, separated from the former by an interval of two or three inches; and the fire-door is perforated, so that a current of air can enter between the two plates of iron, and prevent over-heating. Smoke-box doors are fitted in a similar way, the air entering round the edges of the doors.

The principle of convection enables practical men to ventilate mines and ships (especially steamers), and all places open above, which it may be desirable to keep at a tolerably low temperature, by means of partitions not reaching to the bottom. There is seldom exactly the same temperature in the two compartments; and as the heated air in the one ascends, its place will be supplied by cold air descending down the other compartment, and going under the partition where the air would otherwise be stagnant. Any one may try this by putting a light at the bottom of a tall upright jar, which will be extinguished for want of oxygen; but if the experiment be repeated after a partition has been inserted to within an inch or two of the bottom of the jar, and the light be placed a little on one side, it will burn as vigorously as ever. This principle was first introduced by Captain Priest, R. N., for the purpose of cooling the stoke-hole, and has since been adopted successfully in many instances.

24. *Explanation of some Phenomena depending on the Law of Convection.*

All the oscillations and disturbances of the atmosphere, whether regular or irregular, such as winds and tempests of all kinds, are produced by the shiftings of the atmosphere in consequence of the changes of temperature. A portion of the air, from the long-continued action of the sun in some localities, gets into motion; and as it moves in any direction, its place is supplied by that which is cooler. The laws regulating these phenomena are, from the circumstances of the case, very complicated; but they are all resolvable into this one law of convection, as the simplest assignable cause. In one instance (that of the winds) the results are sufficiently regular to form a beautiful exemplification of the law. They may be briefly explained as follows: The intense action of the sun at the equator causes a vertical ascending current in the tropical regions, and consequently there is a rush of air from the temperate zones to supply the place. If, then, the earth were stationary, it is manifest there would be a north wind blowing in the northern zone, and a south wind in the southern zone; but each portion of the earth's surface has a greater *linear* velocity as we proceed from the pole to the equator, on account of the increase in the distance between the meridians; it follows hence, that the breeze which would be north or south, not having the same motion to the eastward as the earth has, being always met by the earth in its rotation, appears to come from some point of the compass between the north and east or south and east. Hence the northeast trades in the northern, and the southeast in the southern hemisphere.

25. *On the Law of Radiation.*

By radiation a hot body gives out its heat just as a luminous body gives out its light. Although the rays of heat are not visible to the eye, they are sent out in every direction in straight lines, becoming more and more faint as the square of their distance increases; thus the effect of radiant heat is one-fourth at a double distance, one-ninth at three times the distance, and so on. From the want of economical arrangement in common fire-places, *radiant heat* is nearly all that comes into a sitting-room.

26. *To show on what the Radiating Power of Bodies depends.*

The radiating power of bodies depends principally on the nature of the surface. Those bodies whose surfaces are rough radiate most, and polished substances radiate least; also, dark substances radiate more readily than light-colored ones.* We have before stated, that if a steam-

* Recent experiments, however, seem to throw doubt on the influence exerted by color on the radiating property of bodies.

pipe or cylinder be coated with felt, it will diminish the conduction; but let us suppose a portion of the heat to have reached the outer surface of the felt, then, from its roughness, heat would readily escape by radiation. To prevent radiation, therefore, we should coat the felt with canvas, and paint it; the varnish of the paint will give a smooth outer surface, and will diminish the radiation. Meat-covers, metal tea-pots, and other articles of domestic use that are intended to retain the heat, should be well polished, to carry out more fully the object for which they were made, as well as from motives of cleanliness.

27. *On Sea and Land Breezes.*

After sunrise, the land receiving heat by radiation from the sun much faster than the water, the temperature of the land may in time equal, and afterwards exceed, that of the sea; the particles of air immediately in contact with the land, receiving heat from it, will expand and rise, whilst the cooler air over the water, rushing in to supply its place, will in turn be heated, expand, rise, and a current of cool air from the sea to the land will take place. The breeze thus produced in the early part of the day, so common in the tropics, is called the sea-breeze.

In the afternoon, the heat radiated by the sun to this part of the earth diminishes; but the temperature of the land will rise until the heat it thus receives equals that it loses by its own radiation, and that carried off by the air (by convection); and when it shall have reached its maximum temperature, from this time its temperature will begin to fall. It is evident that the time of maximum temperature of the sea will be after that of the land; and since it also loses its heat much slower in proportion, from the time the land has obtained its highest temperature, the temperature of the land and sea will rapidly approach and become equal, and at length the sea will have a higher temperature than the land, when a current of air from the land towards the sea will take place, in a similar manner to that above described. This will be in the evening, and is called the land-breeze.

28. *Capacity for Heat.*

It appears that although bodies have the same degree of temperature, yet it does not necessarily follow that they have the same amount of absolute heat; that is to say, it will require more fuel to raise the temperature of one body one degree, than it will to raise an equal *weight* of another body one degree. Thus the capacity for heat of water is much greater than that of iron; in other words, it requires much more heat to produce a given sensible effect on a mass of water than it will on a mass of iron of the same weight. The quantity of heat required to raise a given *weight* one degree is called its *Capacity for heat.*

29. *Unit of Caloric.*

Some standard of comparison must be adopted as the measure of the quantity of heat, and the quantity sufficient to raise the same *weight* of distilled water one degree is generally chosen. Thus if it take one-tenth as much fuel to raise the temperature of a pound of iron one degree as it does to raise the temperature of a pound of distilled water one degree, the capacity for heat of iron is said to be ·1.* (See Table E in Appendix).

---

* Let w be the weight of one body; t its temperature; c its capacity for heat;

w' the weight of another body; t' its temperature; c' its capacity for heat.

Then, by definition, c will raise the weight 1, one degree.

$\therefore w c$ . . . . w, one degree.

and $w c t$ . . . . w, t degrees.

$\therefore w c t$ expresses the quantity of heat in the first body.

Similarly $w'c't'$ expresses the quantity of heat in the second body.

$\therefore$ the whole quantity of heat in them, if they were mixed, would be $w c t + w'c't'$.

Let now T be the common temperature after mixture;

30. *On Latent Heat.*

Def.—Heat is said to be *latent* when its effects are **not** sensible to the hand or to the thermometer.

31. *Under what circumstances Heat becomes Latent.*

Heat becomes latent whenever a *change of state* takes place; for in such cases the heat is employed solely in producing the change, and has no effect in raising the temperature: thus when ice thaws, or when water is converted into steam, the temperature is unaltered during the progress of this change. For instance, let a piece of ice at 32° be placed in a plate in a warm room; the heat of the room enters into it, and it begins to melt; so that when nearly all is melted, it must contain more heat than it did at first; but until all the ice has disappeared the temperature will be found to be only 32°, exactly what it had before. Again, when water has been raised to the boiling-point (212°), it requires about five times as much heat to convert the boiling water into steam as it did to raise it from the freezing temperature to the boiling; the latent heat of steam is, therefore, about 1000°.

On the other hand, if a vapor be converted into a liquid, or a liquid into a solid, the latent heat becomes again sensible; thus it will require very much more cold water to condense a given *weight* of steam at the temperature 212° into water at temperature 100°, than it will to cool down the same weight of boiling water, of like temperature, to 100°.

This latter statement is of importance in condensing

$\therefore w\,c\,T + w'c'\,T$ also expresses the amount of heat in the mixture.

Hence $\quad w\,c\,t + w'c't' = w\,c\,T + w'c'\,T.$

Cor.—If different weights of the same substance are mixed, $c' = c$; and the formula becomes,

$$w\,c\,t + w'c\,t' = w\,c\,T + w'c\,T$$

or, $$w\,t + w't' = w\,T + w\,T.$$

engines, and accounts for the great quantity of water requisite to condense the steam.*

32. *Heat is the sole Agent in the Liquefaction and Vaporization of Bodies.*

We can easily convince ourselves that heat is necessary to liquefy and vaporize bodies; for we may take a lump of ice and pound it till it be reduced to dust, yet, unless heat be applied, it will never be liquefied; we may, therefore, regard solids, liquids, and gases as substances differing from each other only in this, that the one contains heat sufficient to preserve it in the fluid or gaseous state, which the other does not possess. It is true that many bodies have never been found in more than one state, and no means have been devised to make them alter that state; but yet again many, which till within the last few years were considered as permanently fixed, have been made to take up the three different grades. As an example, we may mention carbonic-acid gas, which has lately been made to assume the liquid and even the frozen or solid form. Mercury generally exists as a fluid metal, but it becomes solid at —38·2 Fahrenheit, and vaporizes at 600° F. Water becomes solid when reduced to 32° F., and, in the open air, boils at 212° F. Hence we may conclude, that solid bodies remain in that state till they arrive at a certain fixed temperature, which is invariably the same for the same substance; after which melting commences; and also that a liquid will, by increase of temperature beyond a certain degree, be converted into gas.

---

* Let w be a given weight of steam; t its temperature;
w' the weight of water to be mixed with it; t' its temperature;
and let L = the latent heat of the steam;
T = the temperature of the mixture.

Then the case is similar to what it would be if water of temperature $L+t$ were mixed with water of temperature t'. Hence the formula before proved will apply, and we shall have

$$w(L+t)+w't'=wT+w'T.$$

33. *The Calorimeter.*

To measure the amount of heat contained in any body, Lavoisier invented an instrument called the calorimeter. Its principle consists in an attempt to ascertain the exact amount of ice at 32° that the body will melt; and the only difficulty experienced is in preventing any of the ice from being melted by any extraneous causes, such as the heat imparted by the atmosphere, etc. To attain this object, imagine two similar cup-shaped vessels, each of which is furnished with a cover, the one contained within the other, with a hollow space between them; and let this hollow space be filled with ice broken into small fragments and packed into the hollow, so as to form a complete envelope to the inner vessel. Then it is clear that if a pipe be fitted to the lower part of the outer vessel, and furnished with a stop-cock, the inner vessel will, so long as any of the ice remains, never surpass 32°; for so soon as the temperature rises above that, the ice will melt and the water formed escape through the pipe, carrying off the heat with it. We may, therefore, suppose the effects of the external air and other disturbing causes annihilated. Again, let the ice (minutely pounded) to be melted by the warm substance be placed in the inner cup, leaving a space in the interior for an iron net which is to contain the body to be experimented on. The inner cup has likewise a pipe and stop-cock similar to the outer one. After fitting on the covers, the interior will, after a greater or less interval of time, have arrived at 32°, and in so doing will have melted a certain amount of the ice, which will flow out of the tube into a vessel prepared to receive it. When the water ceases to flow, let the body to be experimented on be placed in the iron net, and the communication with the external air suspended, as before; then a certain amount of ice will be melted by this substance, which must be carefully weighed, and thus we shall obtain a measure of the quantity of heat contained in a body on cooling down to 32°.

34. *On the Sources of Heat.*

The principal sources of heat are the solar rays, mechanical operations, and chemical combinations; and of these the most important for our consideration are those arising from mechanical operations and chemical combinations, the latter of them giving rise to the class of phenomena included under the term combustion.

35. *On Heat generated by Mechanical Operations.*

Heat may be generated by the friction of solid bodies against each other. This is the cause of much annoyance to the engineer. If, for instance, the bearings of an engine be screwed down too tightly, they will soon become very hot; the heat will in its turn expand the masses of metal in contact, and the evil will be increased. A very serious difficulty arising from the same cause, presented itself in the early days of screw propulsion. The screw-shaft must press against what is called the pushing-post with the whole force necessary to propel the ship; and, on account of the great velocity of rotation, the heat thus generated has been so great as to set fire to the wood in its neighborhood, and in one or two instances to cause the end of the shaft to be firmly welded to the plate against which it is pressed. Sudden percussion will also generate heat: thus a bar of iron may be made red-hot by hammering it; and if a quantity of air be suddenly compressed, the heat developed will ignite tinder.

36. *On Combustion.*

Under ordinary circumstances, combustion means the chemical union of a combustible with oxygen at a sufficiently high temperature. Thus three things are necessary for the combustion of fuel; for, in addition to the fuel itself, it must be supplied with a sufficient quantity of oxygen, and the temperature must not be below a certain amount. The oxygen is usually supplied by the surrounding atmosphere, but in certain cases artificial means are used to increase the supply. Thus the Bude light is fed by pure oxygen independently of the atmosphere; and to supply what are called blast-furnaces, the air is driven into the fire by fans. This latter process is adopted in our steam-ships of great draught of water; the air not coming down the hatchways rapidly enough, the fires would burn languidly were it not for fans worked by the engines. Secondly, a combustible is required. Now the goodness of any species of coal or wood depends on the amount of combustible in any given quantity. By referring to the tables in the last chapter containing the results of the experiments on coals made by Sir H. de la Beche and Dr. Playfare, we see that coal is composed of the following chemical substances: carbon, hydrogen, nitrogen, sulphur, oxygen, and ashes. Of these substances, carbon and hydrogen are called the combustibles, and by their chemical union at a high temperature with the oxygen of the atmosphere combustion is effected and heat generated.

37. *On the Temperature necessary for Combustion.*

It is true that combustible substances will unite with oxygen at all temperatures; but that union is effected so slowly at low temperatures, and the heat developed so slight, that for all purposes for which fuel is required, it is so minute that it may be considered not to exist in a practical sense. It must not, however, be entirely unnoticed; for it is owing to this chemical change that coals become deteriorated by exposure to the open air, and this change is facilitated by the action of the sun and rain; in the latter case the oxygen of the water supplying the place of that from the atmosphere. Spontaneous combustion also is owing to the same cause. Let us suppose a quantity of damp coal shut up so that any heat which may be generated will not be able to escape readily. The water becoming decomposed into its two gases, oxygen and hydrogen, the oxygen unites with the carbon of the coal, and a slight development of heat is the result. The heat thus developed fosters the same process between other particles of carbon and oxygen, and the combinations proceed with increasing rapidity, the temperature at the same time rapidly increasing till the coal becomes red-hot; and in addition, a considerable quantity of hydrogen, which was one of the ingredients of the water before its decomposition, is contained within the mass; this is another combustible substance, ready to burst into a blaze as soon as, in endeavoring to put out the fire, an opening is made for the atmospheric air. The same explanation will serve for the heating, smoking, and, lastly, ignition of hay-stacks, if put together damp. It is only, however, at an elevated temperature that a common fire burns; and if from any cause the temperature of the surrounding substances be lowered, the fire will cease to burn briskly. For this reason the air is frequently heated before it is allowed to enter a furnace; and from want of attending to this fact, common fires are often extinguished by putting on too much coal when they are low.

38. *On Oxidation.*

When speaking of combustion, we stated that it resulted, properly speaking, from the union of some substance, called a combustible, with oxygen at a sufficiently high temperature; and that a chemical union frequently takes place without the sensible development of heat, when the temperature is not high enough for combustion. In this latter case the substance, whatever it may be, is said to be oxidated. The baser metals rapidly tarnish or waste away from this cause when influenced by air or water, each of which contains oxygen. Most metals get coated with a film of oxide, which serves to preserve them from further deterioration; but this is not the case with iron, which wastes away because the oxidation or rust does not adhere to it.

39. *Effects of Galvanic Action.*

It is generally known that when two different metals are in contact, under such circumstances that each of them would ordinarily become oxidated, the fact of their being in contact produces a very marked difference in the effect of the action of the oxygen upon each of them. This is due to what is called Galvanic Action, into which it is not our province to enter; but we will confine ourselves to the consideration of the results. One of the metals will oxidate much more rapidly than it otherwise would, and, on the contrary, the other will be partially or entirely protected. Cases of this kind are of daily occurrence. For instance, if iron railings be fitted in lead and exposed to the damp atmosphere, the lower ends, which are in contact with the lead, will rapidly waste. If brass hinges be fixed with iron screws, the heads of the screws will begin to rust in a few hours. To prevent the injurious effects arising from this cause, screw-shafts are cased with brass; otherwise, from being in contact with the ship's copper, they would be soon unserviceable. It ought also to be stated, that the same effect will take place when portions of the metals only which are in contact are immersed in a fluid, as is seen in the case of the iron-work of paddle-wheels, which rapidly wastes where not coated with paint or tar, although the connection between them and the copper must be traced by going from them to the engines, and thus to the ship's copper. Copper pipes are at times secured together by iron bolts and nuts, which are soon destroyed if acted on by bilge-water. The following list will be found of some service, showing the relative electro-chemical position of the metals in common use to each other:

Electro-negative.

Gold.
Platinum.
Mercury.

Silver.
Copper.
Tin.
Lead.
Iron.
Zinc.

Electro-positive.

Each of these metals is electro-negative to all those that follow it, and consequently if any one of them be placed in contact with any one standing below it, and placed in a fluid, the lower one will oxidate and the upper one be protected. Thus, if lead and iron be in contact, the lead will be protected and the iron will waste; if iron and zinc be in contact, the iron will be protected and the zinc will waste; and the further apart the metals are in the above scale, the more active the influence will be. It was this which induced Sir H. Davy to recommend zinc as a protector to the copper sheathing of ships. Muntz's metal for sheathing is composed of copper and zinc combined in the sheet itself, and is less rapidly corrosive than the copper would be by itself.

40. *On the Boiling Temperature.*

Each liquid, when heated in the open air, has a certain fixed temperature at which ebullition commences. This temperature is called the boiling-point of the substance. Liquids which boil at a low temperature are called "Volatile." (For boiling-points of various liquids see Table B, in Appendix.)

41. *Boiling-point influenced by Pressure.*

In the last article, where it was stated that each liquid has a certain fixed boiling-point, it was supposed that ebullition would take place in the open air, and that the pressure of the atmosphere remained the same. If, however, the elastic pressure vary, the boiling-point will vary; consequently, even in cases where fluids are boiling in the open air, the temperature at which ebullition commences will vary slightly with the state of the weather, being higher or lower according as the barometer rises or falls. If a vessel containing warm water be placed under the receiver of an air-pump, and the superincumbent atmosphere be partially removed by exhaustion, the water will commence boiling, and will continue to do so if the steam be pumped away as fast as it is formed. The boiling-point of water may be lowered about 140°, if it be relieved of the pressure. On the other hand, if the pressure be increased, the temperature will rise above what is called the boiling-point before ebullition commences. Table A gives the boiling-point of water for the various pressures. We can easily infer from that table, that at the pressure of the atmosphere ($14\frac{3}{4}$ lbs. per square inch), the boiling-point is 212°.

42. *On the Temperature of Steam.*

While any gaseous fluid, such as steam, is in contact with the water from which it was formed, their temperatures are the same; so that the temperature of steam in a boiler is the same as that of the surface-water within the boiler; but it is evident that, after they are separated from each other, the temperature of either may be altered without affecting the other. If, however, an attempt be made to raise the temperature of the water, more steam will be formed; and if, on the contrary, the temperature of the steam which has been cut off from the boiler be lowered, condensation will take place.

43. *Vapor.*

Vapor is identical with steam, but it is usually applied to that portion of the fluid which *gradually* and insensibly makes its escape whenever it is exposed to the open air, or in any room in which the atmosphere is not saturated with moisture. Air at a certain temperature is capable of sustaining a certain quantity of vapor in solution, and the higher its temperature the more vapor it will absorb; therefore, if we expose a quantity of water to the air, we find it gradually waste, although we do not see the process going on; and if allowed to stay long enough, the water would disappear altogether.

44. *Explanation of the Formation of Dew.*

We have said that the atmosphere consists of a mixture of air and vapor, and that the quantity of vapor held in solution depends on the temperature. If, then, a portion of the atmosphere, already saturated with moisture, be chilled by a cold body coming in contact with it, the vapor will be precipitated on the cold substance in the form of globules. This will take place in a crowded room, where the moisture may be seen, from this cause, running down the walls; the same may frequently be observed when a goblet of cold water is brought into a warm room.* The term *dew*, however, is applied to the same effect when taking place in the open air.

45. *On the Causes influencing the Formation of Dew.*

The principal cause of dew is the radiation of heat from the earth's surface; this goes on much more freely in the summer time than at any other season, and in warm climates especially, which accounts for the heavy dews in the tropics. If any screen be interposed between the ground and sky the radiation is stopped, and any further formation of dew on that spot is prevented; hence on a cloudy night there is no dew; also, if a handkerchief be spread above the ground there will be no dew below it. This has led to the erroneous opinion that dew falls like rain. For instance,

---

* Iron is said to *sweat* when moisture is precipitated on it from the air in this way. Complaints have been made against iron ships on this account.

the deck of a ship in tropical climates will be covered with dew, except on those places where the guns and other bodies are placed, while the upper surface of the guns, etc., will be covered. Indeed, all the appearances are similar to what they would have been if the dew had descended through the air, and had fallen on the ship; but such is not the case; there is no dew beneath the gun, because the air there is not sufficiently chilled, the deck retaining its warmth. There is but little dew on those nights when there is any wind; for a breeze will carry off the particles before the cooling process has advanced so far as to allow of the deposition. The formation of dew is a manifest provision by which plants are enabled to exist during dry weather. Parasitical plants, such as the ivy, that have but small roots, are able to feed themselves freely by the precipitation of dew on their leaves, and they will appear green and flourishing even when vegetation that derives its moisture from the earth is languishing.

46. *To distinguish between Vapor and Steam.*

Vapor is formed only from the *surface*, steam from the *body* of a liquid. Evaporation proceeds at *all* temperatures; steam is only formed when the fluid has arrived at a *certain fixed* temperature. The formation of steam is a *violent* process; the formation of vapor is *gradual* and *insensible*.

47. *On the Formation of Steam.*

When a fire is placed under a boiler containing water, a rapid interchange of the particles take place, the colder continually descending, and the hotter rising to the surface. This will go on for some time, and may be easily observed by throwing into the water an insoluble powder having nearly the same specific gravity: the particles will then be seen to rise in a stream. After a while, small bubbles will be observed to form at the bottom of the vessel, and rise towards the surface; these are particles of steam; but they will not at first *reach* the surface, because they will be condensed again before they arrive there: still they give out their heat to the general mass; every instant the bubbles of steam become larger and more frequent, and soon the whole mass appears to be in violent commotion, and the steam escapes freely from the water. This fluid (steam) is very different in its nature from the water of which it was formed; for while in this state it has all the properties of a gas. It will become more elastic by compression, and loses its elasticity by being allowed to expand. The elasticity is also influenced by heat, the same as other gases. While in this state it is perfectly invisible, unless on the point of condensing. Those who are conversant with boilers will not fail to have noticed that the steam in the upper part of the glass water-gauge is always invisible.

48. *Distinction between Steam and most other Elastic Fluids.*

Steam is readily converted into water by lowering its temperature; this is of immense importance in steam-engines made on what is called the condensing principle; for when the steam has done its work, it is comparatively easy to get rid of it by the injection of cold water; the space it will occupy is trifling compared with that which it had in a state of steam, and consequently there is but little resistance on that account to the return-stroke of the engine.

49. *On the Boiling-point of Fresh Water.*

The boiling-point depends on the pressure exerted on its surface; for if this pressure be increased, the rising of the steam will be checked till the increased temperature gives it sufficient elasticity to make its escape. The temperature of fresh water when boiling in the open air is 212°, but, as before stated, it varies slightly with the state of the atmosphere; or, in other words, with the height of the mercury in the weather-barometer. The temperature at which water boils under different pressures will be seen by referring to the Table of Pressures of Steam and the corresponding Temperatures in the Appendix. (Table A.)

50. *On the Temperature of Sea-water when Boiling in the Open Air.*

The temperature of sea-water when boiling in the open air is higher than that of fresh water, being about 213·2; indeed the boiling-point of water is increased by *any* substance that enters *chemically* into combination with it: but the boiling-point is not altered by the introduction of particles which are only held in *mechanical* suspension; thus the boiling-point of *muddy* water is the same as that of *pure* water.

51. *Steam from Salt Water.*

The steam which is formed from sea-water is fresh, which is a point of much importance to the naval engineer; for if a boiler be filled with salt water, the water will become more and more impregnated with salt, unless means be taken to get rid of the brine. When the boiling-point of the water is raised to 215°, means should be used to prevent its increasing in saltness.

52. *The Process of Distillation.*

When it becomes necessary to separate alcohol from the water with which it is mixed, it is put into a vessel called a *still*, and the temperature is raised by means of a fire: but care is taken not to elevate it to 212°, because all spirits will boil at a much lower temperature than 212°, and therefore it must be so contrived that the spirit may boil while the water is kept below its boiling-point, and is therefore quiescent. A pipe leads away from the top of the still and terminates in a *worm*, as it is called; that is to say, a long spiral tube which winds about in a vessel of cold water, and the extremity is outside the vessel; so that the steam of the spirit becomes chilled and condensed in its passage, and flows out at the open end. It must, however, be remarked, that the spirit, in boiling, forcibly carries up with it some of the aqueous particles; and hence, if it be thought advisable to get rid of these, the still is emptied of its water, and the spirit returned to it to undergo a repetition of the process, when more of the water is left behind, and it is now said to be double distilled.

53. *Peculiarity in High-pressure Steam.*

High-pressure steam does not scald a hand applied near the orifice from which it is issuing. This arises from the fact, that on its first escape it expands so rapidly that the heat becomes latent.

54. *On the Pressure of Steam.*

The elastic pressure of the atmosphere is 14·75 lbs. (or in round numbers 15 lbs.) per square inch; and if steam have the absolute pressure of 15 lbs., it is said to be atmospheric steam, or steam of one atmosphere; if it have a pressure of 30 lbs. per square inch, it is called steam of two atmospheres, and so on. If we were to take away the safety valve from a boiler, the steam would be called atmospheric steam.

55. *On the Laws regulating the Pressure of Steam.*

When the steam is in the boiler and in contact with the water, it does *not* obey the law which regulates other elastic fluids; but when separated from the water, while in the gaseous state, it does obey those laws: for when in contact with the generating fluid, the water and steam increase in temperature together; but as the water gets hotter, it gives out more steam to *add* to that already formed, which mixes with it and keeps it at the greatest density it can have for its temperature; but, on the other hand, the mass cannot be altered when it is cut off from the boiler.

56. *Pressure of Steam* when in contact *with Water.*

No *law* has ever been discovered connecting together the pressure, density, and temperature of steam when in contact with the water which formed it, although the labor bestowed upon it has been very great; but tables have been formed from the results of the experiments of members of the Academy of Sciences and others, and empirical formulæ have been proposed that agree with those tables sufficiently well for practical purposes. (See Table A in the Appendix.) One fact, however, is well established, viz., that the same temperature corresponds to the same pressure; so that if the *temperature* of the steam *in a boiler* is known, the *pressure* can be ascertained from the tables, and *vice versâ.*

57. *Pressure of Steam* when not in contact *with* Water.

Since this follows the same law as other gases, we must adopt the formulæ used in those cases.*

---

* *On the Expansion of Steam and other Gases.*

Case I.—It has been found by experiments made by M. Regnault, that all gases expand by heat $\frac{1}{459}$ of their volume for each degree Fahrenheit, *while their elastic pressure remains unaltered.*

Let, then, V_1 be the volume of a gas at temperature t_1;

V_2 its volume at temperature t_2.

Hence, if its volume at temperature $0° = V$

the addition of volume for one degree $= \frac{V}{459}$

and for t_1 degrees $= \frac{V}{459} \times t_1$.

Hence the actual volume is $V + \frac{V}{459} \times t_1$

$$= V . \frac{459 + t_1}{459}$$

Again, the actual volume when the temperature is t_2

$$= V . \frac{459 + t_2}{459}$$

and therefore $$\frac{V_1}{V_2} = \frac{459 + t_1}{459 + t_2}$$

Hence the following rule: Add the number 459 to each of the temperatures; divide the one result by the other, and the quotient will give us the relation of the bulks which the gases will occupy without having their elasticities affected.

Case II.—Again: it is a well-established fact, that so long as the

In stating the pressure of steam in a boiler, the excess of that pressure *above the atmosphere* is usually given, and not its actual pressure.

This is because it is what the gauge on the boiler for measuring the steam indicates, and it is this excess that gives the effort to burst the boiler. Thus when we speak of steam of 20 lbs. pressure, we mean steam whose absolute pressure is $20+15=35$ lbs. nearly; but since the external air acts with a pressure of 15 lbs., the effort to rend the boiler is only 20 lbs.

58. *On the Specific Gravity of Steam.*

The specific gravity of steam is much less than that of the atmosphere, under similar pressures. At the temperature 212° it is ·4575, taking atmospheric air as the standard.

---

temperature of a gas remains unaltered, its elastic pressure will vary inversely as the volume.

If, therefore, M be the volume a gas occupied at a given temperature, its pressure being p_1, and N the volume at the same temperature, its pressure being p_2; then

$$\frac{p_1}{p_2}=\frac{N}{M}$$

Hence the following rule: As the pressure p_1 is to the pressure p_2, so is the volume of the gas at the pressure p_2 to its volume at the pressure p_1.

CASE III.—If, now, we have a gas at a certain pressure, volume, and temperature, and we wish to find what its pressure is when the volume and temperature are both changed, we must proceed as follows:

1. Let the temperature alone be changed from t_1 to t_2, and let A and B be the volumes; then

$$\frac{B}{A}=\frac{459+t_2}{459+t_1}$$

2. And having changed the temperature to t_2, let the temperature now remain unaltered, while the pressure is changed from p_1 to p_2 by changing the volume from B to C; then

$$\frac{p_2}{p_1}=\frac{B}{C} \quad \text{But } B=\frac{459+t_2}{459+t_1}\cdot A$$

$$\frac{p_2}{p_1}=\frac{A}{C}\cdot\frac{459+t_2}{459+t_1}$$

59. *Common Steam.*

Steam when in contact with the generating fluid, or if it be not heated after the separation has taken place, is called *common* steam. If we reflect on the mode of its production, we shall see that since, on receiving fresh accessions of temperature, additional particles of steam were invariably added to the previous mass, it will follow conversely, that directly the temperature is lowered, whether it be in contact with the generating water, or be shut up in the cylinder, or be in the steam-pipe, in any such case a portion of the steam will return to the liquid state. This forms what is called the *jacket-water* of an engine.

60. *Superheated Steam.*

If steam be heated after it leaves the boiler, it can evidently be cooled again to its original temperature without returning into the liquid state. When the temperature is thus raised, it is called superheated steam. Recent experiments appear to show that great advantages, in an economical point of view accrue from superheating a portion of the steam that has been generated by a boiler before it enters the cylinder. Under ordinary circumstances, when steam which is on the point of condensing comes into contact with the cylinder, a portion of it is converted into water, which is a manifest disadvantage and loss; and this is obviated in the case of superheated steam, and consequently less water will be required from the boiler to fill the cylinder with steam. Suppose, for instance, that 1000 cubic feet of steam were required to fill the cylinder, and that 1000 cubic inches of water were required to produce this amount of steam; let us suppose further, that condensation takes place in the cylinder to the amount of 200 cubic inches of water; then in ordinary cases the boiler must supply 1000+200, or 1200 cubic inches of water for every stroke of the piston; but if the steam were superheated,

1000 cubic inches would suffice. An amount of fuel will therefore be saved which would be necessary to evaporate 200 cubic inches of water; less feed-water also will be required, and less injection-water to cool down the whole mass to 100°. The practical mode of carrying out this principle will be treated of in Chapter II.

61. *Analysis of Sea-water.*

The water of Kingstown Harbor, as tested by Mr. Mallet, was found to contain in 1 cubic foot, 12,661 grains of solid matter, which, analyzed with precaution, had the following constituents, reduced to per cent.:

Chloride of sodium (or common salt) . .	71·32
Chloride of magnesium	10·79
Bromide of magnesium	0·60
Sulphate of lime (or gypsum)	4·87
Sulphate of magnesia	5·30
Carbonate of lime (or chalk)	1·73
Organic matter	5·27
Loss	0·12
	100·00

Of these the most injurious, as forming solid incrustations within the boiler, are the sulphate of lime and carbonate of lime; and the first-mentioned, namely, common salt, will accumulate in large quantities within the boiler, unless care be taken to remove it. The sulphates are, by their decomposition and re-arrangement with hydrogen, the cause of the offensive odor of bilge-water, which is owing to the presence of sulphuretted hydrogen.

The specific gravity of sea-water = 1027·80; and 100 cubic inches of water, taken from the surface, contain in combination 1·43 cubic inch of gas, which consists of atmospheric air with traces of carbonic acid.

62. *Table of the Amount of Saline Contents in* 1000 *parts of Sea-water from different Localities.**

Arctic Sea . . .	28·30	Black Sea . . .	21·60
North Atlantic . .	42·60	Baltic	6·60
Equator	39·42	Dead Sea . . .	385·00
South Atlantic . .	41·20	British Channel .	35·50
Mediterranean . .	39·40	Irish Sea . . .	33·76
Sea of Marmora .	42·00		

63. *On the Quantity of Carbonic Acid in Sea-water.*

One thousand volumes of sea-water are stated, on the authority of Laurent, etc., to contain 62 volumes of carbonic acid.

---

* From the report of Mr. Mallet in the *Transactions of the British Association*, 1840, p. 223.

CHAPTER II.

THE BOILER.

STEAM being the motive power in all machines called steam-engines, the supply must be obtained by boiling water in some vessel. This vessel is the boiler.

64. *Marine Boilers distinguished from Land Boilers.*

In land boilers the heated gases, after passing through the boiler, were formerly allowed to return along the outside of the shell before entering the chimney; but in marine boilers they must, for the safety of the ship, be kept within the flues or tubes, and these tubes must be enclosed within the shell of the boiler.

Again, since the boiler is supplied with sea-water, contrivances are necessary by which the salts that are left in the boiler as the steam escapes may be got rid of. In addition to this, many operations must be regulated by hand which on shore would be accomplished by machinery connected with the engine itself. This will be necessary because the water-level in the boiler does not preserve its horizontality, on account of the pitching and rolling of the ship.

65. *Gear connected with Boilers.*

It is very evident that steam, if allowed continually to collect in a vessel, without any escape being afforded to it, would at length produce most destructive effects, rending the containing vessel, and dispersing its fragments in every direction; consequently these accidents must be provided against by fitting to each boiler a *safety-valve,* together with a mercurial column called the *steam-gauge*, by which the eye can discover the amount of pressure the boiler sustains.

Again, the height of the water within the boiler is ascertained by *gauge-cocks* and *glass water-gauges*.

Moreover, to prevent the external air from crushing or collapsing the boiler, valves, called *reverse-valves*, are fitted to the boilers of condensing engines. This apparatus is not, however, required for the boilers of non-condensing engines, on account of their extra strength.

At the junction of the steam-pipe with the boiler there is a valve, called a *communication* or *stop valve*, for making free egress for the steam or stopping it, according as the valve is open or closed, and thus isolating one boiler from the rest when necessary.*

And lastly, since the boiler is filled with sea-water, the earthy matter of which is constantly accumulating within it, there are pipes and cocks communicating with the sea for the purpose of getting rid of the brine, and called *blow-out cocks* and *pipes*.

In the front part of each boiler there are openings, about 4 feet high, and reaching nearly down to the floor of the engine-room. These are divided into two parts, one above the other, by a series of bars sloping downwards, called fire-bars. That part of the fire-place on which the bars rest in front is the *dead-plate*, and sufficient room is left here for the bars to expand: the bars are usually in two lengths, and are supported by two cross pieces, one across the middle of the fire-place, and the other at the farther end; these are called *bearing-bars*. On these bars the fuel is placed. The portions of the orifices below these bars are the *ash-pits*, and those above it the *fire-places* or *furnaces*. The upper and lower part have their separate doors, called *fire-places* and *ash-pit doors* respectively. These openings go back into the boiler about 5 or 6 feet, where the fire-places cease. The currents of hot air from the separate fire-places

* Some old boilers have, however, no communication-valve.

now unite into one space; and the boiler is called a *flue* boiler or a *tubular* boiler, according to the construction of the passages of the heated air between the fires and the steam funnel. The heated air, after passing from the fire-places, has not yet been sufficiently robbed of its caloric to permit it to pass at once into the *funnel;* therefore, in flue boilers, it is compelled to take a circuitous path through the boiler in a passage called the flue, the water of the boiler surrounding this flue on every side. After winding backwards and forwards by these means, till it is supposed that the water will have absorbed all the heat, it then passes through the uptake into the funnel. This kind of boiler, called the flue-boiler, was generally used in her Majesty's service till lately; but within the last few years has given place to another kind, in which the gases, after escaping from the fire, have to pass through a series of small tubes before entering the funnel. This latter is called

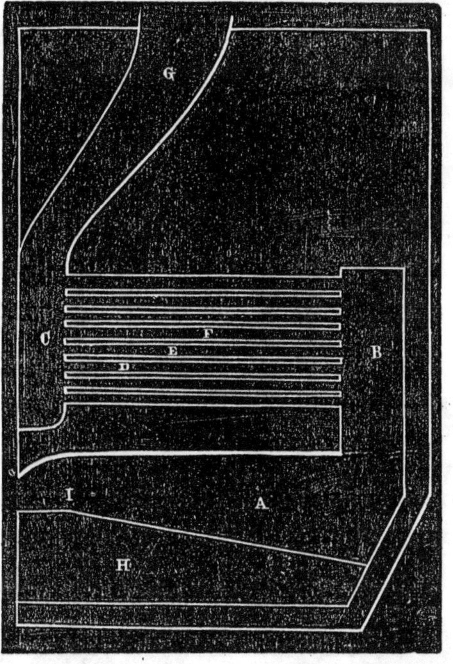

66. *The Tubular Boiler.*

The accompanying diagram represents a section of a tubular boiler, as they are made at Portsmouth. Here A represents the fire-place and H the ash-pit; B is called the fire-box; F E D, etc., the tubes;* C the smoke-box; G the uptake, which is connected with the funnel. Between A and H are the fire-bars, sloping downwards towards the back of the boiler. The fuel is supplied at the opening I; and the smoke from the fire enters B, then through the tubes F E D, etc., into C, from whence it ascends to G, and so through the funnel.

The accompanying Figure exhibits a transverse section of a tubular boiler. A B C are sections of the furnaces, the upper part of each containing the burning fuel, and the lower part being the ash-pit; the ends of the tubes are seen above the flues. The same boilers have their tubes inclining slightly downwards towards the smoke-box. There seems to be some advantage from this arrangement; for the heated air, not having so ready a passage through the tubes, exerts its effect on the boiler longer than it otherwise would; and the soot will not remain in the tubes so long as it would if they were horizontal; it will be partly blown out by the draught.

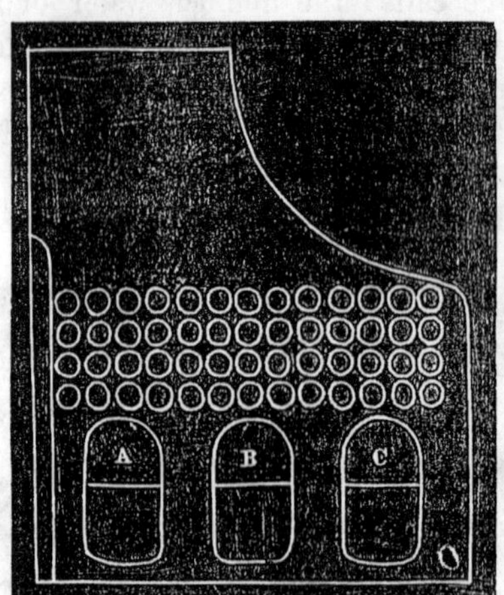

The advantage gained by these boilers over the common or flue boilers consists in the amount of *surface* in the series of tubes through which the heated air has to pass being much greater than that in the flue-boilers, when the sum of the orifices of the tubes is equal to a section of the flues.† The greater the amount of heating surface, the less

* The tubes used in the Navy vary from 2 to 3 inches external diameter.

† The advantage of small tubes over large ones in giving a greater

the quantity of water the boiler will have to hold. The use of a great quantity of water in the boiler consists in its acting as a reservoir of heat, and thus preventing the chilling effects that would otherwise result from the admission of feed-water at each stroke of the pump.

67. *The Number of Boilers in each Steam-vessel.*

There are generally four or more distinct boilers in each steam-vessel of any magnitude, so that steam may be got from all or any according to the number of fires that are lighted. To enable them to act independently, each boiler is provided with all the gear it would have if it were alone; but, generally speaking, the smoke and spare steam go into only one funnel and waste-steam pipe. The steam from each boiler goes into one main steam pipe before entering the cylinders; and by means of the *communication-valves,* the connection which would otherwise exist between all the boilers may be suspended when the use of any boiler is not required. The boilers were usually four in number, and placed side by side, forming a square, having one stoke-hole forward and the other aft; but in the present arrangement they are separated, having one long passage amidships for the stoke-hole, the fire-places of the two sets of fires facing each other. The only objection to this plan lies in the difficulty of supplying the fires with fuel when working all the boilers. Probably the arrangement in the

---

amount of heating-surface with the same opening for smoke, may be thus apparent:

Let l = length of a tube;
r = its radius;
n = number of tubes;

$\therefore$ the whole heating tube-surface $= 2\pi r l \times n$;
and the volume for the heated gases to pass through $= \pi r^2 l n$;

Let $\therefore$ $S = 2\pi r l n$, and $V = \pi r^2 l n$

$$\therefore \quad S = \frac{2V}{r}$$

which increases as the radius of the tubes decreases, provided the space occupied by them is constant.

Great Eastern is better, where the boilers are placed back to back; the fire-places facing the coal bunkers.

68. *The Steam-chest.*

The space in the boiler above the upper surface of the water is called the steam-chest; and this part of the boiler should be as large as it can be made, for with small steam-chests the pressure of the steam is continually varying: small steam-chests are for this reason a chief cause of priming. Large steam-chests are also more economical in fuel. If the steam-chest be too small, it will become manifest in the oscillating motion of the steam-gauge. With small steam-chests the fires must be always kept in an active state, otherwise the steam falls. Some boilers show this defect very plainly: for want of a reservoir of steam, at one moment it is blowing off, and at another it is below the boiler-pressure.

69. *The Fire-bridge.*

There used to be two kinds of bridges, one made of brick and the other of iron; the latter is hollow, and contains water, and the upper edge is sloping, to allow the generated steam to escape. There are several advantages in brick bridges over those made of iron: they can easily be altered if necessary, or knocked away to carry on any internal repairs; and if the fire-places are too long, they can be shortened. Again, if the tubes leak, the lower part of the flues will be filled with water; which can easily be got rid of by knocking out a brick, and thus allowing it to escape by the ash-pit, instead of accumulating till it flows over the bridge. When boilers are fitted with bridges, they are now made of brick. A hole may, when the steam is down, be made through the iron bridge for the same purpose, and a tube inserted. The fire-bars are always inclined to the bridge at an angle inclining downwards, so as to facilitate the stoking, and at the same time to diffuse the air better: the grate-surface is thereby likewise increased. A *hanging* bridge has been fitted to some of the high-pressure boilers, to keep the tubes from clinkering up.

70. *Ash-pits.*

The ash-pits of most boilers are made with round bottoms. They are consequently much stronger; and as the steam is not pent up underneath them, they are not so liable to buckle up towards the fires. When the bottoms of the ash-pits were made flat, they were the weakest parts of the boilers, from the pressure of the steam and the great weight of the superincumbent column of water. Since there is no angle-iron to round-bottomed ash-pits, they last much longer; for dirt accumulates at the edges of the angle-iron, and occasions oxidation.

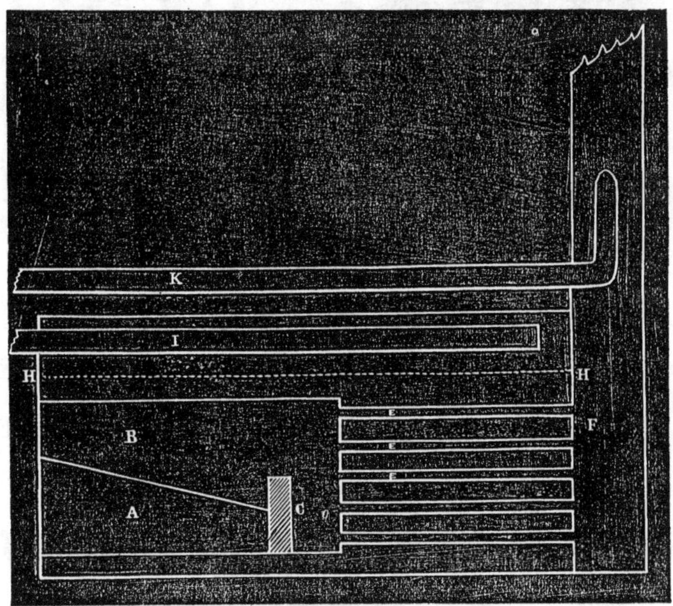

71. *Gun-boat Boilers.*

Fig. 1.

Gun-boat boilers are of a cylindrical form, of which Fig.

1 represents a longitudinal, and Fig. 2 gives the transversal section.

In these diagrams, A is the ash-pit; B the fire-place or furnace, separated by the fire-bars, which slope downwards towards the bridge C; E E E, etc., are the tubes conveying the heated gases into the smoke-box, F, which leads into the funnel; H H the water-line; all above this being the steam-space. The steam pipe I runs nearly the whole length of the boiler, within the steam-space of the boiler; it is closed at the end, but slotted along the top to allow the steam to enter, and at the same time prevent priming. K is the exhaust-pipe, which, in the case of high-pressure engines, leads from the engines into the funnel. A blast-pipe of a similar construction, and acting in the same manner, is fitted to all boilers. These two are separately treated of in the next articles.

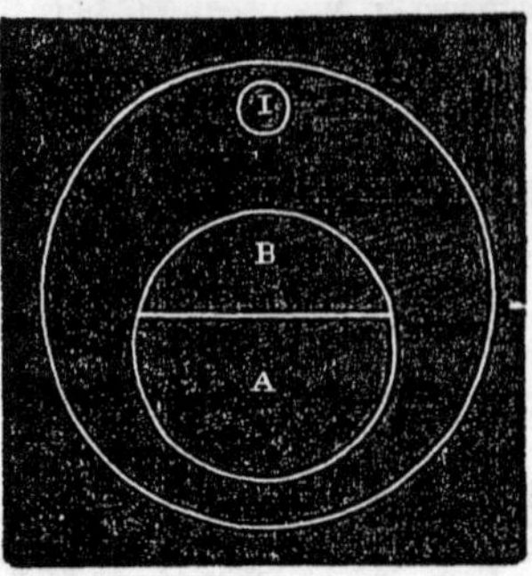

Fig. 2.

72. *Exhaust-pipe.*

This pipe serves to convey the steam from the cylinder, after it has done its work, into the funnel, as is shown in the last article. The force with which the steam issues from it drives the air before it, and creates a draught through the tubes. The end is contracted, as in the diagram, to increase the effect.

73. *Blast-pipe.*

This pipe leads from the steam-chest into the funnel, whereas the exhaust-pipe leads from the cylinder. It is fitted to all boilers, whether high or low pressure, but is only used when getting up steam or working at slow speeds. When used, the escape of steam is not intermittent, as in the case of the exhaust-pipe, but continuous.

74. *Feed or Donkey Engine.*

Tubular boilers contain so small a quantity of water in comparison of the flue-boilers, that the water above the tubes is apt to be soon evaporated, unless the supply be kept up continually. It becomes necessary, therefore, to have means of keeping up the supply of water to the boilers when the steam is up and the engine stationary; for at such times the feed-pump is not at work. These boilers, therefore, are fitted with a small engine, for the express purpose of supplying the boiler with water while the engines are not working.

In H. M. S. Ajax, a small engine, in addition to the auxiliary engine, is fitted to work a fan to ventilate the engine-room, and to exhaust the condensers, so as to keep them free from injection-water. This engine is supplied from a boiler of its own,* whereas the common auxiliary engine is supplied from the other boilers.

75. *Boiler Hand-pumps.*

These are pumps worked entirely by hand in some vessels; but in most vessels fitted with tubular boilers there are means of connecting them with the engines, so that, if the feed-pumps fail to supply sufficient water to the boilers, this pump can be set to work to make up the deficiency. It can also be made available for pumping the ship out, pumping water on deck, or pumping the boilers out when the ship is in port, if the steam does not blow out the boiler dry enough. Indeed, there is always some water left in the boiler from the condensation of the steam. This should be drained out by the hand-pump as soon as the boiler has cooled down; for the particles of water dropping from the internal steam-pipe, and other metallic fittings, are impregnated with copper, and oxidate the lower parts of the boiler.

* This engine will prove very valuable in putting out fire during an action, when perhaps the steam in the large boilers has been kept at reduced pressure.

Many of our readers may find it difficult to understand how the same pump can be used to pump water *into* the boiler, and pump water *from* the boiler. The following explanation, with the help of the diagram, may make it

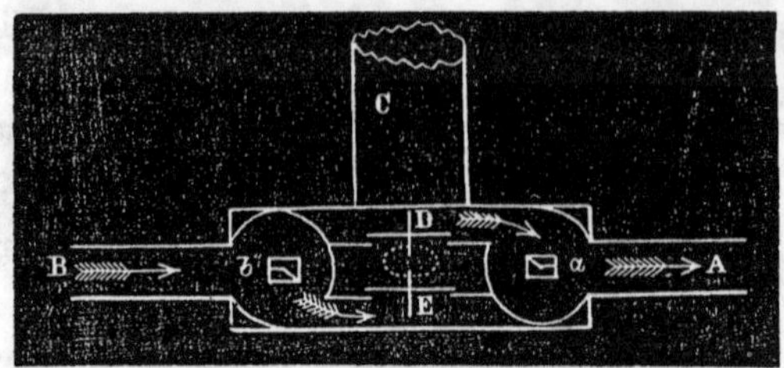

intelligible. B is the pipe communicating with the sea, and A the pipe communicating with the boiler; C is the pump (part only of which can be seen, the remaining part being behind the space B A); *b a* are two cocks, by turning which the circular spaces surrounding them may be brought into the position they have in the figure; D and

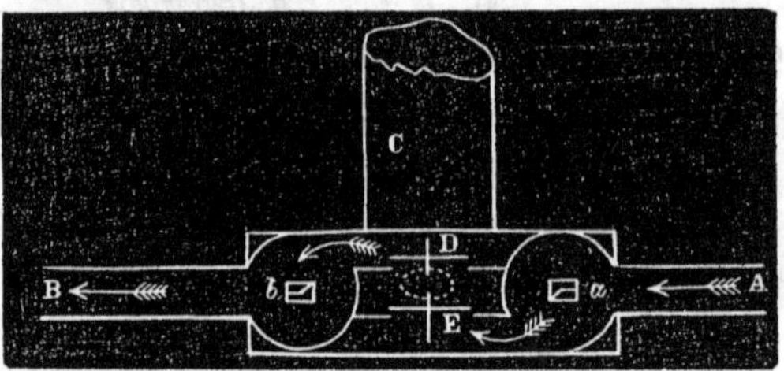

E are two valves, between which is an opening to the pump-bucket C: this opening is represented in the figure by dotted lines. If we look at the arrows, which represent the direction in which the water is to pass, and suppose the valve of the pump to be raised, we shall perceive that, a vacuum being formed in the pump, the water will pass through the valve-passage at E and go into the barrel of the pump; but that on forcing down the piston, this water, being sent back again, is forced through D in the channel marked by the arrows through the pipe A to the boiler.

If the cocks *b* and *a* be turned into the position as represented in the adjoining figure, the same explanation will show that water will flow from A towards B; that is to say, the boiler will be emptied. There are scores, or a slotway, on the outsides, which may be seen at *b* and *a*, where the key for turning the cock is placed; and these scores serve to show the engineer whether the cocks are properly set or not.

76. *The Safety-valve.*

The safety-valve derives its name from its office, which is, to open the communication between the boiler and the external air, when the internal pressure may be considered to have arrived at the limit the manufacturer intends the engines to work at, while it effectually closes that communication so long as the steam retains a pressure that is below that limit.

A circular orifice is made in the upper horizontal surface of the boiler, large enough to allow the steam to escape as fast as it is generated.* Upon this a valve is placed. This valve is weighted by hanging weights from it on a spindle within the boiler, or placing them upon a spindle outside the boiler. The weights must be arranged so that each square inch of the valve shall be kept down with the pressure the boiler is required to bear. Suppose, for instance, that it be desirable the boiler should not sustain a greater pressure than 7 lbs.; in other words, that the pressure of the steam be not greater than (15 + 7) 22 lbs.; we shall have to load the valve till the pressure on every square inch is 7 lbs.; and the same rule will hold with all other pressures. As the safety-valve is supposed to be loaded as high as the manufacturer deems safe, it is clear the engineer should never trifle with it by putting on additional weights. Two valves are usually fitted to each boiler, that if one of them by any accident becomes fixed in its seat (or gagged,

---

* It should, therefore, be in proportion to the heating-surface.

as it is technically termed), the other may allow a free egress to the steam, and prevent injury. If the orifices be not large enough, the steam will accumulate within the boiler, and increase in density, till one of two events happens: the pressure increasing with the density, the boiler will explode; or, if the boiler be strong enough to sustain the increased pressure, as the density increases, the quantity of steam that escapes in a given time also increases, and at length it will find its exit as fast as it is generated. This explains a fact frequently noticed, that on stopping engines suddenly, when the fires are strong, the boiler-pressure, as exhibited by the steam-gauge, is considerably greater than that to which the valves are weighted. We observe this more particularly in those cases where tubular boilers have been substituted for the old flue-boilers, and the same safety-valves have been used. The pressure in many cases has been altered from 4 lbs. per inch in the old boilers to 14 lbs. or 16 lbs. in the new ones. We see, therefore, how necessary it is that the valve should be proportioned to the heating-surface. Sometimes the pressure will rise as high as a pound, or a pound and a half, above the greatest pressure as limited by the safety-valve. This is more likely to be attended with danger in tubular boilers than in the common flue-boilers, on account of their great evaporative power. Annular safety-valves are now sometimes fitted, giving the same amount of egress for steam with a smaller opening. These valves are similar to the delivery-valve of annular air-pumps.

77. *On the Gear attached to the Safety-valve.*

It is necessary that the engineer, without leaving his station in the engine-room, should have the means of convincing himself at any instant of the good working condition of the safety-valve; and to that end a system of levers is fitted, one extremity coming in front, and terminating in a handle within reach; the other presses against the under-surface of the valve, but is not secured to it; so that the engineer can, when he pleases, press on the valve-spindle and raise it, and thus determine whether it is in action: but this does not offer any obstacle to its free motion when forced up by the steam, because it can separate itself from the lever when the pressure of the steam becomes sufficiently great. The spindles of the valves, and all the gear connected with them, require looking to occasionally; for when iron spindles are employed they are apt to set fast. By means of these levers also the steam can be allowed to escape from the boiler, when its pressure is not great enough to lift the valves; as, for instance, when it is necessary in harbor to do any thing to the boiler, which requires the pressure of the steam to be removed; or in case of repair to the engine when no stop-valve is fitted.

78. *Under what circumstances the Weights of the Safety-valves may be increased.*

They should not be altered unless it be sanctioned by proper authority; and the only authorities to sanction such a step are the engine-makers. But there are many cases when such an operation would be highly advantageous; as, for instance, when chasing an enemy, when towing, or on a lee-shore; because in either of these cases, if the vessel be fitted with paddle-wheels, the number of revolutions is sensibly diminished, and consequently the condenser would be able to maintain a good vacuum, although the steam were supplied to the cylinder of greater density. Under these circumstances, therefore, it would appear not imprudent to intrust the engineer with certain weights, previously supplied by the manufacturer, which he would be authorized to use under the sanction of his commanding officer.

79. *The Safety-valve Box.*

In the accompanying diagram C is the valve-box fitted

to the steam-chest E F, *a b* are two safety-valves seating in orifices opening into this box. The safety-valves are retained in their places by the weights A and B attached to the valves by spindles. C D is the steam-pipe proceeding from the valve-box, and *c g a* is called the drip-pipe, coming down by the side of the steam-pipe, for carrying away the condensed steam from the top of the steam-pipe.

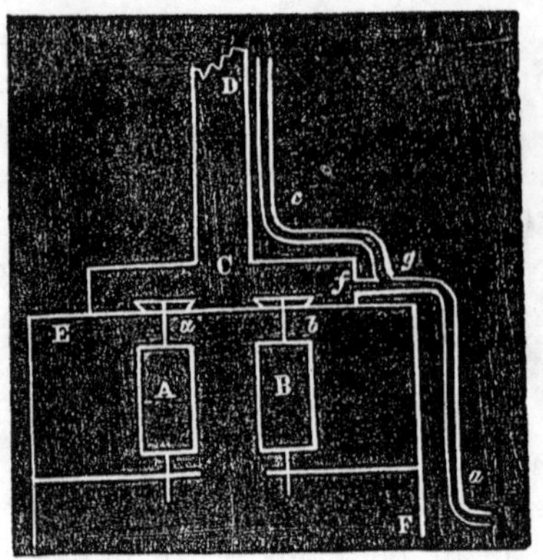

80. *Waste-steam Funnel and Drip-pipe.*

The steam-funnel is an upright tube, by which the steam escaping by the safety-valve finds a passage into the open air. The lower part was shown in the previous figure. It is kept upright by stays from the funnel; and to many of them there is fitted at the upper part a bulb, or steam-trap, serving to check the upward violence of the mud and water sent up from the boiler when priming takes place. A B is the steam-trap, into which the waste-steam pipe enters. The pipe is carried nearly through it, and has a *blank* top; the steam, therefore, makes its way through orifices in the sides, as is shown by the arrows. Attached to the bulb is a small pipe B C, which passes down by the side of the waste-steam funnel, as in the previous figure, and through the ship's side, to carry off what has accumulated in the trap. This is called the drip-pipe. There is also another pipe (*f g*, Fig. p. 64) connected with the safety-valve box, which

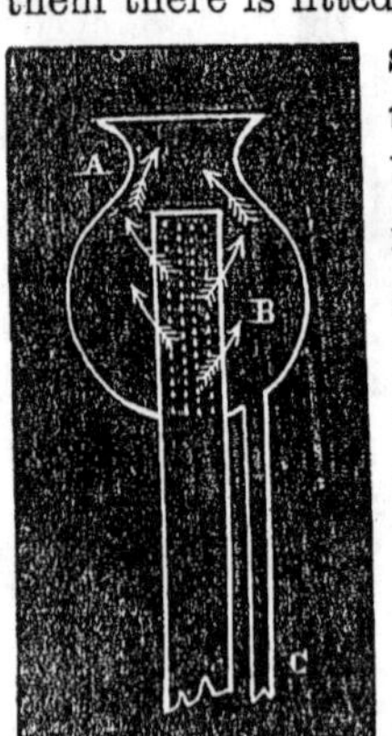

runs horizontally, and serves to carry off whatever may accumulate in the valve-box. This pipe generally discharges into the drip-pipe, so that one orifice through the ship's side suffices for both. Many steamers in the merchant-service, and a few in her Majesty's navy, have a pipe fitted to the boiler to blow off the steam *under water* when the vessel stops; and thus whatever comes up with the steam passes off by the same passage into the water, and is prevented from falling on the deck. In this case the steam-trap, or bulb, is unnecessary. The only objection to this arises from the violent noise and unpleasant tremulous motion caused by the sudden condensation of the steam on entering the water. These are now becoming obsolete.

81. *The Steam-gauge.*

The pressure of the steam within the boiler is ascertained by means of the steam-gauge. Imagine a hollow iron tube to be bent into the form of the letter U, as in the diagram, very much elongated, the one end communicating with the boiler B, and the other C opening into the engine-room. This tube is partially filled with mercury. Now if the pressure of steam in the boiler be the same as that of the atmosphere, the mercury will stand at the same level in both legs, as at a c; but as the pressure in the boiler increases over that of the atmosphere, it forces the mercury down the leg A D, and it consequently rises in the other D C till the balance is restored. And since, if the legs be of the same bore, which is supposed to be the case, every rise of an inch in the one leg is accompanied with the depression of an inch in the other, therefore every rise of an inch shows a difference of level of two inches. But two inches of mercury correspond approximately to one pound

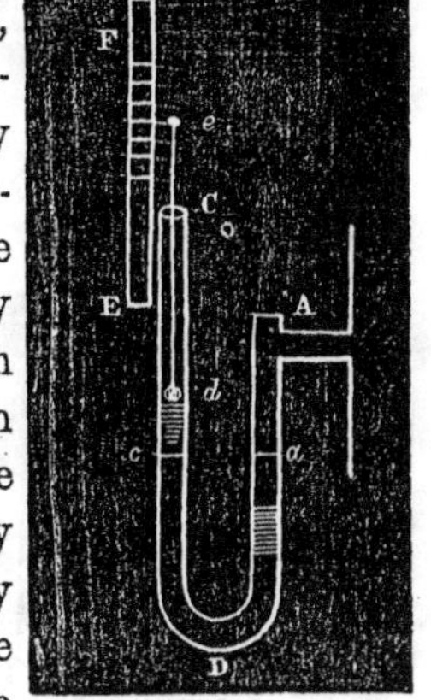

pressure; hence it follows that every inch that the mercury rises corresponds to an additional pound in the pressure of the steam. Now if the tube had been made of glass instead of iron, we might, by inspection, determine how high the mercury had risen; but since this is not the case, a small float *d e* rests on it, and having its upper end above the top of the tube, is pushed up by the force of the steam. The upper end of the tube is brought into contact with a scale of inches E F, and thus the number of pounds pressure becomes readily discernible. These gauges are valuable in cases where the safety-valve does not act; for if the pressure be unduly increased, the mercury is blown out, and notice is given of danger.

82. *Steam-gauge for High-pressure Boilers.*

The mercurial gauge described in the last article is evidently not suitable for high-pressure boilers; for if, as an instance, the pressure of the steam were supposed to be 60 lbs., the total length of the gauge would be 120 inches (or 12 feet). For this reason, a gauge which exhibits the effects of pressure on a thin plate of metal is adopted, the principle and construction being as follows: Let A B be a thin plate of corrugated steel, going across an orifice of the boiler, and therefore acted on by the steam-pressure; to the middle of this plate let a rod *a b* be attached, the upper end of which is in connection with an extremely short bar *b c*. To the same bar is connected the rack *f g*, so that if the rod *a b* be pushed upwards by the action

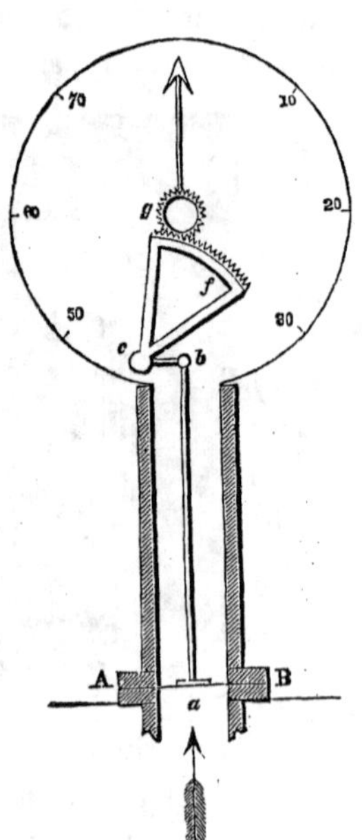

of the steam on the steel plate, the rack will begin to revolve round *c* in direction opposite to the hands of a watch. The rack works in a pinion *g*, and consequently the index will revolve. Round this pinion is coiled a hair-spring, to bring the index back as the pressure is taken off.

83. *Gauge-cocks.*

There are three gauge-cocks fitted to each boiler, for the purpose of ascertaining the height of water within it. They are placed at different heights, the middle one being on the level of the water-surface in the boiler; and consequently the lower one is below that level, and the upper one above it. If, then, they be opened in succession, water should flow from the lowest, a mixture of water and steam from the middle one, and steam ought to rush from the upper one. These cocks are sometimes placed so that they can be reached by hand, although the level of the water in the boiler is out of reach. To effect this, pipes connected with the cocks run up inside the boiler to the proper height. These cocks are frequently tried; for the salt and silt from the water boils into them, and would soon stop them up.

84. *Boiler Water-gauge.*

The water-gauge serves to make the height of water in the boiler visible to the eye. Outside the boiler A B, and generally not far from the gauge-cocks, is a vertical glass tube C D, about 16 inches long. The ends of this tube fit into metal tubes A C and B D, of which the lower one enters the water, and the other the steam; hence the height of the water in the tube is the same as that in the boiler. For convenience sake, it is fitted with a stop-cock E at the upper, and F at the lower end, to cut off the communication with the boilers; there is also a third cock G at the lower

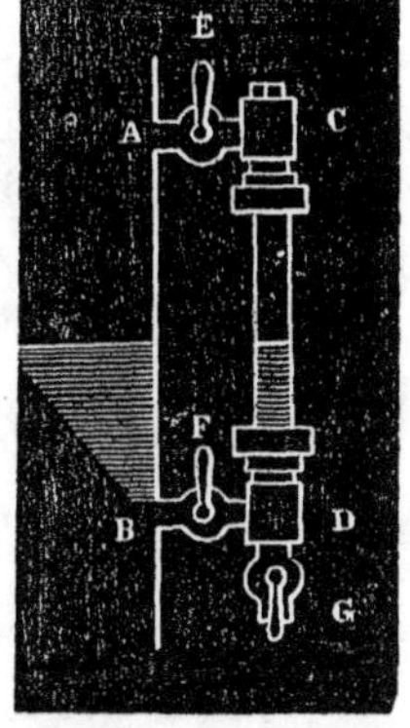

end communicating with the stoke-hole, to clear it, when it becomes choked, by forcing steam through it. This gauge continues to indicate the height of the water when the pressure of the steam is below that of the atmosphere, in which case the gauge cocks fail.

85. *Kingston's Valves.*

These valves are fitted to every orifice through the ship's bottom in connection with the machinery. They are invaluable. It is simply a conical valve, fitted to the conical hole in the ship's bottom, the larger part of the orifice being outside: a spindle is attached to this valve, which works perfectly tight in a stuffing-box; and the inner end of the spindle terminates in a cross handle, by which the valve can be pulled in or forced out. If, for instance, the blow-out

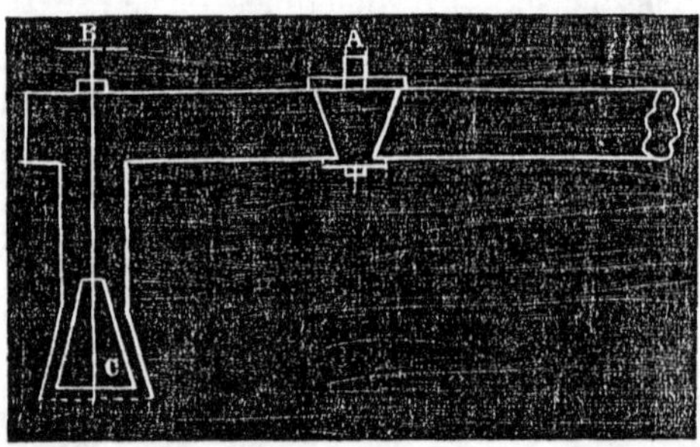

cock A should set fast when open, we have simply to pull the handle B of the valve C, and the orifice becomes closed, and the water is prevented from passing out of the boiler. These valves are equally valuable to the sea injection-orifice; for if the sea injection-cock should leak, there is then no necessity for docking the vessel to repair, as was formerly done. We have but to close the valve, and the sea-cock can be taken out and reground.

86. *Wash-plates, or Dash-plates.*

In the old rectangular flue-boilers, plates so called were used to prevent the send of the water when the vessel rolled or lurched heavily; they were placed in a fore-and-aft direction, and secured to the upper part of the flues and the shell of the boiler, a space being left under them to allow the water to maintain its level. They might, perhaps, be usefully applied to our screw-ships, which are frequently sailing and steaming at the same time. When a ship lurches, and the water leaves the weather-side of the boiler, there is risk of injuring the crowns of the fire-places or upper tubes.

87. *Dampers.*

In most of our steamers there is a damper fitted across the funnel, and in some instances worked on deck. It is merely a disc, or two half-discs, as the case may be, attached to a spindle, to which is fitted a handle; and by this the damper is placed horizontally across the funnel, thus obstructing the upward current; or vertically, so as to allow a free passage. If the construction and use of the throttle-valve are understood, the damper presents no difficulty, for it answers the same purpose in the funnel as the throttle valve does in the steam-pipe. The damper is of great use when the engines are not in motion, and the fires are banked up; and also when the vessel is steaming head to wind and sea; and, indeed, in every instance where the draught should be checked, and much steam is not required.

88. *The Reverse-valve.*

Although, generally speaking, the pressure of the steam is greater than that of the atmosphere, and therefore what we usually have to guard against is, the effect of a *bursting* pressure; yet, under certain circumstances, the contrary effects may take place, unless a remedy be provided. For instance, after the engines have done their work, and the fires have been drawn, the outside of the boiler will cool down by radiation and contact with the atmosphere of the engine-room, and consequently the steam within the boilers wili rapidly condense and lose its pressure. Or, again, if the fires be not properly kept up, the engines will use the steam more freely than it is generated. Now either of these cases, unless proper precautions were taken, would be a source of danger to the boilers; for if the pressure of the external air become much greater than the internal steam-pressure, this force may make the boilers collapse. This is prevented by the use of a valve to each boiler, commonly called the reverse-valve, which is opened by the pressure of the atmosphere before the crisis arrives, and supplies the place of the steam with air.

Other names are sometimes given to the reverse-valve, such as internal safety-valve, vacuum-valve, or atmospheric valve.

This valve is commonly made of the same form as the safety-valve, but it opens inwards, instead of outwards. It requires, however, to be kept in its place by some means. If a weight be used, the weight must be connected to one end of a lever of the first order, the valve being attached to the other end; and it must be so regulated that the atmosphere may open the valve when the steam has diminished to a certain pressure previously fixed on. Generally speaking, however, it is kept up in its place by means of a spring.

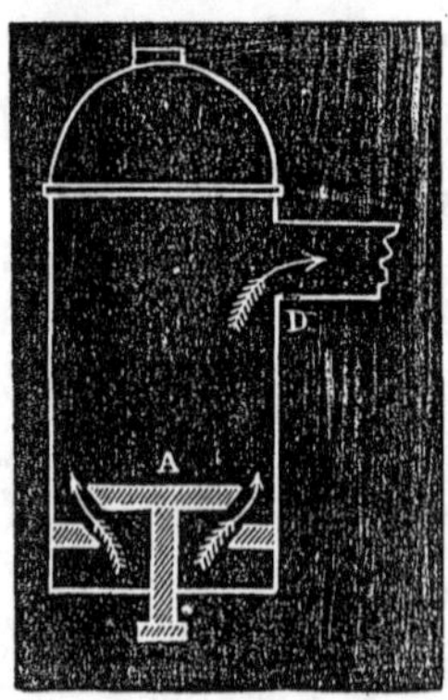

It is more convenient to place it in front of the boiler, and not on the top. Here it will be less exposed to injury, and less likely to be choked up with dirt, and thus rendered useless.

The following kind of reverse-valve is very frequently adopted in our steam-vessels, and has the advantage of not being likely to be affected by any thing lying or falling upon it, because it opens upwards, instead of downwards. A is the valve attached to the spindle A B, which works in guides; the valve fits down on the seat by its own weight; D C communicates with the boiler at C. Now when the pressure of the air is greater than that of the steam in the boiler, it will have a tendency, by acting on the under-surface of the valve, to open it, and so enter the boiler, thus preventing too great exhaustion. Reverse-valves are not needed for high-pressure boilers, on account of their great strength.

89. *Communication or Stop Valve.*

In some boilers there is a free passage for the steam to pass at all times from the boiler into the steam-pipe; but connected with most boilers of the present day there is a valve, called the communication-valve, or stop-valve, which can be screwed down or raised at the will of the engineer. This valve is very useful; for it enables the engineer to isolate any boiler from the rest, whenever it becomes convenient or important to do so. For instance, in large vessels, having several boilers, all of them are only used on emergencies; and were it not for the communication-valve, the steam from the others would find its way into the empty one, and there condense, causing great loss. Again, it is of especial service when the fires are banked up. It is usual at these times to keep them in such a state of combustion that the steam may be got up quickly, if requisite. To that end the steam is kept at, or rather above, the atmospheric pressure. Now if no communication-valve were fitted, the steam, as it is evolved from the water, would pass into the steam-pipe, from thence to the jacket, and ultimately become jacket-water; so that every hour the water in the boilers would become salter, because that which is holding the salt in solution is passing off as steam, and leaving the earthy particles behind. Hence it becomes necessary to displace a portion occasionally, and pump in more. But this would not be the case if the communication-valve were fitted, and kept shut; the steam, as fast as it is generated, would be retained within the boiler; a portion would be condensed by the cooling effect of the atmosphere on the shell of the boiler, but it would mix with the water again; and consequently, however long the fires were banked up, every thing would remain in the same state. The engine-room also is kept cool by this plan, because the heat is confined to the boiler alone.

War-steamers are now always fitted with these valves; for if the steam-pipe were knocked away, or perforated by shot, the steam would thus be prevented from issuing into the engine-room; and the engineers might endeavor, without impediment, to repair the damage.

In the accompanying diagram, B D C is the steam-pipe, of which B communicates with the boiler, and C leads towards the engines. A is the stop or communication valve, which can be screwed up or down by turning the handle F. When open, as in the figure, there is a free passage for the steam; but when screwed down on the seat D E, the communication is interrupted. If the boilers have a tendency to prime, it is as well on first starting the engines, to open the communication-valve only partially at first, to keep back the water. It serves as a sort of dash-plate.

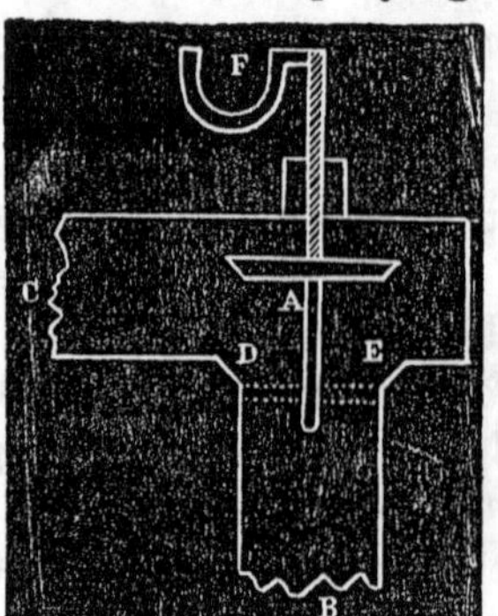

90. *Blow-out Cocks.*

Blow-out cocks are fitted to all marine boilers; they are for the purpose of enabling the engineer to change the water in the boiler as it becomes saturated with salt. A pipe is fitted to the *bottom* of the boiler, and is continued to some convenient part of the stoke-hole, from whence it proceeds to the outside of the ship. In that part of the pipe where it communicates with the stoke-hole there is a simple stop-cock; and a portable box-spanner fits this cock for the purpose of opening or shutting the orifice. Generally speaking, this spanner can only be *taken off* when the cock is closed: this is to guard against the possibility of accidents.

91. *Brine-pumps, Brine-valves, and Refrigerators.*

The boilers of marine engines are mostly supplied with salt water. Now as the water evaporates, and is converted into steam, the solid matter is left behind; and after a time, when the water becomes fully saturated, and can contain no more salt in solution, a deposit begins to take place within the boiler, which indurates as it is precipitated, and forms a *non*-conducting substance between the metal of the boiler and the water in it.* The evil of this is of two kinds. Loss of fuel takes place, because the heat is not able to penetrate so freely to the water; and secondly, the heat, not being spread throughout the mass, acts on the material of the boiler itself, by which means it becomes rapidly deteriorated. To remedy these evils, it is commonly the practice to "blow out" a certain portion of the water at stated periods, the place of the supersalted water (or brine) being supplied with an extra quantity introduced by means of the feed-pumps.

This process involves a trifling waste of fuel; for the water blown out is discharged into the sea at a temperature above 212°, while its place is supplied with water at a temperature not usually exceeding 100°.

To obviate these disadvantages, Messrs. Maudslay and Field have fitted brine-pumps to their boilers, which are worked by the engine; so that a small portion of brine is drawn off at every stroke. They are so adjusted, with ref-

* Dr. Davy experimented on various specimens of incrustation, and found that, "without any exception, they were composed chiefly of sulphate of lime; so much so, indeed, that unless chemically viewed, the other ingredients may be held to be of little moment, and rarely amounting to 5 per cent. on the whole."—*Trans. Br. Ass.* 1850.

erence to the size of the feed-pumps, that the quantity they draw off, together with the quantity of water evaporated, shall be equal to that supplied by the feed-pumps.* The saltness of the water is therefore by these means preserved at a uniform standard, and the danger of injurious deposits is prevented.

Another contrivance, by the same makers, is called a refrigerator, by which it is proposed to obviate almost entirely the waste occasioned by expelling the brine.

The water supplied from the feed-pumps is made to pass through a series of small tubes inside a closed vessel, through which the heated brine passes; and by these means the brine gives out its superfluous heat in raising the temperature of the feed-water previously to its discharging itself into the sea.

92. *Surface Blow-out Pipe.*

The water in the boiler is changed from the surface, and not from the bottom of the boiler, as formerly; for when tubular boilers were adopted, it was discovered that the

---

* If the brine drawn off be supposed to contain m times as much salt as the sea-water, the brine-pumps must extract $\frac{1}{m}$-th part as much as the feed-pump supply.

For let the sea-water contain $\frac{1}{32}$ part of salt;

$\therefore$ the brine contains $\frac{m}{32}$ parts of salt;

and let x = quantity of water supplied by the feed-pump;
y = quantity of water extracted by the brine-pumps:

$\therefore$ $\frac{x}{32}$ = quantity of salt injected into the boiler;

and $\frac{my}{32}$ = quantity of brine extracted;

and if these be equal, $\frac{x}{32}=\frac{my}{32}$

or $$y=\frac{1}{m}x.$$

tubes became much more rapidly incrusted than other parts of the boiler. A pipe with a stop-cock is fitted to each boiler, passing in half way between the upper tubes and the surface, the other end being connected with the blow-out pipe, or otherwise passing overboard, by which means a continuous change of water is going on. The cock is regulated by hand, and varied according to the circumstances under which the boiler is generating steam.

93. *Seaward's Brine-valve.*

This is an apparatus for allowing the escape of the brine from the boiler at every stroke of the feed-pump. It consists of two valves fixed on the same vertical spindle; the one valve is in the passage between the feed-pump and the boiler, and the other to the brine-discharge; the feed-water acts on the under surface of the upper valve, by which means it is raised, and allows the feed-water to enter the boiler. But in rising it raises also the lower valve, because they are connected together by the spindle, and thus the brine is permitted to escape; on the up-stroke of the feed-pump the feed-water ceases to flow, and the entrance of water and exit of brine stop at the same time. A difference in the areas of the valve regulates the proportion between the quantity admitted and that expelled.

94. *Brine and Feed Valves, as fitted at the Factory, Portsmouth Dockyard.*

A B (diagram, p. 76) is the brine-valve box, separated into two compartments by the partition C D; and into two other compartments by the horizontal partition E F, thus dividing it into four chambers; G H are two orifices forming the seatings of the two valves represented in the figure. K is a pipe leading to the boiler, and L is another pipe coming from the water-space of the boiler, and serving as a passage for the exit of water. The valves are connected by spindles with the lever M N, and a spring acting on the lever keeps both valves in their places. P is the feed-pipe, and Q that for brine. Now, when the feed-pump forces water through P, it opens the valve G, and enters

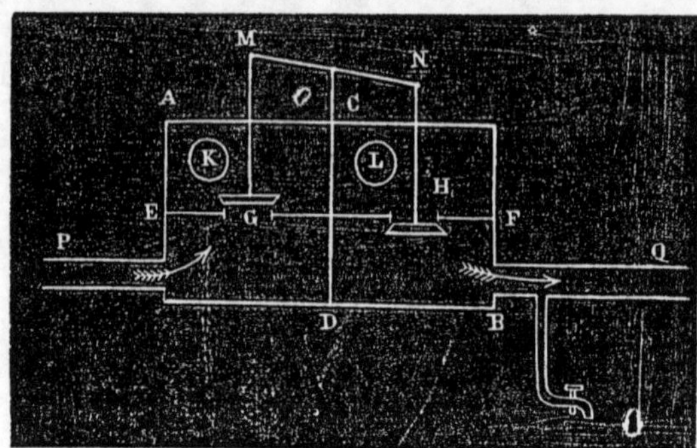

the boiler by means of the passage at K; and as the valve opens, the orifice at H is opened likewise, and the brine will issue from L through the pipe Q. The feed-valve G is four times the size of the brine-valve.

CHAPTER III.

THE ENGINE.

95. DEFINITION.—*The Steam-Engine is a Machine in which Steam is the only or principal Agent, and Heat the Moving Power.*

To illustrate the employment of elastic fluids to drive machinery, let us imagine a very large hollow vessel, called a cylinder, in which a thick circular plate of metal fits so closely as to prevent the passage of the air or other fluid between its edges and the surface of the cylinder. Now the pressure of the air will be equal on its two sides, and the piston, as it is called, will remain stationary; but we may make it move by any one of the three following methods:

1. We may *reduce* the pressure of the atmosphere on the one side, and allow the other to remain unaltered.

2. We may *increase* it considerably on the one side, and allow the other to remain unaltered.

3. We may increase it on the one side, and diminish it on the other.

And in each one of these instances the motion of the piston will ensue.

96. *Instances of the employment of these several Methods in Engines and Machines.*

The first method was applied on what were called atmospheric railways. Steam-engines were employed at intervals of a few miles to pump out the air from a long horizontal tube. In this tube was a solid piston connected with the railway carriages, which were placed above the tube; and consequently, when the equilibrium was sufficiently disturbed by the reduction of the atmospheric pressure on the one side, the *unreduced* pressure on the other side tended to urge the piston, and with it the train of carriages, etc., onwards. This method of propulsion was never generally adopted: the many practical difficulties, and a great loss of power beyond what was expected by its projectors, arising from the development of latent heat, have compelled the companies that adopted it to return to the usual methods.

2d. A gun is the most familiar instance of the application of the second principle. The ignition of the powder produces a gas of great elastic power, which drives the shot against the pressure of the atmosphere. The air-gun also acts on the same principle.

3d. The third principle is but a modification of the two former.

Steam being an elastic fluid, similar in most respects to air, is used in one of these three ways, either with or without the assistance of the atmosphere.

97. *Engines in use before the time of Watt.*

The engines employed were those commonly called atmospheric engines. They were used chiefly in pumping water from mines.

98. *Newcomen's Engine.*

G (diagram, p. 79) is the upper part of a boiler, which serves as a reservoir for the steam, the supply being kept up by the ebullition of the water in the lower part of the boiler. In this engine the steam has a pressure not much greater than that of the atmosphere. The hollow cylinder D F is placed directly over the boiler, and is connected with it by a pipe, as shown in the diagram. The communication can be stopped at will by means of a stop-cock F. D E is a movable piston, fitting steam-tight in the hollow cylinder, the upper end of which is open to the pressure of the atmosphere (a leading feature in all atmospheric engines).

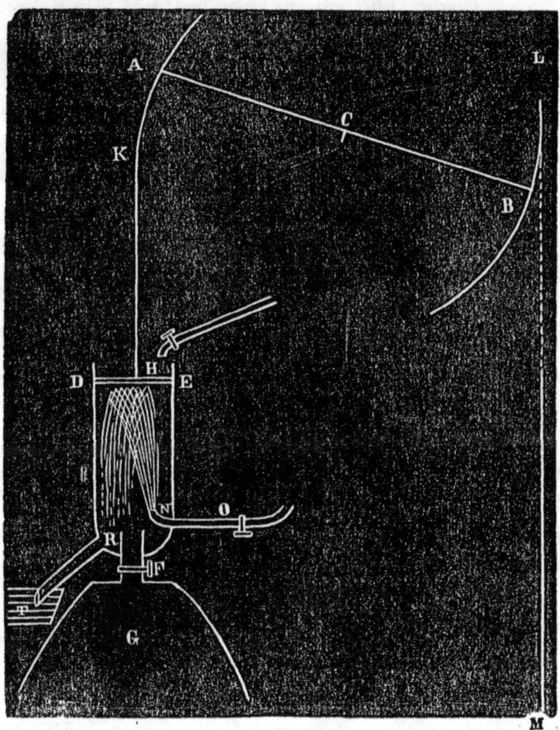

A B is a sway-beam, movable about a fixed centre C; each end of the beam terminating in a circular arc. To the upper ends of the arcs chains are attached, the one chain being fastened to the piston-rod H K, and the other to the rod L M for working the pumps. N O is a pipe leading from a reservoir of cold water, the supply of which to the cylinder is regulated by the cock O. A smaller pipe also leads from the same cistern to the upper part of the piston, and was useful at that stage of steam invention for keeping the piston steam-tight. (In the present day the correctness of workmanship would obviate the necessity of this second pipe.) There is another pipe R T from the lower part of the cylinder, having its lower extremity in a reservoir of cold water; it has a valve at the bottom, which opens outward, and when closed will not allow the water of the reservoir to ascend. One point more requires especial notice. The pressure of the atmosphere on the upper surface of the piston is about 14·75 lbs. per square inch. Now, whatever be the pressure the atmosphere exerts on the whole of the piston, the weight of the pump-rods, etc., must be half that amount. Thus, if the pressure of the atmosphere on the upper surface be 2000 lbs., the weight of the pump-rods, etc., must be 1000.

Let us now proceed to describe the action of the engine. Suppose it to be arranged as in the preceding diagram, with the cock O closed, and the whole of the cylinder occupied with steam; then, since the elastic pressure of the steam is nearly the same as that of the air, the pressure on the two sides of the piston will be equal, and consequently the weight of the pump-rods, etc., will preponderate, and the piston would ascend, and be pulled completely out of the cylinder; but when in the position represented in the figure, we will suppose the cocks F and O to be turned. The steam will no longer enter, and that already in the cylinder will be condensed by a jet of water from N; a partial vacuum will be produced; and if this vacuum were perfect, since the pressure of the air on D E = twice the weight of the pump-rods, etc., the piston will begin to descend with the same moving force that it ascended before. Again, when at its lowest point, the cock O is closed and F is opened; fresh steam enters, and the piston reascends. The water used in condensation, and the condensed steam, will run out of the pipe R T into the cistern T; and when a vacuum is produced in the cylinder, the valve at T will prevent the ascent of the water. This is an outline of the engine principally in use before the time of Watt; but even then the cocks O and F were worked by the engine itself, and not by hand, as the diagram would lead us to suppose. It is not intended in this description to give any detailed account of the engine, and for the generality of students such a description of an engine now obsolete would be useless; but the foregoing will perhaps serve as a basis to further instruction.

99. *The Discoveries of Watt.*

The engine had not advanced beyond this point till the time of Watt, when his attention was called to the subject from having to repair a model for the lecture-room of Glasgow University. He tried various methods; and for a time it seemed impossible to propose any improvement, because the learner will see that it is necessary the cylinder should be hot at one time and cool at another for the efficient working of the engine. At length he conceived it possible to have two distinct chambers, the one being the steam-cylinder, which should *always* be kept hot, and, connected with this, another called "the condenser," into which after the steam had done its duty, it should make its exit and there be condensed by a jet of cold water *continually* entering from a reservoir. The two conditions may therefore be fulfilled at the same time; for the cylinder may be always kept hot, and the condenser kept cold, during the whole time the engine is working; and hence it follows, that the steam, instantly it enters the cylinder, will be ready to act with effect; and again, directly the communication is opened to the condenser, it will make its escape; and by its condensation a partial vacuum will be kept up in the condenser. But now another difficulty arises; it is evident the water would soon fill up the condenser unless removed as fast as it entered; and besides this, the gaseous matter evolved from the water in boiling, not being capable of condensation, would destroy the vacuum. To provide against this, there must be a pump in connection with the condenser, and worked by the sway-beam, to carry off the water and air as fast as they enter. A (diagram, p. 82) is the passage connecting the cylinder with the condensing chamber B; D is the air-pump; E F is the bucket worked by the rod G, which is attached to the sway-beam of the

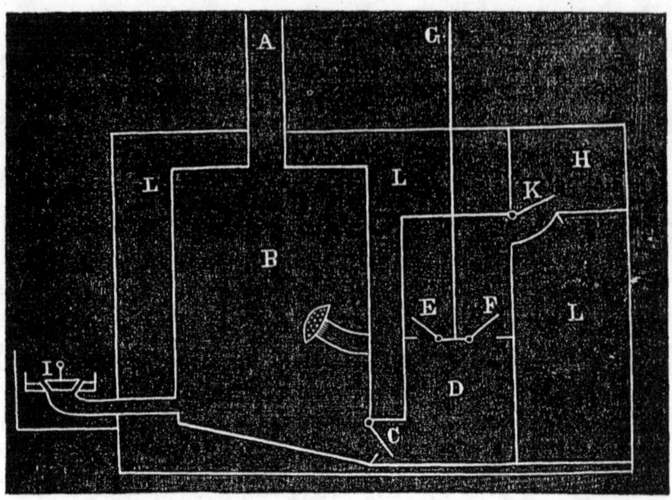

engine; C and K are valves moving on spindles at their upper edge, and opening towards the right. In the bucket of the pump are two valves, commonly called butterfly-valves, E and F, their motion being somewhat similar to that of the butterfly's wings. The lower valve C is called the *foot-valve*, and the upper one K is named the *delivery-valve.* The injection-pipe opens into the condenser as in the figure; and a jet of cold water is continually playing while the engine is at work. In land engines the whole of this apparatus is usually underground, and surrounded by a well of cold water, such as L L in the figure, from which the condenser is supplied. The water of condensation coming from the air-pump is discharged into a vessel H, called the *hot-well.* From this reservoir the boiler is again supplied; and this is a great additional source of economy in the engine, for the water thus returned to the boiler is warm, and therefore sooner boiled than cold water would be.

100. *Principle of the Single-acting Engine.*

Watt conceived the idea that it might be possible, after

the steam had forced the piston downwards to the end of the cylinder, to allow it a free access to the under side; when, *an equilibrium being thus established*, the counterbalancing weight will draw the piston up; and when it has arrived at the top, a communication being opened with the condenser, the steam will be condensed, and fresh steam coming in above will perform similar functions. To accomplish this, the cylinder must be closed at both ends. The steam must act to force the piston downwards, and not upwards, as in the atmospheric engine. A peculiar system of valves becomes necessary to effect the several operations.

101. *Explanation of the Single-acting Engine.*

Referring to the diagram, p. 84, we will first premise that the lower parts of the engine, consisting of the condenser, air-pump, hot-well, etc., are the same as those already described, page 82, and therefore a repetition will be unnecessary. The pipe H serves to convey the steam into the condenser, of which the top is represented in the figure. To explain the mode of ingress and egress for steam to the cylinder, let G G be the cylinder, closed at *both* ends, as in the figure, the cover on the upper end being made to take off, for repairs, etc., as occasion requires; R is a piston-rod moving air and steam tight through an orifice in the centre of the cylinder-cover; E is the piston; S is the steam-pipe; A, B, and C are three valves connected to spindles, and worked by machinery outside the engine, which it is not worth our while to explain here. But we must notice that B is always closed when A and C are open, and *vice versâ*. A rod outside the engine, however, connected with the valves, retains A and C open, and B closed, till the piston has nearly reached the bottom of the stroke; and then, during nearly the whole of the up-stroke of the piston, this rod takes the position it ought to have if the valves A and C were to fit down on their seats, and consequently the valve B opened.

Now, in the first position it may be readily seen that the steam can pass along the steam-pipe S to the top of the piston; and since C is also open, whatever be the quantity of

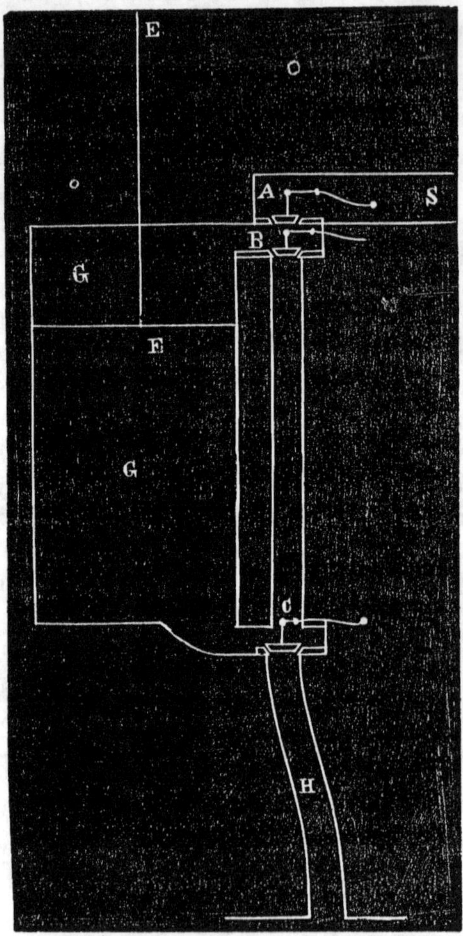

steam below the piston, it will find a ready egress through H to the condenser. Again, when the valves are pushed down, since B is open, the steam which was above the piston, and has forced it down, is at liberty to act either above or below, and on that account its effects are neutralized. The counterbalance at the other end of the sway beam now comes into operation, and draws up the piston

102. *Double-acting Engine.*

Its principle is easily understood, being more intelligible than the single-acting engine. In this class of engines the steam is allowed to act on the upper side of the piston; and having forced it to the bottom, a communication is opened with the condenser, into which it escapes. Then another supply is admitted below the piston, to force it up, which, when it has done its work, escapes also into the condenser. By these means the alternate motion of the piston is produced without the counterbalancing weight, which is, therefore, dispensed with in these engines.

103. *Alteration in the Moving Parts of the Engine introduced by the use of the Double-action principle.*

In engines hitherto described, since the power is exerted downwards at each end of the sway-beam alternately, it sufficed to have the piston and pump rods attached by *chains* to the ends of circular arcs, whose centre was the middle point of the sway-beam (see diagram, p. 79); but in the double-acting engine the *cylinder-end* of the sway-beam is to be first forced downwards by the steam, and then upwards, and consequently the connections must be *rigid;* and hence arises a difficulty, for the piston-rod moves in a vertical line, and must necessarily do so, because it passes through a steam-tight opening in the cylinder. But the end of the sway-beam describes a portion of a circle. It is, therefore, very evident that if the top of the piston-rod were in *direct* connection with the extremity of the sway-beam, the machinery would be strained. Hence a modification becomes necessary. This was also invented by Watt, and called the "parallel motion," because a parallelogram is always the most prominent feature in its outline. For a description of the parallel motion, see p. 96.

104. *Non-condensing Engine.*

This engine is mostly on the double-acting principle, but it has no condenser, air-pump, etc., and the steam is allowed to escape into the atmosphere after passing through the cylinder. For this purpose an exhaust-pipe conducts it to some place where it can be emitted. Since it occupies much less room than the condensing engine, and requires no water for condensing the steam, this species of engine is always used on railways and in some river boats, where saving of space is a great object. In locomotive engines the exhaust pipe passes into the funnel, and as the steam rushes out it serves to create a draught.

105. *The Marine Steam-Engine.*

The marine engine is one whose construction is modified so as to enable it to be placed in a steam-vessel, and, by working, to propel it through the water. In land engines the machinery is not in general limited in the space it occupies; part of it may, if more convenient, be placed underground—this frequently happens with the condenser and air-pump; the cylinder and sway-beams may be of any height, and the beams and rods may be of any convenient length. But it is not so with the marine engine. Here the sleepers in the bottom of the vessel determine the lowest level of the engine; and the upper deck in most cases limits the height.* Moreover, every foot by which the engine can be conveniently shortened or narrowed is so much gain to the ship, by giving more room for the men and officers, passengers, stores, coals, etc.

106. *Side-lever Marine Engine.*

The side-lever engine is a modification of the sway-beam engine on shore. When steam was first used as a motive power to propel vessels, this was the only kind of

*In most vessels of recent construction the whole engine is below the water-level, and this, of course, determines its height.

engine adopted; but they are not so frequently introduced at present, because engine makers are trying all means to construct engines occupying less space.

Plate I. is intended to represent a section of the engine of H. M. S. Bee, of 10 horse-power, and is drawn so as to present to the eye the exterior and interior at the same time. All the moving parts outside the cylinder are, however, omitted in this figure, and will be given subsequently, because it was thought that much complexity would be thus avoided. In this figure the half of every part is represented; and the student must imagine, while reading the description, every separate part to be doubled, so as to form a complete engine. A_1 A_2 represents the interior of the steam cylinder. This is surrounded, as in the figure, by a hollow space, B B, called the cylinder-jacket.* The pipe *a* conveying the steam from the boiler to the cylinder has free access to this jacket, which it keeps continually filled with steam, ready to enter the cylinder whenever it has an opportunity. In the meantime it becomes useful in keeping the cylinder warm, so that no condensation takes place *within the cylinder*. At C is a valve, called the expansion-valve, which, during the ordinary working of the engine, remains open. We shall refer to it again hereafter; but at present we will suppose it *kept open*. The steam can, therefore, make its escape from the jacket into the hollow space D, surrounded by the semicircular casing, of which E E E represents the half. If allowed to make its way, it would enter both the steam ports F F at the top and bottom of the cylinder; but this must not be permitted. That the engine may receive the steam at proper and regular intervals, a valve, called from its shape "the D-slide," is introduced. This valve is represented by itself

---

* Jackets are now seldom used, but a coating of felt covered with wood is put on instead. Fuel would most probably be saved if the jacket were retained, and covered over with non-conducting substances.

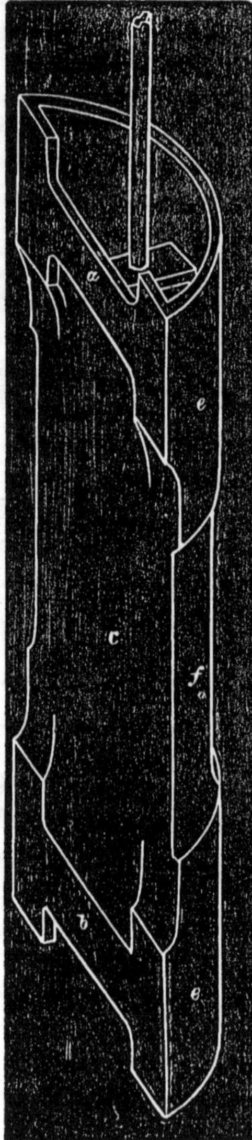

in the adjoining diagram. The flat projecting surfaces *a b* press against the projecting faces of the steam-ports FF (Pl. I.); the middle portion *c* recedes a little, as also does the middle of the semicircular back of the slide *f*.* The slide is hollow, and is usually of such a length that the faces *a b* may cover both ports FF at the same time.† Suppose, now, the valve to be in its place, and put in such a position as to cover both ports; then the steam from the boiler, passing by the pipe, enters the jacket, and making its way through the orifice at C, can surround the middle part of the slide, but can proceed no farther. Let, however, a force act on the rod *d* to draw it up a few inches; then the upper port is opened to the steam, and the lower port is uncovered, permitting a free communication between the portion of the cylinder below the piston and the condensing-chamber G G G. The steam entering by the upper port will consequently be unopposed in its endeavor to force down the piston H H. It will therefore descend, and bring down the rod I I, and whatever part of the machinery outside the cylinder may be connected with it. When

* The space between *e e* and the interior of the slide-casing is packed, to prevent steam from passing up or down.

† The slide in the annexed figure is made larger than necessary, to give a clearer representation.

the piston has come to the bottom of the cylinder, let the slide-rod be pushed down some inches, till the face *b* has uncovered the lower port to the steam; that which has entered above the piston H by the upper port F will be able to make its escape, by the same port, over the upper edge of the face *a* down the hollow of the slide into the condenser G; and at the same time the steam entering by the lower port, meeting with no opposition, forces up the piston, together with the piston-rod. Hence by moving the slide-rod up and down, the *reciprocating* motion of the piston and rod is produced, and with them the parts outside the engine to which we wish to communicate motion. The vacuum in the condenser is kept up by a jet of cold sea-water flowing in by means of a pipe through the ship's side, and called the *injection-pipe.* This supply is regulated by a cock in it, called the *injection-cock,* which is worked by hand. L L is the air-pump: it is similar to those in land engines; it has its bucket M M fitted with butterfly-valves N N, which turn on their spindles, and allow the water below them to pass above the bucket. K is a section of the *foot-valve** (as it is called), which permits the passage of water from the condenser to the pump, but prevents its return into the condenser on the down-stroke of the pump. The valve Q is called the *delivery-valve.* Its office is to take off the load of water from the top of the bucket as it descends. O is the *hot-well;* and above that, in many engines, is a conical vessel P, open at the top, called the *air-cone,* its only use being to prevent any chance of the water in the hot-well escaping into the engine-room; it is not, however, generally fitted now, having been found unnecessary. There are two orifices in the hot-well, the diameter of one being nearly six times that of the other. The larger one communicates with the sea through a pipe, called the *waste-water pipe,* by means of a

---

* The foot-valve, which is usually rectangular, has generally a guard at the back; but this would have confused the diagram.

valve called the *discharge* or *sluice* valve; the smaller one leads to a forcing-pump, by which the boiler is supplied with water of about 100° temperature. In the waste-water pipe is fitted a valve, close to the ship's side, which is called the sluice or discharge valve.

107. *Blow-through Valve.*

The accompanying diagram represents the section of a D-slide, with its casing and the steam-ports of the cylinder. C is the section of the slide, D E the casing, A and B the upper and lower steam-ports; the shaded part at D represents the packing at the upper port; and E that at the lower port. E F H is the part of the casing where the blow-valve is fitted, which contains a partition E G. This partition has a circular orifice, which is closed by the valve G (when in its seating). Now when the orifice is thus closed, the steam which surrounds the *waist* of the slide cannot pass below the partition E G. This is the state in which it ought to be while the engine is working; but so soon as the valve G is raised by the spindle F, a passage is made for it into the condenser through the lower part of the casing at H, and thus the steam can enter the condenser and expel the air without entering the cylinder.

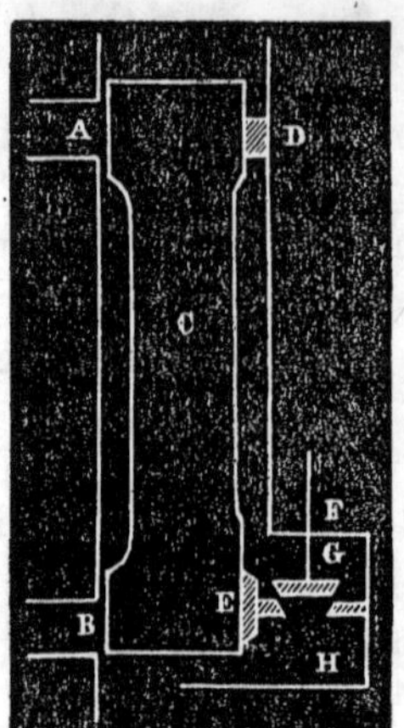

108. *Method adopted for keeping the Cylinder, Air-pump, Slide-valve, etc., air and steam tight.*

Referring to the middle of the cylinder-cover, where the piston-rod passes through it, we see that the orifice is shaped in the form of a circular cup, having a deep projecting flange; it is represented by R R, etc., in Plates I. and II. This is called the *stuffing-box*, for the following reason: the hollow cup is made much larger than the piston-rod, and the space between the stuffing-box and piston-rod is filled with a gasket of plaited hemp. On the inside of the stuffing-box, and below the packing, is a small brass bush, fitting tight round the piston-rod, but so as to let it move in it. This will prevent any packing from being forced down into the cylinder by the piston-rod. Above the stuffing-box is the "stuffing-box *cover*," or "*gland*," SSS; it has a projecting flange similar to that of the stuffing-box, and the two are connected by bolts and nuts. Reference to the figures will show that by screwing down the gland of the stuffing-box the packing is forced into contact with the piston-rod and stuffing-box at the same time, and thus escape of steam is prevented. We ought perhaps to notice here, that an engineer must not be satisfied that the packing fits tight; for unless the whole space between the cup and the piston-rod be filled up, steam will escape. The upper part of the "gland" in contact with the piston is hollowed out; it is kept full of melted tallow, for lubricating the packing. A similar description applies to all those parts where a rod has to work air-tight through an orifice, as may be seen in the figure by referring to the rod of the air-pump and slide valve.

109. *Details of the Piston of the Steam-cylinder.*

HH is a section of the piston. It will be seen that it is hollow, for the sake of lightness, and of considerable depth, to prevent the force of the steam at the edges from deflecting it. Formerly it was the custom to keep it steam tight in the cylinder by hemp-packing, interposed in a hollow groove TT at its circumference, between it and the cylinder; but in the present day, metallic rings, placed within this groove, surround the piston, and are forced out towards the cylinder by springs or packing. A flat horizontal ring, as shown in the figure, is then bolted down to the outer edge of the piston, and keeps the rings in their place. The lower surface to the right is cut away, that when the piston is at the bottom of its stroke, the steam entering at the lower port may have free access to the under-side of the piston, and force it up again. The piston is not allowed to come in contact with the top or bottom of the cylinder; and the space between it and the top or bottom, when at the extreme of its stroke, is called the *clearance.*

The piston-rod is conical at its lower end, and in some cases is kept in its place by a key driven through it and the central part of the piston. But the usual mode at present is to have a thread cut in the rod and a nut to correspond, by which means the piston is secured more firmly to the rod.

The air-pump bucket is kept tight in its cylinder by means of hemp-packing.

110. *Working Parts of side-lever Engines.*

The part U U (Plate II.), going across the cylinder, and connected to the piston-rod I, is called the cylinder cross-head. The smaller cross-piece *v v* is called the air-pump cross-head. The rods X X are termed the cylinder side-rods; and *y y* the air-pump side-rods. Z_1Z_2, Z_1Z_2, are called the sway-beams, or side-levers. Now it will be seen, by inspecting the figure, that as the piston-rod moves down, the cylinder cross-head U U, the side-rods X X, and the ends Z_1Z_1 of the side-levers, will move down with it. But the side-levers move round their middle point *p* (which is called the main centre); and therefore as Z_1Z_1 descend, the ends Z_2Z_2 will ascend. Again, *q q* are the paddle-shafts, that is to say, the shafts to which the paddles are to be attached, and the revolution of these shafts will cause the revolution of the paddles. These shafts are in connection with the parts *r r*, called the cranks, the farther extremities of which are connected together by the crank-pin. Also, the upper end of the connecting-rod *s* embraces this pin by means of the connecting-rod brasses *t t*, while its lower end passes through the cross-piece *g g*, to which it is rigidly secured. This cross-piece is called by some the *fork-head*, and by others it is termed the *cross-tail.* Let now the ends Z_2Z_2 of the sway-beams be supposed to move up, as before, by the admission of steam into the cylinder above the piston. Then the fork-head and connecting-rod, being forced up, will cause the cranks *r r* to rotate; and as they revolve, the shafts *q q* will revolve with them, and produce a revolution of the paddles. This motion will continue till the cranks are vertical; and if the engine have acquired sufficient momentum, they will pass the highest point, and be in a proper position to commence the other semi-revolution. We have before shown that the upward motion of the crank was produced by the pressure acting on the upper side of the piston forcing it down. Let us now, in the next place, imagine that the steam has been admitted below the piston, which is nearly at the bottom of the cylinder; then, on the contrary, the connecting-rod will be dragged down, and the cranks will descend, till they come to their lowest position, causing the paddles to perform the other half of their revolution through the water.

We will next proceed to describe the action of the air-pump. The reader should have Plates I. and II. before him, and refer to each as occasion requires. First, looking at Plate II., we see that the air-pump rod is connected to the air-pump side-rods *y y* by means of the cross-head *v v;* and hence, as the side-levers ascend and descend (vibrating round their main centre *p*), the piston-rod is forced up and down again. The air-pump is lined with brass, to give a better surface for the packing of the bucket to travel over: otherwise the salt water would oxydize the iron, and the packing (being of hemp) would soon be worn away. This is not necessary in the steam-cylinder, because the steam does not act so injuriously on the iron, and the packing is usually metallic. Metallic packing has also been tried in the air-pump. The action may be more clearly seen by referring to Plate I. As the rod of the air-pump is pushed up, the valve K, which is called the foot-valve, is raised by the pressure of the water under it in the condenser, and it by these means fills the body of the pump under the bucket. Again, as the rod is forced down, the bucket M M coming in contact with the water, the valves N N will open, and admit the water above the bucket. When, then, the bucket is raised the next time, the water is lifted with it, and, pressing against the under-surface of the *delivery-valve* (as it is called) Q, makes its escape into the *hot-well* O, where it would accumulate, were it not that an escape is provided through the ship's side by the waste-water pipe. The waste-pipe must be of considerable size, because it has to afford a passage, during a very short period of the stroke, for all the water that has accumulated in the engine during the whole stroke.

111. *Method of working the Slide.*

The shaft 11, called the weigh-shaft, is fixed to some part of the framework of the engine by plomer-blocks, in which it can revolve; so that when a force acts on the stud 2, at the end of the arm 12, to push and pull it alternately, it will make it move either from left to right or from right to left, as the case may be. It will be seen that two arms 34, 34, are fixed to the shaft 11, and therefore the vibrating motion of the shaft through a small angle will be productive of an oscillating motion of these horizontal levers; hence the points 33 will alternately rise and fall. To these points are attached side-rods 35, 35; and their upper ends being connected together by the cross-head 55, its middle point supports the slide, by means of the end of the slide-rod, at the point 6. It will be observed that there is a weight 44 at the end of the levers. The office of this weight is to balance the weight of the slide, so as to keep the slide in its position when the engine is stopped, viz., with both ports closed for steam: or otherwise the slide would drop, and thus open the port for steam, and move the engine. If the slide be thus balanced, the only power requisite to work it will be that which suffices to overcome its friction.

The names of the machinery just described, connected with the slide, are as follow:

The part 11 is called the *weigh-shaft.*

The weight 44 is called the *back-balance.*

That part of the lever from the weigh-shaft to 33 is called the *valve-lifter* or *slide-lever.*

The rod 12 is called the *gab-lever* or *eccentric-lever.*

The cross-piece 55 is called the *valve cross-head.*

112. *Strap, Gib, and Cutter.*

This contrivance is used to connect the working parts of a steam-engine together, and the advantage of using it consists in the facility it gives to the engineer of tightening up the parts of the engine that become worn, together with the power of taking the engine apart when necessary. In the adjoining diagram, *a* is a bearing which is to be connected with the rod *b*, so as to be freely movable. The shaded parts of the diagram represent two brasses; one of which, viz., the lower, rests on the end of the rod, and the upper one on the bearing *a*, leaving a space between them, each brass being hollowed out to hold the bearing. *c c c* is a *strap* surrounding these brasses and the sides of the rod. The rod and the strap have a key-way cut through them, into which first of all the piece of iron *d d d* (called the *gib*) is inserted, and then the *cutter* or *key e e* is driven in, securing the whole firmly together; and as the bearing wears, by driving up the key, the parts are brought close together again. To effect this, spaces are purposely left in the slot-way. It is the practice with engineers to drive all *keys* towards the main centre of side-lever engines.

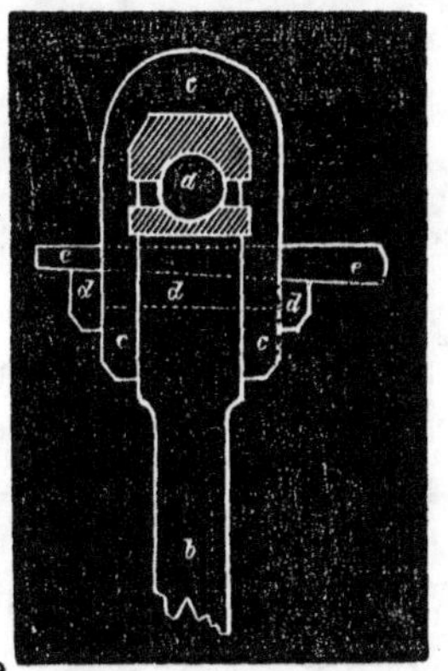

113. *The Cylinder Escape-valves.*

If we watch the action of the slide, we perceive that all ingress or egress to or from the cylinder is cut off by the slide as the piston is coming towards the end of its stroke; and consequently whatever is contained within the cylinder must remain there, unless some means of escape be provided. Now, from various causes (such as condensation, priming, etc.), water is apt to collect in the cylinder, both above and below the piston; and, since it is incompressible, if it accumulate to any considerable extent, the engine will either be stopped or some accident will happen. Either of these may, however, be prevented by providing the cylinder with valves for allowing the water to escape; that for the space above the piston is in the cylinder-cover, and is mostly retained in its place by a spring: the lower one is exhibited in Plates I. and II.; the letter Z represents the weight for keeping it in its place. The valve and orifice communicating with the cylinder are both shown in Plate I., and the outside appearance is seen in Plate II. These valves are generally loaded with a weight greater than that of the safety-valve, otherwise they would open with every fresh introduction of steam.

In engines working at great speed, such as those driving the propellers of most of our block-ships, the load on the escape-valves is not greater than that on the safety-valve. At first starting the engines, it is a common thing to see them open, and allow the steam and water to escape; this goes on till the engine is fairly under weigh, when they remain closed. The object of this is, that the engine may not be overtaxed; and, as is observed in Article 116, cocks are fitted to assist the valves, or other means are adopted of allowing the water to escape. It is a good plan to have a brass or copper case over the upper escape-valve, fitted with a nozzel to emit the water clear of the persons standing in the engine-room.

114. *Parallel Motion.*

By the term "parallel motion" we understand a set of bars and rods fitted to the cylinder side-rods X X, and intended to keep their upper extremity in a vertical straight line, or nearly so, during the whole of the stroke. The necessity of some such contrivance is obvious (see Art. 103); for, as we have before observed, the end of the side-levers Z_1Z_1 describes a circular arc, and this would have the effect of alternately thrusting the piston-rod against one side or other of the stuffing-box. In Plate II. we have, for simplicity's sake, left out the parallel motion; but the accompanying diagram will enable us to suppose those parts that are wanting, and the figure will not become too complicated. Let D F represent the side-rod; F O half the sway-beam; O the main centre; B G, B C, two rods, connected to each other at B, and to the side-rod and sway-beam at G and C respectively (and thus forming a parallelogram); A B another rod, connected with the two former at B, and moving round a fixed point A. This series of rods is called the parallel motion; and our object is to determine their *proper lengths*, that they may effectually perform their duties. To do this, we shall have to show that there is always some point *c* in B C which describes approximately a straight line, and then to find the proportionate lengths of the various rods, that the path of D (where the piston cross-head is attached) and *c* may be made *similar*. We will first, however, give to these rods the names they generally receive: F O being the half sway-beam, and D F the cylinder side-rod; A B is called the radius-bar, or

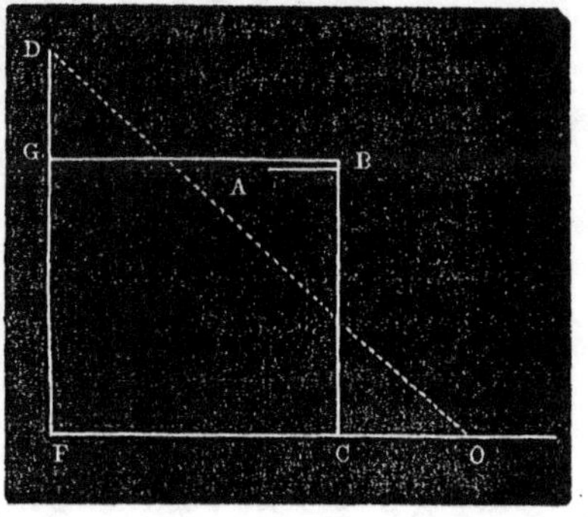

bridle-rod; BC the parallel-motion side-rod; and G B the parallel-motion bar.

The accompanying figure represents the three lines A B, B C, C O, which form part of the previous figure, but are separated from it, because the rest is not wanted in our

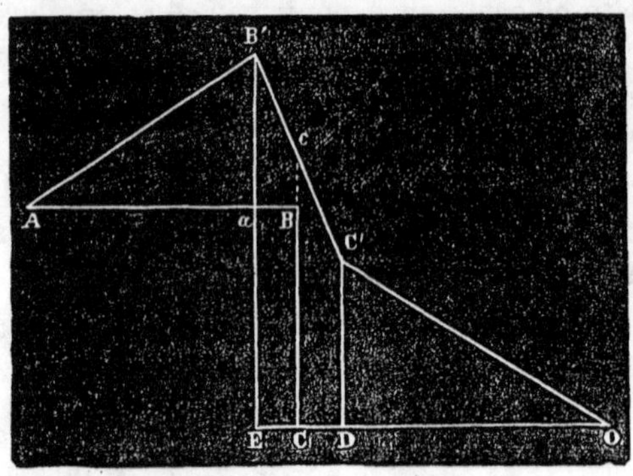

present consideration of the subject. Now as C O moves round the main centre O, A B will revolve about A, and the rods A B, B C, C O will come into some other position A B′, B′C′, C′O, the point B′ being drawn to the left, and the lower point C′ to the right. Again, when it comes into the similar position below C O, the same will take place. But if we produce B C both ways, it will cut B′C′ in some point *c*, which is evidently the point of which we were speaking; for since the whole of the line B C is vertical when C O is horizontal, and since *c* is in this vertical line (produced) at both extremes of the motion, it follows that it cannot be out of that vertical line to any sensible extent at any period of the motion, and therefore the point *c* describes, approximately, a straight line. It is found by a geometrical investigation (given in the Appendix), that unless A B′ be small, the point *c* divides B C into two parts, which are reciprocally proportional to A B and C O; that is to say, B′*c* : *c* C′ : : C′O : A B′.

Our next object is to insure that the point D (the point of connection between the cross-head and cylinder side-rod) shall move vertically, or nearly so. To affect this, our endeavor is to make it move in a path similar to *c*. Now the line D F is, throughout the stroke, parallel to B C, because it is constrained by the bar B G. Let us, therefore, join O *c*, and produce it to cut F D, and the point where it cuts should be the extremity of the rod D F. For since D F is parallel to *c* C, and F C O is a straight line, the triangle D F O, however it may alter its form, is similar to *c* C O in corresponding positions; and since the point O of each triangle is fixed, and the points F and C describe circular, and therefore similar, arcs, it follows that D and *c* will describe similar paths, and D will move in a straight line if *c* moves in a straight line.*

115. *Surface Condensation.*

To avoid the inconvenience attending the employment of salt water in the boilers, Messrs. Hall of Basingford invented a species of condenser which would return the condensed steam to the boilers; and consequently, if the vessel started with fresh water, and had within the boiler a small distilling apparatus for the purpose of generating a quan-

* *To find the Length of the several Parts that the point D may move in a straight Line.*

By the investigation (see Appendix):

$$\frac{CO}{AB}=\frac{Bc}{Cc}=\frac{BC-Cc}{Cc}$$

$$=\frac{BC}{Cc}-1 \quad \ldots\ldots\ldots\ldots \quad (1)$$

But, by similar triangles,

$$\frac{Cc}{CO}=\frac{DF}{FO}$$

$$\therefore \quad Cc=\frac{CO.DF}{FO}$$

$$\text{and} \quad \frac{1}{Cc}=\frac{FO}{CO.DF}$$

$$\therefore \text{by (1)} \quad \frac{CO}{AB}=\frac{BC.FO}{CO.DF}-1$$

And if this relation exist among the several parts, the point D will move in a straight line.

tity equal to that which was wasted by the steam-pipe, etc., the engines might proceed for any length of time without admitting salt water to the boilers. The principle of the condenser employed for this purpose is, that instead of allowing the steam, after escaping from the cylinder, to rush at once into a vessel to be condensed, it is here compelled to pass through a series of small copper pipes, placed vertically; these pipes being placed in a large rectangular vessel, called the condensing-chamber. The injection-water is admitted into the lower part of this vessel, and is pumped out again from the upper part: and the water thus admitted surrounds the pipes, and chills the steam, thereby converting it into water. The air-pump is much smaller with these condensers than with those where the common plan of injection is used, because the injection-water is carried off by a separate process. The only attention these condensers require consists in keeping the tubes clear, and there are means supplied for effecting this. The first cost of these condensers is, however, considerable; they have great weight, and occupy considerable space. There is also difficulty in keeping the tubes clear from incrustation on the outside, and unless that be done, the heat is prevented from passing out; and the copper tubes have also the effect of impregnating the water with a formidable galvanizing agent. These objections have prevented this ingenious idea from being generally adopted in all our steamers.

116. *Test-cocks.*

When engines have very little *clearance* in the cylinder, cocks are fitted at the top and bottom with pipes to them; these are for allowing water to escape independently of the escape-valves, and are kept open till the engine is fairly under weigh. They are so constructed as to allow water to escape as the piston ascends or descends, but not to admit the air on the vacuum side, or otherwise they would militate against the good working of the engine.

117. *The Foot-valve not absolutely necessary.*

Although most engines are fitted with a foot-valve, yet they may be, and are, contrived so as to do without it. But then the steam must not enter the condenser so low down as in other engines; and the air-pump must work as near the bottom of the condenser as possible, that the bucket may plunge into the water at every stroke, to enable it to extract a portion each time, and prevent the engine from becoming choked. Messrs. Napier of Glasgow have constructed some engines to work without foot-valves; but instead of allowing the steam to enter the condenser *down* the slide, they have reversed the operation, and exhaust *up* the slide, and thus into the condenser; so that the water in the condenser may rise to almost any height without entering the slide, because the steam-orifice is at the top.

118. *The Annular Air-pump Bucket.*

The annular air-pump bucket may be conceived by supposing a piston from which two annular spaces have been taken out, as in the following diagram, of which Fig. 1 is the plan, and Fig. 2 at A exhibits the section. The annular spaces are connected together by radii, as is shown in Fig. 1.

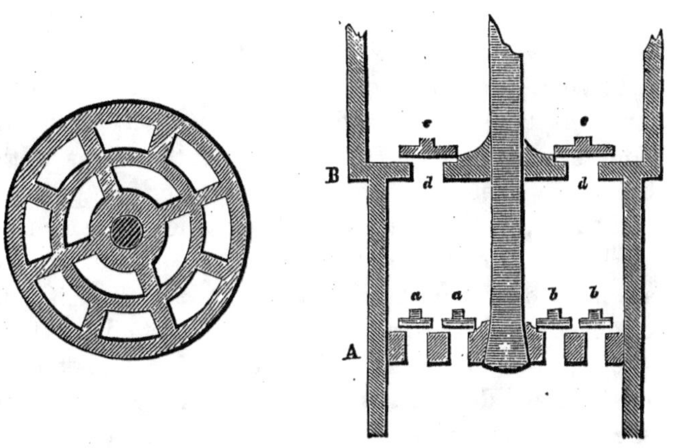

Fig. 1. Fig. 2.

Over these annular spaces circular rings of metal are fitted, and these rings are called the valves. The valves are shown in section in Fig. 2, at *a a* and *b b*. They work in guides, and are only allowed a certain amount of lift.

119. *Annular Delivery-valves.*

Annular delivery-valves are of the same kind as the valves of the air-pump bucket. There is, however, but one circular orifice in the seat, and consequently only one annular valve. It is shown in section in Fig. 2 at B; *c c* is the valve, and *d d* the orifice. Maudslay's double-cylinder engines are fitted with these.

120. *Peculiarity in the Air-pump of a Steam-engine.*

If we look upon the condenser as the well from which the water is to be pumped, we notice a manifest difference between the duty of the air-pumps and that of other pumps, inasmuch as the condenser is not open to the air, and the ascent of the water cannot be assisted by the pressure of the atmosphere. The bucket therefore cannot be raised to any great height above the condenser, with the expectation that the water will follow the bucket on its up-stroke.

121. *Air-pump without a Delivery-valve.*

Instances have occurred in which engines have worked for some time after the delivery-valve had given way. For example, H.M.S. Vixen, when on the China station, broke the spindle of her delivery-valve, and proceeded without it; and scarcely any appreciable difference in the working of the engine could be perceived. But it is clear she must have been fitted with a foot-valve, and it is also evident that the air-pump had more work to do in the up-stroke; and though the mean amount of work is the same in an up and down stroke, yet the bucket would be more strained; and, unless it had been in good condition, it would not have lasted long when subjected to this trial.

In quick-working engines, the shock on the delivery-valve on the ascent of the bucket of the air-pump is very great, producing great wear and tear and a disagreeable noise. To prevent this, a small valve is sometimes fitted to admit air above the bucket as it descends; and lately canvas or vulcanized India-rubber delivery-valves have been fitted. These work very well; but the former leak when the engine stops, so that it becomes necessary to blow through frequently to keep the condenser clear. In some engines the delivery-valve is divided into two parts, these parts being set at different angles. These valves will open at different portions of the stroke, and divide the shock between them. Annular delivery-valves are less noisy than those that work on spindles.

122. *Double-actiny Air-pump.*

For a description of this pump the reader is referred to the last article of Chapter IV.

123. *Discharge or Sluice Valve.*

This valve is fitted in the waste (or discharge) water pipe, at its junction with the ship's side. In some ships there are two valves; one a common lifting-valve, and the other a sluice-valve, which is screwed across the opening of the pipe. This valve must of course be opened before attempting to start the engine, or otherwise the hot-well will burst, or the air-pump break down. The use of this sluice-valve is to cut off the communication with the sea when the engine is not at work.

124. *Slides fitted to Marine Engines.*

They are called the Long D-Slide, the Short D-Slide, the Locomotive Slide, Seaward's Slides, and Cylindrical Slides.

125. *Details of the Long D-Slide.*

This slide has been partially described in giving the details of the beam-engines; but there are still some points that require consideration; for as it is the apparatus by which the supply and exit of steam are managed, *all* its peculiarities deserve attention. With this slide, the steam, after entering the lower port, and doing its work, commonly makes its exit through the same aperture (by raising the slide) direct into the condenser; while that which enters the upper port has to make its way down the hollow of the slide before it can reach the condenser. This, however, is not always the arrangement; for, as we have said, in some engines of Napier's construction the steam from the upper port rushes at once into the condenser, while that from the lower port has to make its way up the slide into the condenser.

Slides are at times hard to move, because of the vacuum in the cylinder when the engine has stopped. In such case the grease-cock of the cylinder should be opened and the air admitted, which will get over the difficulty.

126. *Short D-Slide.*

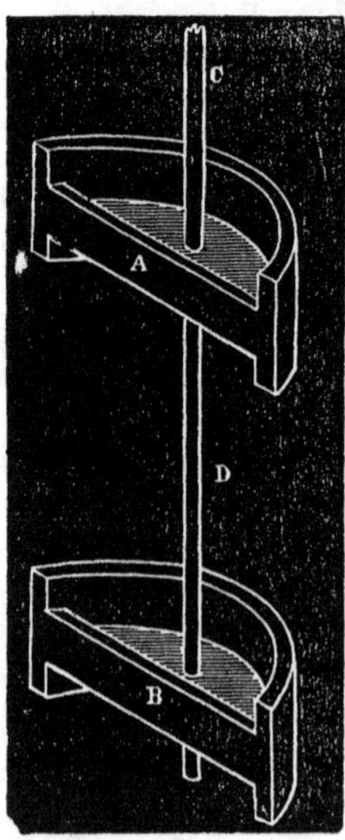

The Long D is made with a passage entirely through it, and has but one exhaust passage; but the short D has two separate exhaust or eduction passages, fitted to allow the steam to pass to the condenser, one at the top of the slide-case, and the other at the bottom.

The accompanying diagram represents the Short D-slide. A and B are the upper and lower slide-faces, and C D is the rod by which they are both worked. At the back of each slide-face may be seen a flat partition to separate the steam from the exhaust side of the slide.

127. *Locomotive Slide.*

If we conceive the condenser and boiler to change their duties, the common slide will then perform its office in the manner the slide of a locomotive engine does. In other words, we must suppose the steam from the boiler to make its way to the cylinder by the back of the slide, and to escape from the face. This construction is generally adopted for all horizontal engines, as also in oscillating engines.

The locomotive slide is more difficult to move than a D-slide, because the pressure acting on the back forces it against the steam-ports, whereas in the other slides the steam surrounds the slide; and the exhaust-port being much greater than the steam-port, the pressure hence arising is more than that caused by the packing of the commoner kind. This want of equilibrium in the pressures has been practically remedied by a COCK to admit steam on the vacuum or exhaust side of the slide at the time of starting. Locomotive slides, as, indeed, all short slides, are more expensive in steam than the Long D, the latter having shorter steam-passages than the former.

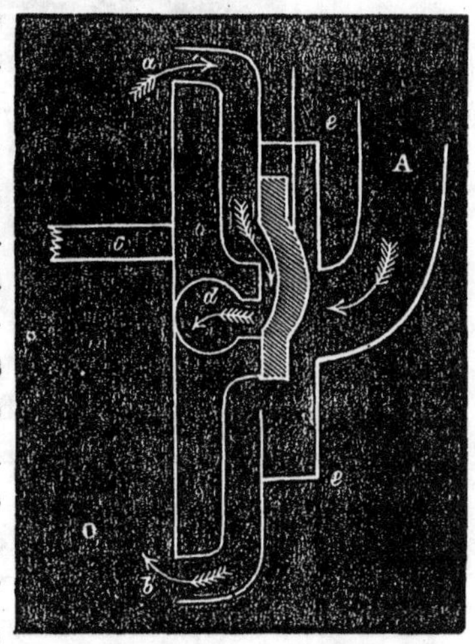

The accompanying diagram represents a section of a locomotive slide and its casing. A is the steam-pipe, *e e* the slide-casing, and the shaded portion represents the slide; *a* and *b* are the upper and lower steam-ports, and *d* is the place of egress to the condenser; *c* is a portion of the piston. As the slide is at present situated, steam from the pipe A can enter the lower port, and that which is above the piston *c* may escape from the upper port through *d* to the condenser. And if the slide be moved down, the reverse of this will take place.

128. *Seaward's Slides.*

In engines fitted with these slides there are four apertures or ports to each cylinder: two on the one side nearest the steam-pipe, for admitting the steam; and two on the other side nearest the condenser, for allowing it to rush into the condenser. In the accompanying diagram A and C are

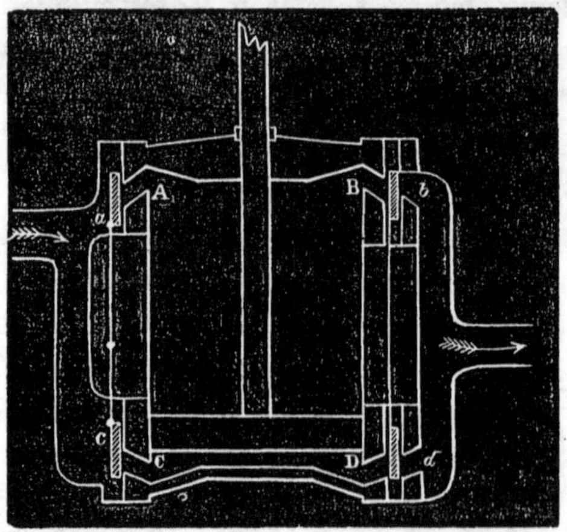

the induction-ports, as they are called, serving to admit steam from the steam-pipe to the top and bottom of the cylinder alternately; and B and D are called the eduction-ports, their office being to allow the steam, which has been previously admitted to the cylinder, to make its escape to the condenser. The arrows show the direction of the steam at ingress and egress.

The slides *a, c, b, d,* are fitted to the rods of the steam and eduction slides *a c* and *b d* with rule-joints, and are kept against the nozzles of the slides by the pressure of the steam. The exhaust-slides at B and D press against the nozzles on the condenser-sides, and the vacuum in the condenser keeps them close when the port-ways are covered; but both slides are assisted by curved springs. If there be any water in the cylinder, it is forced thence into the steam-pipe by the ascent or descent of the piston, the joints of the slide allowing them to be forced back. Again, when the slides do not cover the ports, there is not much friction, because they are then only pressed against the nozzles by the force of the springs; whereas with valves of other construction the pressure is always very great, on account of the packing by which the slide is constantly kept steam-tight against the nozzles. In some instances these slides are worked by cams instead of eccentrics.

129. *Cylindrical Slides.*

These slides are fitted to those engines of Messrs. Maudslay's construction which are called double-cylinder engines, and for an explanation of them we must refer to the description of the engine given in Chap. III.

130. *Meaning of the term "Cushioning."*

The slide is set in such a manner that the passage to the *condenser* shall be shut off by it before the piston arrives at the end of the stroke. Now there is not a perfect vacuum in the condenser, and therefore there is also steam of a certain density and pressure opposing the piston's motion. This is not great in amount so long as a free communication exists between the cylinder and condenser; but immediately that is interrupted, this pressure begins to increase and act as a retarding force, increasing as the steam-pressure on the opposite side diminishes, and thus acting with the latter cause in gradually bringing the engine to a state of rest before it is started in the opposite direction. For instance, if the *cushioning* (for this is the name given) commence when the piston is eight inches from the end of its path, and the pressure be two lbs., then, when at the distance of four inches the pressure will be four lbs.; and when at the distance of two inches the pressure will be eight lbs.; and when at the distance of one inch the pressure will be sixteen lbs. Cushioning at a comparatively early period of the stroke, or, in other words, closing the communication with the condenser early, is of great advantage when locomotive slides are used; for the long steam-passages (see diagram, p. 105) then become filled with tolerably dense steam, so that when the slide opens there is much less demand on the boiler to fill these passages and the clearance at the top and bottom of the cylinder.

131. *Lead of the Slide.*

The stop of the eccentric is so arranged that the port may begin to open for the admission of fresh steam an instant before the piston arrives at the end of its stroke, and the *space the port is open for steam* when the piston is at the end of the stroke is called the *lead* of the slide. The advantage of this becomes evident if we consider the inertia of the engine when an attempt is made to bring it to a state of rest, and the time that must elapse before the steam, coming through a very narrow orifice, would sufficiently influence it; so that if uniformity of motion be desirable, it becomes necessary to have the port wider open; and this can only be attained by making it commence its motion rather sooner. On account of the lap on the slide, we see that the orifice for *exhaustion* will be open earlier than for the *admission* of steam; and, on commencing the return-stroke, the steam that drove the piston the opposite way is escaping freely. The accompanying diagram will exhibit the position of the slide when the piston is about to commence its downward course: the steam has already begun to enter the upper port, and that which has done its work is making its way out of the lower port.

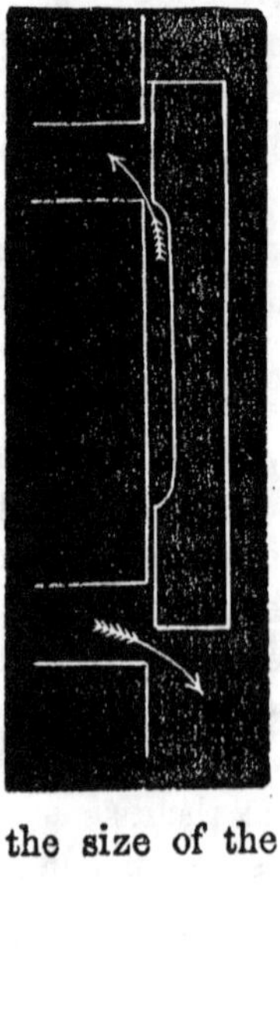

The amount of lead given depends upon the size of the ports and the velocity of the piston. A locomotive engine, for instance, requires considerable lead, as likewise many of our marine engines which are driven at high velocities, particularly those which work the screw without the intervention of any multiplying gear; and, on the contrary, where the velocity is small, and consequently there is little momentum to be overcome, the lead is but trifling in amount. If there were no lead, and the piston moved very rapidly, the crank would, by its momentum, be compelled to drive the piston, instead of being driven by it. To use a technical expression, the steam would be *too late* in its action.

The team *lead* is likewise at times applied to the *exhaust*-side of the slide; for instance, when the exhaust commences sooner at the top than at the bottom, as with direct-action engines, in such cases the engine is said to have more *lead* on the exhaust-side at the top than at the bottom. And again, to take another instance, if the lap on the *steam*-side is reduced for any reason, a portion of the slide-face is cut off from that portion of the opposite end in communication with the condenser. When this is done, it is said that more lead has been given on the exhaust-side.

132. *Lap or Cover of the Slide.*

In the early steam-engines it was customary to allow the steam to flow into the cylinder throughout the whole stroke, or nearly so; but it was found, particularly when the velocity of the piston was considerable, that a very imperfect condensation took place, arising from the great quantity of steam to be condensed, and the little time to effect it. Hence it was found necessary to shut off the steam before the piston had completed its stroke. This was effected by putting *lap*, as it is termed, on the steam-side of the slide. In Fig. 1 (p. 110) let *a b e* represent the slide at half-stroke, *a b* the faces, and *c d* the port-ways into the cylinder. Then, as is represented by the figure, the depth of the slide face is the same as that of the port; in other words, the slide *has no lap*. Again, in Figs. 2 and

than the ports; in other words, the slide has *lap* both at the upper and lower ports. Also, in Fig. 2, the slide is in 3, it will be observed that the depths of the face are greater

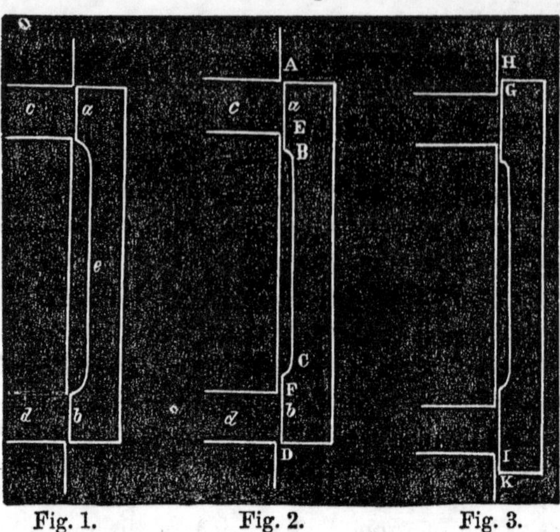

Fig. 1. Fig. 2. Fig. 3.

the middle of its stroke; and it may be seen that the excesses E B and F C are on that part of the slide from which the steam comes. This is expressed by saying there is lap on the steam-side only. In Fig. 3, however, it will be observed that, in addition to the lap on the steam-side, there is an excess H G at the upper and I K at the lower extremity of the slide, which is where the egress to the condenser takes place. In such case, it is said that there is *lap* both on the *steam* and *exhaust* sides. The lap, both on the steam and exhaust sides, is sometimes called the *cover*.

Many engines have a deficiency instead of an excess of lap on the exhaust-side. It is then said that the slide has *negative lap, or cover*, on the exhaust-side.

Def. The word *lap* means the excess of the slide over the port when the slide is in the middle of its stroke.

133. *The Effect of Lap on the Steam-side.*

The lap or cover on the steam-side serves to cut off the

steam at an earlier period of the stroke than it would otherwise do. For if we look at Figs. 1 and 2, and suppose the stroke of the slide to be the same in both, it is evident the lower edge B in Fig. 2 will cut off the steam sooner than the slide in Fig. 1, and thus the steam will work expansively by means of the slide. This expansion cannot be varied at the will of the engineer, like that produced by the expansion-valve, which can be arranged to cut off the steam at different portions of the stroke.

134. *Lap on the Exhaust-side.*

This is necessary when the lap on the steam-side is excessive; because, let us suppose a considerable quantity of additional lap put on the steam-side of the lower slide; then in order to open the lower port at the proper time, that is, when the piston is near the bottom of the stroke, it is clear it must commence its motion sooner than it would if the lap were not so great. But in such case the upper port would open to the condenser too soon, unless lap be added to the upper edge of the upper slide-face. And the same may be said of the lower edge of the lower slide-face.

It must be borne in mind that whenever an alteration is made in the lap of a slide, the stop for the eccentric,* or rather, the position of the eccentric, must be altered so as to preserve the same lead.

135. *On the difference in the working of Two Engines, one of which has Lap on the Steam-sides of the Slides, and the other has none.*

In the latter, the steam being continued the whole length of the stroke, a violent jar takes place as the engine passes its centre, from the full force of the steam being continued so far; because, it must be observed that the steam on the down-stroke will flow in till that on the opposite side of the piston meets it and drives the piston back. In the

* See Art. 136.

former, on the contrary, after the further ingress of steam is prevented, the pent-up·steam, though still aiding the piston in its descent, is constantly losing its elastic force, and, by the time the fresh steam is admitted, offers but small opposition, and the engine works more uniformly. This applies chiefly to pumping-engines.

136. *Method of Working the Slides.*

The slides of steam-engines are mostly worked by what is called an "eccentric." We have before said, "that if the gab-lever or eccentric-lever (marked 2 in Plate II.) be moved backwards and forwards through a certain space, the valve will be raised and depressed through the distance necessary to admit the steam and allow of its egress, according to the judgment of the manufacturer. Now it is very evident this requisite motion might be given by a crank on the paddle-shaft; but this would be attended with a great disadvantage, for the required throw is so small, that the crank itself would be of inconsiderable dimensions, and it would be necessary to separate the shaft to effect it. Thus let 1 2 in the accompanying diagram be the gab-lever; if we suppose a connecting-rod *a d* to be connected with the stud marked 2, and the end *a* of the connecting-rod to traverse round the centre *c* of the shaft by means of the small crank *a c*, the required motion of the stud 2 may be insured by making $a\,c =$ half of its traverse. It is, however, more convenient to avoid using the crank in practice, and merely preserve it in our minds for the sake of elucidating the principle of the movement. Instead, therefore, of a crank, let us suppose a circular disk to envelop the paddle-shaft (which shaft is represented by the shaded part of the figure), taking care that the centre of the circle be at the point *a*, which, under other circumstances, would have been the point of junction between the connecting-rod *a d* and the crank *a c*. This circle may be of any size, but in practice is only made large enough to envelop the shaft; for if the pulley be larger than necessary, there will be a greater loss arising from friction. Now it is evident that as this circle revolves round the centre of the shaft *c*, the line *a c* will describe precisely the same path that it would have done if it had been a crank. Let now this circle revolve freely within the brass circular ring A B, and to this ring suppose the long rod B C, called the *eccentric-rod*, to be attached, having diagonal braces connecting it with the ring, so as to prevent any twisting of the rod. Since, then, from its construction, the eccentric-rod is a *normal** to the circle of the eccentric-pulley, the dotted line *d* B will pass through the centre *a* in all positions of the circle, and consequently the motion of *d* will be identically the same as if *a d* were the connecting-rod, and *a c* the crank.

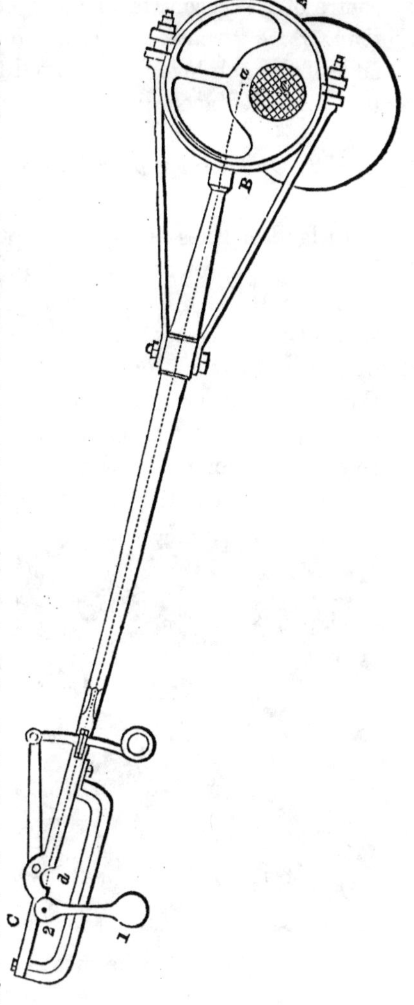

* The normal to a circle is a straight line passing through the centre.

137. *Throw of Eccentric.*

Def. The line *a c*, that is to say, the distance between the centre of the eccentric and the centre of the shaft, is the *throw of the eccentric*, and is equal to half the travel of the slide if the gab-lever and valve-lifter be equal; but if not, it is regulated according to the rule in p. 115.

138. *On the Stops placed upon the Eccentric-pulley and Paddle-shaft.*

In land engines the eccentric-pulley is *keyed* on the shaft, because the crank is always required to revolve in one direction. But a different arrangement becomes necessary with marine engines, because these engines must be capable of having their motion *reversed*, for the purpose of checking the vessel's speed, or giving her sternway; and consequently they must be provided with the means of effecting this. To understand how it is performed, we must see how the disposition of the relative parts of the engines must be altered to reverse the motion. Let, then, *q* be the centre of the engine-shaft, *q a* the crank, *a b* the connecting-rod; and suppose, for the sake of example, that the force of the steam is acting upwards, as is represented by the arrow *b*; then the crank will manifestly be revolving from right to left round the point *q*. This will, we may suppose, be the means of giving the vessel headway. Let us next suppose the engine to have been stopped when the crank is in the position now represented. This is done, as we have before said, by throwing the eccentric out of gear and closing the steam-ports. The engine being at rest, if we were to move the slide into the position it

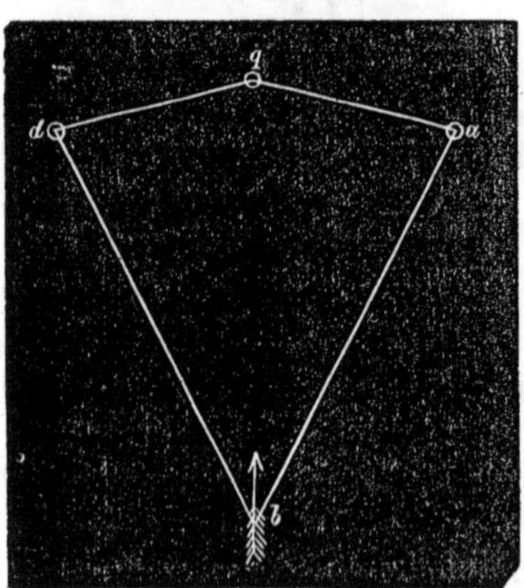

had originally, the eccentric would fall into gear, and the shaft and eccentric-pulley would again commence revolving round *q* as before. But, instead of this, let us suppose the starting-bar to be moved to the opposite direction, so as to let the steam act on the other side of the piston, the point *a* will then descend instead of ascending; and we will suppose further, that in this direction the shaft can revolve freely without moving the eccentric pulley and rod. Let the engine be moved thus till the point *a* comes to *d*, that is, till it is in the middle of its path, but on the opposite side of the vertical. Now since the eccentric-pulley has not been moved, and the piston is in the middle of its stroke, the whole engine is in precisely the same circumstances it was at first, except that *q a* and *a b* occupy the position *q d*, *d b*. Let the eccentric be now thrown into gear, and we shall find as the steam acts on the piston, and forces up the point *b* in the direction of the arrow, the crank *d q* will move from *left* to *right:* and causing the paddles to revolve in this same direction, the vessel will gather sternway. It is clear, therefore, that the shaft must be free to rotate backwards within the eccentric-pulley during half a revolution of the engine, to enable the engine to be put in the second position while working it by hand; and afterwards the engine, as soon as the eccentric is thrown into gear, must of itself act upon it. This is accomplished thus: On the shaft A is placed a stop *c d*; and on the eccentric B is cast another stop *a b*. Then, as the shaft revolves from right to left, the point *a* comes into contact with *c*, and so the eccentric and shaft revolve together so long as the motion continues in the same direction; but so soon as the engine is reversed, these stops become detached; and after passing through the position they occupy in the diagram, the face *b* comes (after half a revolution) into con-

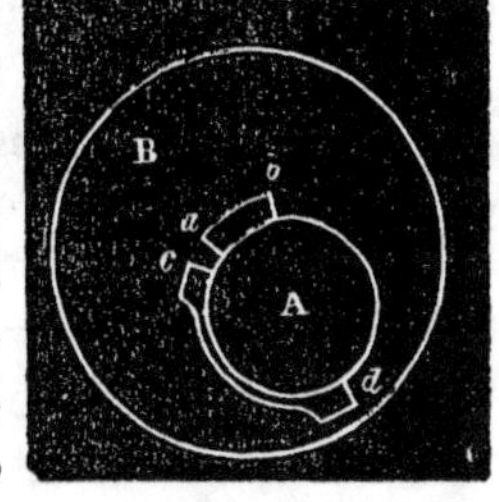

tact with *d*, and the engine is in the position to work the reverse way.

139. *To find the Travel of the Slide from the Throw of the Eccentric and* vice versâ.

If the length of the gab-lever 12 (in Plate II.) be equal to that of the valve-lifter 13, the travel of the slide will be double the throw of the eccentric; but this is oftentimes not the case: still, however, the one may be approximately found from the other by a very simple proportion; for let *a b* be the gab-lever and *c b* the valve-lifter, each of them being supposed at the extreme of its stroke; then suppose the point *a* to come to *e* and *c* to *d*, *e* and *d* being the other extreme positions of the levers; therefore *a e* is the throw of the eccentric, and *c d* the travel of the slide. Now *a b e* and *c b d* are two similar triangles; therefore *a e* : *a b* : : *d c* : *c b*; or, in other words, twice the throw of the eccentric : length of gab-lever : : travel of slide : valve-lifter.

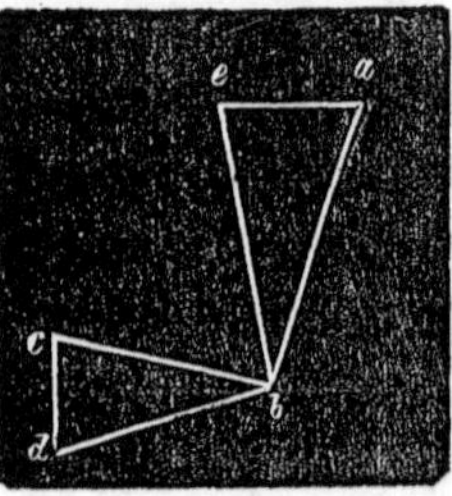

140. *The Double Eccentric, or Link Motion.*

In a locomotive engine it is usual to have two eccentrics keyed to the shaft, to produce the head and back motion. This is sometimes called Stephenson's link motion, and it is being very commonly introduced into our steam navy, particularly for engines to turn the screw-propeller, because a sudden reversing action is more desirable than with paddle propulsion.* The accompanying figure represents the double eccentric. There are no stops on the shaft as in the common single eccentric, but they are keyed to it, and all back-lash is therefore prevented. A and C are the

* The use of these eccentrics is not limited to engines for driving the screw; the Sampson and Bulldog have engines fitted with them, and these are paddle-wheel vessels.

two eccentrics, and B is the shaft; D E is the arc of a circle connecting the ends D and E of the eccentric-rods A D and C E; F is the gab-lever pin, which travels in the slot-way D E. By means of suitable machinery, worked by hand, the arc D E may be raised or lowered so as to cause the pin F to traverse the space from D to E. There are joints at the ends of the rods at D and E, and B is the centre of

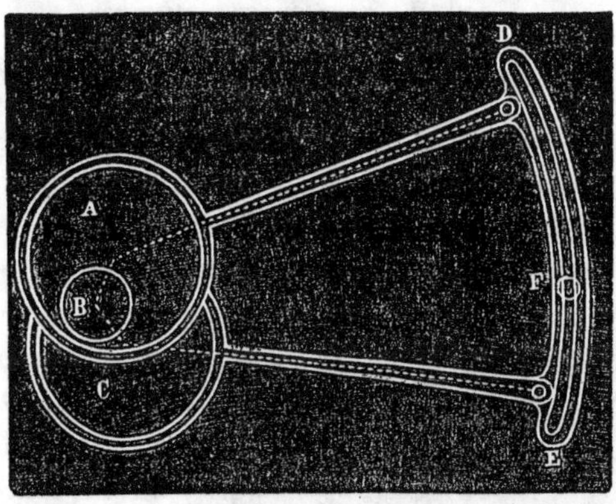

the circular arc D E; therefore F can traverse the slot-way freely. Now when F is at D, the eccentric A D works the slides horizontally, and when it is at E the eccentric C E works it. And one is set for producing the motion for head-way, and the other for stern-way. Lastly, when F is half-way between D and E, the slide will be stationary. When fitted with the double eccentric, the engines cannot be worked by hand.

141. *The Throttle-valve.*

This valve is for the purpose of regulating the supply of steam to the cylinder, and is worked by hand in marine engines. In land engines it is usually regulated by the governor. In some engines it is fitted in the steam-pipe, not far from the cylinder, and in others in a port-way between the jacket and slide-casing. This valve is circular when fitted in the steam-pipe, and rectangular when fitted in the port-way. Where no expansion-valve is fitted, it is used to economize fuel; but its general value is, that it enables the engines to proceed more slowly when orders are given to ease them, or on first getting under weigh, that the steam may be admitted gradually; as also when they would use more steam than the boiler can readily supply.

142. *The Expansion-valve.*

The expansion-valve is for the purpose of cutting off the steam from the cylinder at various portions of the stroke of the piston, in order to economize fuel. The principle by which this is accomplished will become apparent from the accompanying figure. Let A D represent the steam-pressure at the commencement of the stroke of the engine, which is represented by A B; and suppose the steam to act with uniform force throughout the space A C, supposed to be an exact fractional part of A B; make C F, F G, etc., each equal to A C. Through the points C F G, etc., draw C E, F L, G M, etc., perpendicular to A B. Make C E = A D, F L = $\frac{1}{2}$ A D, G M = $\frac{1}{3}$ A D, and so on. Join D E, and through E, L, M, N, etc., draw a free curve. Then since, by the law of the elastic pressure of a gas, the pressure diminishes as the space it occupies is increased, it will follow that, if a perpendicular be drawn from any point of A B to meet the upper curve, the part intercepted by these two lines will represent the pressure of the steam at the corresponding portion of the stroke; for at F, where the space A F = twice A C, L F has been made equal to half A D. Again, at G, where the space A G is three times A C, we have G M = one-third of A D, and so on: the per-

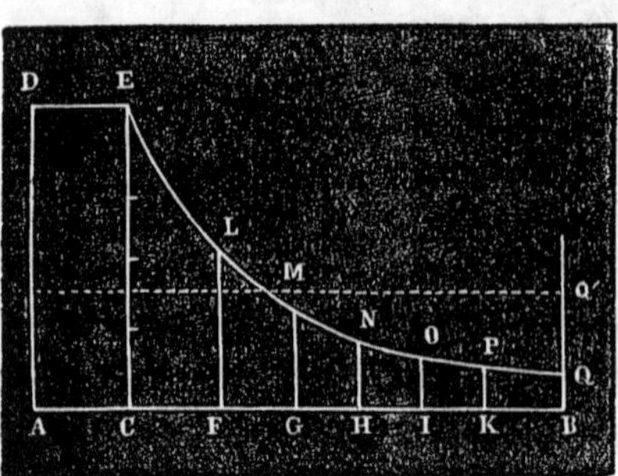

pendiculars, therefore, at all these points being inversely as the corresponding spaces, it will be the case also at all intermediate points, and consequently generally true through out the curve. Perpendiculars, therefore, from all points from A to C, will represent the pressure of the steam before its expansion; and those drawn between C and B, and intersected by the curve, will represent the pressures after expansion. The *sum* of all such lines, therefore, will represent the whole sum of the pressures during the stroke. These we may suppose the same in amount as the sum of a series of lines intercepted between the *upper* dotted line and A B.

Hence the mean pressure during the stroke will be represented by some line Q′B.

But, since at the *end* of the stroke the pressure of the steam is Q B, it follows (the whole cylinder being filled with steam of that pressure) that the quantity of steam used in one stroke may be represented by Q B; we arrive, therefore, at the following result, viz., that steam whose quantity is represented by the line Q B has been enabled, by giving so great an initial force, to perform work whose mean effect is Q′B. Hence the evident advantage of working expansively; that is, of letting in the steam at first at a high pressure, and cutting it off at an early period of the stroke. Lastly, the higher the pressure at first, and the earlier the period at which the expansion commences, the greater the advantage; the only limit being, that the final pressure must never be less than the resistances caused by the engine itself, such as the friction, labor in working the air-pump, etc.; and the initial pressure must not be greater than that which the safety of the boiler and strength of the machinery would warrant.*

* If, when the space traversed by the piston $= n$ times A C, we call the space x and the perpendicular y, we shall have

$$x = n\,\mathrm{A\,C}, \text{ and } y = \frac{1}{n}\mathrm{E\,C}$$

∴ multiply these together, we have

$$xy = \mathrm{A\,C}\,.\,\mathrm{C\,E}$$

143. *Expansion-valves.*

The valve used is generally of the Cornish double-beat description; it is sometimes, however, the throttle-valve or the gridiron-valve. The latter is fitted to most of the Scotch engines.

144. *Hornblower's Valve.*

When the practice became general of working engines at a higher pressure, it was found necessary to introduce this valve. Let us suppose, for the sake of illustration, the pressure on one side of a valve to be greater than that on the other by 20 lbs. per inch, and that the valve has an area of 50 inches; then the valve will be held down by a force of 1000 lbs., and will remain fixed, unless a power greater than 1000 lbs. be applied to it; and in consequence the valve will not only be raised with difficulty, but the power required will soon cause it to loosen and detach itself from its rod. To remedy this, Hornblower conceived the idea of having a valve similar to the common valve, only fixed; and a portion of a pipe was made to slide within another portion, like the tubes of a telescope, so as to fit down on this valve, and prevent the progress of the steam, or to rise up and allow it a passage. The resisting pressure being now only exerted on the edge of the tube, does not produce the same injurious effects as it did before. The accompanying figure will explain it more clearly. A B C D E F is the steam-pipe, G the fixed valve, H K a section of the sliding tube. In the present position the steam can pass between the

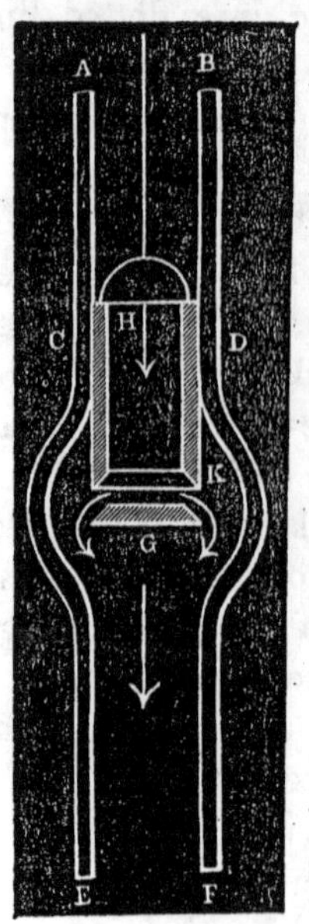

---

which is the equation to a hyperbola whose asymptotes are A B and A D. The curve E M N Q is therefore a hyperbola.

valve G and the lower rim of the tube K; but if the two are brought into contact, the passage is obstructed, and the progress of the steam below G is prevented. This may be considered as the first origin of the Cornish double-beat valve.

145. *The Cornish Double-beat Valve.*

The principle on which this valve is constructed can be readily understood after a personal inspection; but, like many other pieces of machinery, there is great difficulty in representing it clearly to those who are not accustomed to inspect drawings. Imagine, however, A B to be the section of a solid circular plate of metal supported by the cylindrical surface A B C D, in which cylindrical surface are narrow vertical apertures, as represented in the figure, for the purpose of allowing the passage of steam; F G is a section of a casing which surrounds all this. This casing is open at the top, and is connected with the rod H K by radii, which allow steam to pass between them. When this casing is pushed down, the annular apertures at A B and C D are closed; but when raised, as in the figure, they are open. Let now steam be proceeding from the boiler in the direction of the arrow S; if the apertures at A B and C D are closed, it can proceed no farther than the outside of the casing; but if open, it can pass through all the vertical openings and down the steam-pipe C L, entering at both the upper and lower annular orifices. A small vertical motion, therefore, of the valve-rod will be enough to give a large aperture for steam,

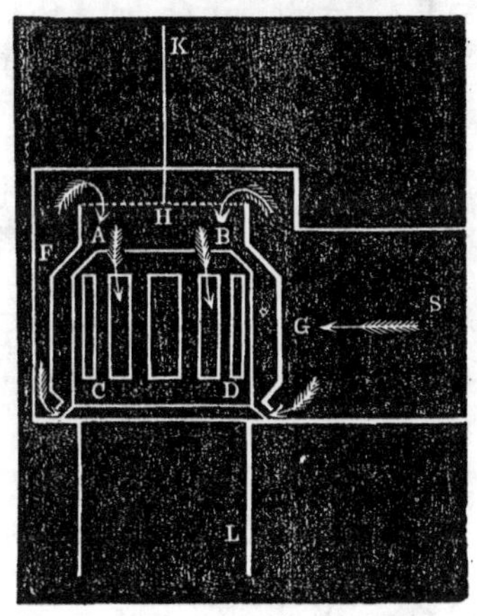

and the valve will open with comparatively inconsiderable force.

The common throttle-valve is, however, probably equally useful: see page 118. It answers the same end as the Cornish valve in cutting off the steam, and is a truly-*balanced* valve, which is not strictly the case with the latter; so that no force is necessary to open it, except in overcoming the spring that keeps it in its place, and that which is required to overcome the friction of the spindle. It may be objected against the use of the throttle-valve, that it is apt to be leaky; but the leakage will at most be but trifling, sufficient perhaps to tell on an Indicator diagram (see "Indicator and Dynamometer," p. 26), but not so important as to be worth regarding when considered with reference to the working of the engine. The throttle-valve is, moreover, a cheaper valve in the first instance, and is not so likely to get out of order: and probably, after a few months wear, the latter would be found equally leaky, for its seatings are very soon injured by the scales of iron becoming detached from the valve-box.

146. *Equilibrium-valve.*

This valve, which is called the equilibrium-valve, is very valuable, because it unites all the properties of the Cornish double-beat valve, and is somewhat simpler. Its principle is easily understood by inspecting the accompanying figure. E B F is the steam-pipe, and the arrows show the course of the steam proceeding from E towards F; A B are two circular and conical valves on one spindle C D, and they are represented in the diagram raised up from their seats, so that there is a passage for the steam all round their edges; but when the spindle is depressed by the machinery of the engine, the further passage of the steam is intercepted. It is evident, in this construction, as well as in the common Cornish valve, that a small motion of the spindle gives a large space for the steam. The upper valve A is made rather larger than the lower valve

B, that the pressure on its upper side may predominate and keep it firmly in its seat.

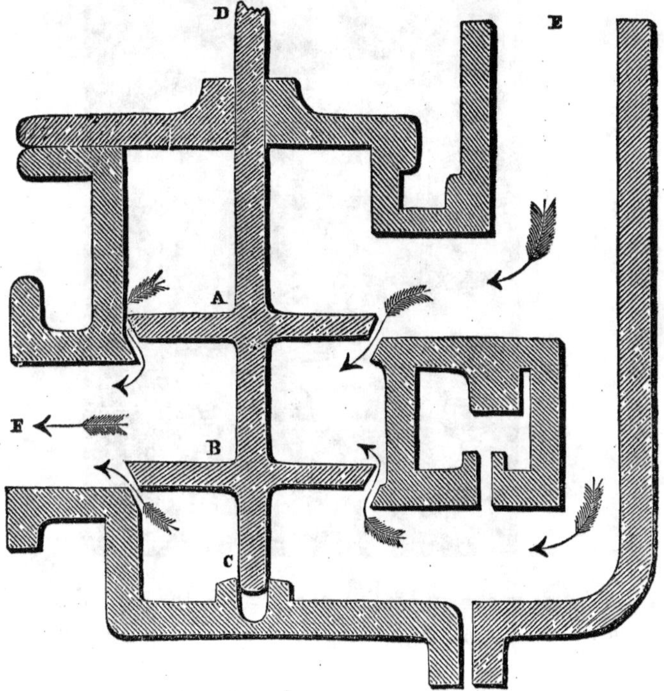

147. *Equilibrium-valves as fitted to H.M.S. Penelope.*

It is difficult to gain a very clear conception of the arrangement of these valves without a model; but the following description may be of some service. Each cylinder has four equilibrium valves, represented by A, B, C, D, in the figure. Two of which, viz., A and C, serve for the admission of steam, and the other two, B and D, for the exhaust; S S is the steam-pipe, E E the eduction-pipe. A *transversal* section of A and B is shown below, and the passage leading to the upper port in the former, and from the port in the latter. When the valves on the spindle at A are raised, the steam passing through the orifices proceeds in the direction of the arrow, as shown at F, to the upper side of the piston; again, as the valves on the spindle at B are raised, the steam leaving the upper port proceeds, as is shown by the arrow at G, through the orifices down the eduction-pipe E, and so to the condenser.

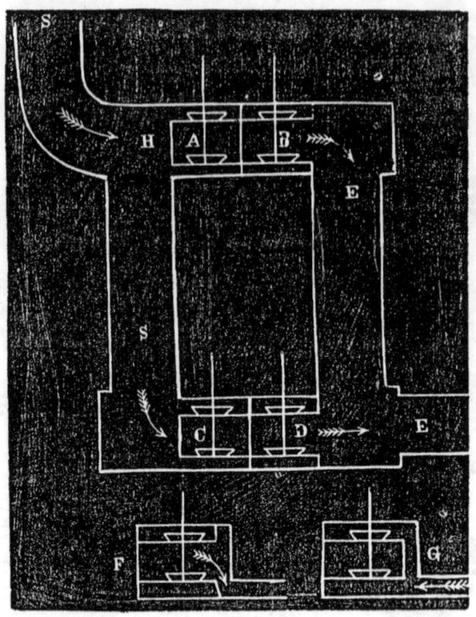

148. *The Gridiron-valve.*

This valve receives its name from its shape and appearance, and serves the same purpose as the Cornish double-beat valve, viz., that a small motion of the valve produces a considerable opening. Let A B C be three portways in the plate of metal D E, through which it is desirable to allow the steam to pass at certain intervals. If now another plate of metal of the same size and shape be placed on this, so that the orifices correspond, a free passage will be left for the steam through each

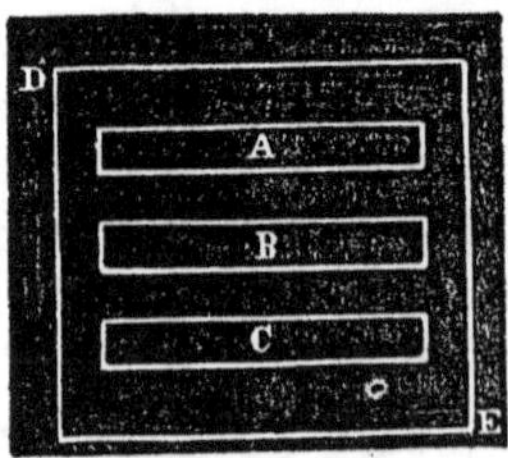

orifice; but if the second plate be moved up a slight space, until the orifices in the one plate are opposed to the solid metal in the other, the passage will be intercepted at each port-way at the same instant, and the communication will be cut off. It will be readily perceived that this contrivance gives three times as great an opening for steam, with the same motion of the rod, as would have been produced if there had been only one port-way. And consequently the depth of the port-way need only be one-third what would otherwise be necessary.

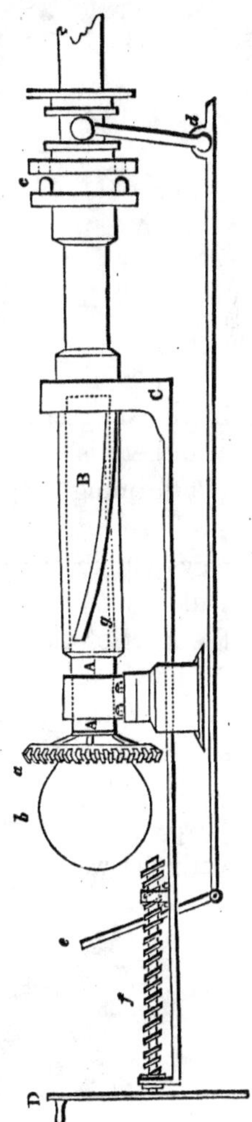

149. *Other kinds of Expansion valves.*

The common throttle-valve is frequently fitted for this purpose, as in H.M.S. Edinburgh; it is either a rectangular or circular valve with a spindle across its centre, acted on by a crank on the outside, to which is attached a weight or spiral spring, so as to close the orifice after the expansion-cam has opened it. This valve is marked C in Plate I.

150. *Maudslay and Field's Rotary Expansion-valve.*

The form of this valve is the same as that of the common throttle-valve (see plate, p. 127); but, instead of having a reciprocating action, it rotates in the steam-pipe, thus opening and closing the orifice alternately.

To show how this is effected, and the mode of adjusting it to give any required amount of expansion, let A A be a spindle, which has a slot-way *g* for some portion of its length; B is a *hollow* spindle, continued to the right, to the extremity of which the valve is fitted, as represented

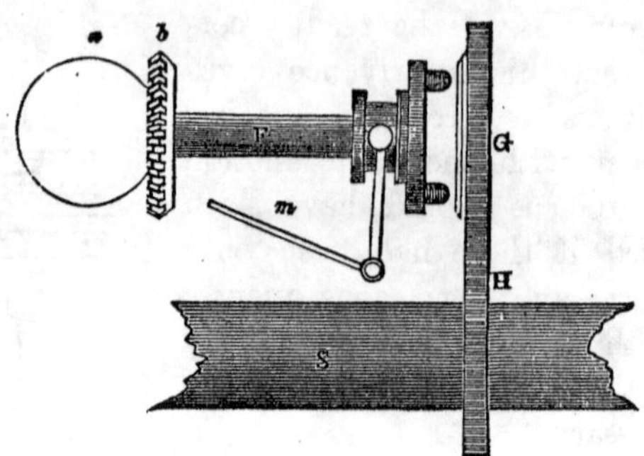

in the diagram on the preceding page. In this spindle also there is a slot-way, not in the direction of its length, but forming a spiral upon it, as shown at B. Now, it is easily seen that when a feather passing through both slot-ways connects these spindles together, the position the valve will occupy in the steam-pipe will, relatively, depend on the part of the spiral slot-way brought by means of the feather in connection with the other slot-way in the spindle A A. This is effected by the following contrivance: The screw *f* is worked by the handle D, and thus moves a collar C. This collar carries with it the feather; and it will be perceived, that as this feather, which passes through both slot-ways, travels to the left, the outer spindle, as also the valve, will commence rotating in opposition to the hands of a watch, and *vice versâ*, if the screw be turned in the opposite direction; and therefore the positions of the two spindles become shifted with relation to each other. Having, by these means, set the valve, here shown, so as to cut off

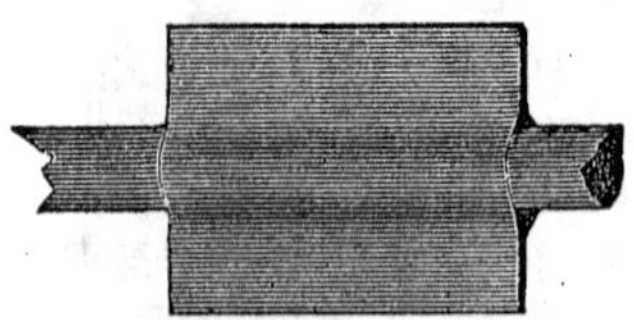

the steam at any portion of the stroke, the whole is made to revolve by a pair of wheels G and H (see Fig. p. 126). G is a wheel gearing into H, and admits of being connected with or disconnected from the engine-shaft S by means of a lever *m*. F is a fore and aft shaft, terminating at *b*, where a pair of bevelled wheels communicate its motion to the valve-spindle at right angles to it. *e* and *d* are levers acting upon the clutch *c* to connect or disconnect the expansion-gear. One other particular requires explanation. A difficulty would evidently arise in setting the slide to work expansively from the circumstance that the earlier the steam is cut off, the earlier it would be readmitted. This is provided against by giving the slide considerable thickness, so that it may close the orifice during some considerable portion of its revolution, as in the annexed figure; care being taken that the valve when working at its highest grade of expansion shall open for steam before the slide has cut off the steam.

151. *Barometer or Condenser-gauge.*

The gauge for ascertaining the state of the vacuum in the condenser is so called, because its principle and mode of action are similar to that of a weather-glass, having a small quantity of air in the upper part of the tube. The principle of the weather-glass is as follows: A glass tube 33 or 34 inches long is filled with mercury, and then (the orifice having been stopped with a finger) it is inverted over a basin of mercury. The finger is then taken away, and it will be found that the mercury will immediately sink in the tube, and consequently rise in the cistern, till its weight balances the pressure of the atmosphere, which, by its elasticity, is endeavoring to force it up the tube. And it will be found that the height of the mercury in the tube above that in the basin is about 30 inches, varying slightly from day to day according to the state of the atmosphere. Now, in order to show how to make this principle available for a condenser-gauge, we will next conceive that some air has made an entrance into the upper portion of the tube; the pressure of this will assist the mercury in counterbalancing the atmosphere, and therefore the mercurial column will not be so high as it otherwise would have been; and we can further perceive, that the greater the pressure of the air above the column, the shorter that column will be. Hence we can use this instrument, not only to exhibit the pressure of the external air, but likewise the elasticity of *any* gaseous fluid admitted above the mercury in the tube. This, then, is the method of using the mercurial column in connection with the condenser; for we have only to make a communication with the upper part of the glass tube and the condenser, and the pressure of the steam in the condenser will be discovered from inspection by observing how much the column is below what it would have stood at had a perfect vacuum existed. The contrivance by which this is effected is as follows: A C D is an iron tube, open at A, and communicating with the condenser at D; C is an iron cup surrounding the tube,

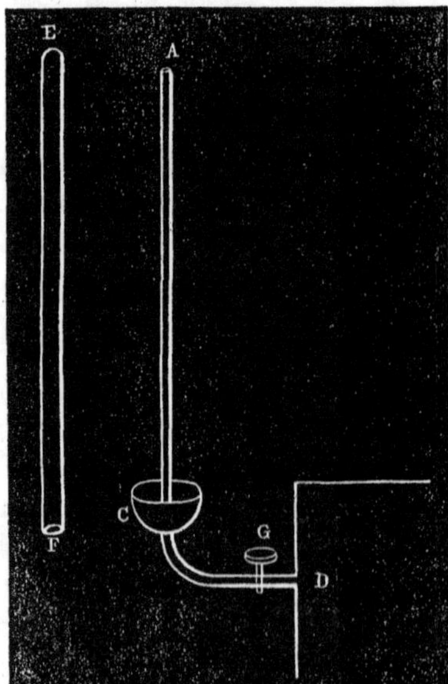

and filled with mercury; G is a stop-cock; E F is a glass tube, open at the lower end F, but closed at E. When this glass tube is placed over the iron tube A C, the end A is near the top of the glass E, while the open end of the glass F stands in the mercury-cup C; and while the stop-cock G is closed, the mercury does not rise in the glass; but (supposing a partial vacuum in the condenser) directly G is opened, there will be the same amount of vacuum in the tube as in the condenser, and the atmospheric pressure on the surface of the mercury in the cup will force it up the space between the two tubes, till a balance of forces is produced, when it will rise no higher. A piece of cork should be inserted in the upper end of the tube A C, to prevent the descent of the mercury into the condenser, which it is apt to do if there is not sufficient mercury in the cup to form a column whose height will balance the pressure of the air, or in the event of the vessel rolling. The cork is usually porous enough, if not pushed in hard, to allow the communication to be kept up; but if not, a small hole must be made in it.

152. *To estimate the Pressure by the Barometer-gauge.*

Since 30 inches of mercury press downwards with the same force as the atmosphere (which, *in round numbers,* is 15 lbs. on the square inch), therefore every two inches of mercury correspond to 1 lb. pressure; and consequently, wishing to estimate the pressure, a scale of *inches* is fixed by the side of the glass tube, the number of inches on the scale being supposed to be measured from the surface of the mercury in the cup; but as the vacuum is supposed to be tolerably good while the engine is working, the scale is only graduated for a few inches below 30. If, then (after what has been said), the mercury stand at 28 inches, the pressure in the condenser is 1 lb.; if at 26, it is 2 lbs.; if at 24, 3 lbs., and so forth; every fall of 2 inches denoting an additional pound of pressure in the condenser.

153. *Errors in the preceding Mode of estimating the Vacuum.* There are two sources of error. In the first place, the pressure of the atmosphere in the cup is always liable to change; this is, however, not a very important defect compared with the following. For, as was said in describing the scale, the graduations are made on the supposition that the level of the surface of the mercury in the cup is stationary, because it is from this level that the scale commences; and therefore a fixed scale must be erroneous, on account of the sinking of the mercury in the cup as it rises in the tube. In the weather-barometer this defect is sometimes remedied by taking care that each *adequate* fraction of an inch shall be graduated as an inch; but the same process cannot be adopted here; for the glass tubes being liable to accidents, they are at times replaced by others of larger or smaller bore, and this would completely frustrate all attempts at accuracy by these means. Another cause of error will arise if any of the mercury be lost from the cup by accident; for by such means the scale may be wrong as much as an inch.

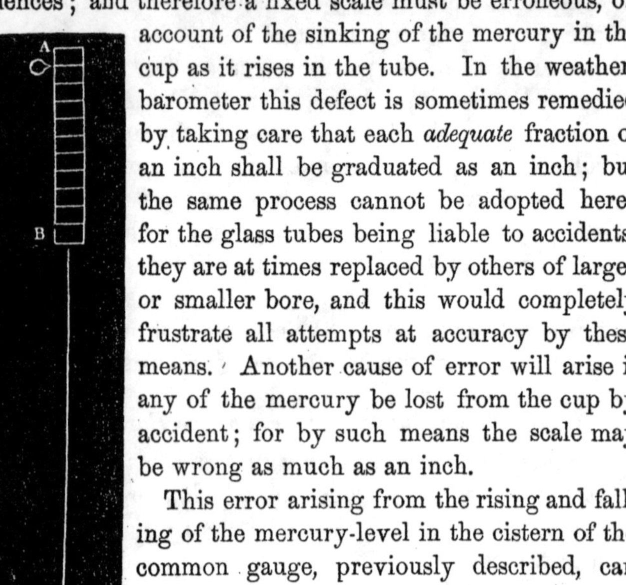

Fig. 1.

This error arising from the rising and falling of the mercury-level in the cistern of the common gauge, previously described, can only be obviated by having a shifting instead of a fixed scale. The scale of inches A B, in Fig. 1, which is usually fixed to the framework of the engine, is detached, and a stout wire, B C, of the proper length,* is fitted to it, and terminating in a pointer at C. Let, now, the scale be allowed to slide in a groove, and when an observation has to be made, it must be moved till

* That is to say, of such length that any number of inches on the scale may designate the requisite number of inches from C.

C comes into contact with the surface of the mercury in the cup. It will be convenient to have a small handle, as at A, to raise and depress it.

154. *Short Barometer-gauge.*

This error may also be corrected with sufficient accuracy by having a barometer-gauge precisely similar to what a weather-barometer would become if it were quite enclosed in a space communicating with the condenser; it would then be found that, before a vacuum was created, the mercury would stand as high in the glass tube as in the weather-barometer: but on creating a vacuum, and thus taking off the pressure from the mercury in the cistern, the mercury would fall in the tube. In this instrument, therefore, the less the height of the mercury in the tube the better the vacuum, whereas in the common gauge the reverse was the case.

This is the principle of what is called the short barometer, of which Fig. 2 is a representation. A is the cistern, which communicates with the condenser by means of the tube B E, having a stop-cock at B. C D is a short tube opening into the cistern A, but closed at C. The dark part is supposed to be filled with mercury. Now, as the vacuum is created above A, the reaction of the glass at the top of the tube at C will become less, till (the vapor not being able to sustain the whole column C D) it will begin to descend; and, leaving a pure vacuum at the upper end, will give the actual pressure. This barometer is made short, because the upper extremity would be of no service, since the instrument is only used when a partial vacuum has been attained.

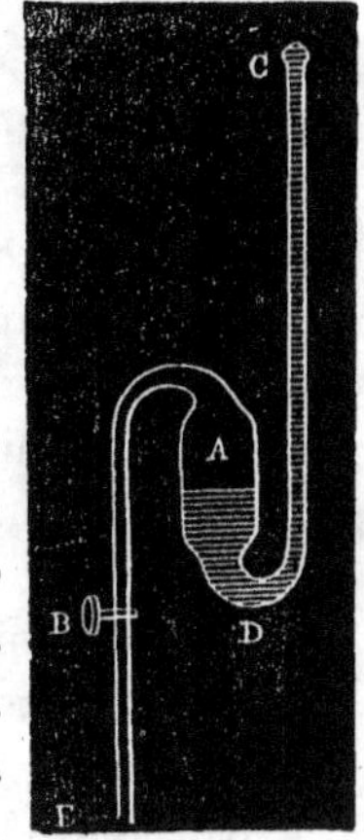

Fig. 2.

155. *Lubricators.*

These are brass cups or vessels, into which oil is put to

lubricate the bearings and other moving parts of the machinery. The object of lubricators is to have the bearings lubricated *gradually,* and prevent the necessity of oiling the bearings so very frequently as the engineers were compelled to do before their introduction. The common kind consists of a cup with a tube passing through the bottom, and rising nearly to the level of the upper edge. Five or six worsted threads pass down this tube, and their upper ends hang over into the cup, which is kept supplied with oil, into which the worsted dips. These threads form, therefore, what is called a *capillary syphon,* and the oil, by the capillary action, creeps up the worsted into the tube, and runs out of the lower end by drops. This end is placed in a hole of the engine communicating with the bearing, and thus it becomes incessantly lubricated, so long as the lubricator is supplied with oil.

156. *Expansion-gear.*

Where expansion-gear is fitted, the expansion-valves are closed and opened by *cams* (as they are called).* These cams are for the purpose of instantaneous action, which an eccentric does not give. The description of the eccentric shows that it opens an orifice but slowly, and closes it in the same manner. The steam during this process is said to be *wire-drawn;* in other words, it is passing through an orifice becoming *gradually* narrower or wider. To gain the full benefits of expansive working, however, it is thought better to shut off the communication with the boiler as suddenly as possible. Let us, then, imagine the expansion-valve to be kept on its seat by means of a spring or weight; and that a lever E connects the expansion-valve with the expansion-rod levers F F, to which the pulley G is connected. The spring will therefore always keep the pulley

* The slides themselves of some of Messrs. Seaward's engines are worked by cams instead of an eccentric, and thus do away with the necessity of expansion-gear.

in contact with the shaft. The diagram, however, shows that the portion of the shaft under the pulley G is not uniform; but that a part of the circumference is raised about an inch above the general level. There is a series of these elevations, B B, etc., each of which is called a step of the

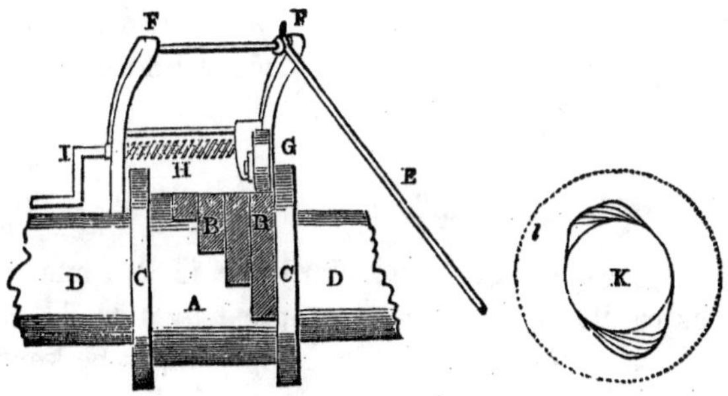

cam, and the portion of the circumference of the shaft they occupy becomes less and less as we proceed from right to left; so that the end view of the shaft is represented by K, *l l* being a representation of the collars which are exhibited in the first diagram by C C. Now, as the shaft revolves, whenever any one of the steps B comes under the pulley, the pulley is pushed back, and the levers F F acting on the expansion-rod E, opens the expansion-valve; but immediately the raised portion has passed the pulley G, the spring re-acts, and closes the valve again. It will be seen that the engineer, by turning the handle I, can bring the pulley into contact with any one of the steps at his discretion, and thus can regulate the portion of the stroke during which the valve shall be open. When the pulley is in the position represented in the figure, the expansion-valve will be open during a considerable portion of the stroke; and the engine is said to be working on a *low* grade of expansion. Some engines have as many as seven grades, others have but two. It is a practice with some engine-makers to arrange their expansion in the following manner: Let the stroke of the engine be 6 feet, and let the steam be cut off, if working most expansively, when the piston has traversed one foot; by the next step let it be cut off when the piston has traversed two feet, and so on, till we arrive at the point where the slide itself cuts off the steam, which is called the fixed expansion, and is beyond the control of the engineer. Students should take an early opportunity of inspecting the expansion-gear, as both description and drawing will fail to supply the place of information gained by actual inspection.

157. *Feed-pumps.*

As the water during its ebullition is continually being expended, its place must be supplied by a fresh accession from some other source. The supply might be kept up by the boiler hand-pumps, as they are called—that is to say,

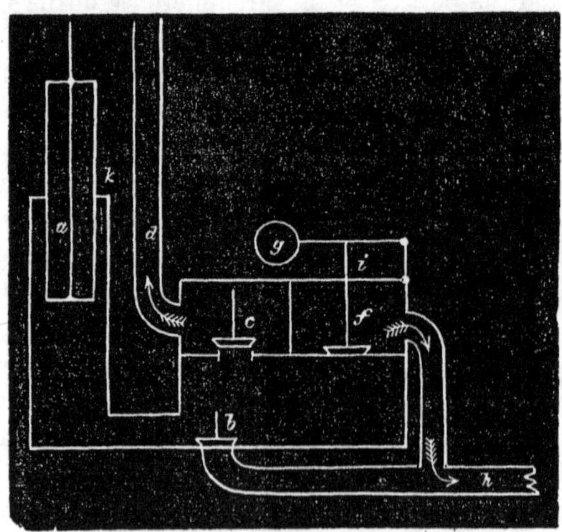

by pumps worked by hand forcing water into the boiler; but to obviate the necessity of manual labor, there is, connected with each engine, and worked by it, a feed-pump, whose duty it is to send a jet of water into each boiler at every stroke of the engine. The feed-pump is of greater capacity than is absolutely necessary to supply the waste by evaporation in the boiler together with the amount of water blown out, in order to have a reserve that would be necessary in case the boiler were leaky. The quantity that can be supplied is usually from three to four times that consumed by evaporation. The feed-pump is a forcing-pump, with solid plunger, as at *a*; having a valve, called the foot-valve, *b*, for allowing the admission of water to the barrel on the up-stroke, and a second valve, called the delivery-valve, *c*, through which the water, thus admitted, passes as the plunger makes its down-stroke. The water, after passing through the delivery-valve, is conveyed by a pipe *d*, called the feed-pipe, to the boiler. There is a cock at the farther end of this pipe, by which means the supply to the boiler can be regulated. Now, since this cock may be partially closed, it will sometimes happen that the pump will raise more water than can pass through the orifice. A valve *f*, contrived to obviate this difficulty, is called the surplus or overflow valve.* This valve is kept in its place by a weight *g*, or spiral spring; and when at any time the water cannot escape freely into the boiler, it acts, by its increased pressure, on the under-surface of this valve, opens it, and either returns to the hot-well, from whence it came, by the pipe *h*, or is directed into the waste-pipe of the engine, and so goes overboard. There is a small stuffing-box at *i*, to keep the valve-spindle water-tight, as also one for the plunger at *k*. The feed-water is usually taken from the hot-well, because the water there is fresher than common salt water, being mixed with the condensed steam, and also because it is warmer, the temperature of the hot-well being about 100°. The surplus-valve must be loaded to a greater amount per square inch than the pressure of steam in the boiler, to insure the passage of water when the cock is open. Some feed-pumps are fitted with valves in a bucket similar to the air-pump, instead of having a

* This valve is sometimes called the escape-valve of the feed-pump.

solid plunger; these act, therefore, on the lifting instead of the forcing principle. In the old side-lever engines, the plunger of the feed-pump is worked by the cross-head of the air-pump.

158. *Bilge-pumps.*

Since water is always finding its way into the bilge, even if the vessel be not leaky, from the jackets of the cylinders (when fitted), from the various cocks opening into the engine-room, and, when the engines are stopped, from the water driven out of the snifting-valve on blowing through; therefore a pump, called a bilge-pump, is fitted to each engine, for the purpose of keeping the bilge clear. It is generally of the same kind as the feed-pump; that is to say, it is a plunger-pump, with its foot-valve and delivery-valve. In the accompanying diagram A represents the plunger, B the foot-valve, C the delivery-valve, D a rose-head surrounded by the water of the bilge, B D is called the suction-pipe, C E the delivery-pipe. The plunger is mostly worked by the air-pump cross-head, on the opposite side of the engine to the feed-pump. In some cases, the pump discharges the water by a pipe into the hot-well; in others, the pipe leads directly overboard. This latter plan is much to be preferred, for the pump is apt to bring up solid substances, such as pieces of chip or oakum; and if the valves in the valve-box become gagged up with any thing of this kind, the pump offers a free communication, through which the contents of the hot-well will find their way into the bilge. This has, at times, been attended with some inconvenience, the water getting into the after-hold, damaging the stores, etc.

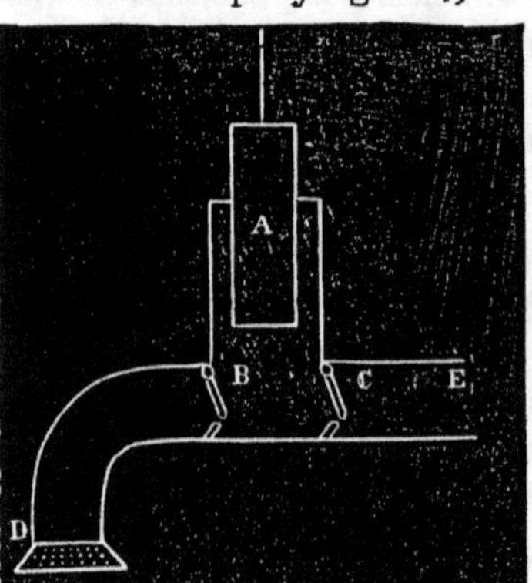

In one ship the water was nearly up to the fires before the cause of the mischief was discovered.

Where the bilge-pipe is carried directly overboard, the end of the pipe should be considerably above the water; for when the ship is deeply immersed, the water may, by the rolling of the ship, be driven down the pipe, and if the valves happen to be up, it will pass into the bilge. Where the pipe is brought near the surface of the water, it is a good plan to have a cock fitted in the upper pipe, so as to cut off the communication with the sea. The suction-pipes of the bilge-pumps, and indeed all other pipes in the bilge, should be of copper, and fitted with brass flanges and copper bolts. Lead pipes have been used for bilge-pumps; but they are apt to choke up, and are easily bent and damaged.

159. *Modes of Propulsion.*

There are two methods of rendering the force of steam-engines available in propelling vessels, viz., Paddle-wheels and Screws.

160. *Paddle-wheels.*

The general construction of the common paddle-wheel is so simple, that scarcely any one who has ever seen a steamer finds any difficulty in comprehending it; and indeed it is understood by most people who scarcely comprehend any other part of the machinery. We have already called the shafts *q q* the paddle-shafts. If there be but one engine to the vessel, as is the case with H.M.S. Bee, these shafts protrude beyond the sides of the vessel, and sustain a circular framework of iron to which rectangular boards, called paddles, are fastened; these boards being placed at equal distances round the circumference, and radiating from the centre.* As the crank causes the shafts, and therefore the wheels also, to revolve, the pres-

* The diameter of the wheel is generally about eight times the length of the crank; and the number of paddles is nearly the same as the number of feet in the diameter.

sure of the boards against the water causes a reaction to be exerted, which becomes effective in propelling the vessel. If they revolve in one direction, the vessel goes ahead; and if in the contrary direction, this motion is checked, and she goes astern. The paddles are secured to the radiating arms of the wheels by hook-bolts, a species of bolt by which they are hooked on to the arms of the wheels, and can be detached when convenient. The paddles are generally made of one single board, but at times they are divided into two, and sometimes into three, by horizontal sections. When the board is divided, it is for the purpose of setting the parts that are farthest from the centre on the opposite side of the arms to those which are nearer; so that they are arranged on each arm like a series of steps, the lower one being on the after part of the arm, when entering the water, and the upper at the back of the arm.* Each portion of the paddle is then supposed to dip nearly into the same place in the water When two engines are used, as is the case with almost all the vessels in our steam navy, the shaft connecting the two engines together is called the *intermediate* shaft, and the shafts attached to the wheels are called the paddle-shafts.

161. *Feathering-paddles.*

Besides the common paddle-wheel, there are others with what are called feathering-paddles; the object of these being to enable each paddle to enter and leave the water nearly in a vertical position, and thus avoid the loss of power caused by the obliquity of the common paddle-wheel.

162. *Reefing the Paddles.*

When the wheels are teo deeply immersed, the paddles may be disconnected from the paddle-arms and secured again nearer to the centre of the wheel: this process is

* This wheel is usually called the cycloidal wheel, because the boards are arranged in that curve on each paddle arm.

called reefing the paddles. Any method of doing this with ease and rapidity would do away with one of the chief objections to paddles, viz., the difficulty of preserving the same immersion of the paddle as the ship's draught varies.

163. *Disconnecting the Wheels.*

Most vessels are fitted with means of disengaging the wheels from the engines whenever it is intended that the ship should sail without steaming, to prevent the resistance the paddles would exert while being dragged through the water. Many engine-makers have plans of their own; but others use a plan called, from its inventor, Braithwaite's disconnecting-strap, which will be given in the next article.

164. *Methods of disconnecting Paddle-wheels.*

1. Maudslay's Method. In this plan the wheel, the paddle-shaft, and the crank with which the paddle-shaft is connected, are drawn from the engine in a lateral direction, till the crank-pin, which, when the engine is at work, connects the two cranks together, ceases to be in contact with the paddle-shaft crank, and therefore the wheel may revolve freely. If this plan be adopted, the paddle-boxes must be a few inches wider than otherwise would be necessary, to allow the wheel to be pushed out far enough.

2. Seaward's Methods. 1. There is a boss on the end of the paddle-crank, which, when turned in a particular direction by levers provided for that purpose, allows the crank-pin to escape from the boss. 2. A slot-way is cut through the face of the paddle-crank, and the pin is retained in it by two bolts which run up the crank on each side of the pin, their heads being in sight close to the paddle-shaft. When these are withdrawn far enough, the pin escapes through the slot-way, and the wheel is free to revolve.

3. Braithwaite's Method. To understand this method, conceive the *paddle*-crank to be a complete disc, having the

paddle-shaft for the centre. The intermediate shaft has the usual crank, the pin of which is attached to a ring passing round the disc, in the same manner as the ring of the eccentric surrounds the pulley. Now while the ring fits loosely on the disc, the engines or paddle-wheels may revolve independently of each other; but if a key be so fitted as to connect the ring with the disc, which it does by friction, the wheel must revolve with the engine. It is found, in practice, that when disconnected, there is a great deal of friction to be overcome between the disc and the ring; and that when connected, it is difficult to connect them so firmly by the key as to prevent all motion of the disc in the ring. The ring is fitted with a key, half into itself, and half into the discs, in the same manner as the cranks are secured to the shafts.

165. *The Immersion of Paddle-wheels.*

The paddle-wheels of sea-going steamers should be about one-sixth of their diameter immersed in the water. For river-boats, the upper edge of the lowest paddle should be what is termed *a-wash*, or on a level with the water. In giving this rule, we are, however, supposing the boilers' productive power to be proportioned to that immersion. But if that be not the case, we must be guided by it: what we must aim at is, to use up the steam supplied by the boilers without urging the fires, so as neither to let a great quantity escape on the one hand, nor, on the other, to allow the steam-pressure in the boiler to fall below its proper standard.

166. *Paddle-wheel Brakes.*

The most common description of brake is the friction-strap, which, by the application of a tackle, is pressed on the shaft; but this is not found to be sufficient in a sea-way. The best method is that which consists of wedges driven, or rather screwed down, between the *outer segment* of the wheel and the *paddle-beams.*

167. *The Screw-Propeller.*

The paddle-wheel has some serious defects, particularly when applied to vessels of war, which have caused inventive minds to introduce other modes of propulsion free from such grave objections. It is evident that the paddle-shaft of a steamer must be at a considerable distance above the water-line of the vessel, and there must be machinery connected with this shaft; therefore, so long as paddles are employed, it would be impossible to place the engine below the water-line, out of reach of shot. Again, the paddles are a serious inconvenience to a man-of-war steamer, preventing, to a great extent, the use of broadside guns, and frequently causing difficulties in transporting guns from one end of the ship to the other, on account of the shaft rising above the deck in some instances. These and other inconveniences—such as the resistance caused by the paddle-boxes when going head to wind, and the impossibility of taking full advantage of the sails of the ship—have caused another instrument to be adopted. This is usually called the Screw, and sometimes the Propeller. The name *screw* is given to a set of metallic blades, placed obliquely on a horizontal shaft, and revolving by means of the engines. The form of each blade may be conceived by imagining a straight line to be always perpendicular to the shaft while it travels along it, and at the same time revolves round it. Thus let A′B′ be the shaft (which, when working, would be horizontal, although placed vertical in the diagram for the convenience of describing it); and suppose the line A′P to commence travelling down A′B′, always remaining at right angles to it, while at the same time it revolves round it; so that when A′ comes to B′, P has

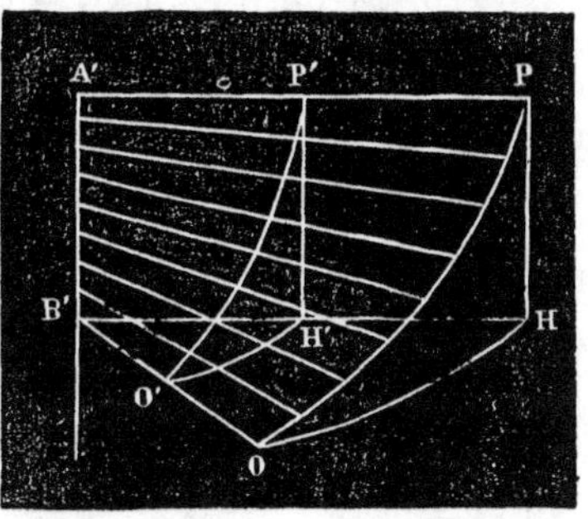

come to O instead of being at H, where it would have been had it not revolved through the angle H B′O. If the rate at which the line revolves round A′B′ be in a constant ratio to the rate at which it moves along it, the screw is called Smith's screw; if, however, the rate of revolution be not uniform, while the motion along A′B′ is uniform, then the surface would form a blade of Woodcroft's screw. Vessels in her Majesty's service using submarine propellers are mostly fitted with a double-threaded screw; the second blade being on the side of the axis opposite to the one we have drawn, like two of the opposite sails of a windmill. When the draught of water is not great, a three-bladed screw has some advantages, especially in a sea-way.

Definitions.

168. Length of Screw.—The space A′B′ along the axis, which is occupied by the screw-blade, is called the *length* of the screw.

169. Angle of Screw.—The angle P O H, between the outer edge O P of the screw, and plane perpendicular to the axis of the propeller, is called the *angle* of the screw; and this, according to the mode of description, we see is always constant for Smith's screws. By observing the angle P′O′H′, we discover that the angle of the screw increases (*cœteris paribus*) as the radius A′P decreases.

170. Pitch of Screw.—If we suppose A′P to make a complete revolution round the axis A′ B′, continuing its uniform motion along the axis, the length A′B′ would, in such case, be called the *pitch* of the screw.

171. Slip of the Screw.—The screw-propeller, if working in a medium that could not yield, would advance a distance equal to the pitch during each revolution. But such is not the case in the yielding medium in which it actually does rotate; and therefore it is found that the knots per hour passed over by the ship are less than those which ought to have been passed over on the supposition that the screw was working in an unyielding medium. If,

then, the former be taken from the latter, the difference is called the *slip of the screw in knots:* and if this difference be divided by the speed of the screw in knots, we shall have the fraction of the speed lost; this, again, if multiplied by 100, will give the percentage of loss.

172. AREA OF A SCREW.—By the area of a screw is meant the surface of the blade of the screw, which is usually expressed in square feet. It will be seen in the Appendix that the resistance a screw exerts does not depend simply on the area, but that it is a complicated function of the diameter and the angle.

173. THREAD OF SCREW.—The thread of a screw is the outer edge of the blade. In the diagram, O P would be the thread.

174. DIAMETER OF SCREW.—The diameter of a screw is the diameter of the cylinder on which the spiral thread is traced. A′P is the radius of the screw; and twice A′P would be the diameter.

The screw is placed in a rectangular orifice, made expressly for it in the dead-wood at the vessel's stern, immediately on the fore-side of the rudder. The axis A′ B′ is placed horizontally; and, passing through a stuffing-box in the dead-wood, is connected with the engines, either immediately as in some of our largest ships, or intermediately by means of gearing.* The screw-blades are made to revolve round the axis in this orifice; and if we look at their form, we shall see that they press obliquely on the water, in which the screw is supposed to be entirely immersed: the force caused by the reaction of the water is in the opposite direction, and that *part* alone of the force which is in the direction of the axis is effective in propelling the ship. Hence it has been found, both theoretically and practically, that the slip is less when the angle P O H is small and the screw revolves at a great speed. The

* There is a stuffing-box in the stern-post for keeping the shaft water-tight.

practical difficulties lying in the way of obtaining this result, however, are, that the engine must work at very great speed, or multiplying gear must be used of a high multiple.

The practical limit of speed is often pointed out by the heating of the bearings of the screw-shaft, and at the place where the thrust is exerted.

Other advantages, as far as the ship is concerned, arise from the fine-pitch screw, viz., that the hole in the deadwood and the size of the trunk are less.

175. *Disconnecting the Screw.*

There are but two ways of disconnecting the screw-shaft from the engine-shaft. According to one method, the engine-shaft is withdrawn from the screw-shaft, and the latter is then free to be moved. In the other method, the screw-shaft is fitted with a ⊢ end, and the engine-shaft has a slot-way in it to receive the end of the screw-shaft. When the screw has been lowered, a keep is put across the slot-way to retain it in its place; and when it is required to raise the screw, the slot-way in the shaft must be placed vertically and the keep removed, when the screw-frame can be raised.

176. *Methods of raising the Screw.*

There are several methods of raising the screw; that most commonly adopted is as follows: A couple of sheaves are fitted in the upper part of the screw-frame, and rope-falls run through them, and being passed through blocks or sheaves, are led away to the capstan or otherwise, according to the weight to be lifted. In some ships, long vertical screws are fitted in the trunk for raising the frame of the propeller. One or two ships are furnished with means of raising the propeller by the pressure of water, according to the principle of the Bramah Press. The same principle is also employed in one or two ships to withdraw the engine-shaft from the screw-shaft.

177. *Governors in Screw-vessels.*

The principle of this apparatus is the same as that of the land-engines, being a machine for controlling the throttle-valve as occasion requires. Two heavy balls are suspended by means of arms to an axis revolving with the engines. The upper ends of these arms are jointed to the axis, and therefore as the axis rotates the balls will fly out from it; and their distance from the axis will depend on the velocity. The arms by which the balls are suspended are connected with rods, which give motion to the throttle-valve, and are so arranged that as the engines move faster, and therefore the balls fly out farther, the valve shall begin to close; and if the engine relax in its speed, and the balls droop towards the revolving axis, the valve will open. Governors are sometimes fitted to screw-steamers of light draught of water, to limit the supply of steam to the cylinders when the ship pitches. For since the propeller is at one extremity of the vessel, it will at times, by the pitching of the ship, be performing its revolutions in the air: the engines will then be relieved of their load; and if the supply of steam were not reduced, they would fly off at a great velocity, which would again be checked as the stern of the vessel became immersed in the water. This would be detrimental to the machinery. The governor is so adjusted that when the speed of the engines is much above what ought to be their maximum, the throttle-valve closes, and admits no more steam till the revolutions decrease, and thus lessen the centrifugal force acting on the balls.

CHAPTER IV.

178. *Direct-action Engines.*

A DIRECT-ACTION engine is one in which the piston produces a rotary motion of the crank without the intervention of sway-beams or side-levers.

These engines are so varied in their forms and in the adaptation of their parts, that no general outline can be given. Scarcely any two are alike: but some are more commonly in use than others, and we shall therefore give such a description of these as will enable the reader to form an adequate idea of their construction; remarking, at the same time, that such information as can be gained by books will not supply the place of personal inspection.

The kinds of direct engines most commonly introduced into our steam-ships are those which have received the following names:

Gorgon engines.
Fairbairn's engines.
Double-cylinder engines.
Oscillating engines.
Trunk engines.

These engines are for propulsion by means of paddles. We have also every modification of these for driving the screw, the chief difference being that the same kind of engines for such purposes is placed with its cylinders horizontal, and the power is either applied in a direct manner to the screw-shaft or by means of gearing.

It must be understood that the internal arrangements are the same in these as in the side-lever engines, all of them having cylinders, in which the steam causes the piston to move from the one end to the other; as also condensers, air-pumps, etc. The principal difference, therefore, between them lies in the means by which the power exerted on the piston is transmitted to the crank, and in the configuration of the several parts; the chief object proposed by the manufacturers being to confine the space occupied by their engines within the narrowest limits. In most engines of this kind, however, the connecting-rod is necessarily short.

179. *Gorgon Engines.**

The principle of construction of these engines will be more clearly seen by reference to the accompanying figure, which represents a section of one of such engines; and the several parts are, for simplicity's sake, represented only by lines. Here A B C D represents the cylinder; F is the centre of the shaft, directly over the middle of the cylinder (and therefore the engine is of the class called "direct-action"); I E is a section of the piston; I H the piston-rod, working steam-tight in a stuffing-box at K; H G is the connecting-rod, and G F the crank. It is easily seen, that as the piston is forced up and down by the steam, the crank will be made to revolve, and consequently cause the paddle-wheel to rotate. The remaining parts of the engine will be readily understood: L is the condenser, M the air-pump, N the hot-well, *a* and *b* are the foot-valve and delivery-valves respectively, and *c* is the snifting-valve. There are two particulars deserving special notice in this engine, viz., the slides for admitting the steam and allowing it to escape, and the parallel motion, or the means of keeping the piston-rod in its vertical line. It is observable that there are four sides, viz., A, B, C, and D: two of which, A and C, are for allowing the ingress of steam; and the other two,

* The following ships are fitted with this kind of engines: Ardent, Caradoc, Cyclops, Driver, Firebrand, Geyser, Gorgon, Penelope, Polyphemus, Prometheus, Sidon, Styx, and Vixen.

B and D, for allowing it to escape to the condenser L.* The following is an outline of the parallel motion: H O is a beam called the "rocking-beam," one end of which is fitted to the upper extremity H of the piston-rod. P Q is a vertical frame, called the "rocking-standard;" the lower

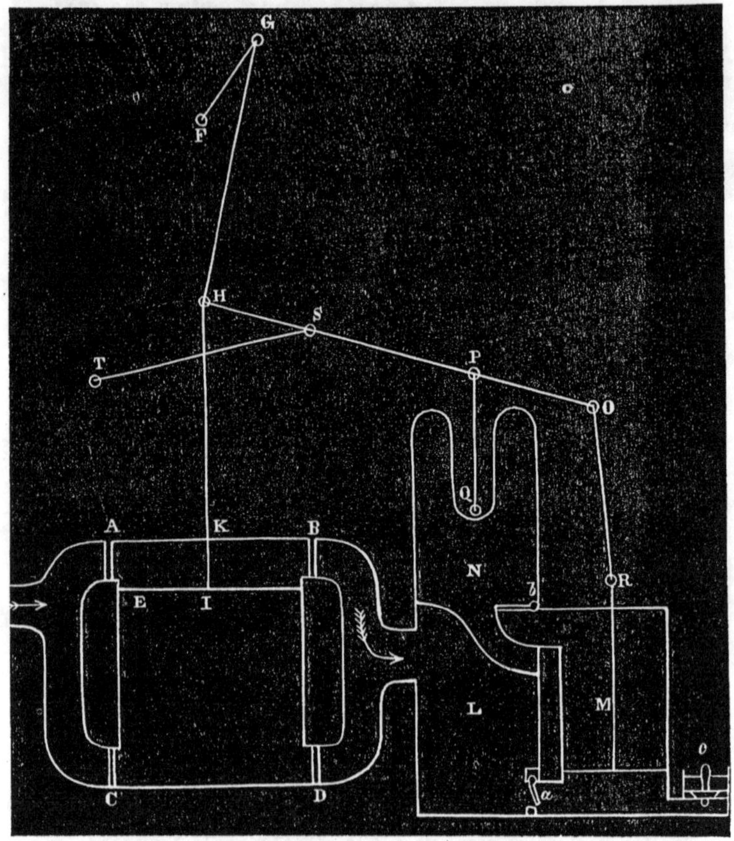

end of this is connected with some convenient point Q, about which it can move, and the upper end P will therefore describe a small circular arc about Q; but this arc will be so small, that it may be practically looked upon as

* See description of these slides.

a straight line. T S is a radius-bar, attached at one end T to the framework of the engine, and at the other to the rocking-beam. If now these rods have the proper proportions, the motion of H will be vertical. The parallel motion will be investigated completely in the next article. The rocking-beam is continued along to O, and the air-pump rod is fitted to it by means of the intermediate rod R O. The air-pump rod is kept in a vertical line by means of guides.

180. *To find the Length of the Radius-rod, etc., of the Gorgon Engine.*

Let T S be the radius or bridle-rod, H P the rocking-

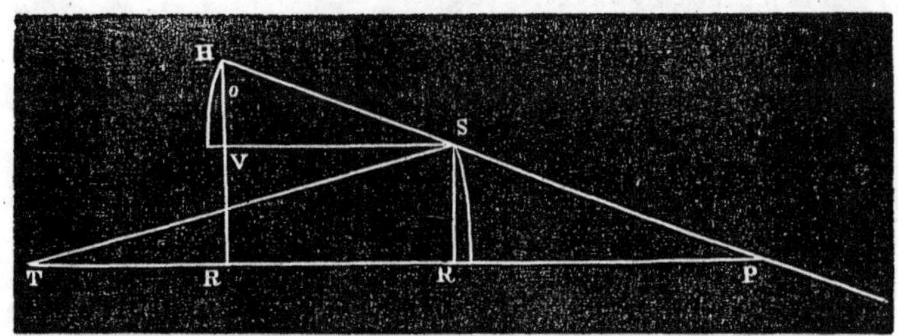

beam, P the point to which the rocking-standard is connected, S the point of attachment of the radius-bar; then it will be found that S P is a mean proportional between T S and H S; that is to say, T S : S P :: S P : S H (1).*
Also, if we wish to get the actual length of T S, S H, and S P, we shall have

---

* This may be proved as follows:
Let $TS = a$, $SH = b$, $SP = c$, $SR = x$, $HV = z$.

Then $$TR = \sqrt{TS^2 - SR^2} = \sqrt{a^2 - x^2} = a - \frac{x^2}{2a} \text{ nearly.}$$

Also $$SV = \sqrt{HS^2 - HV^2} = \sqrt{b^2 - z^2} = b - \frac{z^2}{2b} \text{ nearly.}$$

$\therefore$ $$TK = TR - VS = a - b - \frac{x^2}{2a} + \frac{z^2}{2b} \text{ nearly.}$$

$$TS=\frac{(HP+TK)^2}{TK+2HP} \quad . \quad . \quad . \quad . \quad . \quad . \quad . \quad . \quad (2)$$

$$SH=\frac{HP^2}{TK+2HP} \quad . \quad . \quad . \quad . \quad . \quad . \quad . \quad . \quad (3)$$

$$SP=\frac{HP(HP+2TK)}{TK+2HP} \quad . \quad . \quad . \quad . \quad . \quad (4)$$

and having T K and H P given, we may by these formulæ find the length of the radius-rod, and the point S, to which it is to be fitted.

But $TK=a-b$, because the point H will coincide with K when the engine is at half-stroke.

$$\therefore \qquad \frac{x^2}{2a}-\frac{z^2}{2b}=0 \text{ or } \frac{x^2}{z^2}=\frac{a}{b}$$

Again, since, by similar triangles,

$$\frac{z}{b}=\frac{x}{c} \qquad \therefore \frac{x}{z}=\frac{c}{b}$$

$$\text{and} \qquad \frac{x^2}{z^2}=\frac{c^2}{b^2}$$

$$\text{Hence} \qquad \frac{c^2}{b^2}=\frac{a}{b}$$

$$\text{or} \qquad c^2=a\,.\,b$$

$$\text{and} \therefore \qquad SP^2=TS\,.\,SH$$

$\therefore$ TS:SP::SP:SH, which proves . . . . (1)

Again, let HP $=m$, TK $=n$, (known quantities)

$$\therefore \quad b+c=m \quad . \quad . \quad . \quad . \quad . \quad . \quad . \quad . \quad . \quad . \quad . \quad (\alpha)$$

$$\text{and} \quad a-b=n \quad . \quad . \quad . \quad . \quad . \quad . \quad . \quad . \quad . \quad . \quad . \quad (\beta)$$

also we have proved that $c^2=ab$ . . . . (γ)

$$\therefore \quad b+\sqrt{ab}=m \quad . \quad . \quad . \quad . \quad \text{by } (\alpha) \text{ and } (\gamma)$$

$$\text{or} \quad \sqrt{b}(\sqrt{b}+\sqrt{a})=m$$

$$\text{also} \quad (\sqrt{a}-\sqrt{b})(\sqrt{a}+\sqrt{b})=n. \quad . \text{by } (\beta)$$

$$\therefore \quad \frac{\sqrt{b}}{\sqrt{a}-\sqrt{b}}=\frac{m}{n}$$

$$\text{hence} \quad \sqrt{b}=m\sqrt{a}-m\sqrt{b}$$

$$\therefore \quad \sqrt{b}=\frac{m}{m+n}\sqrt{a}$$

$$\text{or} \quad b=\frac{m^2a}{(m+n)^2}$$

$$\textbf{But} \quad a-b=n$$

$$\therefore \quad a-\frac{m^2a}{(m+n)^2}=n$$

181. *Fairbairn's Direct-Action Engines.**

The chief peculiarity of these engines is in the parallel

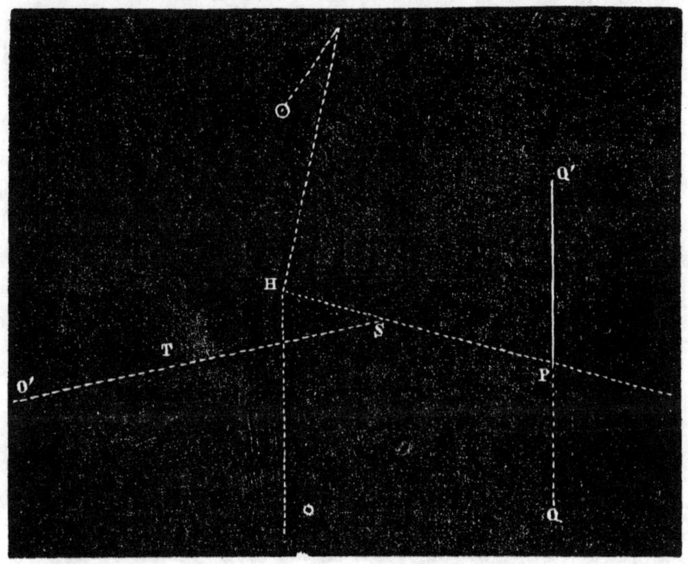

motion, which, after all, is somewhat similar to that of the Gorgon engines.

The dotted lines represent the Gorgon engines. H P O

---

or $$\frac{a(n^2+2mn)}{(m+n)^2}=n$$

$$\therefore \quad a=\frac{(m+n)^2}{n+2m}$$

that is, $$TS=\frac{(HP+TK)^2}{TK+2HP} \quad . \quad . \quad . \quad . \quad (2)$$

Again, $$SH=b=\frac{m^2a}{(m+n)^2}=\frac{m^2}{n+2m}=\frac{HP^2}{TK+2HP} \quad . \quad . \quad (3)$$

Also, $$SP^2=SH.ST=\frac{HP^2.(HP+TK)^2}{(TK+2HP)^2}$$

$$\therefore \quad SP=\frac{HP.(HP+TK)}{TK+2HP} \quad . \quad . \quad . \quad . \quad (4)$$

* The following ships are fitted with this kind of engines: Dragon, Odin, and Vulture.

is the rocking-beam, H the point to which the piston-rod and connecting-rod are attached, P the point of attachment of the rocking-standard; then, to construct Fairbairn's parallel motion, let the rocking-standard P Q be inverted, as in the figure, so as to hang down from a point Q′ in the entablature of the engine. In the Gorgon engines H P is prolonged to O, as before described, and the air-pump is worked from this extremity; but in Fairbairn's engines the radius-bar S T will be produced to some point O′, and O′T serves as the beam for working the air-pump. The steam is admitted and allowed to escape by means of a D slide-valve, worked by an eccentric.

The four main parts of each engine, viz., the cylinder, slide-valves, condenser, and air-pump, form a square, and thus occupy the least possible area.

182. *Maudslay's Double-Cylinder Engines.**

In the foregoing direct engines the connecting-rod is necessarily shorter than it would have been if side-levers had been used; and consequently the force exerted on the crank alters more suddenly as the motion is alternated from the down to the up stroke, and *vice versâ*, than would have been the case had the connecting-rod been longer; therefore, although, as a mechanical principle, the whole force exerted by the steam in the up and down stroke is given off in each revolution of the crank,† still it has been objected by many practical men, that these sudden and violent changes are liable to cause derangement in the machinery; and also, from the shortness of the crank compared with the length of the radius of the paddle-wheel, the engine is

---

* The following ships are fitted with this kind of engine: Devastation, Hermes, Medea, Scourge, Terrible, and Osborn.

† The mean effect produced through the intervention of a crank is the same as if $\frac{7}{11}$ of the pressure exerted on the piston had been applied at the extremity of the crank through the whole revolution. This may be shown thus: let P be the pressure on the piston, and Q be a power which, exerted at the extremity of the crank and at

more apt to be checked if struck by a heavy sea when near the top centre than it would if the connecting-rod and crank had been of greater length.

Now in most direct engines a long connecting-rod is an

impossibility; for the distance from the shaft to the bottom of the vessel being limited, the depth of the cylinder, the radius of the crank, and the length of the connecting-rod,

---

right angles to it, would produce the same effect: then $P \times 2l = Q \times 2\pi r$; where l = length of stroke, and r = radius of crank.

$$\therefore \quad Q = \frac{l}{\pi r} \times P$$

$$\text{But} \quad l = 2r$$

$$\therefore \quad Q = \frac{2}{\pi} P = \frac{7}{11} P \text{ very nearly.}$$

must all be accommodated to it. Messrs. Maudslay and Field, seeing this evil, proposed to remedy it by adapting two cylinders to each engine, instead of one; the cylinders having one connecting-rod *between* them. In the accompanying figures A_1 and A_2 are the two cylinders of one of the engines; a_1 a_2 the piston-rods; these rods are connected together at their upper extremities by the cross-piece B C D, called (from its form) the T-plate or cross-head; the lower end C of the T cross-head is connected with the connecting-rod C E, which again being connected with the crank E F, communicates with the paddle-shaft F. The condenser G is underneath the cylinders. It is clear that if steam be admitted below both pistons at the same time, the pistons, in rising, will force up the T cross-head, and with it the connecting-rod, etc.; and conversely these will again descend as the piston is forced down. Hence the working part of the engine can be comprehended. It remains to be shown how the steam is admitted to both cylinders simultaneously. Looking at the plan of the figure, the circle S represents a slide-valve, different in form from the common slide-valve, inasmuch as it is circular instead of being semicircular; it has one upper and lower face in contact with the ports of the cylinder A_1, and one of each in contact with the cylinder A_2; so that as the valve is raised or depressed, the steam is admitted above or below both pistons at the same instant of time. H is the air-pump, the bucket of which is worked by the beam K L moving round the centre I. The slides being circular, admit of a simple kind of metallic packing, similar to that of a steam-piston. The face or nozzle of the cylinder must of course be concaved.

183. *Boulton and Watt's Direct-action Marine Engines.**

"In this plan of engine the condensers are situated be-

---

* The following ships are fitted with this kind of engines: Centaur and Virago.

tween the cylinders, and at the extremity of each condenser an air-pump is situated. These air-pumps are wrought by a beam, the centre of which rests on the condenser-top, and which derives its motion from a crank on the intermediate shaft—a rod extending from this crank to one of the ends of the beam, which is made something of the bell-crank fashion, to communicate the movement. The top of the piston-rod is maintained in the vertical position by guides."*

184. *Messrs. Miller and Ravenhill's Direct-action Marine Engines.*†

"No engine can occupy less space than this, for its length is very little more than the diameter of the cylinder. The condensers extend from cylinder to cylinder, having the air-pumps within them; so that the whole of the cast-iron part of the engine is bound together in a solid mass. The air-pump buckets are wrought by means of cranks on the intermediate shaft."‡

185. *Oscillating Engines.*§

In these engines the connecting-rod is altogether dispensed with, the piston-rod being attached directly to the crank; and because the piston-rod, from this mode of connection, must either be bent when motion ensues, or the top of the cylinder must move laterally, this is provided for by suspending the cylinder on two hollow trunnions, round which it can oscillate backwards and forwards as the crank moves from one side of the shaft to the other The steam from the pipe enters a belt on the cylinders

---

* *Artizan*, vol. ii. p. 4.

† The following ships are fitted with Miller and Ravenhill's direct engines: Gladiator and Rosamond.

‡ *Artizan*, vol. ii. p. 4.

§ The following ships are fitted with oscillating engines: Antelope, Banshee, Basilisk, Black Eagle, Oberon, Sphinx, Trident, Vivid, Fairy, Minx, Phœnix, Rifleman, Teazer, Wasp, etc.

through the trunnions nearest the ship's side. From this belt it passes through the valve, by which means its distribution is regulated, and escapes from the cylinder to the condenser by the trunnion on the opposite side to that at which it entered. There are two air-pumps, lying at an angle with the keel, and they are both worked by a single crank on the intermediate shaft;* the due position of the air-pump rods being maintained by means of guides. The slide-valves are provided with guides, and are worked by means of an eccentric in the usual manner: but the eccentric-rod is not attached immediately to the valve-lever, but to a curved transverse link, guided between the columns that support the shaft, and susceptible of a vertical motion. The curve of this link is concentric with the arc described by the cylinder in its oscillations; and its design is to obviate the distortion that would result from the combined movement of the cylinder and eccentric.†

186. *Engines for working the Screw-Propeller.*

These engines may be said to be of two kinds, viz., those having the axis of their cylinders vertical, and those whose cylinders lie horizontally. The former kind cause a longitudinal shaft above the cylinder to rotate by means of cranks. This shaft is connected with a large driving-wheel, which, acting on a smaller wheel connected with the screw-shaft, causes it to revolve with a greater velocity than it would otherwise do.

The second kind of engines consist of those whose cylinders are horizontal: these are destined to work the screw shaft direct, that is, without the intervention of any cog-wheels or gearing. They work at higher velocities than would be necessary if multiplying gear were used, and the shaft is made to revolve by means of cranks. The cylinders are mostly placed on different sides of the

---

* In small engines the air-pumps are worked by an eccentric.

† See *Artizan*, vol. ii. p. 92.

shaft, as also the air-pumps, etc. To avoid the wearing away of the cylinder by the weight of the piston, the piston-rod is prolonged, and projects beyond the farther end of the cylinder:* so that the piston is supported by two stuffing-boxes, one at each end of the cylinder. The chief obstacle to be overcome by the manufacturers of these engines is, that on account of the narrow space in which the engines have to work, especially when placed low down, the cylinder is necessarily brought closer to the shaft than could be wished, and consequently all the difficulties arising from the common direct-action system apply also here. These engines are mostly fitted with double eccentrics, for the purpose of rapidly reversing the motion, since this is more essential for screw-ships than for those fitted with paddles.

187. *Direct-acting Screw-Engines.*

There are several ships fitted with this class of engines. By inspecting the diagram it will be seen that A B, C D, are two cylinders lying horizontally on opposite sides of the screw-shaft whose section is S; E and F are the pistons; E G, H F, the piston-rods; G L, L H, the connecting-rods, attached to the same crank S L; and if the steam be in the portions of the cylinders A F C F, it tends to turn

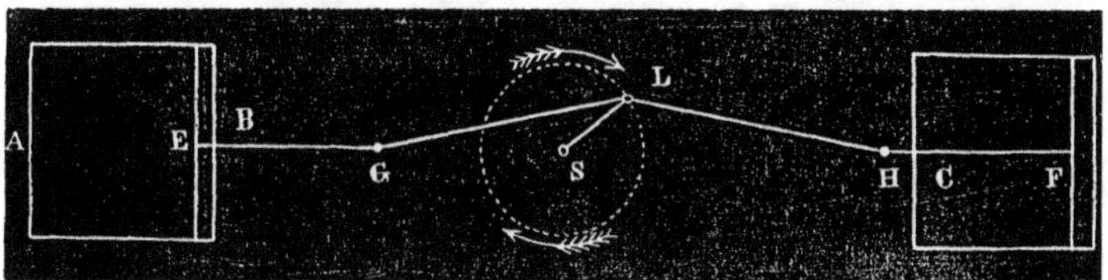

the crank in the direction of the arrows, and thus produces a revolution of the shaft. There are usually four of these cylinders, two on each side of the shaft; but if two only, they do not work the same crank as in the diagram, or the engines would both be on the centre at the same time. To

* This is not fitted in all cases.

give a tolerably long connecting-rod, the cylinders are placed as far from the shaft as can be done conveniently. The air-pumps of these engines are usually placed under the main shaft, and worked from it by means of eccentrics. They are fitted with locomotive slides (Article 127), and are worked either with double eccentrics or two single eccentrics (Article 140).*

188. *Direct-acting Geared Engines for Screw-Ships.*

The accompanying diagram will suffice for a sketch of

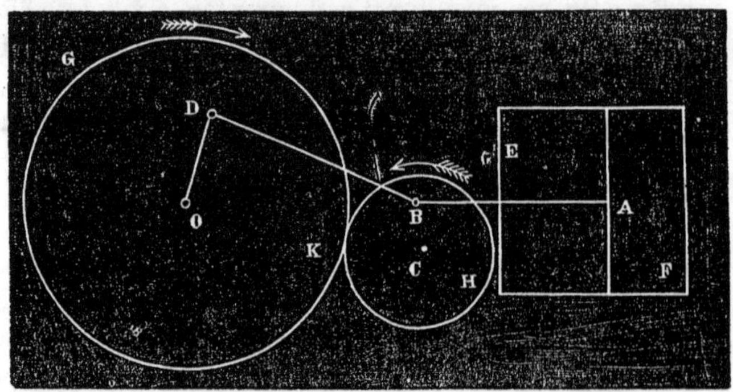

this class of engines. E F is a horizontal cylinder, of which A is the piston and A B the piston-rod; B D the connecting-rod, turning the crank D O, and with it the driving-wheel K G, which is geared to the pinion K H: therefore as this wheel revolves in the direction of the arrow, the pinion revolves in the opposite direction, as is shown in the diagram; C is a section of the screw-shaft, and consequently by these means rotation of the shaft is produced. It is easily seen that this is the same kind of engine as the direct-acting engine for paddle-steamers, the cylinder lying horizontally, and the driving-wheel taking

* The following ships are furnished with this kind of engines: Ajax, Blenheim, Conflict, Desperate, Euphrates, Edinburgh, Hogue, Horatio, James Watt, Niger, Megæra, and Vulcan (worked with four cylinders); Amphion, Archer, Cressy, Tribune, and Princess Royal (worked with two cylinders).

the place of the paddle-wheel. Gearing is introduced to increase the number of revolutions of the shaft, and thus enable the screw to make revolutions enough without giving undue velocity to the piston. This kind of engine is therefore useful for driving screws of small diameter and fine pitch.*

189. *Oscillating Horizontal Engines.*

The accompanying diagram will show the application of the oscillating engine as fitted for screw-propellers. There

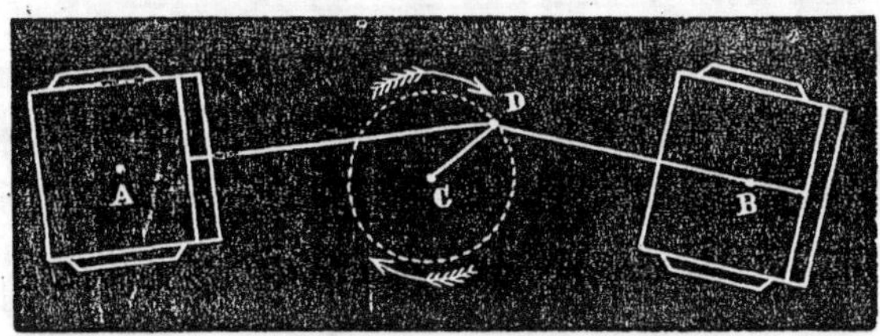

are usually four cylinders, two pistons being coupled to each crank, as represented in the drawing; and as is also the case with the direct-acting horizontal screw-engines. In the diagram A and B are the two cylinders on opposite sides of the shaft, whose centre is C, the cylinders being allowed to oscillate about their steam and eduction pipes; A D and D B are the piston-rods, which also serve as connecting-rods, and unite in turning the crank C D, by which means the rotation of the screw is effected. The air-pumps are worked from the main shaft as in the direct-action engines, but are placed at an angle instead of being vertical, that they may be worked by one crank.†

190. *Trunk Engines.*

The cylinders of these engines are horizontal, and connected at once to the screw-shaft. Imagine a hollow trunk, *a b c d*, to pass through the cylinder A B C D and to pro-

* The following ships are fitted with this class of engines: Duke of Wellington, Dauntless, Highflyer, and Sharpshooter.

† The following ships are fitted with this kind of engines: Simoom and Sanspareil.

ject beyond it at both ends, passing through the covers A B and C D. Where the trunk comes in contact with the cylinder, a stuffing-box and gland are fitted to keep the trunk air and steam tight. The middle portion of the

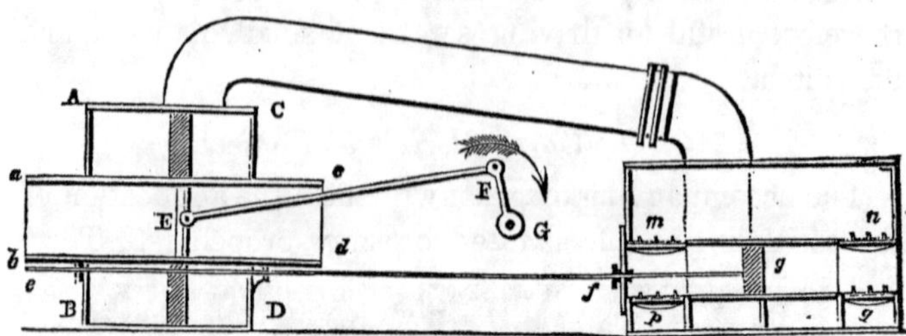

trunk is rigidly connected with the piston of the cylinder (represented by the shaded portion of the diagram), and to the central part E of the hollow space the connecting-rod E F is attached, which turns the crank F G of the screw-shaft G. The piston surface becomes for this reason an annular ring. Now as the crank revolves, the crank end of the connecting-rod must vibrate; and this it will be at free liberty to do, although there is no piston-rod, because the size of the trunk will admit of a vibratory motion within it. These engines are fitted with locomotive slides, and are worked with double eccentrics, rendering the back and head turns at all times to be depended on. The air-pump, like the cylinder, is horizontal; and, indeed, all the parts of the engines are as low as they can possibly be, for the purpose of bringing the machinery below the water-line. The air-pump is worked directly by the piston, the pump-rod, *e f g*, passing through the covers of the cylinder as represented in the diagram. The pipe shown in the figure, which is taken by many at first sight as the steam-pipe, is, in fact, the eduction pipe for conveying the waste steam from the cylinder to the con denser. The principle of the air-pump, as it is not confined alone to this sort of engine, will be explained in the next article.

191. *The Double-acting Air-pump.*

There are no valves in the bucket of this kind of pump, *g* being a solid piston, which is worked horizontally by the rod *e g*; *p q* are foot-valves, and *m n* delivery-valves; the lower chamber represents the condenser, and the upper one the hot-well.

Suppose, now, the piston to be at the extreme left, and to commence moving to the right: if there be any water above *g*, it will be driven through the valve *n* into the hot-well; at the same time the valve *p* will open, and allow the water of the condenser to pass through it; on the return-stroke of the piston, this water will be forced through *m* into the hot-well, and so on. Since this pump acts during the return-stroke, the area of the piston need only be half as great as that of the common description.

192. *Maudslay and Field's Return Connecting-rod Engine.*

This engine takes its name from a peculiarity in the construction, viz., that the connecting-rod lies between the extremity of the piston-rods and the cylinder, instead of being in the opposite direction. There are also two piston-rods to each cylinder. Fig. 1 represents an end view

Fig. 1. Fig. 2.

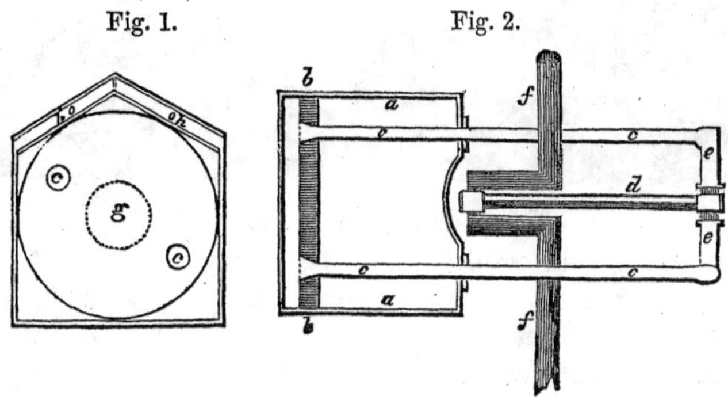

of the cylinder, showing the cover, with the two glands *c c* for the piston-rods, and a recessed space *g* in the centre, to prevent the crank from striking the cover. *h* and *h* are the sections of two locomotive slides, with which each engine is fitted. In Fig. 2 *a a* is a horizontal section of the cylinder, etc.; *b b* is the piston; *c c* the two rods, one working above the shaft, and the other below it; *e e* a sort of cross-head connecting the piston-rods. This cross-head is necessarily at an angle with the horizontal plane; *d* is the connecting-rod, working the crank, as in the figure, and turning the screw-shaft *f f*. With this kind of engine, it is clear that a longer connecting-rod may be adopted than in most cases of horizontal engines, because, although the cylinder is brought very close to the screw-shaft, yet the piston-rods may be prolonged on the opposite side to any convenient distance, by which means additional length is gained.

193. *Humphrey's Engine for Screw-Ships.*

The principle of construction of the engine will be easily understood by the accompanying diagram. Here *a a* is the

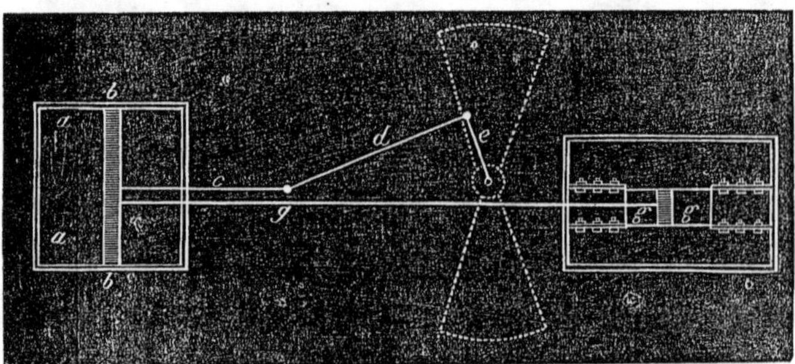

cylinder; *b b* the piston; *c* the piston-rod; *a* the connecting-rod; *e* the crank turning the screw-shaft; *g* is a rod also worked by the piston, and forming the air-pump rod for the double-acting pump *g g*, the construction and working of which were explained in Art. 191.

CHAPTER V.

GETTING UP THE STEAM.

194. *Filling the Boilers.*

THE first thing to be done is to get the water into the boilers. To do this, let the blow-out cocks and Kingston's valves be opened, and the water will of course commence running in. To prevent any obstruction caused by the pressure of the air in the boiler on the surface of the water, let the guage-cocks be opened; and, as the water rises, the air will be driven through their orifices into the engine-room. If expedition be required, the safety-valve may be opened likewise until the water is up, to take the superincumbent pressure from the water: the water would evidently run in till it has the same level as that outside the ship. If the vessel be deeply immersed, so that too much would enter, let the blow-out cocks be closed, when the fires can be lighted with safety. In ships of light draught of water, the level of the water in the boiler must be higher than that of the sea; consequently, when the water ceases to enter, the blow-out cocks must be closed, and the boiler hand-pumps set to work. We can ascertain when the water ceases to flow in of its own accord by putting the hand, or a lighted candle, to the orifice of the guage-cocks; for if the safety valves be closed, air will rush out so long as the water rises, and will then cease.

These remarks, however, apply principally to the case where an engineer is not well acquainted with his engine, boilers, etc.; for, after once or twice filling, he knows with sufficient accuracy the time the water will be flowing in, and acts accordingly; making due allowance for variations in the draught of water outside, depending on the load.

195. *To know when the Blow-out Cocks are closed.*

It is the practice of engine-makers to cut a slot-way or score across the plug of the cock in the same direction as the hole through it; so that when this slot-way lies across the pipe, the orifice is necessarily closed; and when we wish to open it, the plug must be turned till the score lies in the direction of the pipe.

196. *On the Height to which the Water is to be raised at first.*

The steam will be got up most rapidly when the height of the water above the flues or tubes is not greater than it should be to ensure the safety of the boiler. Therefore the fires may be lighted as soon as the flues or tubes are all covered; and when the water is an inch or two deep over them, the pumping need not proceed further for some little time; and if the water be running in, it should be stopped till that within the boiler has gained a sufficiently high temperature. The chilling effect of the cold iron is detrimental to the effective combustion of the coal. Every one must have experienced the effect of putting on a quantity of cold coals on a fire that is nearly going out. The fire will probably be extinguished by the process that was intended to revive it.

197. *Laying the Fires.*

Unless the fires have been previously laid, this operation is generally performed while the water is running up into the boilers. It is, however, mostly done after the fire-places are cleaned out and put to rights. It is done as follows: Let the fire-bars be covered with coals from one end to the other: this is done to prevent a current of cold air passing through the back of the ash-pit into the tubes, and to cause all the air that enters the tubes to pass over the fresh lighted wood, etc. The coals being arranged, some fire-wood is placed in front, with some of the oily cotton, waste oakum, etc., put under it. Then, having set a light to the oakum, the ash-pit doors are kept shut, to concentrate the draught on the ignited part. In a few minutes the wood and the coals placed on the top will be thoroughly ignited. The upper part of the fire must now be pushed back over the new coal: and it will be striking to observe how rapidly the combustion will proceed, the blast of air over the upper surface of the coals carrying the heat and flame from mass to mass with great rapidity. When the fire has well burnt up, the ash-pit doors are opened, to obtain the greatest draught possible.

198. *When wishing to get up the Steam expeditiously.*

When in a hurry to get up the steam, every hatchway in the engine-room should be opened, that the fires may get a good supply of air, in order that the oxygen may combine freely with the combustible. The time taken in getting up the steam will vary with the moisture of the air and the force of the wind.

199. *Duties to various parts of the Engine, etc., while the Steam is getting up.*

1. SAFETY-VALVE.—It is a common practice to leave the safety-valves open after the fires are lighted: this is not a good plan. The object of doing so evidently is, to allow the air to escape that had been mechanically mixed with the water, and is liberated by the heating process. As this air becomes disengaged, its pressure acts on the surface of the water, and checks ebullition. Hence the safety-valves are commonly opened. But it is more judicious to let the heated air pass through the engines, where it will help to warm them.

It is, however, possible that when the steam-pipe is of great length, time might be saved by keeping the communication-valve closed until the steam is up, as a great deal of steam will be condensed in this pipe and in the jacket.

A loss from this cause must ensue whenever the starting of the steamer is delayed after the steam begins to form beyond the time necessary to heat the steam-pipe, jacket, etc., and the effects will depend on the amount of radiating surface. In a steamer in which the boiler was at a great distance from the cylinder, it was found that eight or ten minutes was saved by keeping the communication-valve closed until the steam was up sufficiently to start. It would be well to try in each steamer which method ought to be adopted for the sake of saving time.

2. THROTTLE-VALVE.—The throttle-valves should be opened shortly after the fires are lighted, to prevent their setting fast, which they will do, if kept shut; for the steam and heated air will expand the valve; and when set fast in its place, it will be impossible to get the steam into the cylinder. Cases of this kind have at times happened. Indeed, in one instance the engineer, whilst endeavoring to open the valve, was obliged to use such force that the lever broke off, and effectually prevented the ship from proceeding for some time.

3. LUBRICATORS.—The lubricators are generally trimmed and filled up before starting; because it cannot be so well done afterwards: it is true, it must still be done afterwards when under way; but as this cannot be prevented, the waste consequent upon so doing must be borne with, and must not obviate the rule of carefully seizing the opportunity while stationary.

4. THE MOVING PARTS OF THE ENGINE.—Great care should be taken to ascertain whether any thing will interfere with the free working of the engine, particularly where it comes near some fixed part of the ship; as, for example, while repairing the engine, blocks of wood are interposed to support some of the heavy portions; and these are frequently left afterwards, and become a cause of serious mischief. Where the cylinder-covers are recessed to admit of the piston cross-head working into them, so as to give greater length to the connecting-rod,

these hollow spaces must be carefully cleared. In cold climates ice may have formed above and below the air-pump buckets, under the feed and bilge pumps, and all this requires consideration and care. When starting the engines, and hence, as we shall hereafter observe, when the use of the engines is no longer required (at least for a time), in cold climates the engines should be well blown through to get rid of all the water from them. If there be water above the bucket which cannot be got rid of by blowing through, the engines should be moved round as slowly as possible to drive the water into the hot-well.

5. Funnel-Stays.—While getting up the steam, attention should be paid to the funnel-stays. It is a practice in some steam-ships to tighten up the funnel-stays for the sake of appearances: they become slack after the steam has escaped, and the boiler cools down, because all the heated parts, such as boiler, uptake, funnel, etc., contract as they cool; and the crown of the boiler, which had been in all likelihood somewhat forced up by the steam, recovers its shape. We must, therefore, when the fires have been lighted, take the precaution of slacking off the funnel-stays till the steam is up, when they may be tightened again. Now it will generally happen, that, if the funnel be taunt, and the stays not too much spread, they will require a second setting up; and it is for the following reason: After the steam has been up some time, the heat from the funnel communicates with the stays, being conducted down them, so that they become lengthened, and slack again. If the stays are much spread, the heat is carried off while endeavoring to ascend vertically, and consequently the stay does not expand so much. If no attention is paid to the stays, to slack them off as the top of the boiler rises, and the expansion goes on, either the stay or its fastenings will yield. It is a common thing to see funnels, when much decayed, crippled (*i.e.* bulged out in places); this doubtless is owing to the stays being too taunt, as the funnel expands when raising the steam. In

one instance, the hoop round the funnel to which the stays were attached gave way, and nearly proved fatal to those who were walking on the deck at the time. The bolts in the gunwale have occasionally been drawn, when in a heavy sea, by the want of spread in the stays. The foremost stays are most affected in this way; for, as the ship pitches, the funnel has a tendency to fall aft. To remedy this, the eye-bolts should be driven in at right angles to the direction of the strain. The plan has been adopted in some steamers, and effectually prevented the drawing out of the bolts. Whilst speaking of funnel-stays, we may observe that it is usual, where the funnel is taunt, in gales of wind to put up extra stays, midway between the deck and the other stays. These are sometimes called belly-stays, but more properly preventer-stays. They are particularly useful in despatch vessels, where the stays have not much spread.

200. *Injection-Orifice Choked up.*

On getting under way, it will at times be found that the injection-orifice is choked up. This is to be expected, in iron steamers especially, from the rapidity with which seaweed grows on iron when long stationary in salt-water. It will also be the case with copper-bottomed vessels after lying at anchor for any considerable time, unless the copper wastes quickly; but more particularly if it happen in the spring of the year; for seaweed, like all other vegetation, is found to grow most rapidly at that season. To clear this, whenever it takes place, let the snifting-valve be secured down, and the valve in the waste-water pipe closed also; then open the injection-cock and blow-through valve, and blow the engine through; the steam not escaping by the snifting-valve, nor by the more tortuous passage through the air-pump and waste-pipe, will exert a pressure on the seaweed at the mouth of the injection-pipe, and in all probability will force a passage. Mud will at times block up the orifices, particularly when they are low down, and the ship has been put ashore, or has taken the ground; this may be cleared in the same way. It may be objected, that, since the injection-orifice is very low down, the steam will not have sufficient force to produce any good effect against the pressure of water on the outside; but this can scarcely be the case with our present steamers, for very few have their steam-pressure less than 8 lbs. above that of the atmosphere; and if we consider every two feet of water to produce one lb. pressure, the steam will have some effect if the depth is any thing less than 16 feet. If the pressure be 10 lbs. the depth may be increased to 20, and so on. The effective pressure will, however, manifestly be less as the depth is greater.* In block-ships there may be some difficulty from the great draught of water, and because the injection sea-cock is so near the vessel's keel. The same method may be adopted to clear the orifice if choked up with ice. A vessel in the Thames was trying to force her way through a floe of ice; and when just in the midst of it, she stopped for want of water to condense the steam; for in those days the steam-pressure was so low in the boiler that the engines could not be worked without injection-water. The steam, however, was blown through the pipe, and it thawed the ice so as to admit the water again. The vessel was but a small one, and consequently the orifice not far below the surface, and the steam-pressure in the boiler overcame the column of water. There may be some difficulty at times in discovering whether the orifice is cleared; for the steam in the injection-pipe will

---

* Let $p =$ the pressure in the boiler,

$a =$ depth of injection-cock below the surface of the water;

$\therefore$ since 34 feet of water give a pressure equal to that of the atmosphere, or 14·75 lbs. per square inch;

$$\therefore \quad 34 : 14{\cdot}75 :: a : {\cdot}434a \text{ nearly.}$$

Multiply, therefore, the depth by ·434, and we shall have the pressure of the water opposing the steam.

Hence the available pressure is $p - {\cdot}434a$.

Moreover, if $a = \frac{p}{{\cdot}434}$ the force will be zero.

prevent the injection-water from entering, and we shall therefore be led to suppose the orifice is still choked up. If, however, there be any suspicion of this, shut the blow-valve, and apply the hand to the outside of the pipe; and if it be found that the pipe is cold near the ship's side, and as we pass the hand along we suddenly arrive at a part where the steam still keeps the pipe hot, we may be certain that the water and steam are struggling for the mastery, and that eventually the water will make its way. Its progress will be expedited by the application of cold water to the outside of the pipe and condenser.

201. *Danger to the Engine from Solid Bodies under the moving parts.*

In frosty weather the water in some parts of the engine may become frozen, and be the source of danger to the engine, particularly under the plungers of the feed and bilge pumps. If not moved before the pumps are set in operation, the stroke of the plungers may knock out the bottoms of the pumps. In the case of the feed-pump, the ice may be removed by blowing through, if the waste-water pipe and snifting-valve be previously closed. In case of the bilge-pump, heat must be applied externally. Ice is apt to form also in the air-pump, and may be thawed by blowing through. If the vessel take the ground, great difficulty is frequently experienced from sand and dirt getting into the engines. Sand, for instance, will accumulate under the air-pump bucket, and prevent the complete downward stroke; the engine in this case must break down. When a steamer is on shore with a sandy or muddy bottom, it is well not to work the engines too long with a view to start her, for all propellers stir up the sand, etc. If a ship do not start with the first few turns of the engines there is not much chance of their effecting it.

202. *The Snifting-valve "drawing Air."*

On first getting up the steam, and attempting to get a

vacuum in the condenser, it is sometimes found that the snifting-valve is "drawing air," as it is termed; that is to say, from the valve not fitting tight, air is making its way by these means into the condenser. This is liable to happen from a piece of chip or coal, or a piece of seaweed, having passed into the condenser, and becoming jammed under the valve, which allows air to pass in and destroy the vacuum under the air-pump bucket. It is usually remedied by a bucket of water being poured on the valve. If this be repeated two or three times, it will generally clear it. Sometimes a piece of oakum will get under the valve, which is generally the source of great trouble; for it is apt to wind itself round the spindle, and the water will not be able to wash it away. The consequences of air getting into the engine through the snifting-valve have proved to be more serious than could at first sight be imagined. The snifting-valve not being closed, we shall in many engines have a pressure of air against one side of the foot-valve; and the injection-water producing a vacuum in the condenser, that valve will not open on the up-stroke of the air-pump, and the water not being pumped off will rapidly accumulate in the condenser, and at length find its way into the cylinder; and consequently the engine will, in all probability, be broken down. Such an accumulated catastrophe, arising from so slight a cause, reminds one of the nursery-tale commencing with, "For want of a nail the shoe was lost," and terminating with the catastrophe of the rider being slain by the enemy; and serves to show the value of much of our early legendary information, if we would but bring it to mind occasionally. For the case is by no means exaggerated, as the accident actually happened to a steam-boat in Scotland some time since from a thread of seaweed getting under the snifting-valve.

203. *The Foot-valve gagged, owing to the Engine having become hot.*

The foot-valve may become gagged from the following

cause. Should the engine have become hot owing to excessive blowing-through, leaky slides, leaky blow-valve, etc., and too much injection-water be admitted while the whole engine is hot in consequence of the steam, the water will have the effect of condensing the steam in the condenser, but not in the air-pump, and the result may be the same as in the last article. In some old engines a cock was fitted to the condenser to admit air and equalize the pressure, if needful, in the condenser and air-pump; but since escape-valves have been fitted to the cylinder this cock has been dispensed with.

204. *Starting the Engines.*

The first thing to be done is to ascertain with what kind of *slide* the engines are fitted; if with the long D-slide, it must be raised to admit steam *above* the piston, and depressed to admit the steam *below* the piston; but if with the locomotive slide or Seaward's slides, the reverse must take place. Having ascertained this, we may look at the slide to see how it is worked by means of the starting-gear.* Let this gear be so moved as to give the necessary motion of the piston, and consequently to the crank. This part of the manipulation requires some careful consideration; and each engineer must lay down a technical rule for himself on which he can act without hesitation when he receives his orders, because there is then no time for reflection. The best rule, generally speaking, is to leave the piston and slide out of consideration, and notice whether the motion of the starting-gear in one direction will produce a motion of the *crank* in the *same*, or in the *opposite*, direction. The engines should be worked a few turns by hand, in nearly all cases, before being thrown into gear, to let the steam act on the piston *throughout the stroke*, which it will not do when the slide is worked by the eccen-

* In Plate II. the long horizontal lever connected with the gab-lever is called the starting-bar, because it is the lever by which the slide is moved by hand.

tric, on account of the lap. When working by hand, any water that may happen to be in the cylinder will be at liberty to escape through the ports. When the slide is moved to admit steam to the piston, the injection-cock should be open to admit water to the condensers, otherwise the engines will move sluggishly. Some engines will not start unless the injection-cock be opened. In starting an engine, it is a good plan to commence the motion with the throttle-valve only partially open, and increase the supply of steam and injection as the ship gathers way: in most cases, the injection should be supplied very gradually, or the water will be liable to get into the cylinders, and the work thrown on the air-pump will be too much while the engine is moving but slowly.

205. *Starting with one Engine in Gear.*

In case the engines are fitted with single eccentrics, this may be done when there is a scarcity of hands in the engine-room. One engine must have been thrown out of gear at the time the slide of the other was at half-stroke, and therefore both ports were closed. If in this position the engine not in gear be worked by hand, steam will immediately be admitted to the other engine, because the slide is on the point of opening to steam. This plan can only be adopted when continuing to go the same way. To reverse the engine, both engines must evidently be thrown out of gear.

206. *Working the Engine at the Moorings.*

When the steam is nearly up, it is a common and very useful rule to work the engines by hand a turn or two before starting, to see that all is right; and it is well to throw them into gear (if fitted with single eccentrics), to see whether the eccentrics are at liberty to slip round on the shaft; for at times they set fast, and perhaps it may be midway *between* the stops for the head and sternway; so that on being thrown into gear the engine stops, for the ports to the cylinder are not opened at the proper time.* If we refer to the article on Setting the Slides, we shall see that the stops are placed on the eccentric so as to admit the steam at a particular part of the stroke, that is to say, near the end; but if the eccentric become fixed on the shaft from any cause, it evidently comes to the same thing as if the stops had originally been put on wrong, and the steam were therefore admitted at an improper time. Water dropping into the engine-room from leaky hatchways will tend to cause the eccentric to rust on the shaft; or if the bearings get hot, and it becomes necessary to use water to cool them, the oil will be washed off from all the parts in the neighborhood of the bearing. The eccentric will sometimes not work freely for another reason. The brass ring of the eccentric is at times tightened up while in harbor; and by so doing it may become fixed, so as not to allow the gab to fall on to the pin, the rod remaining suspended on account of the friction. This defect can in most cases be remedied while the engine is being worked by hand.

207. *Whether a Steam-ship may start before the Steam is well up.*

This will depend on the anchorage of the steamer. If she have to go for any distance where no accident could happen provided the steam became low in the boiler—as for instance, in an open roadstead, or a harbor not crowded—then there would be no necessity for waiting till the steam has reached its full pressure. Thus if the full steam were 8 or 10 lbs., it is not necessary to wait till it blows off; as soon as the guage has risen 2 or 3 inches, the process of blowing-through might be effected; and as soon as the boiler has recovered from this, the vessel may be considered ready to start, on condition that she gets up the steam to its full pressure as she proceeds. Of course, if no after-precautions be observed, since the demand is

* This refers to engines fitted with single eccentrics.

greater than the supply, the engines would shortly stop for want of steam. To avoid this, a high grade of the expansive gear must be put on; or if that be not fitted, the steam must be well throttled. The supply of steam is limited at first for several reasons, but chiefly because the ebullition proceeding from the bottom of the water serves mostly to heat the upper strata, and a great deal of heat will be lost in raising the temperature of the boiler: besides this, more than a due proportion of feed-water must enter the boiler to raise the water-level; yet, notwithstanding all these drawbacks, the steam will gradually rise if kept back in the boiler by the methods prescribed, and distance will eventually be gained. This method does not apply where sufficient notice has been given beforehand for making the necessary preparations, but to those cases only where despatch is the great object. By these means the ship will proceed at perhaps two-thirds her usual rate; and to start at full speed, she must have waited a considerable time; and after all, it is probable the pressure in the boiler would have lowered at first starting.

208. *Steaming through an intricate Passage on first Starting.*

If the vessel have to steam through a difficult passage on first starting, or to leave a lee shore in bad weather, she should not be allowed to get under way till after the steam has been up some time; for to neglect this precaution may be attended with dangerous consequences, because, as was before stated, unless the expansion gear or throttle-valve be attended to, the steam will fall in the boiler, and the engine will stop, perhaps at the very time it is wanted to exert its greatest power. The better plan is to give the engines a few turns at the anchorage, or at moorings, before starting, so as thoroughly to heat them, and at the same time to have the steam well up in the boiler; and it will be as well to blow out some of the water from the *lower* part of the boiler, that its place may be taken by hotter water from the upper part; if these

12

precautions be adopted, and the feed be shut off for a few minutes, the boiler will keep its steam, unless it have some radical defect.

209. *On Opening the Communication with a Boiler in which the Steam is of less Pressure than the other.*

The danger arising from this is similar to that last mentioned, because the colder boiler serves as a condenser for the steam of the other one; so that instead of going into the cylinders, it is condensed by the cold boiler. And what has been said of passing through a difficult passage with steam low applies equally well to those instances in which a collision between two vessels is expected; for on attempting to reverse the engines, it will perhaps be found with low steam that the pressure is not great enough to overcome the onward momentum of the ship.

210. *Priming on first starting the Engine.*

One cause of priming on first starting the engines arises from the pressure being taken off the surface of the water in the boiler, and thus enabling the ebullition to go on with greater violence; but this is not the principal cause: the chief reason is, that many foreign substances become mechanically mixed with the water; for instance, on getting up the steam in a muddy river, such as the Thames, the mud will, by boiling, be driven up to the surface of the water, and accumulating there, will prevent the free course of steam to the steam-chest, and consequently it forces up the water and mud before it. If there be any mucilage in the water, priming will also take place. Such water is formed in deep bays and harbors, especially at particular times of tide, from the mixture of seaweed and decomposing vegetable matter. There are few persons who have not noticed this fact one way or another. A boiler will likewise prime as the vessel goes out of salt water into fresh, and also in going out of fresh water into the salt: the first of these cases can be accounted for from the fact, that fresh water boils at a lower temperature than salt water, and therefore, as the fresh water enters the boiler previously heated, the ebullition is more violent; but the contrary case is difficult to explain; and, indeed, this latter instance would almost lead one to suppose the former explanation not to be the true one. The same difficulty occurs in attempting remedies for priming; for melted tallow on the surface of some boilers will check the priming, and in others it will increase it.

We will not enter here into one of the principal causes of priming, namely, the form and dimensions of the boiler and steam-chest, because that is a matter beyond the control of the engineer and officers of the ship; but it is very clear, that if a larger steam space were allowed, and combustion took place more slowly, and the boilers were not so contracted at the water-surface as many of our marine boilers are, we should not hear so much of priming. It is probably true, that those who have the management of the Cornish engines scarcely know the meaning of the phrase.

211. *Priming while getting up the Steam.*

If the boiler prime while getting up the steam, as may happen if it be filled with fresh water, the dampers should be shut, the fires put back, and, at the same time, an extra quantity of water should be thrown in by the hand-pump or the auxiliary engine; by thus checking the ebullition, the priming will probably cease. If the boiler be liable to prime, the stop-valves should be carefully closed, to prevent water from getting into the engines by the sudden ebullition, and only partially opened on first starting.

212. *Remedies against Priming.*

The remedy usually adopted to prevent priming is the introduction of tallow. Some boilers have a syringe fitted on purpose; others have a stop-cock attached to the feed-pump, so as to charge it for one stroke with tallow. The auxiliary engine, if fitted, may also be employed to force tallow into the boiler. If the steam-pressure be reduced, it may be introduced through the reverse-valve or through the glass water-gauge.

Priming has been successfully got rid of in some vessels by placing two flat pieces of perforated iron near the steam-pipe, taking care that the perforations of the two plates are not in the line of the pipe. Any water that gets through the perforations of the first plate will impinge on the solid portion of the second and be stopped. It will also be reduced by increasing the size of the steam-chest. If a steam-dome be added for this purpose, it is right not to cut the piece entirely out of the boiler, but to perforate it, that it may serve as a strainer of the steam.

213. *On the Effect produced on Fires by Cold Surfaces.*

If the water in a boiler be cold, there are two distinct causes for delay in getting up the steam. The first is because time will be lost in warming the water; the second is, that the flame will not burn so briskly when coming in contact with cold iron as it would do if it were hotter, This may be proved experimentally by any one who is desirous of putting it to the test: let him take *a very small* cotton-wick, and float it in oil; after applying a light to it, let him bring down a ring of cold metal, so as to surround the flame, and it will shortly be extinguished.

214. *On Banking up the Fires.*

Banking up the fires is an economical measure. It is practised whenever circumstances require that the engine should be stopped and started again after a short notice given, such as twenty minutes or half an hour, for preparation. If the service on which the vessel be employed ad mit of a delay of from one hour to an hour and a half after orders are received to start, economy may generally be effected by putting the fires out and retaining the water in the boilers (allowing it to cool down),* and closing the communication-valves.

---

* This has been clearly established by some experiments of Lieutenant Halkett's.

The operation of banking up may be described as follows: the fires are put back against the bridge; small wet coals and ashes are thrown on them, and the dampers closed; if dampers are not fitted, or if they do not fit tight, the ash-pit doors are closed. "Banking up" has been practised on the following occasions: for instance, after anchoring, when it is probable the vessel will have to get under way in the course of a short time; or if, owing to a gale of wind or a strong tide, it is expected that it may be necessary to use the steam for easing the strain on the cables. In these cases the steam may be allowed to fall to atmospheric pressure, if it be known that it will not be required till after sufficient notice. If, however, the vessel be anchored in a roadstead, it may be necessary to have the steam in such readiness as to be able to blow through and move ahead at very short notice. In this case the pressure must be kept higher. When banking up under sail, the pressure at which the steam is retained is determined by the nature of the service and the strength and variableness of the wind. If the steam has been allowed to fall to atmospheric pressure, from twenty to thirty minutes will be required to get it up. This will depend on the nature of the coal (Welsh coal requiring more time than north-country coal). The temperature to which the boiler is cooled in a given time will have an effect on the time to heat it again, as also will the temperature and humidity of the air.

215. *Putting the Fires back.*

If an order be given to stop for a few minutes only, the dampers or ash-pits are to be closed, and the fires are only put back so as to diminish for the time the consumption of fuel and production of steam. As the engine must be ready to start the instant the order is given, the steam is not allowed to fall below the maximum pressure. Where tubular boilers are fitted, simply opening the lower part of the smoke-box doors is sufficient to check the production of steam.

216. *The Safety-valves with Fires banked up.*

It is a custom in some cases, when the fires are banked up, to keep the safety-valves open, their object being not to tax the boiler when it is unnecessary to do so; but the prudence of such a plan is much to be questioned, for we may be injuring the boiler in another way, namely, by the saturation of the water. For as long as the safety-valve remains open, steam will be escaping, and the water in the boiler will become highly saturated, so that it becomes necessary, after a time, to displace a certain quantity of the brine by blowing off. Now this will certainly be unnecessary if the safety-valve be kept closed, for the danger from closing it is not to be mentioned, since it will always be possible to keep the steam below the point at which it escapes. Let, therefore, the safety and communication valves be closed, and endeavor by these means to keep all the steam in the boiler: we shall be able to effect this, provided the heat of the fires, when banked up, is only sufficient to counteract the loss attendant on radiation. The steam will, when generated, condense on the inner surface of the boiler, and trickling down its sides, will fall again into the water, to be reconverted into steam, and undergo a repetition of the process. If this can be managed, it will be quite unnecessary to blow out.

217. *Steam-gauges of a strange Vessel's Boilers.*

On first getting up the steam in strange boilers, the steam-gauges should be carefully examined when the fires are lighted, to see if the floats be resting on the mercury. The following device has been adopted at times for the purpose of making the steam-pressure seem less than it actually is, and to make it appear that the engine is doing a great amount of work with weak steam. Two or three inches are cut off the steam-gauge float, and a cork or plate, with a hole in it, is inserted in the gauge-tube, so that the ball of the float rests on this, and the float does not come into contact with the mercury till the latter has risen up to it; and as the rod is raised above its proper level, it will then appear to stand at zero, when the actual pressure is 2 or 3 lbs.; and whatever be the pressure indicated, the actual pressure will be 2 or 3 lbs. more. It is necessary, therefore, to attend to this point on first taking charge of a fresh steamer.

218. *Attention to be paid to the Jackets, if the Engines be fitted with them.*

If the cylinders be surrounded with jackets, and the communication-valve left open, they should be emptied as the steam is getting up, or the water remaining in them will condense some of the steam as it enters. Indeed, the jacket-cock should be always left a little open while under steam, for the same reason; and also because the attention of the engineer may be called off, and he may thus forget that it is shut, when the condensed steam will collect as water in the jacket, will fill it, and eventually, if unnoticed, enter the slide-casing, and from thence pass to the cylinders.

219. *To ascertain on board a strange Steamer if the Throttle-valve or Blow-out Cocks be open or shut.*

On taking charge of a strange engine-room, it is sometimes difficult to ascertain whether the throttle-valve be open or shut, because there may be no marks by which to discover it. We have already shown how necessary it is to have the throttle-valve at least partially open while getting up the steam (see p. 166). The following plan may be adopted: Move the lever, or whatever means are supplied for opening and shutting the valve, to its fullest extent both ways, then let it be placed midway between these two extremes. Now since when at one extreme it will be quite closed, and at the other quite open, when placed half-way it will be partially open. This is all we want till the engine starts, for it will prevent any of the afore-mentioned casualties to the throttle-valve. Again, when the steam is up, open the blow-valve, and move the throttle-valve spindle to one extreme. Notice whether, by so doing, the passage of the steam is obstructed; if so, the valve is closed, and the place of the spindle should be marked "shut;" but if not, it should be marked "open," and the other extreme marked accordingly.

The same method may be pursued with blow-out cocks, if there are no distinguishing marks on them to show when they are open or when shut: the water passing in or out of the boiler would indicate when they are open and when shut.

We may ascertain whether the expansion-valve be open or shut, by inspection of the cam at the shaft: if the roller be on the shaft, it is closed; if on the cam, it is open.

CHAPTER VI.

DUTIES TO MACHINERY WHEN UNDER STEAM.

220. *The Boiler.*

The boiler requires the constant attention of the engineer, because it is the source of power; and not only so, but, being urged by heat, is more likely to become deranged, when neglected, than any other part of the machine.

Accidents are sure to occur if the water be allowed to get low; and therefore we readily infer that tubular boilers, having less water-surface, are a subject of greater anxiety than flue-boilers, that are not so contracted. As was previously stated, the glass water-gauge shows us the water-level, and therefore the engineer's eye is continually upon it; the gauge-cocks also are occasionally tried, for fear the glass gauge should be choked, and fail to show the water-level, as also to keep them from choking up.

221. *On the choking up of the Glass Water-gauge.*

This is most likely to happen when the boiler is filled with muddy water. Let us suppose that from this cause the upper orifice chokes up, while the lower one is clear; then the steam which is in the upper part of the glass will condense (partially at least), from the cooling effect of the atmosphere, and consequently the water will rise higher in the gauge than in the boiler; indeed, the gauge will be nearly full, although it may happen that the water is only just above the lower orifice within the boiler, and low enough perhaps to subject part of the upper tier of tubes, or the top of the flues, to the action of the fire. Again, if we suppose both orifices to have become choked, or the lower one only, the water-level in the gauge will not alter, however much it may vary in the boiler; so that it will be of no use in indicating the quantity of water in the boiler. In explaining the construction of the glass water-gauge (see p. 67), it was said to be generally constructed in such a manner as to allow steam to be blown through it occasionally, to clear away any mud that may accumulate.

222. *On "Blowing out while under Steam."*

Blowing out should be strictly attended to while under steam at sea, to keep the boiler free from salt and incrustation. The common practice has been to displace 5 or 6 inches every hour; but as the necessary number of inches must depend on the capacity of the boiler and the degree of saturation at which it is determined to keep the boiler, the table D in Appendix should be consulted. If brine-pumps are properly proportioned, blowing out will evidently not be necessary; but let not the blow-out cocks be neglected altogether, for they then act as a reserve in case the brine-pumps fail; and if not attended to for some time, they will probably be found inefficient when wanted. Let them, therefore, be opened once a day at least, to keep them clear and in good working condition.

When water which contains solid substances in solution is evaporated, these are left behind, and therefore increase the state of saturation of the water remaining in the vessel, till the limit of saturation is reached. If *pure* water equal in amount to that which has been evaporated be now added, the ratio of the saturation will return to the same state as before the evaporation commenced.

If we are unable to obtain pure water, yet if the water that is available have a less degree of saturation than that in the vessel before evaporation commenced, we shall be enabled to recover the original state of the fluid; but it will be necessary to throw in a larger amount of water than that evaporated.

The water thus introduced is the feed-water, and it is clear that its amount must depend on its own amount of saturation, the amount of water that has been evaporated, and the state of saturation at which we wish to keep the fluid.

It has been stated that more feed-water, if not pure, must be thrown in than that evaporated; therefore the vessel containing it would continually get fuller. To avoid this, a certain portion must be got rid of; this quantity is what is "blown out" of a marine boiler at certain intervals.

Hence the amount of feed-water to a boiler is equal to the amount evaporated and the amount "blown out."*

Table D has been formed with the view of showing the ratio of feed, and amount blown out, to the evaporation, at the various degrees of saturation between that of sea-water and the highest point; and likewise the probable loss of coal attending the process. This latter column has been determined as follows: Let us take the degree of saturation $\frac{3}{33}$; the coal, if used beneficially, must raise the temperature from 100° to 1212°, that is, 1112°; and if blown out, the temperature of that loss is water at 243·5°, hence 143·5° are lost, and their volumes are as $1:\frac{1}{2}$; hence the

---

* Let A = area of base of boiler,
x = number of inches blown out,
y = number of inches evaporated,
$x+y$ = amount introduced by feed in same time,
a = degree of saturation of sea-water,
b = degree of saturation at which boiler is to be kept,

$$\therefore \quad A\,a\,(x+y) = A\,b\,x$$

and
$$x+y = \frac{b\,y}{b-a}$$

or
$$(b-a)\,x = a\,y$$

$$x = \frac{a\,y}{b-a}$$

amount of heat used : that lost as 1112 : 71·75, and the amount lost : the whole amount

$$
\begin{aligned}
&:: 71{\cdot}75 : 1112 + 71{\cdot}75 \\
&:: 71{\cdot}75 : 1183{\cdot}75 \\
&:: {\cdot}0606 : 1 \\
\text{or } &:: 6{\cdot}06 : 100^{*}
\end{aligned}
$$

The only practical way of determining whether the amount of feed at any given rate of the ship is sufficient, is to let the evaporation go on for a certain time, within the limits of safety to the boiler, without feeding or blowing out, and notice the amount to which the water falls in the gauge-glass: call this m; then setting on the feed, let the evaporation go on for the same time, and call the rise in the water n. Then $\frac{m+n}{m} = \frac{\text{feed}}{\text{evaporation}}$. Compare this with table D, and we shall see the corresponding amount of saturation at which the feed then supplied will keep the water.

223. *On the point of Saturation, or the limit which the Boiler should not exceed.*

It is necessary to have some tests by which the saltness of the water in the boiler may be ascertained; for if the amount of brine expelled by blowing out be not equal to that supplied by the feed-pumps, it follows that saturation will proceed, although a certain amount may be regularly got rid of. There are two methods of ascertaining the degree of saltness of the water, viz., either by the *thermometer* or the *hydrometer*.

1. We have before noticed (Chapter I.) that the boiling-point of water is influenced by the amount of salts it holds in solution. The following table will serve to show how far this is true with solutions of brine of various degrees of saturation. Common sea-water contains about $\frac{1}{33}$ of its

* For a general investigation on this subject, see the Miscellaneous Chapter.

volume of salt and earthy matter, and therefore stands immediately under fresh water; in the next line the solution is supposed to contain $\frac{2}{33}$ of its volume, or twice as much; and so on, till we arrive at $\frac{12}{33}$, which is called a saturated solution; after which the water can contain no more in a dissolved state. The proportion of solid matter should never exceed $\frac{4}{33}$, as incrustation commences shortly before that point; therefore 216° is considered to be the extreme limit of the boiling-point, although no salt will be precipitated till the boiling-point reaches 226°, as we have said above.

Proportion of salt in 100 parts of water . . .		0	Boiling point . .	212·0°
"	"	$\frac{1}{33}$	"	213·2
"	"	$\frac{2}{33}$	"	214·4
"	"	$\frac{3}{33}$	"	215·5
"	"	$\frac{4}{33}$	"	216·6
"	"	$\frac{5}{33}$	"	217·9
"	"	$\frac{6}{33}$	"	219·0
"	"	$\frac{7}{33}$	"	220·2
"	"	$\frac{8}{33}$	"	221·4
"	"	$\frac{9}{33}$	"	222·5
"	"	$\frac{10}{33}$	"	223·7
"	"	$\frac{11}{33}$	"	224·9
"	"	$\frac{12}{33}$	"	226·0

Advantage, therefore, may be taken of this fact by drawing off a small quantity of water from the boiler, and boiling it in the engine-room. For this purpose it is convenient to boil it in a long copper vessel deep enough to hold the thermometer; and the water should be kept in a good state of ebullition while the height of the thermometer is observed.* The point at which the thermometer stands must be read off carefully; and, indeed, to perform the experiment properly, a thermometer specially adapted

* Care should also be taken to make use of a thermometer on which some dependence may be placed. To this end, let the thermometer be first placed in pure fresh water when boiling, and observe whether the mercury stands at 212° when the weather-barometer stands at 30 inches

o this purpose should be supplied, graduated with extreme care at and near the boiling-point, such as those constructed for ascertaining the heights of mountains by similar means.

2. We may also ascertain the degree of saturation by the hydrometer, of which we will first give a description. The hydrometer consists of a hollow ball of glass or metal, with another small weight, or glass bulb partly filled with mercury, below it, to give it stability, and to sink it to a given depth. From the upper part of the bulb there rises a slender stem, which is graduated; and since the instrument will sink to different depths in fluids of different specific gravities, it follows that the hydrometer may be conveniently made use of to determine the specific gravity, and therefore the saltness, of water from the boiler. But there is one particular on which the efficiency of this instrument depends; and for want of paying sufficient attention to this point it becomes frequently quite useless when placed in charge of those who are not accustomed to minute accuracy in observations. It is very evident that the density of the water depends on its temperature as well as on its saltness, and therefore the saturated solution of a high temperature will frequently be of less specific gravity than that which is not so highly saturated at a lower temperature. To convince ourselves of the material change which takes place in the density of the water, let us place the hydrometer in cold fresh water, and place the vessel containing it on the fire: as the water becomes heated, it will gradually sink; and if the experiment be made with one of those supplied to our steamers, it will sink altogether before the water boils. Therefore on the side of the stem opposite the graduations we find the number 55°, which expresses the temperature the water ought to have when the hydrometer is placed in it. Now the hydrometers at present used in the naval service are very inconvenient, unless they are differently constructed from those we have seen; for this temperature 55° is considerably too low, for two reasons. In the first place, it would be impossible,

when on board a steamer in very hot countries, to cool down the water so low as 55°; and in all cases it would be so long cooling down to this temperature, after being drawn off from the boiler in a boiling state, that all observations would necessarily be very protracted. And secondly, there is no paper accompanying the instrument, and giving an explanation of its principles and the meaning of the graduations on the stem. The mark W, however, is evidently the point to which the hydrometer should sink when floating in fresh water at 55°; but beyond this we have no information. Feeling, in common with others, the want of something more definite to make the instrument practically useful, we have made some observations, which will, it is hoped, be of service.

Boiling-point of water from the boiler.	When the water had cooled down to 200°, the hydrometer stood at	When it had cooled down to 64°, the hydrometer stood at
213°	W or 0	12
214	6	20
215	11	25
216	16	30
217	24	40
218	35	51

These results are not so regular as could be wished; and if the experiments had been continued over a longer time, it would have been advantageous. Any engineer, however, may make similar experiments, and will probably be enabled to make the table more perfect, and at the same time gain great practical knowledge of the hydrometer. The two points to be carefully attended to in all such experiments are, the height of the weather-barometer and a full state of ebullition of the water when the thermometer is placed in it. In forming the above table, the weather-barometer stood at 30 inches. Since the boiling-point of water from the boiler should never exceed 216°, it follows that the hydrometer should always sink till the mark 16 comes to the level of the water when at 200°, or till the mark 30 comes to the surface at 64°.

224. *The Salinometer.*

This name is given to a peculiar kind of boiler water-gauge; it contains within it a hydrometer and thermometer, so that the temperature and density of the water can at all times be ascertained by inspection.

225. *Ash-pits not to be choked up with Ashes, etc.—Results of throwing Water there.*

Whatever kind of coal is used in a steamer, it is a practice to get the ashes out of the ash-pit every four hours (the vessel being supposed to be going at full speed, and not burning the ashes). But if large quantities of them are retained in the ash-pits, they absorb the oxygen of the air, because they are necessarily very hot, and consequently the supply to the fires is diminished. Besides which, they take up some of the space within the ash-pits. They should, therefore, be hauled out frequently; and when the boiler, from want of evaporative power, will not allow the ashes to be reburnt, let them be heaped up between the fireplaces, and when they have accummulated in sufficient quantity, let them be thrown overboard. In some vessels a practice is adopted, which is much to be reprehended, viz., that of throwing water into the ash-pits, with a view to cool the ashes: this will, in a short time, destroy the bottom; the water thrown in evaporates, and the salt is left behind, which will rapidly oxidate the plates. Boilers have been known to require new ash-pit bottoms in the short space of time of eighteen months, and the sides immediately above the angle-iron required patching: this arose from the cause above mentioned. But it should be stated, that this happened ten or twelve years ago, before engineers had gained their present experience. Moreover, stokers have been scalded from throwing water on the hot ashes, and generating steam in the ash-pit rapidly, which not finding vent through the fire-bars, comes into the engine-room, bringing with it impalpable ashes, that settle on the various parts of the engine, to be washed into the bearings the first time the parts are oiled. The ashes should be quenched on the stoke-hole plates, and it might be advisable to have buckets made on purpose, with half-rose tops; the arms of the stoker would thus be saved, as steam would not be generated so fast, and the dust would not be so great. A watering-pot, such as is used in some men-of-war for laying the dust on the decks, would answer the purpose. The fire-bars are subject to rapid oxidation from wetting the ashes in the ash-pits; the steam evolved from the ashes, acting upon them, cools them, and the water becoming decomposed, scales of oxide of iron come off, and the bars are deteriorated and weakened.

226. *On Stoking.**

The economy of the working of an engine depends very materially on the attention paid to the stoking. The state in which the fires should be kept to obtain the maximum effect varies slightly with different boilers and different kinds of coal. Fireplaces with great draught should have a thicker layer of coals on the bars than those of sluggish draught.

Welsh coal does not adhere or stick together like north-country coal; the former, not being bituminous, should be kept somewhat thicker than the latter. If anthracite coal be used by itself, the fires should be very thick. When Welsh and north-country coal are mixed, the usual thickness may be preserved.

As a general rule, the fires should be kept thin towards the back, to allow air to get in at the back of the furnace; and by so doing, create a greater rush of air through the ash-pits, which will more thoroughly ignite the gases.

---

* The remarks on fuel in the Appendix, which are the results of researches by Sir H. De la Beche and Dr. Lyon Playfair, should be read before proceeding further.

With Welsh coal, it will be found necessary to have the fire-bars wider apart than when using other kinds of fuel, so as to admit the air freely.

227. *Fires to be cleaned out occasionally.*

The fires should be cleaned out as they require it, that is to say, the clinkers* that form on the fire-bars should be removed; for it is easily seen, that a mass of the dross of the coal, settling itself on the fire-bars, must choke up the intervening spaces, and check the draught. The clinkers are to be removed as follows. The fires are allowed to burn down (to speak technically), then an instrument called a slice is pushed under the clinker, so as to raise it off the bars and detach it; after this is done, the rake is made use of to haul it out. We may form some idea of the evil arising from allowing the clinkers to remain, when it is known that they are sometimes too large to come out of the fire-doors whole. Before hauling out the clinkers, the fires should be put back; they are afterwards hauled forward again, and fresh coal laid upon them.

After all the clinkers are out, it is as well to shut the door, and haul the ashes out of the ash-pit; for when the fresh coal is thrown in, some small coal will fall through the bars and be wasted, if any ashes be there; but if the pit have been previously cleared out, what falls through may be afterwards raked out and burned.

Clearing the fire-bars will, as a matter of course, depress the steam for some time; for the water will not only lose the effect of the fire, but the cold air entering at the open door will check the other fires. The amount of depression will depend on the evaporating power of the boiler and the smallness of the steam-chest. In a boiler that keeps its steam easily, and has a large steam-chest, the deficiency will not be felt; for the supply will be tolerably well kept

* Clinkers are composed of the earthy matter, silica, etc., of the coal, which, separated from it during combustion, and falling through the burning mass, runs down on the bars, to which they adhere.

up, and the quantity of steam previously in the steam-chest will act as a reservoir, from which the engine may fearlessly draw for some time.

228. *On Feeding the Boilers.*

In attending to the feeding of the boilers, care must be taken that the water be not allowed to get either too high or too low. This is regulated by the feed-cocks or feed-valves. If the water be allowed to get too high, and so overflow the internal steam-pipe, it will make its way into the cylinder, and perhaps the engine will break down. Priming, again, is frequently caused by the water getting too high in the boilers, for in *so doing* we necessarily contract the steam-space. If the water be allowed to get too low, we shall be in danger of burning the flues or tubes of the boilers. The proper water-level is a matter of some nicety in many vessels; some boilers keep steam better with the water well up than others. This takes place where there is a large uptake; for if the passage from the fires to the uptake is very direct, the latter will be very hot, and will give out a considerable quantity of heat to the surrounding water.

229. *Method to be adopted in case the Blow-out Cocks set fast, or Blow-out Pipes get stopped up with Scales, etc., and Brine-pumps are not fitted.*

When under steam, should the blow-out cocks set fast, so that they cannot be opened, and the vessel be not fitted with brine-pumps, or any other means of getting rid of the brine, it is evident the saltness of the water must rapidly increase. Some means must be taken to allow the water to escape from the boiler into the bilge, and thus make the bilge-pumps do the duty of brine-pumps.

When the blow-out cocks set fast, and the brine-pumps do not act, it sometimes happens that the cocks of the boiler hand-pump or the auxiliary engine can be reversed; and one of these can be used to pump water out of, instead of into, the boiler. This plan was once adopted in the Terrible: the auxiliary engine was employed to extract the brine from the boiler.

230. *Steam blowing off with violence when the Vessel is pitching and rolling.*

It must be borne in mind that the boiler of a marine engine is not under the same conditions as that of a land-engine. In the first place, the water-level is not preserved; for the violent pitching and rolling of the ship produces its effect on the level of the water-surface. As the vessel pitches, the water rises violently at the fore part of the boiler, and acts on the steam, which is recumbent, as it were, upon its surface. So suddenly does this take place, that the steam is driven up against the safety-valve before it can make its way to the place the water has left, and the valve will be found to lift, and the steam makes its escape. Again, as the vessel pitches, or rolls, the safety-valve (if loaded by a weight) does not press with such force as it would if the boiler were upright: to find the effective pressure, we must multiply the nominal pressure by the cosine of the angle between the direction of the spindle and the vertical line. To see how this applies, we have only to take a very extreme case; let, for instance, the ship be supposed on her beam-ends, so that the top of the boiler, instead of being horizontal, is vertical: it is plain that in such position the valve would not press on the seat at all, however highly it be loaded; and if the boiler were made to revolve still further, the valve would actually tumble out.

231. *Blowing out to be limited when the Vessel is going slow.*

When head to wind, and sea, or towing (unless fitted with a second motion), or when working very expansively, it will not be necessary to blow out so much as when going at full speed; for as we evaporate less water, there is less brine left behind. Of course it is here supposed that the engineer does not allow the steam which would have gone into the engines, if they had been going at full speed, to escape by the waste-steam funnel.

Again, it sometimes happens, either from the vessel having been supplied with bad coals, or some other cause, that the minimum quantity of water consistent with safety has been blown out for some time, for fear of diminishing the quantity of steam produced. We will therefore suppose the water to have become highly saturated. The engineer will then take advantage of the vessel going slower, or any other adverse circumstances, and get rid of as much of the saturated water as can possibly be spared. It must be borne in mind, however, that this case is an exception to the general rule, viz., that the amount of saturation depends on the ratio of the feed to the evaporation, and that the quantity blown out is merely the quantity that accumulates in the boiler by the excess of feed

232. *Number of Boilers to be used when not at full speed.*

There is a common practice in our steam navy, when employed on a service in which particular despatch is not the object, to use half the number of boilers, and proceed at a speed proportionably less, in order to consume less fuel in traversing the distance. The saving thus effected depends on the fact, that the consumption of fuel *per hour* varies as the *cube* of the speed, and the consumption of fuel *per mile* depends on the *square* of the speed (see Miscellaneous Chapter). Suppose, for instance, a vessel to be furnished with four boilers, and that her speed when using all four is ten knots; her speed with two boilers would be eight knots nearly. Let us suppose, for argument sake, each boiler consumed half a ton an hour; then, at full speed, four half-tons, or two tons, would drive the ship over ten knots, or one ton would propel her over five knots. Again, in the second case, two half-tons, or one ton, would send her over eight knots. Hence we should by this method gain three knots in distance for every ton of coal:

and we may set it down as a general maxim, that the slower a vessel goes, the greater the distance she will steam over with the same consumption of fuel. This is on the supposition that she meets with no strong head-winds, etc., such as to force her to use all her power. If, however, the wind or tide would have the effect of making her go astern, her rate through the water for the greatest economy of fuel should be at least half as great again as she would have gone in the opposite direction if no power had been used. Thus if a vessel be steaming up a river which flows at the rate of four knots, her most economical speed would not be less than six knots, making good two knots over the ground.

But it is a question for mature consideration, whether a still further saving might not be effected by a different mode of managing the fires. Suppose, for instance, as we had at first arranged, that the vessel be going at eight knots, using two boilers instead of four. The alteration we would propose is, that instead of using two boilers she should use three or more;* but that the speed of the ship should still not exceed eight knots, which she would have had with two boilers. To effect this, the engineer must do all he can to produce a slow combustion; and it will be found that by this slow combustion a considerable saving will be effected. Those of our readers who are conversant with the mode of producing steam on the Cornish system will be more likely to appreciate this; for our endeavor is to make the two methods approximate, by spreading the fuel over a greater number of tubes, and so allowing more sur-

* In the Report of the trials made on the French screw ship-of-war Charlemagne, contained in the *Artizan* for September, 1853, we have the following fact corroborating the above remarks:

"The commission wished to assure themselves if any economy of fuel could be obtained by using three boilers, and maintaining the same number of revolutions. With this view a third boiler was lighted. The consumption of coal with the three boilers was 66,679 lbs. per 24 hours, as against 73,558 lbs. with the two boilers, being a saving of 9·3 per cent."

face to impart their heat to the water. The Cornish boiler, however, is not suitable for marine purposes, as, owing to its peculiar construction, it would take up too much room, the amount of heating surface being much greater in proportion than the common boilers. This plan was tried for a short time on board H. M. S. Avenger, though not long enough to obtain any measured results. An order had been given to go on with two boilers, and the fires in them were worked in the usual way, and kept in an active state of combustion. Shortly afterwards the order was given to proceed with three boilers, but no additional orders were received to go on faster than with the two. It was then found to be scarcely possible to cover the fire-bars in all the boilers with fuel, the rapid absorption from the great quantity of surface was so effective in keeping up the steam, and the amount required being so small. The saving of fuel was very great; but the limited time of the trial would not allow the actual quantity to be ascertained. If difficulties should arise, when using large boilers, in obtaining a small supply of steam—that is to say, if it be found that, when all the fire-bars are covered, too much is generated—let one or more fires in each boiler clinker up, and their ash-pit doors be closed. And in using the boilers in this way, the ashes may be repeatedly burned over again, merely throwing the clinkers away.

In working expansively, it has generally been supposed that it is more economical to use as few of the boilers as possible. But if the boilers are in close contact, without any non-conducting substance between them, a great deal of heat will escape into the empty boiler: and in this case it will be found more economical to use all the boilers.

233. *Superheating Apparatus.*

The principle on which superheated steam is applied has been stated in the preliminary chapter, and very little remains to be done but to describe the process by which the waste heat ascending the funnel is utilized for this purpose.

In the accompanying diagram, let A A represent the upper part of the boiler, B B the uptake, C C tubes through which the steam passes (the heated gases circulating round them); D_1D_2 two chambers or boxes, one, D_1, the induction, and the other, D_2, the eduction; G the main steam-pipe, in which is a stop-valve, shown by a dotted line, to prevent, at will, the steam from passing to the engines the usual way; b_1 b_2 also two stop-valves, for the purpose of shutting off the superheating apparatus if required. We have here shown the application of the above as fitted to one boiler. If more than one be fitted, an induction and eduction chamber must be brought from each boiler to the superheated chambers. The heating surface of the tubes is from two and a half to three square feet per horse-power.

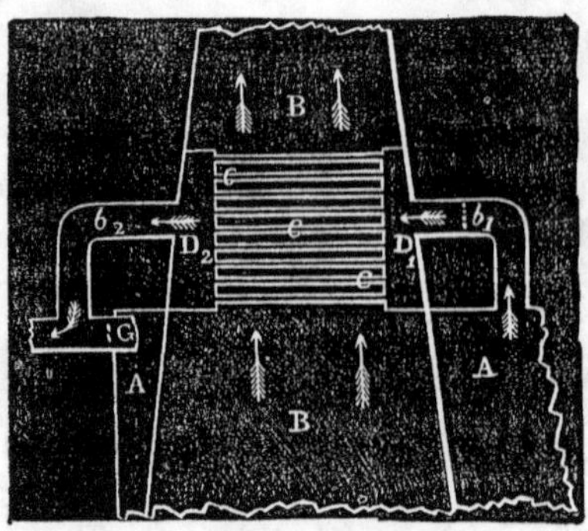

234. *On Ashes and burning Coal escaping from the Funnel.*

Sometimes hot ashes and burning coal will be forced from the fires through the flues or tubes up the funnel, from which they will fall on the deck, and may set fire to the awnings. This can only arise from a defect in the construction of the boiler, and cannot be remedied, except perhaps by an alteration in the position of the fire-bridge. It does not follow that an alteration in the bridge, by shortening the fireplace, will necessarily damage the steam-producing power of the boiler. Indeed, the opposite effect may be produced if done judiciously, when the transition from the fireplace to the flues is too abrupt and tortuous; otherwise the damper must be partially closed, to let the fires burn less briskly, and check the draught. If, when the alteration has been made, the boiler do not keep its steam, the expansive-gear or throttle-valve must be brought into use; but if, on the other hand, great speed be our object, the primary evil will perhaps have to be put up with. However, it must be borne in mind that it may probably be checked by consenting to lose one or two revolutions of the engines, and this will not tell much upon the speed of the vessel, while a considerable saving of fuel will be effected; for whenever we have to guard against the evil of ashes coming out of the funnel, we may be sure that fuel is being wasted, and a great deal of heat expended on the funnel and lost in the atmosphere, instead of being absorbed by the boilers. To prevent this, the boiler-tubes are sometimes ferruled at the smoke-box end.

235. *Flame appearing to issue from the Funnel.*

In Chapter I. we stated that three things were, under ordinary circumstances, necessary for the combustion of fuel, viz., the combustible itself, the oxygen of the atmosphere, and a sufficiently high temperature; but if either or both of the latter be wanting, combustion will not take place. Now to apply this to the case in point, we readily see, that if a boiler is badly constructed, and a proper supply of air be not admitted to the furnaces, proper combustion cannot take place so long as the heated gases remain in the funnel; but directly they come in contact with the atmosphere, unless the temperature be too much reduced, chemical union takes place, and flame is produced. Again, if fires be too thick on the bars, carbonic acid will be formed by the union of oxygen with the carbon which lies nearest to the bars, and the carbonic acid thus formed in passing through the upper strata of coals gets robbed by them of a portion of the oxygen, and is by this process converted into carbonic oxide, being thus reconverted into a combustible, which, if supplied with more oxygen, burns with a lambent bluish flame. Most persons must have noticed this on the top of a common fire that is beginning to burn clear; and it is sometimes observable on the top of a steamer's funnel.

236. *On the Draught of Air to the Fires.*

Some vessels have difficulty in keeping up the steam, from a deficiency in the draught. From whatever cause this may arise—whether from some inherent defect in the boiler, or from a defect in the engine-room, whereby a free current of air cannot make its way to the fires—it can be obviated, to a great extent, by fitting a small pipe with a stop-cock leading from the steam-chest into the funnel or uptake: the principle of this is the same as that of the blast-pipe opening into the funnel of a locomotive engine. The improved draught will more than make up for the loss of steam by which it is effected. The only objection to this appears to be that it oxidates the funnel, and the rust and soot are blown about the decks.

The draught depends very much upon the state of the atmosphere; the greater the elasticity of the atmosphere, the better the draught: and, in addition to this, the elastic pressure of the air on the safety-valve alters from day to day; so that on a day in which the barometer stands high, the engine is working with stronger steam than on other days.

237. *What is necessary to be done when the Water is low in the Boiler.*

The water is apt to get low at times; as, for instance, if the blow-out cock cannot be closed fast enough after blowing out. It is a bad plan in such cases to pump in water; for if the fireplaces or tubes be red-hot, or nearly so, the consequences of injecting cold water would be the sudden production of steam in such quantity that the safety-valve would not allow it to pass off as fast as it is generated; and even if an explosion did not take place, the iron of the boiler would be injured by the sudden cooling: this is likely to produce a crack in the boiler, or oxidate it, and so thin it down. Again, if allowed to remain hot, and no remedies be used, the pressure of the steam, acting on the crown of the heated fireplaces, will force them down: this will happen, even though some water be above the flues, unless there be enough to keep the lower particles in contact with the iron to carry off the heat; to prevent which, the following remedy must be adopted. The fires must be pushed back, or hauled out, and the boiler allowed to cool down of itself, the safety-valve being eased to get rid of the steam-pressure, as before; but on no account should water be pumped in when there is any apprehension that the boiler has become over-heated. If, however, by any accident the water be low in the boiler, but not so low as to lay the tubes or flues bare, no time should be lost in opening all the feed, by putting on the second feed-pump, setting the auxiliary engine to work, opening the communication-pipes, easing the safety-valve to blow off some of the steam from the boiler, and relieve it of the pressure.

238. *On the depression of the Steam-pressure from admitting a great quantity of Water too suddenly.*

If we are obliged, as in the forementioned instance, to admit a great quantity of water, it must be expected that the steam will lose its elasticity, because it will not be produced so rapidly for some time on account of the presence of the cold water. We shall, therefore, be under the necessity of throttling or working expansively till the boiler has recovered its energy, otherwise the engines will exhaust the boiler, and they will be brought to a stand-still. There is no danger to the engine, as some imagine, in working on a vacuum, as it is called: the only thing we have to dread is, that the engine will stop; or that the boiler will collapse, if the reverse-valves are not in good working order.

239. *Attention to be paid to Injection-cocks.*

Where there is much fluctuation in the steam-pressure, and likewise if the speed of the engine be liable to vary, the injection-cock should be well attended to, else the engine may choke with too much water; or, on the other hand, it may be working hot from having too little water. The best temperature of the condenser in these latitudes, and in vessels of light draught of water, is somewhat less than 100° Fah.; but the temperature for the most economic working of the engine depends on *three* things, viz., the *temperature of the injection-water;* the load on the pumps, or, in other words, *the depth of the condenser below the surface of the sea;* and lastly, the *pressure of the steam on its exit from the cylinder* to the condenser; and if any of these quantities be increased, the necessary temperature of the condenser, and therefore the deficiency from the vacuum, will increase with it. Therefore in hot climates, where the sea is warmer, such as the coast of Africa, or the East or West Indies; or, secondly, in our line-of-battle ships, where the waste water has to be forced out of the ships against a considerable pressure of the water outside; or, lastly, if the engine have but little lap on the slide, so that the pressure of the steam at the end of the stroke is considerable—we shall, in any of these cases, have to increase the temperature of the condenser. The investigation connected with this subject will be given in the Miscellaneous Chapter.

If the vessel be in a gale of wind, with a heavy sea, the injection-cock will require strict attention. Here it would be better to work too hot than too cold, as being the lesser evil; for when the engine is relieved of its load, as it will be at times in a sea-way, the quick motion will cause more steam to enter the condenser in a given time; and if the injection-cock have been previously partially closed, the back pressure arising from the imperfect vacuum will prevent the engine from flying off so quickly. If, however, a good supply of water had been maintained, the engine would revolve too quickly at one time, and at another, when its motion was checked from the immersion of the wheels or the screw, there would have been too much water for the quantity of steam, and the engine would choke. In long voyages, where the consumption of fuel is an important question, to work the engine rather warm will conduce to a saving of fuel, and more especially where refrigerators are not fitted for the purpose of warming the water that enters the boiler.

Again, if we wish in hot climates to use the same quantity of injection-water as in the country where the engines were made, we may arrive, with tolerable accuracy, at the temperature the condenser must be kept at by adding 39° to the temperature of the injection water.*

If the injection-cock is left open when stopped, the condenser will fill with water very rapidly; and if the ports

---

* When the temperature of the injection-water is higher than the manufacturer of the engine would naturally expect it to be, we may arrive at the temperature of the condenser, subject to the above condition, as follows:

Let the temperature of the condenser be 100° when that of the injection-water is 60°.

Then, by p. 33, $$100 = \frac{1212\,w + 60\,w'}{w + w'}$$

$$\therefore \quad 100\,w + 100\,w' = 1212\,w + 60\,w'$$

or $$40\,w' = 1112\,w$$

$$\frac{w'}{w} = \frac{1112}{40} = \frac{139}{5}$$

Let us now suppose the engine to have been originally constructed so that the weight of injection-water is $\frac{139}{5}$ times the weight of steam; and therefore that if the proportion of injection-water be increased much above this, the engine will be overtaxed, owing to the extra work thrown on the air-pump. Hence we may assume the limiting value of this ratio to be 30.

Again, let us assume that x is the temperature of condensation when t' is that of the injection-water.

$$\therefore \quad x = \frac{1212 + \frac{'w}{w}t'}{1 + \frac{w'}{w}} = \frac{1212 + 30\,t'}{1 + 30}$$

$$= \frac{1212 + 30\,t'}{31} = \frac{1212}{31} + t' \text{ nearly.}$$

$$= 39 + t'$$

If, then, we add 39° to the temperature of the injection-water when high, we shall arrive, with tolerable exactness, at the temperature for the condenser.

on the exhaust side are open, the cylinder also will fill: should this happen with only one engine, and the other be the starting-engine, an accident is very likely to occur, for it is not probable that the escape-valves will be able to relieve the cylinder of the water in time to enable the cranks to turn their centres. Cylinder-covers have been broken, and condensers burst, by these means.

If the injection-cock or air-pump be leaky, the engine must be blown through at intervals when stationary, otherwise the water will gradually fill up the condenser, and the steam will not be able to start the piston. But the blowing through must be conducted with some judgment; for if the condenser be made very hot by so doing, the evil from the want of vacuum will be nearly as great as that from too much water: indeed, the condenser may be made so hot, that the entering water will be for some time quite repulsed. When injection-cocks are *very* leaky, the *sea-cocks* should be only *partially* opened when the engine is stopped and started at intervals, having some one stationed to open them when the order is given to start, and close them again when the order is given to stop.

Injection-pipes are mostly unconnected; that is to say, a pipe from each sea-cock passes to one condenser only; but many of the old engines had a pipe across the ship from one sea-cock to the other, and pipes from this went to each condenser.

This plan had the advantage over the present, that if one sea-cock failed, or became stopped with sea-weed, ice, etc., both engines might still be worked.

240. *Kingston's Valves.*

When Kingston's valves are fitted to the sea-cocks, they should be kept open—unless when their working order is being tested—or they may, by the sudden opening of the injection-cock, close, owing to the rush of water on the outside of the valve. This happened to a vessel, and it was some time before the reason why there was no injection-water was discovered.

Kingston's valves are very apt to set fast, and should be frequently moved.

241. *Condensing Engines worked on the High-pressure Principle.*

In a case of emergency, the mere fact of the condenser being useless need not prevent the engines being started. The engines can be worked without injection-water, on account of the much greater amount of the steam-pressure since the introduction of tubular boilers. In H.M.S. Onyx and Vivid, the speed, from being 14 knots, became 9 when working in this way. However, since the feed-pumps, as at present fitted, only obtain their supply from the hot-well, they cannot then be used, and the boiler must be supplied by the auxiliary engine or by hand.

242. *Injecting from the Bilge.*

In case of a ship springing a leak, a vast quantity of water may be taken out of the bilge simply by using it for injection-water; and by so doing we are not at all taxing the engine, because the engine will require this water to perform its work properly. We can form an idea of the quantity of water that may be got rid of in this way by bearing in mind, that every inch of water coming away from the boiler in the form of steam requires about 30 cubic inches of water, at the mean temperature, to condense it. Now the Bee's engine (10-H.P.) demands about 13,000 gallons, or about 13½ tons, per hour for condensation; and we may therefore draw an inference how much would be required for larger engines.

When, however, it is deemed desirable to inject from the bilge, some one should be stationed at the entrance of the injection-pipes to keep pieces of chip or oakum from getting into them through the roses, or the air will force them into the engines, and will eventually stop the engine.

They will be liable to get into the air-pump, and gag the valves, so that the water cannot be pumped out of the condenser, and the engine will choke up. This was experienced in the Thunderbolt; after she was ashore at the Cape of Good Hope, a gale of wind came on, and washed down the bulkheads, and consequently the oakum with which they had been caulked washed into the bilge, and made its way into the engine. The Phœnix was found to be very leaky lately from a defect in the stuffing-box of the screw-shaft; and in crossing the Bay of Biscay she made about a foot more water than the pumps in the ship would clear out; they were obliged, therefore, to inject from the bilge to keep her free: had the injection-pipe leading into the bilge become choked up, in all likelihood the vessel would have foundered.

243. *On Leaks in the Engine-slides, and their remedy.*

At times it will happen on starting (more especially if the engine have been taken to pieces) that the sound of air will be heard entering the engine as the vacuum is formed. It is sometimes difficult to find out the leak; but it is important that it be discovered, for some tons of coals may be saved in a long voyage by having the engine air-tight. Many are apt to fancy that a leak admitting air into the engine is not so important as one that allows the steam to escape. In this, as in many other instances, we are led astray by our senses; the steam coming into the engine-room forces itself on our notice, whereas the air can only be discovered by watching for the sound as it enters the narrow orifice. One way to discover the leak is to light a candle, and pass the flame slowly along the joints, when it will be found that, on arriving at the leak, the draught of air will force the flame towards the joint, whereas at other parts the light will be unmoved. It becomes, therefore, important that the steam should be got up twenty minutes or half an hour before the time of starting, that all these defects may be discovered and remedied.

When ready to start, let the engines be blown well through, and then let them cool down by the action of the external air chilling the condenser. A leak on the steam-side becomes visible on admitting *steam* to the engine, for it will make its escape into the engine-room.

This will also, if the blowing-through be continued for a long time with the waste-water pipe plugged or stopped up, discover a leak on the exhaust side; but if it fail to do so, the candle may be applied after the vacuum has been formed. If the leak be suspected in a joint where the surface is horizontal, it will be discoverable by pouring water on it; for it will evidently be at that part where the water is forced into the vacuum.

When the leak has been found, it must be caulked temporarily with spun-yarn or long hemp soaked in white or red lead; or if the leak do not admit of being stopped by caulking, let a piece of soft wood covered with red or white lead be driven in.

In some parts of the engine it will be found difficult to make good the defect with red or white lead, from the want of sufficient space in the joint. Suppose, for instance, a cylinder-cover be leaky at the joint over the ports, where there are no bolts for some considerable space, so that the cover springs between the two nearest bolts; if lead be interposed, it will be thrust out by its alternate expansion and contraction, and by its want of elasticity will fail to stop the leak. The best substance to apply in such cases is gasket soaked in red or white lead; for as the joint opens the gasket will spread by its elasticity, and keep the orifice closed. If a gasket-joint has been made while the steam was down, it should be screwed well up as soon as the engine is hot, and it will give no trouble afterwards. Gasket-joints are very valuable where the surfaces to be brought into contact are irregular; hence they are always used for boiler joints, man-hole, and mud-hole doors; but such joints as are planed up may be kept air-tight by simply interposing linseed-oil or thin white and red lead. Wire-gauze is also very serviceable for making joints with.

244. *Method of working the Engines if the Slides are leaky.*

If the slides are leaky, it is advisable to work on the first grade of expansion, unless a higher grade be preferred; for with this grade the slide will close the port nearly at the same time the expansion-valve closes, after which no steam can pass to the condenser, and we consequently save the steam that would otherwise pass to the condenser during the interval between the closing of the steam and the opening of the expansion valve.

245. *Leaky Condensers or Air-pumps.*

In old engines the bottom of the condenser is apt to give out, exposed as it is to galvanic action, from the presence of brass in the air-pump and foot-valve, the copper bolts in the ship's bottom, etc., the current being excited by the moisture in the bilge. Air-pumps become defective in the bottom from the same cause. In those engines where the air-pump is separate from the condenser, and only connected with it by means of the foot-valve passage, as in Boulton and Watt's old beam-engines, on the bottom of such pumps are plates to cover the hole through which the boring-bar passed: these plates after a time drop off, the bolts having become eaten away. Now a defect of this kind, whether in the condenser or the air-pump, is very difficult to repair while the vessel is at sea, on account of the closeness of the part to the bottom of the ship. The sleepers would have to be cut away unless it could be repaired from the inside. But the following method will be found a good temporary expedient: Let two partitions be fitted athwartships between the two sleepers, one before the condenser, and the other abaft it; let also the limber-holes be stopped up and be made water-tight, as also the partitions just mentioned. Again, let a pipe be brought from the injection-pipe, or from the water-cock that is fitted to quench the ashes, and, if possible, let this be fitted with a stop-cock; but if that cannot be done, some means must be at hand for plugging up the end of this pipe. By means of this pipe let us fill the tank we have already made with the partitions, and we shall thus effectually cut off the communication between the condenser and the external atmosphere. If a partial vacuum be created in the condenser, the air acting on the surface of the water in our tank will force it through the leak into the condenser, and it will act the part of a second injection-cock. If the leak be large, the injection-cock must be partially closed, as the water is getting into the condenser by another channel. It will be found in almost all cases that the upper edge of the sleepers is above the bottom of the condenser; so that we should have no difficulty in getting the water to surround the condenser. The tank, or whatever name we please to give it, should be kept running over, so as to change the water, and keep the bottom of the condenser cool. There could be no objection to having a small quantity of water overflowing into the bilge, for the bilge-pumps would clear it out, and it would sweeten the bilge. If the vessel had to run any length of time in this way, it would be as well to pitch over the bottom of the tank, to cover the heads of the copper bolts. If a brush cannot be introduced, because of the closeness of the condenser to the bottom, it might be melted and poured in in sufficient quantities to cover the bottom, and cut off the communication with the copper. The water should be let out of this tank on arriving in port, or otherwise what remains in the tank would become impregnated with copper.

If the condenser be above the sleepers, we must build up water-tight bulkheads round the condenser, leaving a sufficient space for water all round. We need not remark, that we are only by this process approaching to the method adopted in land-engines, whose condensers and air-pumps are surrounded by cold water.

246. *Feed-pumps to be looked to occasionally.*

When under steam, the feed-pumps should be looked to occasionally, to discover whether they are getting out of gear; and in case only one pump is needed to keep up the supply of feed-water in the boiler, the means for connecting the other should be at hand, to provide against the danger arising from the water-level being suddenly lowered by any accident, such as a shot in action entering the boiler, or a leak at other times.

The engineer must be strongly impressed with the importance of keeping the flues or tubes of his boilers covered with water while the fires are burning; for if from any cause, whether from blowing-out too freely, feeding too scantily, or from the rolling motion of the ship, they become bare, not only will they become heated and injured, but danger of explosions will arise from the sudden generation of steam. To guard against the danger arising from the rolling motion of the ship, he will find it necessary to keep the water-level higher than he would otherwise do. The feed-pump should be of sufficient capacity to meet this emergency.

247. *Dampers and Ash-pit Doors.*

If a vessel be steaming head to wind and sea, especially if it be a paddle-vessel, the number of revolutions will be materially diminished; and therefore, unless the evaporative power of the boilers be reduced, steam will escape from the safety-valve. To prevent an excess in the generation of steam, the ash-pit doors and dampers should be partly closed; and this is an operation that requires some nice management: for if too much closed, the stokers will have to rake and knock the fires about, and fuel will thus be wasted. If any extra work, therefore, be thrown on the stokers, it is a clear proof the operation has been carried to excess.

248. *Meaning of the term "Back-lash."*

Where parts of the same machine are not rigidly connected together, it will happen that at one time the one part will, from its momentum, have a greater velocity than the part which ought to remain in contact with it. They will therefore separate for an instant. But that portion which does not contain within it the moving power must, after a time, relax its speed; and the other part acquiring additional velocity, the two will come together again, producing a jar more or less unpleasant and injurious as the collision is more or less violent. The series of collisions thus produced is called *back-lash.* A good illustration of this is to be seen in the gearing of screw steamers. So long as the driving-wheel endeavors to move faster than the pinion will allow it, so long do they remain in contact; but directly the driver relaxes its speed, the pinion separates from it, and the jarring noise is produced when they come together again; for this they must do, since the faster wheel is connected with the resistance, and will therefore continually go slower, until contact is again made. The same thing sometimes happens with the eccentrics of marine steam-engines when they are moving slowly. The eccentric being loose upon the shaft, and the engine working slowly, it falls away from the stop at one part of the revolution; and, after a short interval of time, the stop overtakes it again, and thus a noise caused by their meeting is produced. In this case it arises from the eccentric not being properly balanced. In some instances, the weight balancing the eccentric is too heavy; in others, too light. This may be remedied by tightening the slide-packing, or, in some cases, by hanging weights on the eccentric.

These remarks on the back-lash of the eccentric do not apply to the engines for screw-ships which are fitted with double eccentrics, for they are keyed on to the shaft, as was stated in p. 114, for the head and sternway.

249. *Duties to the Bearings of Engines.*

If bearings are too loose, there will be a disagreeable and perhaps dangerous jar; and if too tight, the friction will be too great; they will then get hot, and the attendant evils will follow, viz.: the necessity for cold water, frequent stoppages, and perhaps a break-down of the engine. It is advisable on first starting to have them rather loose, to allow for expansion as the different parts get warm. Set-screws are fitted to some plomer-block caps to relieve the bearing of the weight of the cap, which otherwise acts as a *break.* The brasses are also kept off the shaft by screws. Where these are not fitted, pieces of hard wood should be interposed between the plomer-block and cap, that the wood, and not the bearing, may receive the weight of the cap.

The bearings of some engines require closer attention than others: the direct-action class require to be narrowly watched. When the ship is rolling heavily, or pressed with sail, the collars of the journals should be well lubricated, as well as the journals. Sometimes it is found that oil or tallow will not keep the bearings cool; we must then use water; and this must not be deferred till too late a period; for if we have recourse to water after the engine-bearing has become very hot from friction, we may possibly, by pouring on cold water, split the plomer-block. The superiority of water over oil, in many cases, consists in its boiling at a lower temperature, and carrying off the heat in a latent state, in the form of steam (see p. 33). It does not lubricate in the same manner that oil lubricates; indeed, the friction of the bearings will be greater with water than with oil; but by boiling at 212° it keeps down the temperature, and thus prevents friction. Both cast iron and brass are apt to split from having cold water poured on them in considerable quantities when in a very hot state. One of the plomer-blocks of a large steamer was split in this way. If the bearing be so hot that the application of cold water would be dangerous, let the water be applied hot at first, and still the metal will not be raised above the boiling-point of water. However, in most cases, cold water may be safely applied. Brasses are very apt to crack if cold water be suddenly poured on them; this will be more likely to take place if there be too much zinc in the alloy.

Sulphur, mixed with oil or tallow, will have the effect of cooling down a bearing: this seems to be efficacious for the same reason that water is so; sulphur boils at a low temperature (226° Fah.), and so the heat is carried off.

250. *"Soft Metal" for Bearings.*

"Soft metal" is an alloy consisting of equal parts of antimony and tin, with a small proportion of copper. The proportions are, 19 parts of antimony, 19 parts of tin, and 9 parts of copper. "Soft metal" does not wear away; but if not confined by edges of brass it will be forced out. It is a never-failing remedy for hot bearings; its effects are mechanical, as the bearing alters its shape according to the form of the part working in it; the friction is also considerably less. The thickness is about a quarter of an inch.

251. *On Expansive Working.*

It begins now to be pretty generally understood that advantage is gained by working steam expansively. The advantage over that obtained by throttling arises from the circumstance, that though the steam has but a small pressure at the end of its stroke, and therefore a cylinder full of very weak steam is used, yet during a portion of the stroke, that is, during the portion the piston traverses before the steam is cut off, it has a considerable degree of elastic pressure, much greater than it would have if the steam were throttled. Again, we know that even if the steam be partially throttled, we shall be able to work more economically than if we used the full power of the engine; for, although the vessel would not go so fast, the same quantity of coal would, unless during boisterous weather, with opposing winds, make her traverse a greater space.

But when steamers are working expansively, and they have to stop from any cause, more particularly in cases of collision, the expansive gear should be thrown off before attempting to start again; for, supposing the engine to be working with a high grade of expansion, and the order is given to stop, and then to start again, the cranks of both engines may be in such a position that no steam will enter so long as the expansive gear is in connection with the engine, for both expansion-valves may be closed at once. Let us suppose, for instance, that the steam is cut off when one quarter of the stroke has been accomplished, and that the engine is stopped with one of the pistons near the half-stroke, and descending; the other crank will be approaching its lower centre, neither of the expansion-valves will be open, and therefore, though the slide be moved by hand to admit the steam, no motion will ensue.

Again, if the order be given to go astern, the expansive gear must be disengaged before executing the order, because the expansion-cams are not constructed so as to admit steam for the back motion.

252. *Steam Circle.*

When it is intended that a steamer should make use of the combined advantages of steam and sail, the following rule, suggested by Captain Ryder, R.N., may be found of some practical utility. On steaming directly towards a port with a foul wind and sea, should it become apparent that the quantity of coal remaining on board is not sufficient to enable the ship to reach the harbor, and it therefore becomes necessary to keep her off under sail, putting out the fires or banking up, as may be deemed expedient, it may become useful to estimate the quantity of coal remaining on board in miles of distance from the port; then opening the compasses to that distance, according to the scale of the chart, place one leg on the port to be reached, and describe a circle round it, which call the "steam circle." It will then be evident how long the ship must be kept under sail before the distance can be reached at which she could arrive at the port under steam alone; and if from the place of the ship two tangents be drawn to the circle on opposite sides of it, we shall be able to see how many points the ship may be kept away so as to get with certainty within the steaming distance by the assistance of sail only.

253. *On the Management of the Fuel while under Steam.*

The coal-boxes require to be looked to occasionally, to see if there are any symptoms of spontaneous combustion. If there be, no time should be lost in well deluging the coal-box with water; and the precaution of not taking off the scuttles should be carefully observed, so as not to allow a free supply of air, except in that one through which the water is to be poured. Some steamers are fitted with pipes leading down the coal-boxes, and filled with water. These pipes serve to indicate the temperature of the coal-boxes at intervals; for if the coals become hot, the heat will be conveyed by the water up the tube to the surface, and by ascertaining the temperature of the water we can readily tell whether all is safe in the interior of the mass.

If the steaming qualities of the boiler are sufficiently good, the coal should be wetted, if small, before being put on the fire. With Welsh coal, and particularly if the coal be small, it will be found to be a source of great economy to wet it; for if the coals be thrown on small, a great portion is carried onwards to the tubes, flues, etc., stopping them up with soot (a non-conductor). Again, small coal will lie on the top of the fire like so much sand, and the air cannot get at it to produce a speedy combustion. And if the fire be disturbed, or raked about, to make it burn better, the small coal passes down between the fire-bars, and, in all probability, is cleared out of the ash-pits with the ashes, and eventually thrown overboard. Hence it will be found that by wetting the coal steam will be kept better, and with the consumption of considerably less fuel.

In Wales it is a common practice to mix up small coal with water, or even with mud, so as to enable them to be formed into balls, and they thus make exceedingly good fires.

254. *Preparatory Orders before Stopping the Engines.*

Fuel may be saved if the engineer be made acquainted beforehand with any stoppages likely to take place; as, for instance, for getting soundings, coming to an anchor, or taking a ship in tow, or whenever the speed of the vessel is about to be reduced. As an extreme case, let us consider a vessel of the size of the Terrible, when working all her boilers, with twenty-four fires; suppose an order to be given to stop the ship immediately after the fires have been fresh charged with coal. Now each fire requires about three or four shovelfuls of coal, or about 20 lbs. Therefore all the fires will have required $20 \times 24 = 480$ lbs., nearly a quarter of a ton. If immediately after firing the ship be stopped for some time, this fuel will evaporate water from the boilers, and the steam generated will escape by the waste-steam funnel, whereby so much coal will be wasted, at the same time causing a great noise on deck from the rush of steam, and preventing orders from being distinctly heard, all which might have been avoided if those in charge of the engine-room had been made acquainted with the stoppages likely to take place. In giving the orders, however, it would be well that they were given in such a way as to leave the management and responsibility of the fires in the hands of the chief engineer: it might be productive of bad consequences to order the engineer not to put on any more fuel for a certain time, because those on deck cannot be aware of the state of the fires at the time they give such order. The engineer not being allowed, after such an order has been given, to exercise his discretion, complies with it literally; and if the vessel is going at her full speed, the steam-pressure falls, because the demand is greater than the supply; and should she stop, and it be found necessary to give a back-turn, it might be impossible to do so. This is to be particularly guarded against in crowded harbors.

When about to stop a steamer, for any reason whatever, it is a useful rule to give the previous order to the engineer, "Stand by below;" for in large steam-ships it requires nearly all the engineers, and in some ships quite all, to work the engines by hand. This order will therefore enable the chief engineer to place his men at their stations, and so prevent confusion and loss of time. In some steamers, fitted with single eccentrics, when under way, the gear for working the slides is detached; and the order, "Stand by," gives time for the engineer to make his arrangements, and carry out the coming order quickly. Again, if the order, "Down with the engines," be given after the vessel is fast, it is conducive to the saving of fuel: for otherwise the engineer, not knowing what is likely to occur, keeps the fires forward, and perhaps the dampers open; or, in other words, keeps the fires in such a state that the engines can be instantly moved if wanted; whereas if he had been aware the vessel would not have to start again for some time, and that he should have timely notice previously, he would have put the fires back and closed the dampers, and then a certain amount of fuel would have been saved; or if the stoppage were for any length of time short of two hours, he would have "banked up." (See p. 178.)

This last evil would be greater in tubular boilers, in consequence of the water being so soon evaporated, and from the incessant working of the auxiliary engine when the vessel is stationary, to say nothing of the unpleasant noise arising from the steam blowing off.

CHAPTER VII.

DUTIES TO MACHINERY DURING AN ACTION OR AFTER AN ACCIDENT.

255. *The Gear for repairing Damages during an Action.*

All tools that are likely to be wanted should be arranged in order *in the engine-room,* according to the discretion of the chief engineer, in some place where they will not be liable to be struck with shot. Inside the combings of the hatchways would evidently first suggest itself as the most suitable place for such gear as might be wanted on deck; but such places are too liable to accident, and therefore the engineer must be content to put up with the delay occasioned by sending below for whatever articles he may want.

The following gear should be ready and arranged:

Spanners suited to the paddle-wheels, as many as the ship is supplied with; hand, sledge, and flogging hammers; punches, flogging, cross-cut, and hand-chisels; three or four hack-saws; some fearnaught, canvas, thin sheet-iron and copper plates, swabs, spun-yarn, and shores of convenient length; also plugs for the tubes of the tubular boilers; spare sails, hammocks, etc.; and bags of coal, if time will allow, should be placed round and on the steam-chest, especially if the vessel be likely to be fired on from a height.

256. *Machinery requiring examination before the Action.*

The disconnecting gear should be in such good work ing order as to leave no doubt as to its efficiency; but if, from any cause, we are not quite certain of it, this should be examined, if time permit, because it may happen that a shot or shell will so distort one of the wheels that the vessel will be useless until it be disconnected.

Also the bilge-pumps should be connected, and the apparatus for the process of injecting from the bilge carefully examined.

Note.—Care should always be taken to replace all the tools after each part of the machinery has been examined, to be in readiness when actually wanted.

257. *Preparations to be made in the Engine-room against Fire.*

The boiler hand-pump should be in readiness to supply water in case of fire, and the hose should be screwed on previously. In some steamers, a pipe from the feed-pump is brought on deck to supply water; this also is an advantageous plan, especially if the ship were attacked by pirates, where the laws that usually regulate modern warfare are neglected; for if the engine be worked hot, hot water would be ejected from the pipe.

258. *Regulation of the Fires during Action.*

This must depend entirely on the nature of the service. If the steamer be chasing an enemy's ship, or, on the contrary, be trying to avoid the fire of a superior force, or if the vessel be liable to be sent off with all speed to take up some other position, or to carry reinforcements; or in towing; or, in short, in any important duty where all the power she can command will be required to be brought into play—it is plain that in any such case the steam must be kept up at its full intensity, or nearly so, at whatever hazard. But, on the other hand, if the steamer be employed in bombarding, as was lately the case at Odessa, where speed was no great object, and the ships were merely kept moving to divert the attention of the enemy; or, again, in a general action with other vessels, when there is no probability of her being required to change her position without some minutes previous notice—then in all such cases it becomes important to allow the steam-pressure to decrease till it is but little above the atmospheric pressure: and the reason is obvious, for we know that if a shot enter a boiler filled with very strong steam, steam or water, or both, will rush out with disastrous effect into the engine-room, creating great mischief and confusion; whereas, on the contrary, if the steam have not a pressure much exceeding that of the atmosphere, the damaged part becomes much more manageable. It must be remembered that should the steam be lowered to the atmospheric pressure, the gauge-cocks will not act; and it will be impossible to change the water in the boiler, if the water-level be lower than that outside the vessel. Hence, whenever the authority of the commanding-officer sanctions such a step, let the steam be lowered till near the atmospheric pressure; and as this requires some little management, we will go somewhat into detail. Let the fires be banked up so as not to burn too briskly, and yet be in such a state that, by raking the coals about, a good fire may instantly be excited; this will enable the vessel to start off shortly after the order to do so is given. The next important thing to attend to is the reverse-valve; for we have already seen that when the pressure in the boiler becomes much less than that of the atmosphere, this valve opens, and allows air to enter. Now if the engine have to work at this low pressure—as, for instance, to enable the ship to shift her birth, etc.—the efficiency will depend more on the state of the vacuum than that of the steam; and the vacuum will evidently be much injured by the introduction of air into the boiler, so as to become mechanically mixed with the steam. This is of more importance in unbalanced than in balanced engines; for atmospheric steam entering below the piston will at best have as much as it can struggle with in raising the piston, more particularly if there be a head wind and sea. Let, therefore, the reverse-valve be temporarily loaded, and fit a longer steam-gauge float than that ordinarily used, to enable the engineer to discover the state of the steam,* and so to manage the fires as to prevent a vacuum from being created within the boiler. The reverse-valve should be loaded so as to open when the external pressure exceeds the internal by about 5 lbs.

Another plan may also be tried, which perhaps would be *more* advantageous than the preceding. Keep the fires forward, and in an active state of combustion, and open the *safety-valve* to allow the steam to blow off to atmospheric pressure. But if the steam-chest be small, it will perhaps be found that air will enter the boiler by the safety-valve whenever the engines are worked according to this plan, particularly if the orifice of the internal steam-pipe is near the safety-valves; for the rush of steam to fill the cylinders is so great that a partial void is created, and the air rushes through to supply the place. Should this be found to take place after the steam is blown off, the safety-valve may be partially closed to prevent air from entering the boiler.

259. *Casualties to which Paddle-wheels are liable during Action.*

They are necessarily liable to be struck by shot, and disabled; but the chance of their being disabled seems to have been much magnified by alarmists. Indeed, previous experience does not allow us to bring forward any instance of a steamer's wheel having been disabled in action, although the ship has been struck in the hull in a great number of places.† If, however, the wheel happen to be struck, and it be found to revolve afterwards with the engine, let it continue to work; for the steaming qualities of the ship will be but little affected, although two or three paddle-boards and arms are knocked away. A

* There is now no chance of the mercury being forced into the boiler from the pressure of the air, because in the present day an internal pipe is carried up from the steam-gauge to the upper part of the steam-chest.

† Mackinnon's *Steam Warfare in the Parana*, vol. i. p. 220.

steam-ship when on the coast of Africa worked the engines with one-third of the paddles off each wheel. She had been sailing, and, wanting to go in chase, did not wait to ship the floats. But if it have become so jammed as to prevent the working of the engine, it must be disconnected immediately from the engine, and the ship be steamed with the one wheel; this will give her about two-thirds her full speed. One engineer at least must be present at the work of removing the damaged parts of the wheel, with handy workmen who have been used to hammers, etc. The tools required will be principally flogging chisels and hammers.*

260. *General effect of Shot upon Funnels.*

The danger from shot is not much to be apprehended, unless its velocity has been partially destroyed before striking the funnel. It was formerly supposed that flame would escape from a shot-hole, and be productive of danger to the ship; but serious reflection will convince any person that, on the contrary, the cold air will rush into the funnel, where the gases are much rarefied by heat. This was fully tested on board H.M.S. Echo. The draught will be slightly checked by the cold air rushing into the orifice, but not sufficiently so to produce any appreciable difference in the speed of the ship, or in the revolutions of the engine. And even if a spent shot or a falling spar strike the funnel, and carry it away, the chief mischief that will accrue will be, that the draught will be lessened, and the men on deck will be annoyed with the smoke; but the evil is not so great as might be supposed.† What

* It may not be out of place here to remark, that during a war, an engine-smith and a boiler-maker should be attached to the engine-room. Our West-Indian mail-packets are manned in this way.

† This has been sufficiently tried on board her Majesty's ships Blenheim, Echo, and Bee, by direction of Captain (now Rear-Admiral) Chads, R.N. In the Bee, the effect on the speed from entirely removing the funnel was a loss of about one-fifth.

we have to dread most is, that from some mischance—perhaps from the effects of a falling spar—the funnel will be bent down, because it will in its fall carry over with it the pipe by which the steam makes its escape; for if this pipe be merely bent over, and not carried away entirely, the steam will be stopped, from its not being able to pass the bend. Now let us bear in mind, that the funnel being bent over prevents the production of steam by checking the draught; and that the same accident happening to the waste-steam funnel prevents the overplus steam from getting away from the boiler. It becomes, therefore, a duty, before cutting away the funnel and liberating the smoke, that the waste-steam funnel should be cleared away to enable the safety-valve to act freely: if the vessel be in motion, so much the better, because the engines will then consume the steam as fast as it is generated, and prevent accumulation in the boiler. But the evil may be yet more serious; for it may happen that the engine is stationary at the same time the steam-funnel is bent down, in which case there will be no vent for the surplus steam till the orifice be opened; and unless this be done expeditiously, the steam will accumulate in the boiler, causing an explosion. In addition, therefore, to the obvious method of cutting off the injured pipe, some prompt measure should be adopted to prevent a great accumulation within the boiler. To haul out the fires would but increase the danger; for the very act would put the fires in such a rapid state of combustion, that an additional quantity of steam will be rapidly generated. Again, the future production of steam will be checked by this process; and it would be very imprudent at such a time to put a stop to the further service of the engines. Let, therefore, instead of this, the blow-valve be opened; and that the steam may not inconvenience the engine-room, if the vessel have light draught of water, let the snifting-valve be weighted, or even shored down for the time that the steam may be driven up through the air-pump, hot-well, and lastly through the waste-water pipe into the atmosphere. Should the boiler be overtaxed by this, as can easily be ascertained by the steam-gauge, let the grease-cocks on the cylinder-cover be opened, or the upper escape-valve, and let the slide be placed in such a position as to allow the steam to enter the cylinder above the piston. A weight may also be put on the reverse-valve; or if an inverted one, it may be shored up. The boiler would by these means be relieved; and on the order being given to go on, the engine could in an instant be brought into its normal state, and the working of the engine would carry off the steam. In doing all this, it may happen that the condenser will have been made so hot by the blowing-through that the injection-water will not come into the condenser. If so, let a few buckets of cold water be thrown over the outside of the condenser, if possible, and work the engine as slow as circumstances will admit, keeping the injection-cock open. Even at the worst the engine can be worked for some time at high pressure, if the boiler is loaded to 8 or 10 lbs. This will work off the steam, and save the boiler.

It may be possible to work the engines for a short time by going alternately ahead and astern, even though the vessel be not permitted to shift her berth to any great distance; and in such case this might be done.

261. *Remedies to be adopted in case a Shot enters the Boilers.*

If the shot make an orifice in the water-space of the boiler, hot water will immediately rush out. Let all the scuttles in the stoke-holes be open, that the water may find its way into the bilge; and let the spare gratings be handed down from the decks as quickly as possible into the stoke-hole for the stokers to stand on while firing, especially if one boiler only is struck. If the steam be above the atmospheric pressure, let it be allowed to escape by the safety-valve, open the blow-out cocks of this boiler, put the fires back if they can be got at, close the dampers and ash-pit doors, use the steam from the boiler alone; then the water will not be *forced* out of the boiler, but only *run* out as it would from any other vessel, the force depending on the height of the surface of the water above the orifice. If the shot, however, enter the *steam* part of the boiler only, and the steam be only at atmospheric pressure, it will be of no consequence so far as the effect in the engine-room; but if it be at a pressure much above that of the atmosphere, it will scald all those who come in the direction in which it is issuing. The hole through the boiler may be stopped by placing a piece of wood against it, which may be kept in its place by a shore from the ship's side, etc. A piece of fearnaught, covered with red and white lead, should be placed between the wood and the boiler to render it water-tight.

262. *Whether the Steam should be got up in all the Boilers on going into Action.*

It would be advisable to get up the steam in all the boilers, even though all be not wanted, and the fires should be banked up in those that are not used; for, first, no one can tell from one minute to another what need the vessel may have of all her power; and secondly, the chances are much against all the boilers being struck with shot. The steam might be kept very low in those boilers not immediately wanted, but yet in such a state as to be readily serviceable if required.

263. *Temporary Repair to the Shell of a damaged Boiler.*

It has been previously stated, that iron plates should be prepared, of different sizes, to suit any case that may occur. Let these have one or two holes in the centre, with cross-bars and bolts, together with nuts to screw up the plates, somewhat similar to the man-hole and mud-hole doors. A portion of these patches (half, for instance) should be concave; so that, when having to patch a boiler on the side opposite to that by which the shot entered, the convexity will allow the edge of the patch to come close home. With every patch provided, there should be two or three layers of fearnaught, that the joint may be made tight. If repairing on the side by which the shot entered, no great difficulty probably will present itself beyond that of getting the bar in the hole; but on the other side many of the ragged pieces of the edge will have to be first broken off, the fearnaught must be interposed between the plate and the boiler, and the plate must be screwed home towards the bars, interposing washers between the plate and the nut, to save time. The side of the boiler by which the shot makes its egress will present by far the most formidable difficulties; for, in addition to the jagged appearance of the shot-hole with the pieces projecting outwards, the fragments splintered off the other side will probably make a vast number of ragged holes of various sizes.

264. *Steam-pipe or Feed-pipe struck with Shot.*

If the steam-pipe be struck, the stop or communication valves must be immediately closed, and a handy piece of sheet iron or copper must be curved to suit the form of the pipe. A layer of fearnaught should be interposed between the sheet and the pipe; and the whole may be secured by spun-yarn wound round it.

If the feed-pipe be struck, and the small engine for feeding the boiler be efficient, that must, of course, be set to work, and the feed-apparatus be detached; but if that have been already disabled, it may be that the boilers are fitted with circulating-pipes; then feed into one boiler by that feed-pipe which is still in working condition, and open the communication between the two boilers; or the blow-out cocks may be opened if they happen to lead into one of Kingston's valves. If no such pipes are fitted, we must resort to the following plan: Go on for some time without feeding, that is to say, as long as is consistent with safety, and then blow the steam off from the boiler requiring to be fed; and if the boiler's water-level be below the water-line outside, all we have to do is to open the blow-off cocks, and the water will rise in the boiler to the level of the water outside the vessel: this process may be repeated from time to time, until the feed-pipe has been temporarily repaired, which can be done after the same manner as the steam-pipe, that is, with a piece of sheet-copper, canvas, white-lead, and spun-yarn.

If the waste-water pipe be broken from any cause, the engine must be worked without condensation, to lessen the quantity of water that would have to pass through the pipe. If the injury can be got at, a strong cleat may be nailed to the ship's side, and pieces of wood secured to this and round the pipe; the whole being wrapped round with canvas, white-lead and spun-yarn, forming a sort of faucet or expansion-joint.

In the case of sea-cock pipes breaking at the vessel's bottom, as has sometimes happened, a similar plan should be adopted.

265. *To work with one Engine only if the other be disabled.*

If one of the engines be disabled by any accident, and the other be required to work the ship, there may be some difficulty in making it pass the centres, especially if it be a paddle-steamer worked by a direct-action engine.

If the nature of the service allows, no time should be lost in taking off some of the paddle-boards at that part of the wheel where the weight of the piston is felt. If, for instance, the wheel be fitted with double boards (the cycloidal wheel), let one of the boards be detached from each of the arms of both wheels that happen to be in the water when the engine is in that position in which it is brought to a stand-still. If the wheels be fitted with single boards,* let all the paddle-boards be *reefed*, and thus lessen

* The divided boards are to be preferred for several reasons, particularly because they are not so liable to split, and are more easily removed in parts when fitted as a common board, that is, placed on the same side of the paddle-arm.

the work of the engine: this, indeed, seems the best way even with the cycloidal plan, for it will let the single engine come up to its work, and use its steam; but those paddles which would be in the water when the steam has to contend with the disadvantages of the engine, should be brought nearer to the centre than the others, so as to give an oval form to the curve made by the outer edge of the paddles. If, owing to stress of weather, being chased, or from any other cause, it is found impossible to re-arrange the floats, so as to enable the single engine to turn its centres with facility, it may be found necessary, on first starting after the accident, to put the ship before the wind, that the way of the ship may assist the cranks over the dead centres till the engine have acquired sufficient momentum; after which, on hauling to the wind again, the engine will probably continue to work. As the top centre in direct-action engines offers the greatest difficulty, the lead may with advantage be dispensed with by lowering the slide a small space. With all kinds of marine engines, in whatever duties employed, whether in towing, running with mails, or for war-purposes, the engines should be so managed as to move with the normal velocity of the piston at least, or rather above it; and this more particularly if the engine be leaky on the exhaust-side so that the quick working of the air-pump will keep the exhaustion, much in the same way as a man does who works the handle of a common hand-pump quickly when the bucket is leaky.

266. *Remarks on the Screw-Propeller.*

One great object aimed at by the constructors of engines to work the screw-propeller has been, to keep every part below the water-line of the ship, thereby protecting them in great measure from the effects of shot; and therefore the precautions and rules laid down in the former pages do not apply with so much force to them; although, if any accident were to happen, the same system must be pursued. The screw, however, is liable to be struck if the vessel be pitching at all heavily, and doubtless the mischief would be greater in such case than if a paddle-wheel were struck. If a part be *broken away* by any accident, and the screw be found to revolve, let it go on; remembering that, since the surface of the blade is diminished, the engines will go too fast, and exhaust the boiler; to prevent which, the engines must have their power reduced by working expansively, or throttling the steam. If the screw be injured by becoming twisted, without being knocked clean away, so as to be jammed in the space cut out for it to work in, no general remedy can be stated; but it must be left to circumstances, depending entirely on the nature of the injury, and the time, opportunity, and means the engineer can command.

267. *A Steam-Ship leaky, when the Steam is not required.*

We could evidently disconnect the paddle-wheels or screw from the engine, and work without them, employing the steam-power solely in pumping out the vessel. To do this, we must connect the bilge-pumps, and inject from the bilge. A considerable quantity of water may be allowed to enter to the condenser; because the engine working so freely, the air-pump will carry it off, and therefore we can let in much more water than is sufficient to condense the steam. If the engine be unbalanced, and any difficulty occur from its want of power to turn the centres after having lost its paddles, which serve as the fly-wheel, the slide-rod should be lengthened a little, which can be readily done in most engines; consequently the cushioning on the down-stroke will take place sooner, and the steam will come in earlier; this will prevent too great a downward momentum; and, on the other hand, the steam will be admitted for a longer portion of the up-stroke.*

268. *Necessary precautions if the Vessel be so disabled that she must go ashore.*

The first object should be to increase speedily the ves-

* See *Indicator and Dynamometer*, 2d edition, p. 25.

sel's draught of water, that she may take the ground as early as possible;* so that when all is ready to get her off again, she may be lightened. The boilers should, therefore, be filled up by the pumps to their crowns, and water should also be allowed to enter the bilge. A good way to effect this latter object is to let the injection-cock be opened, and allow the water to find its way through the snifting-valve.

269. *Temporary Repair of Tubes when damaged by Shot or any other cause.*

The remedy in this case is obvious: all that can be done temporarily is to prevent the water from entering the smoke-box; this can be done by driving plugs into them. In some cases, both ends of the tubes must be plugged up; but frequently it will suffice to drive a plug into the tube so as to cover the hole. The plugs should be made of a good length, so as to cover more than one hole.

If several tubes are destroyed at once, so as to render all attempts at repair abortive, the fires should be drawn from that boiler, which must be considered *hors de combat.*

270. *Steamers in Chase.*

When two steamers are keeping the same course, and one of them has *some slight* advantage over the other in speed—say a mile an hour—then if the slow vessel can by any means get so close on the quarter of the other as to be powerfully influenced by the following current of the faster vessel, it will be found that the latter will not be able to escape from her; and the other, although slower, will be enabled to hang upon her quarter as long as she pleases, unless by skilfully altering the course the faster vessel make her escape in another direction. It is a common thing to see one steamer hugging† another in this

---

* See the *Recovery of H.M.S. Gorgon*, p. 6, by Captain A. C. Key, R.N.

† This is the term used on the Thames.

way. The only way to avoid it in the faster vessel is by suddenly and unexpectedly altering the course, so as to change the direction of the current before the chasing ship can be aware of what is done.

271. *Repairing Shot-holes in the Funnel after an Action.*

These may easily be repaired by having some patches of thin sheet-iron got ready, with a sort of double spring attached, one inside and the other outside; the hole may be covered over by one of these patches, since we need not be very careful about its fitting over-tightly. To do away with the fear that exists in many minds lest the fire should come out of these holes, we would instance the doors in front of the smoke-boxes of tubular boilers that are made to ship and unship, and no risk of burning the vessel by the issuing flame is ever entertained.

The observations we have already made respecting the mode of repairing, in a temporary way, the damages of boilers during an action, will apply to them after the action is over; only greater care and more precautions can be adopted than would otherwise be used. If the hole be in such a part that a shore may be interposed between the orifice and the ship's side or the beams overhead, we may, in addition to the plans proposed, press home the plate against the fractured part by these means. In many instances, however, it would be better to empty the boiler, and allow the patch to be introduced from the inside, that the pressure of the steam may make it fit more tightly, instead of tending to force it away. To get an idea of this method, we would refer our readers to the mud-hole doors, the plan proposed being similar in principle.

272. *Necessary precautions when straightening a Piston-rod, or other part of the Machinery.*

To effect a repair of this nature, the part must be put in the fire and softened. Now in doing this, if it be exposed to the open air when hot, it will oxidate, and portions will scale off; to prevent which, the fire that is used must be chiefly of wood, for coal brings off scales from iron when heated to redness. The same reasoning applies to some other parts of the engine; for instance, if a crank-pin or crank-shaft were to scale, the pin would be too small for the eye of the crank. Charcoal should be used if it can be had.

273. *Method of working the Engines without Cylinder-covers.*

It can be effected in this way: Let the broken cover be removed, and the upper steam-port blocked up with a piece of wood so shaped as to prevent its being forced inwards towards the slide by the pressure of the atmosphere: the orifice is made steam-tight by interposing fearnaught between the wood and the edges of the port. The wood must be kept in its place by two shores, one on each side of the piston-rod, pressing with one end against the wood, and with the other against the opposite side of the cylinder. The steam will be admitted, therefore, to the *under* surface of the piston, but not to the *upper* surface: the upper surface will be acted on by the atmosphere alone.* Now, since the pressure to which the steam is raised is considerably above that of the atmosphere, the piston will be forced up against the resistance the air exerts; and on creating a vacuum underneath the piston, it will be forced down by the atmosphere. To prevent irregularity, we should not create too good a vacuum; thus, if the steam have a pressure of 10 lbs. above that of the atmosphere, we have an effective upward pressure of 10 lbs., and consequently the downward pressure should be about 10 lbs. But the pressure of the atmosphere is 15 lbs.; hence we should have a pressure underneath of 5 lbs., arising from

* We have throughout this work used freely the words *upper* and *under:* when speaking of the sides of the piston, these expressions apply strictly to upright cylinders only; but it will be understood that when speaking of horizontal cylinders, the opposite slides are meant.

the uncondensed steam, or a deficiency from a vacuum amounting to 10 inches of mercury; and since a perfect vacuum amounts to 30 inches, the height of the barometer-gauge should be about 20 inches. Subsequent experiments have, however, shown that this precaution is usually unnecessary, and need only be adopted when unpleasant jerks are experienced as the wheels rotate. The vessel's rate was found to be about two-thirds her ordinary speed. If the engines be fitted with Seaward's slides, we need only detach the upper slides on the steam and vacuum sides; the springs at the back will be sufficient to press them against the part and keep them closed. This was successfully carried out in the Reynard.

CHAPTER VIII.

DUTIES TO ENGINE, ETC., ON ARRIVING IN HARBOR.

274. *Blowing-out on arriving in Port.*

IT was formerly the universal practice, and is continued now in many instances, to empty the boilers by "blowing out;" but the introduction of tubes, in many cases made of thin brass, has rendered this practice objectionable. For it has been found, from the contraction of the tubes on cooling, leaks have been caused in the tube-plates. And consequently the boilers are now allowed to cool gradually with the water in them; and if it be thought right to have the boilers empty, the water is pumped out afterwards. The chief thing for consideration is, that hot water will hold many salts in solution that will be precipitated when cold, and therefore previous care should have been taken to have the water well changed. The general practice at present is to "blow out" until the water is as low as is consistent with the safety of the tubes, and then pump the boilers up again by the donkey-engine before hauling out the fires. The safety-valve should be allowed to remain closed, to prevent the water from becoming more saturated with salts.

275. *Blowing through and hauling out Fires.*

The engines should be blown through with steam the last thing, to drive all the water out. The cock at the bottom of the condenser is also useful for this purpose. By taking due precaution, much of the injury to engines from the oxidation of the metal will be prevented: another source of risk will also be avoided; for, as was observed in Art. 201, in frosty weather there is danger of solid ice being formed in the engines, as, for instance, above the air-pump bucket. On one occasion a steamer was detained for hours while attempts were made to melt it; and when the engines began to move, fears were entertained that the air-pump covers would give way.

When the fires have been hauled out after anchoring, it becomes necessary to deluge the burning fuel with water. A ship from neglecting this had to be scuttled: the stoke-hole plates became red-hot and set fire to the platform underneath, and this again to the coal-boxes.

276. *Duties to the Engines on first arriving in Port.*

The engines should first of all be carefully wiped down, after the boilers have been blown out; for while hot the grease is more easily removed, and it can be done with less waste. When this has been done, if the vessel is to be laid up for any considerable time, the packing should be taken out of the slides, glands, etc., for if not, a galvanic action is set up, and the rods, etc., will oxidate rapidly; but otherwise some melted tallow should be poured into the grease-cups round the piston-rods: the object of this is to prevent the entrance of dirt between the bush and the rod. This tallow must be allowed to remain there all the time the vessel is in harbor, to catch the dirt that would otherwise fall into the gland, or get down between the piston-rod and the bush, and having once found its way there, would cut the rod and wear away the packing. A similar plan should be adopted with all the other glands. When the steam is getting up, we are not to allow this tallow to remain there and melt, because it is supposed to have become dirty; but it should be taken out, and clean tallow put in its place. The tallow, after being taken out, need not be thrown away; let it be melted, and any dirt that is in contact will fall to the bottom of the kettle. Again, if the engines are kept bright while in harbor, let the bright work, when about to proceed to sea, be coated over with melted tallow mixed with white-lead, which will resist the corroding influence of the salt water. On arrival in port, all that will be necessary is, to wipe of the tallow and white-lead, and the former bright appearance will be estored.

277. *Lubricators to be Examined.*

Occasionally, on arriving in port, the lubricators should be scalded out with hot water, to remove whatever dirt may have accumulated about them; the necessity for this will depend much on the purity of the oil used. If fitted with Barton's lubricators, a new worsted should be put in at the end of every voyage, for it is apt to become gummy after a time, which prevents the capillary action from going on.

278. *Bearings to be examined.*

When the bearings of the engines are taken apart to be cleaned and examined, it is at times found that the brasses are cut or scored, from some defect in the lubrication. Oil-grooves in the under brasses appear to be bad, for in a short time they become full of dirt, which hardens and cuts the bearing: it may be as well to fill these up with soft metal. The only case in which oil-grooves appear to be of any service is, when cut across the top brass, to conduct the oil, etc., to their extremity.

The bearings should now and then be taken apart, but not oftener than necessary; for detaching the parts of the engine is likely to be attended with mischief, since after so doing the engine will require re-adjusting; and if screwed down too tight, the bearings will heat, and when once hot it is troublesome to get them cool; they may be an annoyance during the whole of the following voyage. Or, on the other hand, if not screwed down tight enough, there will be mischief from jar to the machinery.

If the vessel be fitted with beam engines, the upper side-rod end bearings require great attention, the little motion there is at that point not being enough to produce a good surface, and the wear is all on the upper and lower side of the bearing, which in time wears it oval. Of course, when time and circumstances admit, this oval must be altered into a rounded form again; but where this cannot be done, from want of time and opportunity, great caution must be used in tightening up the bearing; for if too tight, we shall have one oval surface working within another, and if very tight, the side-rods will break just under the strap or eye. Many side-rods have been broken in this way.

279. *Outer Bearings of Paddle-shafts.*

Oxidation goes on here to a great extent, from the action of the salt water on the brass and iron which are in contact in the bearing. They require to be in good order, and the oil-holes free. Two cases have occurred in the Navy in which the paddle-boxes have been set on fire from the heating of the outer bearing. In one instance a broken punch was found in the oil hole.

280. *Piston-glands, Keys, etc.*

The piston-glands of all engines, but more particularly of those with short connecting-rods (in which any derangement of the parallel motion is more likely to produce a transversal strain of the piston), should be kept as high as the motion will allow; for the more packing there is, that is to say, the deeper the stuffing-box (which is produced by keeping up the gland), the better guide it will be to the piston, and the more it will tend to keep it in a straight line.

281. *Screwing down the "Holding-down Bolts."*

When the vessel comes into harbor, the holding-down bolts should be looked to now and then, and screwed down, if necessary, *before the steam is down;* for gales of wind will tend to loosen the engines on their sleepers, and if the operation be not performed before the steam is got rid of, we may not be able to get at the bolts, from the position of the side-levers. In screwing down the bolts, they should be taken diagonally, and one nut should be screwed down as much as another; for it is to be presumed that the engine will thus come into its place more accurately. On the other hand, if the bolts be screwed down on one side only, the engine will probably be out of square with the ship. In vessels that are built diagonally, and also in iron vessels, great care and judgment are required in screwing down the holding-down bolts. And after a vessel has been ashore or in dock, the holding-down bolts should be examined carefully; in the former case it is a common thing to find them broken.

The stays of the engines ought to be slacked when the ship is docked, or when on shore; for at such times the vessel will spread open from being relieved of the pressure of the water outside.

282. *Examining, repairing, and repacking Slides.*

A little reflection will convince any person that, if a flat surface be continually rubbed, the middle will become worn away more than the edges, and from being flat at first it wears into a concave surface. Let us bear this in mind, and examine the action of the packing on the back of the slide. The packing surrounds the back of the slide in the form of a ring; and as the slide is continually moving upwards and downwards, to allow the alternate ingress and egress of the steam, the middle of the portion rubbed by the packing—that is to say, the middle of the upper and lower projecting surfaces at the back—will become hollow, and it will tell upon the working of the engine; for if, when the slide be depressed or elevated, the packing be screwed up tight, it will be slack when the slide is in the middle of its path. Again, if it be screwed up when the slide is half-way down, it will jam when an attempt is made to raise or depress it. The latter case is not unlikely to produce accidents; for if the slide be thrown out of gear when it is at the top or bottom of its stroke, and an order be given to go astern, the engineer will perhaps find it so jammed that he will not be able readily to move it. When the slide is taken out to examine it, therefore, a straight-edge, as long at least as the slide itself, should be brought into contact with the back of the slide lengthways, to see whether it be in contact with the upper and lower projecting portion of the back throughout the length. If it be found to be hollow, the projecting parts should be filed down, and it is as well to leave the backs slightly rounded up in the middle to allow for their wearing away. After the backs have been filed, they should be smoothed carefully to prevent the packing from being cut away.

Having examined and made good the defect at the back, it may happen that the face and nozzles will require looking to. They are apt to get leaky from the alternate expansion and contraction of the metal, and from not attending to the packing with sufficient care; for if the slides are not kept in contact with the nozzles, steam will pass between the slide and the back-plate, and gradually cut a channel for itself, as water would down the face of a chalk-cliff. To get them steam-tight again, the slide must first be made true; that is to say, its faces must be made flat. The slide-faces should then be covered over with red-lead and oil, and the slide should be put in its place: let it now be moved up and down the extent of its travel, and at the same time kept hard against the plate; we shall by these means, on taking off the slide, detect the projecting surfaces of the nozzles. If the mischief have not gone very far, these projections must be scraped down, but if that cannot easily be done, the part must be filed away; this can be performed at the upper port with a crank-handle file, and at the bottom port a long-handle file must be used, having another person below to keep the file in its place. When the surfaces are nearly true, the red-lead and oil must be put on proportionately thin, or the part requiring to be taken off will not be discovered. A sheet of tin or white paper is of great service to reflect light on those parts that are obscured. After the faces are brought to coincide, the slide should be rubbed once or twice against its facing, having previously covered over the surfaces with a little fine emery and oil. Much dependence cannot be placed on this latter plan for grinding the surfaces together; for large pieces of emery will rub hollow places in the facing, if continued long.

In repacking slides, great care is to be taken in making the gaskets; for if the slide have been at work for any considerable time, the space at the back, between the slide and its casing, must necessarily become larger than it was when new. Now the gasket must be made to accommodate itself to this, that is to say, it must be thicker at the back than at the sides, or else the slide will leak. The ends of the gasket must be made to bear well against the nozzle, to prevent the passage of steam from the steam-side to the exhaust-side of the slide without entering the cylinder. Where cotton can be obtained, it is preferable to spun-yarn for packing, because it is more elastic and retains its elasticity much longer. Canvas also when made up into packing answers exceedingly well; it is not destroyed so soon by heat as common packing. A similar remark applies to the trunnions of oscillating engines, which, being circular at first, wear oval, and therefore the packing will not fit if *uniformly* distributed around it.*

Slides require to be examined now more frequently than formerly; for since the introduction of tubular boilers, and generally of boilers having a confined steam-space, and limited at the water-line, priming goes on to a much greater extent than formerly; consequently dirt from the boiler is carried over with the steam, and deposits itself about the slide and its casing; and from the heat of the engine it becomes baked on, which renders the slides hard to move, and injures the packing and slide-facing.

---

* In making up the gaskets, it will be found a good plan to rub the soft soap over the yarn before it is plaited up, to suspend the galvanic action that would be likely to be set up.

283. *To find the Length of Stroke of an Engine.*

Put the engine at the top centre; mark on a batten the distance of the cross-head above the cylinder-cover; then put the engine at the bottom centre, and mark again the height of the cross-head above the cylinder-cover; the distance between these two marks is the exact stroke of the piston.

284. *To adjust the Parallel Motion of Marine Engines.*

1. SIDE-LEVER ENGINES.—If while watching the engine at sea we notice that the cross-head does not move in a vertical straight line, we know that there is something wrong in the parallel motion. This should be set to rights at the earliest opportunity after arriving in port. The difficulty we have to contend with is, first to find out where the error lies, and afterwards to correct it. To do this, we must first of all put the engine exactly at half-stroke; this can be done as follows: Having found the length of stroke as in the last article, bisect it, and make a mark on the piston-rod to correspond, and move the engine round till the cross head comes to the point of bisection, when the engine will be at half-stroke. This being accomplished, let us narrowly examine the parallel motion.

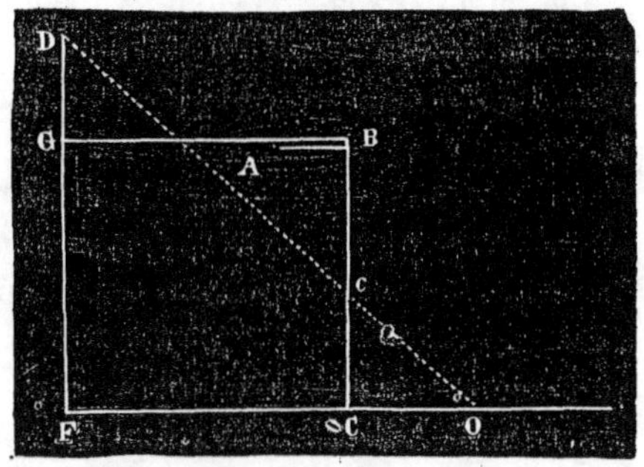

Let F O C represent the half side-lever, O the main centre, D F the cylinder side-rod, B C the parallel-motion side-rod, G B the parallel-motion bar, A B the radius-bar. Now the engine being at half-stroke, let us examine first whether the three points G, A, and B, are in one straight line.* Next, let us carefully measure G B and F C, also F G and B C, to

* They are purposely put out of a line in the figure, to allow the line A B to be seen.

ascertain whether G F B C is a parallelogram, which will be the case if G B = F C and F G = B C. If these conditions are not fulfilled, we must satisfy them by interposing liners at proper places according to our judgment. But we must be careful about the point F; for by interposing a liner there we should elevate the piston, and might endanger its striking the top of the cylinder. If, however, these necessary conditions be fulfilled, and yet the motion is not true, we are sure it must be that the radius-bar A B is not of the proper length. Those who are in the habit of making calculations can discover whether this is the case or not by the formula $\frac{CO}{AB}=\frac{BC.FO}{CO.DF}-1$ (See Chapter III. p. 99). To effect this, multiply together B C and F O, also C O and D F; divide the former by the latter, and take 1 from the quotient. Then divide C O by this result, and the quotient will give the length A B of the radius-bar. Those who are not conversant with such investigations must move round the engine till it comes to the top and bottom centres; and if it be discovered that in so doing the point D moves to the left, the radius-bar A B is too short; if, on the contrary, the point D goes to the right, it is too long. Some engines are so fitted that the point A can be shifted to the right or left, and then by means of liners we can alter the length at our discretion. Some, however, are not fitted in this way; and if any difficulty present itself about the adjustment, the best plan is (supposing the piston-rod to be vertical at the middle of the stroke) to endeavor to correct it when at the bottom, and let it take its chance at the top; for any defect there will not be of such consequence as in other positions, because nearly the whole extent of the piston-rod being outside the cylinder, allows for a little play without having much effect on the stuffing-box; whereas if any defect existed uncorrected when the piston cross-head is down, the strain is brought on the stuffing-box, and then by reaction on the radius-shaft plomer-block. Engineers are at times satisfied with ascertaining that the three points before mentioned, G, A, B, are in the same horizontal line when the engine is at half-stroke; but this evidently will not tell us whether the radius-bar A B, or the parallel-bar G B, is too short or too long, which is clearly an important thing to ascertain.

Many engines have their parallel motions thrown out of adjustment in the following way: The piston perhaps strikes the bottom of the cylinder, because the lower brasses of the side-rod and connecting-rod have worn away: to prevent this, a *liner* is put under the *lower* end of the side-rod to raise the piston in the cylinder; by doing which we throw the parallel motion out of adjustment, because the radius-shaft ought to have been raised at the same time as well as the parallel-motion side-rod. A somewhat similar effect will take place if a *liner* be put under the lower connecting-rod brass. The better way is to line up the brasses of the *upper* end of the side-rods, and by this method we shall not affect the parallel motion.* We must take into consideration that the wear on the brasses of the cylinder side-rods is much greater than on the motion side-rods; for they have the whole pressure on the piston to contend against, whereas the duty of the others is merely the guidance of the piston-rods, so that we shall not have to line up the one so much as the other.

2. Parallel Motion of the Gorgon Engines.—The first thing we have to look to is the wearing away of the brasses of the rocking standard, so that when the engine is at half-stroke the radius-bar and rocking beam centres are not in a straight line. If we examine this kind of engine, we shall readily be convinced that the parallel motion is very liable to get out of order. For the connecting-rod brasses, by wearing away, raise the piston and cross-head, and at the same time the rocking-standard is

* That is to say, if the parallel motion be that usually known by the name of Maudslay and Field's; but if it be that known as Boulton and Watt's, lining up either end of the side-rods will throw it out.

wearing down. It is true the shaft-brasses are wearing also, but they will be found not to wear so fast as the brasses of the connecting-rod.

With engines of this kind we must carefully examine the parallel motion after the entablature has been meddled with. For instance, if the woodwork to which the entablature has been secured shrink, and the entablature be screwed up, and it be screwed up more on the one side than on the other, we shall twist the parallel motion, by shifting the fixed point of the radius-bar without altering the position of the cylinder.

The proportion to be preserved among the lengths of the several parts will be found in the Appendix.

285. *To ascertain geometrically the Length for the Radius-bar in Side-lever Engines.*

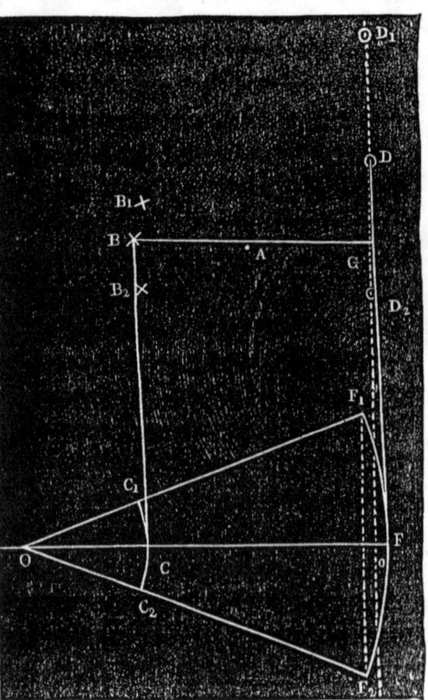

Let O F be the half side-lever, F D the side-rod, C B the parallel-motion side-rod, and B G the parallel-motion bar. Let the side-lever O F come into the positions O F_1 and O F_2 when at the extremes of the stroke, the point F having described the arc F_1 F F_2, and C having described the arc C_1 C C_2. Join F_1 F_2, and bisect the versine in the point *o*; through *o* draw *o* D at right angles to O F, which will contain the point D. Again, let O F_1 be the position of O F when at the extreme of the stroke, the crank being at the bottom centre. On o D produced set off D_1, making $F_1D_1 = FD$; then D_1 is the position of the top of the piston-rod when the piston is at the top of its stroke. From C_1 draw a line parallel to F_1D_1, and make B_1C_1 equal to B C. Again, by the same process find the points C_2, F_2, D_2, and B_2, corresponding to the positions which C, F, D, and B will have when the piston is at the bottom of the stroke. Then the extremity of the radius-bar has during the whole motion come into the three positions B_1, B, and B_2, and the centre of the circle passing through these points will be the fixed point of the radius-bar. Let A be this point, and the length of the radius-bar will be A B.

286. *To get the Paddle-shafts into the same Straight Line.*

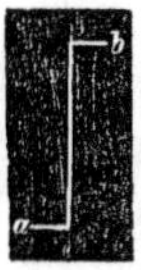

The weight of the paddle-shafts and wheels has a tendency to make them droop bodily by wearing away the brasses; and, in addition to this, they are liable to turn through an angle, because the pressure is always forcing the paddle towards the head of the ship. We will first endeavor to detect whether the paddle-shaft has drooped or not. To do this, place the cranks first of all on the top centre; then take a gauge, of any convenient length, but shorter than the distance between the centre of the shaft and boss of the crank, and made of the form represented by the figure. Let the point a be placed in the centre of the intermediate shaft, and with the end b describe a portion of a circle on the face of the opposite crank, having previously chalked it over so as to see the mark made. Let now the cranks be turned through a quadrant of the circle, and make another mark; turn them round to the bottom centre, and make a third mark; finally, turn it through another quadrant, and make a fourth mark. Now the order in which these marks intersect each other must be noticed; and it is clear that if the centre of the paddle-shaft is in the same line as the centre of the intermediate shaft, these four marks on the face of the crank will coincide; but if the first mark be at a greater distance from the centre of the paddle-shaft than the third mark, then the paddle-shaft has gone bodily down. The same reasoning with the second and fourth marks will tell whether the shaft has come bodily forward.

We have next to examine the outer end; this end is liable to droop, from the weight of the paddle, and likewise to be forced forwards, from the pressure. The way to discover if that be the case is as follows: Let the cranks, as before, be placed on the top centre. Let C A, A B be

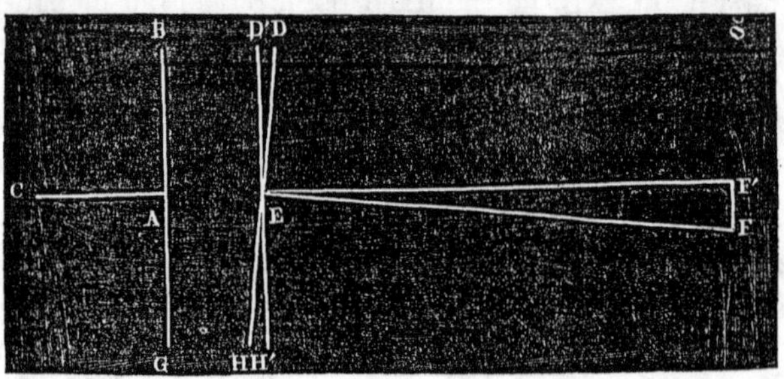

the position of the intermediate shaft and its crank, and E F and D E that of the paddle-shaft and its crank, the end F having drooped through the space F F′, which it is our object to find. Measure the distance B D, between the faces of the two cranks, in a line with the crank-pin. Care should be taken, at the same time, that the shaft does not move endways: in turning round, the ends of the shaft should be gauged, as a test of this. Then turn the engine through two quadrants, till the cranks come to the bottom centre, and measure the space G H, the distance between the faces of the cranks in this position. If B D = G H, it is a proof that the shafts C A and E F are in the same straight line; but if B D be greater than G H, it is a sign that the end F is too low. Turning the brasses end for end will sometimes rectify the defect caused by the *forward* wearing away of the shaft-brasses, and snifting the top and bottom brasses will at times correct the error introduced by the drooping; but if the error be considerable, the brasses must be lined up, or packing pieces introduced under the plomer-blocks.

To allow for the probable drooping of the paddle-end of the shaft, the end of the crank-pin is made to fit loose in the eye of the paddle-crank. This object was formerly gained by the use of the drag-link. The drag-link was a coupling-piece to connect the two crank-pins together, one crank being in advance of the other.

The rule by which we get the thickness of the piece to be interposed at F is given below. From the measured distance B D, take the measured distance G H, and divide the remainder by two. Then multiply this result by the length of the paddle-shaft (from the crank to the outer bearing), and divide by the length of the crank; the quotient is the distance F F′ required.* If the paddle-shaft be wholly below the intermediate shaft, this error should

---

* Let D′H′ be the position D H would assume if F E were in the same straight line with A E; ∴ D′H′ is parallel to B G, and D D′ = H H′, and G H′ = B′D′.

Also since $GH' = GH + HH'$

and $BD' = BD - DD'$

and because $HH' = DD'$

$\therefore \quad GH + HH' = BD - DD' = BD - HH'$

Hence $2HH' = BD - GH$

or $$HH' = \frac{BD - GH}{2}$$

Again, by similar triangles,

$$\frac{FF'}{FE} = \frac{DD'}{DE} = \frac{HH'}{DE}$$

or $$FF' = \frac{FE}{DE}.HH' = \frac{FE}{DE}\cdot\frac{BD - GH}{2}$$

Example.—Let F E = 12 ft. 6 in.; DE = 1 ft. 9 in.; B D = 7 in.; and G H = $6\frac{7}{8}$ in. Then B D − G H = $\frac{1}{8}$ in.

$$\therefore \quad FF' = \frac{12{\cdot}5}{1{\cdot}75} \times \frac{1}{16} = \frac{12{\cdot}5}{28}$$

which is rather less than half an inch. Hence, if the thickness of half an inch be interposed, the defect will be fully compensated.

be corrected first. It will be seen that similar methods will apply to the shafting of screw-engines.

287. *To set the Slides of the Engines; that is to say, to put the Stops on the intermediate Shaft.*

Throughout this work we suppose that the engine is rightly constructed and sent out of hand by the engine-maker; and consequently we must take for granted that the eccentric-rod, gab-lever, valve-lifter, slide-rod, etc., are of the proper length and position when the engines are new. But it becomes the duty of the engineer to shift or alter the position of the stops on the eccentrics from time to time, as these parts are liable to wear, and a little alteration in their position or size affects materially the lead of the slide. We must bear in mind that we are here dealing with a part of the engine where an error of one-eighth of an inch will double or annihilate altogether the lead of the slide.

In setting the slides we must first of all put the crank on its centre. Let us suppose that we wish to set the slide correctly for the upper port; to do this we must get the piston at the top of its stroke, and consequently, in a beam-engine, we must get the crank on its bottom centre, or if a direct engine, on its top centre. Now this we accomplish as follows: If the ship be on an even keel, and the engine square with the ship, or in other words, if a line at right angles to the keel be parallel to the piston-rod, then find, first, the diameter of the crank-pin, and take half of it for a radius; with this radius describe a circle round that end of the shaft to which the crank is affixed, having beforehand chalked over the surface, to render the circle conspicuous; this having been done, take a plumb-line, or one of the engine-nuts fastened to a piece of twine, and place the line in contact with the inner surface of the crank, and let the crank be moved round till the line is in contact with the circle described and the crank-pin at the same time. When this takes place the engine is on its centre, the crank being vertical. The probability, however, is, that the vessel will not be on an even keel; we must consequently have some way of effecting our purpose independently of the plumb-line. Let the circle be described, as before, round the centre of the shaft; next get two battens whose edges have been made quite true, and let them be connected together, so as to be at right angles to each other;* then, if the engine be a beam-engine, let one edge of the square be applied to the flange of the air-pump, the air-pump cover having been removed, and the other edge be brought into contact with the pin of the crank; we must examine whether it is in contact also with the edge of the circle previously described; if not, let the crank be moved round as before, till a contact takes place. A moment's reflection will show that when this happens the engine is on its centre. If the vessel be fitted with direct engines, we must use the flange of the cylinder instead of that of the air-pump. We should not be certain of getting a true result if we were to apply the square to the upper surface of the air-pump or cylinder-cover, instead of taking it off and applying it to the flange, because the cover may not be so true as the flange, if the joint be thicker at any one part, the flange being of necessity planed

---

* *To get two Battens at right angles to each other.*

Measure off, on a board, 17 inches in length, then open a two-foot rule, and extend it as if it were a pair of compasses, till one end is in contact with one extremity of the line, and the other end with the other extremity; the rule will then have its two legs very nearly at right angles with each other; for each side of the rule being 12 inches, the base of the triangle thus formed will be (*Euclid*, Book I., Prop. 47) $\sqrt{12^2+12^2}=\sqrt{288}=16{\cdot}97=17$ inches nearly.

Otherwise, measure off a line 5 inches long, and let the marks corresponding to 3 inches on one leg of the rule, and 4 inches on the other, be brought into contact with its two extremities; the legs of the rule will then be at right angles; for $3^2+4^2=9+16=25=5^2$: the included angle is a right angle.

The same rule will hold if a line 10 inches in length be measured, and the lengths 6 and 8 inches be brought in contact with its extremities; the included angle will be a right angle.

truly, for the purpose of getting the engine true; or we may get the extreme of the stroke by turning the cranks over the dead spaces at the top and bottom of the stroke, and making a mark at the extreme top and bottom on the piston.

After we are satisfied with the placing of the crank, let the slide be put in its place, so as to give the proper amount of "lead" at the upper port; the eccentric must next be moved round till the eccentric-rod falls into gear; then place the stop on the shaft in close contact with that on the eccentric. The crank must next be placed on the top centre, and the slide moved with the engine, so that it may be ascertained whether there is the proper amount of lead for the lower port. If less than the proper quantity, it must be increased by lengthening the slide-rod, and thus compromising the lead to some extent at the upper port, for the sake of giving more to the lower.* To adjust the stops for the reverse motion, let the eccentric-rod be disconnected from the gab-lever pin, and let the eccentric be moved round the back way, without the engine, till the rod again falls into gear. Now place the stop for the back way, and let the slide be examined at both ports by turning the engine, eccentric, and all, to see whether there is the proper amount of lead for the reverse motion at the two ports. If the engines be beam-engines, there is usually the same amount of lead (about $\frac{1}{8}$ of an inch) allowed at the top and bottom port; but more lead is required at the lower than at the upper port with direct engines; this can easily be obtained by lengthening the slide-rod when necessary; with engines of this latter class, it is usual to allow about $\frac{1}{4}$ of an inch, or more, of lead below, and about $\frac{1}{16}$ or less above the piston; thus the increase of momentum on the down-stroke, arising from the weight of the piston, etc., is overcome, and the change of motion from the down to the up-stroke is effected without

*The same thing may be accomplished by shortening or lengthening the eccentric-rod, if considered advisable by the engineer.

any violent jar to the machinery. We shall thus increase also the lead on the exhaust-side at the upper port, which is likewise an advantage in unbalanced engines. The actual amount of lead depends on the velocity with which the wheels are revolving. In locomotive engines, and all that move at high velocities, the lead must be considerable, in consequence of the great speed of the piston; the steam would be ineffective in checking the momentum, were it to enter at so late a period in these engines as in the marine engines. To take the opposite extreme, if we turn round the engine by hand, we want no power to check the momentum, because the piston is moving so slowly; and therefore the slower the piston travels, the less the amount of lead required. The lead of which we have hitherto spoken is called the lead on the steam-side, but most engines have another kind of lead; in them a communication is made with the condenser before the piston has completed its stroke, so that on what is called the steam-side of the piston there are three processes successively employed: 1. The influx of the steam; 2. The steam is cut off, and works by expansion; and 3. Before the stroke is terminated the steam is allowed a passage to the condenser. This latter will of course materially assist us in checking the momentum of the piston, for it is not only checked actively by coming into contact with fresh steam, but the force of that on the side where it was impelled is taken away. The lead is then said to be on the exhaust-side, and it is effected by taking off from the upper and lower edge of the slide; so that when one of the ports is open, the amount of lead required for the steam, the other port shall at the same time be open a little to the exhaust. In Maudslay's direct-action engines, there is considerable lead on the exhaust-side at the upper port, for the same reason that there is more lead on the steam-side at the lower port, viz., to improve the working of the engine.

We have hitherto supposed that the engines are new, or have had a thorough repair; but if the engines have been at work for three or four years, and it becomes necessary to set the slides, the slide-rod and eccentric-rod must be readjusted; because, since the brasses of the weigh-shaft and slide-rod are subject to continual friction, and therefore liable to wear, it will have the effect of depressing the slide, and so give us more than the due amount of lead at the lower port, by taking away the same quantity from the upper port. The brasses of the eccentric-ring are likewise continually wearing, which has the effect of virtually shortening the eccentric-rod. Now this will cause the slide to be elevated or depressed, according to the manner in which the gab-lever is placed on the weigh-shaft.* This latter defect may therefore exaggerate the former defect, or help to counteract it, according to the nature of the engine. We must also notice the wear of the gab and gab-lever pin; the continual jar on them as the slide-stroke is reversed produces great wear, unless they be well case-hardened, and even then it will frequently happen that one side of the pin may be much better hardened than the other, and the softer side will become most worn, and on the return of the stroke there will occur what is technically called back-lash; that is to say, the eccentric will be in motion some little time without acting on the slide. It is manifest that unless these defects of the engine be corrected, or made to compensate each other, it will be useless to attempt giving the requisite amount of lead, because an error in the motion of the slide of $\frac{1}{10}$ of an inch will be a serious thing as far as regards its lead. We will therefore proceed to show the way of correcting and adjusting the length of the eccentric-rod; to do which it will first be necessary to place the slide at the middle of its stroke.

288. *To place the Slide in the Middle of its Stroke.*

Take a batten and place it over the ports when the slide is out, and with a penknife mark off on the batten the

---

* It will depress the slide if the gab-lever hang down, and elevate it if the gab-lever stand up.

depths of the ports; this will give us not only the depth of the port, but the distance between them; let this be placed over the slide, so that the *cover* on the steam-side at top and bottom shall be equal, and we shall get the amount of steam cover that the slide has; shall also ascertain if there be any cover or lap on the exhaust-side, and whether positive or negative. If the gab-lever is at right angles to the eccentric-rod, when the slide is at half-stroke, and the amount of lead is the same at both ports, the laps on the steam-side must be equal to each other

289. *To adjust the Eccentric-rod.*

Place the slide in the middle of its stroke; then let the *throw* of the eccentric be placed in a line with the eccentric-rod. Open a pair of compasses to any convenient distance, and placing one point in the centre of the gab-lever pin, with the other make a mark on the eccentric-rod. Then let the eccentric be turned half round, so as to have the throw again placed in a line with the eccentric-rod; we see that by so doing the gab must have passed over the gab-lever pin. Take the compasses (opened to the same extent as before), and make a mark on the eccentric-rod on the other side of the gab-lever pin; the centre of the gab should be the middle point between these two marks. If that be found not to be the case, the eccentric-rod must be altered accordingly. This is to be effected where the rod is connected to the band or ring by putting on a washer, or, on the other hand, by filing off the part of the bolt that screws up the ring.

290. *Remarks on the Alteration of Slides.*

In speaking of the adjustment of slides, we have not said a word concerning any alterations to be made in the slide itself—such as by taking off some of the lap, or otherwise altering it; and the reason of this is, that such an alteration should never be made without the knowledge and approval of the authorities who are responsible for the ship. We must bear in mind that the slide is regulated by the capacities of the boiler; and that if any lap be taken off with the view of allowing the steam to be admitted through a greater portion of the stroke, the boiler might become exhausted, or it would require the fires to be urged in a wasteful manner to keep up the supply. It would be an improvement to take off a considerable portion, if not all, the lap from many engines driving paddle-wheels, if the engines are fitted with expansive gear, so that the steam can be cut off by expansion under ordinary circumstances by that gear; and then the full power of the steam may be admitted at extraordinary times during the whole stroke, or nearly so. Because in paddle-wheel vessels the number of revolutions is sensibly diminished from any cause producing greater resistance; as, for instance, against opposing wind and sea, or when towing; and when this happens, although the boiler generates its usual quantity of steam, it cannot enter the cylinder, and consequently escapes by the safety-valve. Since the lap on the slide gives it the character of *permanent* expansive gear, this cannot be remedied at the time; but if, on the other hand, we had been working on one of the grades of the expansive gear, it could have been detached; and if there were no fixed lap on the slide, the steam would enter the cylinder instead of being lost in the atmosphere. There are many cases in which the additional work thus to be obtained would extricate a ship from a perilous position; yet still no engineer or commanding-officer would be authorized thus to tamper with the slides without the sanction of his employers, whether it be the Admiralty or the Company to which the vessel belongs.

When lap is taken away from the steam-side of the slide, some portion of the face should also be taken away from the exhaust-side, otherwise the uncondensed steam would produce too much effect in checking the motion of the piston. And it must be remembered that, when any alteration is made in the slide-face, whether it be reduced or added to, the driving-stops on the intermediate shaft must be altered also. If the *lap* is *increased*, the stops must be advanced; and if *decreased*, they must be put back.

291. *On Cleaning out and Scaling the Boiler.*

It is sometimes found to be difficult to get the scale out from the bottom of a boiler, because there is so little space under the flues and fireplaces, and a rake cannot be employed to extract it; this will be found particularly to be the case in the angles or corners of the boiler, for the rake will only jam it up into them. Some boilers will not admit a man underneath the flues and fireplaces to get the scale out; and yet we must be particular in seeing that the boiler is quite clean; for any scale that may remain keeps the heat away from the water, and injures the plate, and serves as a nucleus for any other deposit. The best instrument to use is a slice; this can be forced under the mass, and bring it away by portions; and should any parts of it hang about the water-ways, they should be sliced down and hauled out from the mud-hole. Moreover, it is difficult to get out the stuff in consequence of the interference of the stays supporting the fireplaces and flues above the bottom of the boiler. This difficulty exists more in flue than in tubular boilers. Our great object is not to allow any scale to remain in the boiler to form a nucleus.

After a boiler has been cleaned out, the blow-out cocks should be carefully examined, and the passages leading to them: for if the pipe go in a direct manner through the bottom of the boiler, the scale taken from the boiler is apt to get into the pipe and choke it; the blow-out cocks should be opened to let the water force it out; this should be done before the man-hole door is on, to make sure that they are clear. This seems to be the proper place to call attention to the fact of the blow-out pipes choking when a vessel is at anchor in a roadstead, or any other place where she is rolling. If there be ever so little scale in the boilers, it will find its way into the blow-out pipe. This will take place when the boilers are what is called empty; that is, when there is merely a little water remaining after the boilers are blown out, and washing about from side to side, and drifting portions of scale with it. When the ——— was employed on the north coast of Spain, and at anchor in Sebastian Bay, where there is more or less swell setting in, it was a common thing to find the blow-out pipe of the front boiler choked; but as there were pipes to the after boiler, and circulating pipes fitted, the front boiler could be filled from the others, for the four boilers constituted but one in four pieces; quite a hard mass was at times extracted from the pipe, the heat having had the effect of solidifying it. To prevent the scale working into the pipe, the boiler should be pumped dry. If this cannot be done, the mud-hole doors must be taken off to empty the boiler thoroughly. A coarse grating ought to be fitted over the pipe, and thus large pieces of scale would be prevented from entering the pipe. This can be made in the following way: Two strips of iron should be placed at right angles to each other, and bent over to form a hemisphere, with a bolt screwed into the top; these can be placed over the blow-out pipe, and the bolt unscrewed, so as to bring the head of the bolt hard against the under part of the flue or fireplace, for the sake of keeping it in its place. In the figure, A A is the bottom of the fireplace or flue, B the blow-out pipe, C C the bottom of the boiler, E E one of the strips of iron forming the grating, D the screw-bolt. Now if E E have a greater span than the blow-out pipe, that its shoulders may rest on the bottom of the boiler, it is clear that if we bring the head of the bolt against A A, E E will be pressed down, and secured over the pipe. The strips should evidently be made of the same metal as the boiler, for fear of a galvanic action being set up. Copper was employed in one vessel

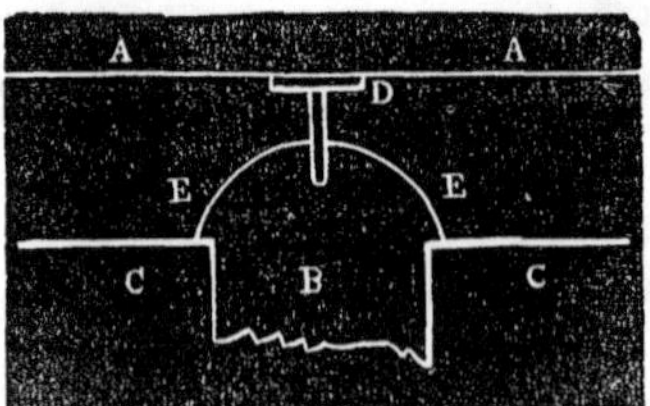

fitted with an iron boiler, and after a time the pipe broke away from the boiler. On examination, the pipe appeared so soft that it could be cut with a knife; the iron had been converted into plumbago.

292. *Rust-Joints.*

This kind of joints is made by mixing together cast-iron borings, sal-ammoniac, and sulphur; it is then caulked into the joints, and when dry becomes a hard mass, perfectly steam and air-tight.

293. *Stopping Cracks in Boilers, and repairing Tubes.*

Cracks generally arise from blisters, which are usually caused by imperfect union of the iron when rolled. When a crack is discovered in the flue of a boiler, it may frequently be prevented from extending farther by drilling a hole at each extremity of the crack, and putting in a rivet. If the crack be of any considerable length, let more rivets be put in, and well riveted down; this will prevent the crack from spreading, and when caulked, will generally put a stop to the leakage; but if the caulking be found inefficient, let some lead be driven in and caulked. Wood may also be used as a temporary expedient to stop leaks in boilers. In patching a boiler, the piece *cut out* should not have angular corners; for if there are such, it will be found that the plate will crack at the angular points. The patch ought to be put on in the inside of the boiler, to prevent its becoming over-heated.*

---

* We have recommended in p. 230 that leaky tubes should be plugged up at their ends with wood. This is only a temporary expedient; a more permanent repair will be to get a smaller tube from some other vessel or dockyard, and place it inside the leaky one, setting on the ends with a conical mandril to render it water-tight. This goes on the supposition that all the spare tubes of the vessel are used up, and that no other of the same size can be obtained.

294. *Repairing the Fire-bridges and Ash-pits.*

Should it become necessary to repair the fire-bridges at any time when in harbor, great care should be taken, when made of iron, if a patch be put on the top, that the piece put on be not hollowed out below, so as to prevent the free escape of steam; that is to say, it should not be convexed upwards. Otherwise, the flame acting on the patch converts the water beneath it into steam, which has a tendency to rise, and instead of ascending to the surface of the water, becomes locked (as it is generally termed) in the hollow; and, as we know, steam, like all gases, is a non-conductor of heat (see p. 25), consequently the iron becomes over-heated, and burns. Fire-bridges have given much trouble when this has not been attended to. In a well-constructed fire-bridge that has a good incline, there is no difficulty; for the steam having free egress, the bridge is preserved. The same remarks hold good respecting repairs to the bottoms of ash-pits; the patch or plate, indeed, should present a rather concave appearance to one looking down on it. If made quite flat at first, the hot ashes being on the upper side and the water below, the upper surface will always be hotter than the lower, and the effect of the heat will therefore be to expand the upper surface more than the lower, and consequently it will shortly present a convex appearance within the ash-pit; or, speaking technically, will *buckle* towards the fire. Hence round-bottomed ash-pits are to be preferred to others. Messrs. Boulton and Watt used to make the water-ways of their boilers wider at the top than at the bottom, to give a free upward motion to the steam.

295. *Staying the Boilers.*

In old boilers, stays were interposed between the top of the fireplaces or flues to support the shell, and they were curved a little, like a very elongated **S**, so that if exhaustion take place at any time in the boiler, and the reverse-valve did not act, they would spring, and the chance of injury to the crowns of the fireplaces or flues was diminished. This hardly affected the tension of the stay so far as the outward pressure was concerned; for if only slightly bent, it would require an enormous strain lengthways to straighten it. Of late years tops of boilers have been stayed from the bottom, and not from the crowns, of the fireplaces, and the stays are straight.

296. *Increasing the Load on the Safety-valve.*

If it be deemed advisable to increase the load on the safety-valve, it will be necessary to increase in the same ratio the weights on the *escape-valves* of the cylinders and the *overflow-valves* of the feed-pumps. In some cases the weights are of iron; and, as space is sometimes an object, it may be as well to ascertain whether the same object may not be gained by substituting a leaden for an iron weight.

297. *Boiler Water-glass.*

It is often found in new vessels, that the water in the gauge-glasses is unsteady. This arises from the high state of ebullition of the water in the neighborhood of the lower end of the gauge-glass, which causes a mixture of steam and water to be found at times in the glass, and the water-level is uncertain. When this happens, an attempt should be made when in harbor to remedy it. This can generally be done by leading up a pipe from the upper end into that part of the boiler where the steam is purer, and also conducting another pipe from the lower end towards the bottom of the boiler into the more solid water. It should not, therefore, terminate over the top of the fireplaces, where the heat is great and the ebullition strong. Gauge-glasses and gauge-cocks should always be placed as nearly as possible directly over the keel, where they will be least influenced by the rolling motion. The pitching and 'scending motion is but of little consequence, the length of the boiler bearing such a small proportion to the length of the ship that the water will not rise or fall much on that account.

The gauge-glass should always be placed in that part of the boiler which is in a plane at *right angles* to the keel, to prevent an inconvenience arising from the rolling of the ship.

298. *Internal Feed-pipe.*

Let the internal feed-pipe be examined, to ascertain whether it is sufficiently under water; otherwise the steam will be apt to get into it, and cause the boiler to feed badly, and make a sharp, cracking noise in the pipe, if the valves of the feed-pump are not tight. The feed-water should not be discharged near the surface of the water, because it checks the ebullition. If the pipe do not go far down, it will be a great annoyance to the engineer, when connected with boilers that are apt to prime.

299. *The Steam-gauge to be examined occasionally.*

The steam-gauge should be taken off occasionally, when in harbor, and cleaned out; for the water is apt to get into it, and render it an incorrect indicator of the steam-pressure. The leg attached to the boiler will oxidate, and therefore from wasting the bore will increase, so that a depression of one inch in that leg will cause more than an elevation of one inch in the other. Therefore, if the rod had risen one inch, the difference of level will be less than two inches, and consequently the real pressure in the boiler will be less than the indicated pressure as shown by the gauge.*

300. *Replacing the Fire-bars.*

When putting the fire-bars in a boiler, the side ones should be placed close alongside the fire-place, that the fire may not be too brisk between it and the iron plate,

* Thus, let the radius of the bore when new be r, and let the radius of the leg in contact with the boiler become r' by oxidation;

least it get over-heated and the water be driven away to the other side, when the plate will crack and the boiler become leaky; this is more particularly to be attended to when using Welsh coal, from the intense heat given out in the fireplaces; whereas, with more bituminous coal, the heat is given out in the tubes or flues to a greater extent.

301. *Sweeping the Funnel, and the attention requisite to be paid to it.*

When the tubes are swept, it is at times necessary to clean the funnel; this necessity does not arise generally because of any fear of the draught becoming lessened; for a *considerable* quantity of soot lodged in the funnel would have but little influence: but if allowed to stay there, and the vessel remain at anchorage any considerable time, especially if it rain, and the funnel be not covered over

---

and suppose the mercury to fall through the space x when it rises one inch in the other leg.

$$\therefore \quad \pi r'^2 x = \pi r^2 . 1$$

or

$$r'^2 x = r^2$$

$$x = \frac{r^2}{r'^2}$$

$$x + 1 = \frac{r'^2 + r'^2}{r'^2}$$

$$\frac{x+1}{2} = \frac{r^2 + r'^2}{2 r'^2}$$

But $x + 1$ is the difference in level caused by the rise of 1 inch in the index, and $\therefore \frac{x+1}{2}$ = the number of pounds pressure in the steam corresponding to the rise of 1 inch. Hence, when the pointer rises an inch, the difference in pressure in pounds is $\frac{r^2 + r'^2}{2 r'^2}$

Example.—Let $r = \frac{1}{2}$, and $r' = \frac{1}{2} + \frac{1}{16} = \frac{9}{16}$

$$\therefore \quad \frac{r^2 + r'^2}{2 r'^2} = \frac{\frac{1}{4} + \frac{81}{256}}{2 \times \frac{81}{256}} = \frac{64 + 81}{162} = \frac{145}{162} = 89 \text{ lb.}$$

the wet will loosen the hard crust of the soot, and the first time the fires are lighted, the vibration of the boiler will detach it, and cause it to fall about the deck; so that it will be essential to get rid of it while the vessel is in harbor. If much time cannot be spared, the greater portion of the soot may be removed by firing a pistol or musket up;* the vibration caused by this is sufficient to shake off that which would otherwise become loose. But if time permit, the better plan is to sweep the funnel in the same manner as the flues. The funnel should likewise be kept well tarred over on the outside, for the sake of preserving it. Coal-tar is mostly used; this looks well; but it is necessary to repeat it often, nor does it protect the funnel for any length of time. Stockholm or vegetable tar, mixed with a small portion of turpentine, will be found a much better material; it will preserve the funnel better, and last much longer. Hot salt water is sometimes mixed with the tar instead of turpentine; but this probably renders the funnel more susceptible of rust. When first coated over with Stockholm tar, the color is bad; but as it dries it turns to a good black color. A good mixture may be obtained by using Stockholm tar combined with an equal quantity of mineral tar. In harbor a canvas funnel-top is used to prevent the rain from running down the funnel and oxidizing the uptake and smoke-box, etc.; or, which is still better, an iron top, the edge of which is made to overhang, and is raised a few inches, to allow egress for the smoke when fires are lighted to preserve the boilers.

302. *Coal-Bunkers to be examined.*

If lined with copper, it will sometimes be found that the ends of the stays which are screwed or driven into the ship's side will be eaten away by galvanic action. The bunkers of a ship have been known to give way from this cause; so much so as to cause apprehensions that the whole

* Care should be taken that blazing soot do not fall down on the band.

contents of them would be discharged into the engine-room. The system of cross-stays is objectionable for this reason, and likewise because they are likely to be bent and drawn when struck by large masses of coal. Angle-iron has been found sufficiently strong and much more suitable; this would of course be riveted up and down the inside of the coal-bunkers. Whenever the weather permits, the coal-box plates should be taken off, to allow the gas that is evolved from the coal to pass off through the gratings. The gas alluded to is chiefly carburetted hydrogen, the fire-damp of our mines, and the gas commonly burnt in our shops, etc.

303. *Coaling Ship.*

The coal remaining in the bunkers should be trimmed towards the doors, or at all events levelled, to be used first; for coals that have been long in the bunkers lose much of their value, owing to the high temperature of the place in which they are confined. The fresh coal should be received as dry as possible. Welsh coal takes up less room than north-country coal. In voyages of considerable length, it would be advisable, where it can be managed, to have a mixture of the above coals: steam will be got up more speedily, and less wood will be required; whereas if none but Welsh coal is used, much wood will be required for lighting fires. Again, with this mixture the fires can be worked thin. For surveying-vessels, and others in which stoppages are frequent, north-country coal is best, because in pushing the fire backwards and bringing them forwards so many ashes are not made. With tubular boilers, in which an accumulation of soot is prejudicial, a smaller amount of north-country coal should be used.

304. *Tools and Rubbish of all kinds should be taken carefully from the Boilers after Repairs.*

Whenever boilers are opened for any purpose, the stokers should not be permitted to take oakum or pieces of wood with them into the boiler to sit on; for these sub stances are apt to be let down between the water-spaces or tubes, and neglected; remaining there, they form a nucleus for deposit, and will ultimately prevent the water from coming in contact with the iron; moreover, they are apt to get to the bottom of the boiler, and, from the vortex occasioned by blowing off, to find their way into the pipe, and completely choke it up. After a vessel has been under repair, the boilers should be examined most carefully, that any thing that may have been left in them may be hauled out through the mud-hole door: rivet-bags have been known to have been left behind. All substances made of hemp should be taken out with care; for calcareous substances seem to have a peculiar affinity for that material. Spare rivets, or pieces of loose iron, are to be looked for. Stokers have been known to put their dirty engine-room clothes in the boiler to give them a good boiling; this should by no means be allowed, for they may get adrift, and stop up the pipes.

305. *Impure Air in the Boilers.*

When the man-hole doors are taken off with a view to sending men in to examine the boilers, the gauge-cocks should be opened, and also the safety-valves; for if all these should be closed it will be found that the air will become vitiated, and after a little time candles or lamps will burn with difficulty, proving that the air will become unfit for respiration.

306. *Screw-gearing in Screw-steamers.*

When screw-steamers are fitted with gearings connecting the engine with the propeller, the gearing should be examined occasionally to discover whether the cogs and teeth are defective. If any of the cogs are loose, they may be secured in their places with pieces of fine canvas and white-lead. The gearing becomes much worn after a time, and it will be necessary to trim up the cogs; the pitch-lines should also be looked to, to see whether they agree. Care should be taken that the cogs do not bottom on the pinions as the shaft-journals wear away: this has been found to be the case in some instances.

307. *Lubricating the Gearing in Screw-vessels.*

Tallow is sometimes used to lubricate the gearing, but it has the disadvantage of becoming hard; moreover, it is difficult to clean the parts of the machinery with which it comes in contact; it is better, therefore, to use a mixture of soft-soap and black-lead: this will be found to lessen the abrasion and noise, and will not be attended with the same difficulties as tallow.

308. *Paddles.*

Some paddles are fitted with two plates to them, one at the back to receive the nip of the arm, and the other the nuts, or else the paddles will be weakened by the screwing up. The hook-bolts should not have their hooks too long, in order that a *few* turns out of the nut may suffice to let the bolt be unhooked, that the boards may be unshipped, bolts and all, and be reshipped with the bolts in; otherwise the bolts may be lost overboard in shipping and unshipping, and time certainly will be wasted in performing this operation when perhaps every moment is most precious. The nuts of the paddle-bolts should be all of one size, that the same spanner may fit them all: much confusion and loss of time will be avoided by attending to this circumstance.

309. *Preserving Boilers when not in use.*

A boiler when not in use should either be *perfectly* dry, or plenty of water should be kept in it: mere moisture is very detrimental to iron, chiefly because the solution of copper from the internal steam-pipe, feed-pipe, etc., carried down with it to the bottom of the boiler, is not so diluted as when it mixes with a boilerful of water. Fires should be lighted at intervals to dry the boilers. Coal-tar, red-lead, and tallow, etc., have been tried as coatings to prevent oxidation; but many parts, from being difficult of access, will escape notice. We would recommend a trial of the following, which has proved successful. Mix a quantity of soft-soap with some hot fresh water, and pour this into the empty boiler; then open the blow-out cock, and let the water run up to the top of the tubes or flues: the solution being carried by these means to every part of the water-space, oxidation will be suspended. There should be about 3 lbs. of soap to every ton of water. Those parts which are above the water, such as the steam-chest, uptake, etc., should be coated with soft-soap and linseed-oil. For this part mix 2 lbs. of soap with every gallon of oil; and let this be put on before the boiler is filled.

310. *Fitting Mud-hole Doors.*

In many steamers the mud-hole doors are fitted on the outside; but it is a better plan to have them fitted on the inside, and the internal pressure will then assist in keeping them in their places. The Meteor some years since returned from Gibraltar with the bolt broken off the mud-hole door, and there was nothing but the pressure of the steam and water to keep it in its place; it had leaked at starting, and on screwing it up it broke off. Now had it been fitted on the outside, the vessel must have been detained, to say nothing of the risk arising from letting the water pour out of the hole into the engine-room. Since the publication of the first edition of this work, a sad accident occurred on board a screw-steamer at London Bridge: the mud-hole door was fitted on the outside, and when getting up the steam, the joint was discovered to be leaky, which the engineer endeavored to remedy by screwing it up; the bolt broke, and the door being forced off, the engineer was driven by the rush of scalding water to the opposite side of the stoke-hole, and scalded to death.

311. *Getting up the Steam occasionally when in Harbor.*

The more any person is in the habit of watching the working of engines that have been remaining still any considerable time, the more he will become convinced of the necessity of having the steam up at short intervals. The steam should be got up every two or three weeks, and the engines worked for a short time. There is not so great an expenditure of coal in this as would at first sight be supposed; considerably less will be used than would be in the inefficient working of the engine, leaving out the wear and tear arising from the rusty state of the machinery. When the engines are thus worked for the sake of keeping them in good order, it will, of course, take place in harbor, or elsewhere where the ship is upright, and not rolling about; and it will not be necessary to have so much water in the boiler as otherwise would be needful, nor will it be important to have so many nor such active fires. One boiler will be sufficient for our purpose; and with a small quantity of water it will soon boil, and will serve to keep the other boilers dry. Let the fires burn slowly by closing the dampers, to allow the water to absorb the heat and not permit it to pass up the funnel. There will be two advantages attending this plan; less fuel will be used, and it will make little or no smoke to black the rigging and sails. The small coal may be used for this purpose; and keeping the fires thus, the steam will soon be got up well enough to give a few round turns to the engine; and this is enough for the purpose. An engine that has stood by two or three months without having the steam up, can hardly be said to be in an efficient state, and the coal used in working it will be paid for tenfold. Moreover, in cold, damp weather, the good effect it will have upon the ship will be very great, both on the score of health, by driving off all damps, and exhausting the noxious vapors from the holds, to say nothing of the preservation of the ship by drying up the wet about the timbers of the bilge.

What has here been said goes on the supposition that

the vessel is supposed to be in readiness to move in the usual time of lighting the fires, in which case the engines must be kept in perfect order; but if the vessel be supposed not to be wanted for any considerable time, it is generally allowed that the better plan is to have the boilers and engines open, to allow the air to keep them dry.

In the latter case, from ten to twelve hours warning may be necessary to enable the engineers to put on the man-hole and mud-hole doors, and replace slides (if taken out), and to repack them and the glands.

It is, however, indispensable that the engines should not be allowed to remain in the same position for any length of time; if, therefore, permission be not given to get the steam up at intervals, means must be adopted to move the engines by turning the wheels by hand.

312. *Turning round the Wheels by hand.*

With a balanced engine this requires but little force—a few hands in the wheel at the extremities of the arms are sufficient; but with an unbalanced engine, tackles must be used, care being taken to raise all the floats out of the water that had been previously immersed.

313. *Turning-Gear.*

Gearing is now fitted to our screw-ships to turn the engines. A wheel is keyed to the propeller-shaft abaft the engines, with an endless screw-gearing in it; a lever is connected with this screw, and a motion being given to it, the whole mass of machinery is moved, the wheel and screw-pinion being so proportioned that sufficient power is obtained.

314. *Raising Cylinder-covers by Tackles.*

This is the usual mode of raising cylinder-covers: As a great strain is required to raise them, the blocks must be arranged so as to grant the greatest purchase. Before the eye-bolts are screwed into the cover, insert pieces of iron under the flange, that the bolts, when screwed in, may press on it; and then, on screwing them in, the cover will be separated from the flange of the cylinder. No one should attempt to work under cylinder-covers when suspended in this way, or supported in any temporary manner, for fear of accidents. They may be supported by two props of stout wood resting on the piston and lashed to the piston-rod.

315. *To get the Cylinder-cover of an Engine into its place by the help of Steam, supposing it to be lashed to the Cross-head; or to raise it by a similar process.*

To do this, we will suppose that the pistons are in working condition within the cylinder, and that the engines likewise are in working order, with the exception of the cylinder-covers. Let us suppose the engine which has its cover raised to be on its top centre. Let both engines be blown through, and a vacuum created in the condenser. Now one engine being on its centre, the other will be at the middle of its stroke. Let the slide of *this latter* engine be moved *carefully* by hand, to effect a communication between the condenser and the lower part of the cylinder; the atmospheric pressure acting on the top will then force the piston of this engine to the bottom of its stroke, and the other piston will now be half-way down. Next perform the same process with the other engine, but very gradually, for fear of letting it down too quickly; and the cover which was before half-way down will come into the required position. The same method may be employed to raise the cylinder-covers by the help of the steam. The piston of the engine whose cover is to be raised being at the bottom of the cylinder, lash the cover to the cross-head, and admit steam above the piston of the other engine which is at half-stroke. As the joint has to be broken, this must of course be done carefully. Then, when the starting engine is at the bottom centre, introduce steam under the piston whose cover is off, and raise it to the point required.

If it be necessary to raise both covers, the second one should be lashed when the first piston is half-way up, and then, when this piston is at the top, the other will be half-way up. The break on the wheels will control the motion, and secure them when high enough. Some modern engines have *man-hole doors* in the cylinder-covers, which can be taken off to effect repairs of the piston. These remarks however, apply only to paddle-engines.

316. *To ascertain if the piston of an engine is tight.*

An engineer is apt to suppose, when the engine does not perform its functions according to his expectation, that the piston is leaky, and thus allows some of the steam to pass from one side to the other without executing any work. This can be ascertained when the vessel arrives in port, or whenever the engine is stopped. Let the lower steam-port be opened for steam, and at the same time open the grease-cocks in the cylinder-cover. Now it is clear, if the steam can pass between the edge of the piston and the cylinder, it will come up through the grease-cups, and make itself visible in the engine-room. The engine should remain stationary a small space of time; for if the leakage be small, it will be some time before the escape of steam can be observed.

317. *Piston loose on the Rod.*

If the piston is loose, and it be impossible to stop and secure it, the steam should be throttled for that engine, to lessen its force on first entering. When tightening the piston on the rod, care must be taken, in driving the key up, that it is really acted upon; that is to say, that there is what is technically called draught in the key-way; and secondly, that it is not driven up so hard as to split the piston, as has been done in some instances. Pistons that are secured by a nut and screw need no precaution. They should be screwed up as tight as possible.

318. *To separate parts of an Engine that have become rusted together.*

Heat is the agent to be employed for this purpose, and the readiest plan is to make a fire round the part; but if that be not enough, a mould of sand may be made round it, and molten metal run into the recess left for that purpose. Heated pigs of ballast, slabs of iron, etc., may perhaps answer the purpose.

319. *Blowing through when the Blow-valve is injured, or in case it be not fitted.*

Let the slide be moved so as to open one of the ports; by this process we shall fill the cylinder with steam: then let the slide be reversed, so as to fill the cylinder with steam on the other side. By so doing, that which was first admitted to the cylinder will pass into the condenser. The cold water in the condenser will gradually condense it, and it will therefore be ineffective at first; but by continuing the process, the water will be more and more heated, until at length, from being no longer condensed, the steam will act on the water, and drive it out of the condenser. This will, of course, be a slow process; but it can eventually be accomplished by this method, and it can be resorted to when other plans fail, or if the blow-valves have become injured and useless.

320. *Blowing through delayed by very cold weather.*

In very cold weather there is such a vast difference between the temperature of the steam and that of the atmosphere within the engine-room, that steam is very rapidly condensed in the steam-pipe as it passes from the boiler to the cylinder. In the Bee, the time that elapsed before the steam could reach the cylinder was on one occasion delayed so long that it was for a time imagined the stop-valve of the boiler was closed. The vessel had lain some time without having the steam up; and as the temperature was very low, the damp in the steam-pipe had become frozen hard, forming a layer of ice round the inner surface of the pipe. Now, although the steam-valve was loaded to 7 lbs., and steam was at the time blowing off freely from the steam-funnel, yet it was condensed as rapidly as it passed over from the boiler. This was ascertained by passing the hand along the pipe, when it was discovered that there was a clear line of demarcation between the part occupied by the steam and that which still continued frozen, the one being hot and the other cold; and it was interesting to notice how gradually the steam prevailed over the ice, till it came to the jacket, when it rushed in violently, and the engine started into motion. Probably this delay might have been avoided if the pipe had been coated with some good non-conductor, such as felt; for the plan has been adopted since that time, and the same thing has never happened again.

321. *Attention to be paid to Engines driving the Screw-Propeller.*

CRANK-BEARINGS.—The crank-bearings of those engines which act directly on the screw-shaft (that is to say, without the intervention of a driving wheel) require great attention; for it will be seen that, as the rotary motion is given to the screw, the necessary reaction of the water being in a line with the keel, and therefore in a line with the shaft, great friction is brought on the sides of the brasses of the connecting-rods; for although the cranks are short and rigid, still they will spring, and in so doing will nip the sides of the brasses, unless the thrust of the screw-shaft be received abaft the engines. In some cases it has been received abaft the stern-post, that the external water might keep it cool. In all screw-boat engines pipes should be brought from the sea-injection to every bearing, to let the water run on the bearings if necessary; for if oil will not keep the bearing cool, water will, because it boils at a lower temperature, and will carry off the heat from the bearing in a latent state. Any one who has observed the good effects of water on a hot bearing must have noticed its superiority over oil in such cases. The good effects of sulphur arise from the same cause; it fuses at a low temperature, and so, like the water, carries off the heat.

In small steamers of easy draught of water, and fitted with the screw, the three-threaded screw will be found more effective in a sea-way, because it takes a greater hold of the water, and the engine is sure to have some part of one of the blades immersed, and always meets with some resistance, instead of flying off, as it is apt to do with a two-bladed screw when the vessel is going head to wind, or before it; but the two-threaded screw will be found the best in still water, and in large deep vessels, such as our line-of-battle ships, because it does not produce so much broken water as the other.

In starting screw-ships, where the draught of water is not great, the engine should at first be set in motion with but little steam, which should be supplied with greater freedom as the vessel gathers way, or otherwise there will be a large amount of slip, from the ship not getting instantaneously any considerable speed. Something similar to this may be noticed on the railroads in starting a locomotive engine, where the wheels slip, or *skid*, as it is termed, upon the rails on the first entrance of the steam.

Screw-ships ought to have a water-tight bulkhead fitted to the fore-side of the stern-post; so that if they should become leaky, the water would not come into the bilge. A hand-pump should be fitted, to pump this out in harbor A pipe, with a cock in it, should also be fitted near the bottom, and the other end be passed into the condenser, that the water may be taken out for the use of the engine while under steam without the labor of pumping.

While in harbor, the cylinders of screw-vessels which lie horizontally ought to be kept particularly dry, other wise water will remain in the lower parts of the concave surface, and in a short time rust and injure the cylinder, and will thus render it oval instead of circular, because the weight of the piston is on the lower part; therefore, when the engine has done its work, plenty of tallow should be put into the cylinder and slides, to protect them against the action of the water.

The screw-propeller should be disconnected from the shaft occasionally, to prevent it *setting* fast, which is found to be the case if it be allowed to remain for any considerable time. The gear by which this is effected should also be looked to, to see if dependence can be placed upon it when the screw is up.

CHAPTER IX.

MISCELLANEOUS.

322. *Methods of measuring the Efficiency of Steam-engines.*

THE efficiency of an engine is evidently measured by the amount of *useful* work it can accomplish in a given time. Now the *useful* work of an engine is the product of the resistance it can overcome multiplied into the space through which that resistance is moved in a unit of time. Hence if P represent the number of pounds a steam-engine overcomes, and v the number of feet through which that resistance is moved in one minute, $P \times v$ is the useful work or *power* of the engine. But it is found that this product for any tolerably-sized engine requires a great number of figures to express it; and it is on that account not only cumbrous, but beyond the powers of the mind to realize at the first glance; on which account it was thought advisable by Watt to divide the product so obtained by some large number, and so to obtain the result in fewer figures more readily appreciable. The first engines made by Watt and others superseded the use of horses in pumping water out of mines; for which reason it was proposed to compare the work of an engine with that which it was supposed a horse would do. This quantity, *i.e.*, the product of the weight a horse would raise in lbs. multiplied into the height in feet through which he would raise it in a minute, was considered to be 33000; and therefore since the time of Watt the measure of an engine's efficiency has has always hitherto been $\frac{P \times v}{33000}$, and this is called the horse-power of the engine.

Mr. Atherton, chief engineer of Woolwich dockyard, in

a recent work on the capability of steam-vessels, remarks that the foregoing measure has, in marine engineering, become practically superseded, inasmuch as the term horse-power, as now applied in marine-engine contracts and practice, does not specially determine or limit the gross working power of the engines; indeed, it is a well-known and expected fact, that the actual power of an engine is frequently 3 or 4 times that which the nominal power would give. He, therefore, to obviate in some measure this defect, proposes to get a new constant, instead of the number 33000, by getting the mean gross effect of several of our best marine engines, and dividing this by the mean of their nominal horse-powers. The quotient thus obtained, after deducting 15 per cent., gives 132000, which number he uses instead of 33000.

323. *Duty of an Engine.*

The duty of an engine is a term used to express the effect produced by a given quantity of fuel. One chief distinction between the power of an engine and its duty lies in the fact, that power has reference to time, but duty has not. The duty of an engine would be the same whether the engine were to work for an hour, a day, or a month, whereas the power developed would vary as the time. In estimating the duty of land-engines, the measure usually taken is the result obtained by dividing the effective horse-power by the consumption of fuel in the same time, which gives the power developed by a unit of fuel. This is expressed by $\frac{\text{effective horse-power}}{\text{consumption of fuel}}$; whereas for marine engines the inverse of this is usually adopted, the duty being measured by $\frac{\text{consumption of fuel}}{\text{effective horse-power}}$. In either case it is useful, as affording a comparison of the economy of engines and boilers of different construction, irrespective of their size, and is more immediately a test of the merit of the *boiler* than of the *engine*.

324. *To obtain the Horse-power of an Engine.*

1. If an indicator can be used, the readiest plan in an engine actually at work is to get by means of the indicator the pressure on the surface of the piston: from this a deduction must be made on account of the pressure of the uncondensed steam and the friction of the engine; the result will give the effective pressure. (See *Indicator and Dynamometer*, p. 38, second edition.)

Again: the space passed over by the piston in one minute may be easily got, by multiplying the number of revolutions of the engine by twice the length of the stroke.

Let now P' be the effective pressure on the piston,
v' its velocity:

Then the effect produced by the steam $= P' v'$ (neglecting friction and useless resistances).

But by the principles of mechanics, $P' v' = P v$.

Hence the horse-power of the engine $= \frac{P' v'}{33000}$.

325. *On Mercantile or nominal Horse-power.*

The method proposed in the last article is evidently only applicable after the engine has been made and commenced its functions. But it is necessary to have some definite rule for gaining an idea of the power of an engine to be constructed, otherwise contracts could not be entered into between the manufacturer and the party for whom the engine is to be made. And therefore, in sending in tenders for engines for Her Majesty's ships, the calculation of the power is made by allowing the effective pressure on each square inch of the piston to be 7 lbs., and the speed of the piston for engines fitted with paddles is as follows:

For	3 ft.	0 in.	stroke,	30	revolutions	per min. =	180	ft.	per min.
	3	6	"	27	"	"	189		"
	4	0	"	$24\frac{1}{2}$	"	"	196		"
	4	6	"	$22\frac{2}{3}$	"	"	204		"
	5	0	"	21	"	"	210		"
	5	6	"	$19\frac{7}{11}$	"	"	216		"

For 6 ft.	0 in.	stroke,	$18\frac{1}{2}$	revolutions	per min.	=222	ft. per min.
6	6	"	$17\frac{5}{13}$	"	"	226	"
7	0	"	$16\frac{1}{2}$	"	"	231	"
7	6	"	$15\frac{11}{15}$	"	"	236	"
8	0	"	15	"	"	240	"
8	6	"	$14\frac{6}{17}$	"	"	244	"
9	0	"	$13\frac{2}{3}$	"	"	247	"

And hence the following rule adopted by the Admiralty for horse-power:

$$\frac{7 \times \cdot 7854 \times d^2 \times \text{feet per minute}}{33000}$$

$$\text{or} \qquad \frac{d^2 \times \text{feet per minute}}{6000} = \text{nominal horse-power.}$$

It is, however, expected that the engines, when tried and tested by the indicator, will exhibit a considerably higher result than that obtained by this formula.

326. *To find the Horse-power from the Evaporation of the Boiler.*

The following rules, adapted to logarithmic computation, are formed from valuable investigations by Comte de Pambour, the substance of which is given below. They are, however, attended with great difficulties in practical application, from the fact that the effective evaporation of engines is not known. If we knew how much pure steam a given boiler is capable of evaporating in a given time, these formulæ would give us every thing that we could desire; but unfortunately this is still a desideratum; and even if the supply of water to boilers of various capabilities were ascertained with the view of getting the desired result, still we must remember that the steam generally used in engines is surcharged with watery vapor, and therefore not altogether effective in producing elastic pressure. And the state of the steam will vary from time to time in the same engine according to the resistance the engine meets with: for it is pretty evident the purer and more elastic the steam, the better the effect. The table of relative volumes and pressures (Table A, Appendix) will not therefore apply. (See also *Indicator and Dynamometer*, 2d ed. p. 43.) But since the investigations and rules which follow proceed on the hypothesis of the applicability of that table to the practical working of engines, the theoretical evaporation deduced from it must be used in the computations that follow. The investigations connected with this subject are given below, and although independently made, are based on those of Comte de Pambour.* But those which are given when *not* working expansively will scarcely ever be of any practical use, since that condition is never fulfilled;

---

*The steam in the steam-chest of a boiler is in a different state from what it would be if it were shut up in a vessel apart from the water which generated it; for in the latter case it might be heated and cooled again, and its elasticity might be increased by diminishing the volume, and afterwards expanded, and it would obey the same laws as other elastic fluids; but such is not the case when in contact with the water from which it was formed, for then additional particles are continually being added to the original steam, or returning from it into the fluid state. Experiments have been made at various times for the purpose of establishing some law connecting the pressure of the steam with its density, but not with any satisfactory result. Empirical formulæ have been proposed by Dulong, Arago, Southern, Tredgold, and others, giving a relation between the pressure and temperature; but these are too complicated to be made available for practical purposes. After stating these, and showing the way in which they ought to have been turned to account, M. de Pambour gives one of his own, which, he says, sufficiently accords with facts to be practically useful, and has the advantage of being tolerably simple when introduced into investigations.

Let S = the quantity of water evaporated each minute;

V = the quantity of steam formed from it under the pressure p (in lbs. per square foot).

Then $\frac{V}{S}$ is called the relative volume of the steam under the pressure p.

and $$\frac{V}{S}=\frac{1}{a+bp}$$

where $a=\cdot 00004227$

and $b=\cdot 000000258$

as in all engines the steam is cut off before the end of the stroke by the slide, although the expansive gear be not used. Practical rules deduced from these investigations will now follow.

Again, if A be the area of the piston in feet, and $n=$ the number of strokes in a minute, l the length of a stroke in feet, c the clearance of the cylinder in feet, and v the velocity of the piston in feet per minute, the space $A\ (l+c)$ is filled with steam at each stroke; and therefore in n strokes the volume of steam $=n\,A\,(l+c)$. But $n=\frac{v}{l}$; and since the volume of steam

is V $\therefore$ $$V=\frac{v\,A(l+c)}{l}.$$

Hence $$\frac{V}{S}=\frac{v\,A(l+c)}{S\,l}$$

But $$\frac{V}{S}=\frac{1}{a+bp}$$

$$\therefore \quad \frac{v\,A(l+c)}{S\,l}=\frac{1}{a+bp} \quad . \quad . \quad . \quad . \quad . \quad \text{(I.)}$$

Now p, the pressure of steam in the cylinder, is, in the case of uniform motion, the same as the resistance to motion on the opposite side of the piston; and this resistance is composed of several parts, viz.:

1. The *useful* load $=$ R (suppose).
2. The pressure of the uncondensed steam $=p_1$ (suppose).
3. The friction of the *unloaded* engine $=f$ (suppose).
4. The additional friction for every unit of load, which varies with the load, and therefore we may call it $\delta\times R$, where δ is some constant quantity.

Hence $$p=R+p_1+f+\delta\times R=(1+\delta)R+p_1+f$$

also since $$a+bp=\frac{S\,l}{vA(l+c)} \quad . \quad . \quad . \quad . \quad . \quad . \quad . \quad \text{(from I.)}$$

$$\therefore \quad a+b\overline{(1+\delta\,R+p_1+f)}=\frac{S\,l}{A\,v(l+c)}$$

and $$b(1+\delta)R+a+b\,\overline{p_1+f}=\frac{S\,l}{Av(l+c)}$$

consequently $$b(1+\delta)R=\frac{S\,l}{Av(l+c)}-(a+b\,\overline{p_1+f})$$

$$\therefore \quad R=\frac{1}{b(1+\delta)}\left\{\frac{Sl}{Av(l+c)}-(a+b\,\overline{p_1+f})\right\}$$

which gives the useful load, R, on a square foot.

RULE I.

Knowing the Evaporation of an Engine, the Speed, and Area of the Piston, to find the Horse-power.

CASE I. *When not working expansively.*—To the logarithm of the evaporation (in cubic feet per minute) add the constant logarithm of 6·510286; take the natural number of the result, and call it A. Again, to constant logarithm 2·747750 add the logarithm of the velocity of piston (in feet per minute), and twice logarithm of diameter of piston (in feet); take natural number of the result, and call it B. Take B from A, which gives the useful effect. Divide the result by 33000, and the quotient will be the horse-power.

$$\text{And} \therefore \ \text{A R} v = \frac{1}{b(1+\delta)}\left\{\frac{\text{S}\,l}{l+c} - \text{A}\,v\,(a+\overline{b\,p_1+f})\right\}$$

But A R v is evidently the useful effect of the engine when not working expansively, and only requires to be put in a practical form by substituting numbers for the constant quantities, and reducing the result to a rule.

Now, according to Comte de Pambour, it has been found by experiment that $\delta = {\cdot}14$ for well-constructed engines in good working order; also p_1 may be taken at 2 lbs. per square inch; and f at 2·5; hence $p_1+f = 4{\cdot}5 \times 144$; also we will suppose $c = \frac{l}{20} \therefore \frac{l}{l+c} = \frac{20}{21}$; substituting these values, we get the useful effect

$$= \frac{1}{{\cdot}000000258 \times 1{\cdot}14}\left\{\frac{20}{21}\text{S} - {\cdot}7854\, d^2\, v\, ({\cdot}00004227 + {\cdot}000000258 \times 144 \times 4{\cdot}5)\right\}$$

Now $\frac{20}{{\cdot}000000258 \times 1{\cdot}14 \times 21} = [6{\cdot}510286]$, the square bracket being used to designate a logarithm.

And $\quad {\cdot}7854 \times ({\cdot}00004227 + {\cdot}000000258 \times 144 \times 4{\cdot}5) = [2{\cdot}747750]$

$$\therefore \quad \text{the horse-power} = \frac{[6{\cdot}510286]\,\text{S} - [2{\cdot}747750]\,d^2 v}{33000} \quad . \ . \ (\text{A})$$

from which we have Rule I., Case I., given above.

If, however, the engine work *expansively*, let l' be the space performed by the piston before the expansion commences; and let p be the pressure of steam *before* expansion, and p' the pressure at any

CASE II. *When the Engine is working expansively.*—To the logarithm of the evaporation add the constant logarithm 6·531475, and to this add logarithm in column 3, Table E (Appendix), corresponding to the degree of expansion as expressed in the left-hand column; take the natural number of the result, and call it A. Then proceed to find B, as before, and divide by 33000.

Example I.—The boilers of a pair of marine engines evaporate 284 cubic feet an hour for each engine; the diameter of the piston is 80 inches, and the velocity 220 feet a minute; find the horse-power.

---

instant of the motion afterwards, the piston at that instant being supposed to have described the space x. Now, if s be the quantity of water that formed the steam with which the cylinder is filled,

$$\frac{A(l'+c)}{s}=\frac{1}{a+bp}$$

and
$$\frac{A(x+c)}{s}=\frac{1}{a+bp'}$$

$$\therefore \quad \frac{l'+c}{x+c}=\frac{a+bp'}{a+bp}$$

$$\therefore \quad a+bp=(a+bp)\frac{l'+c}{x+c}$$

and
$$p'=\left(\frac{a}{b}+p\right)\frac{l'+c}{x+c}-\frac{a}{b}$$

Hence the pressure on the piston being p' A, we have

$$p'A=\left(\frac{a}{b}+p\right)A\frac{l'+c}{x+c}-\frac{a}{b}A$$

And the work done while traversing the small space dx (supposing the pressure invariable for this infinitesimal space) $=p'.A.dx$

$$=\left(\frac{a}{b}+p\right)A(l'+c)\frac{dx}{x+c}-\frac{a}{b}A\,dx$$

and the work done by expansion

$$=\left(\frac{a}{b}+p\right)A(l'+c)\int\frac{dx}{x+c}-\frac{a}{b}A\int dx$$

(the integral being limited by the values $x=l'$ and $x-l$)

$$=\left(\frac{a}{b}+p\right)A(l'+c)\log._{\varepsilon}\overline{x+c}-\frac{a}{b}Ax+\text{Cor.}$$

$$(x=l') \quad =\overline{\frac{a}{-}+p}\,A\overline{l'+c}\log._{\varepsilon}\overline{l'+c}-\frac{a}{b}Al'+\text{Cor.}$$

Here $S=\frac{284}{60}=4\cdot733$ cubic feet a minute.

$$d=\frac{80}{12}=6\cdot666 \text{ feet.}$$

$$v=200$$

Then log. S.	$=\cdot675136$	Constant log.	$=2\cdot747750$
Constant log.	$=6\cdot510286$	log. 220	$=2\cdot342423$
		log. 6·666	$=\cdot823865$
log. 15326000	$=7\cdot185422$	log. 6·666	$=\cdot823865$
		log. 5469000	$=6\cdot737903$

$$A=15326000$$
$$B=\ \ 5469000$$

$$\frac{9857000}{33000}=299 \text{ nearly.}$$

$$(x=l)\quad =\left(\frac{a}{b}+p\right)A(l'+c)\log._\varepsilon(l+c)-\frac{a}{b}Al+\text{Cor.}$$

$$=\left(\frac{a}{b}+p\right)A(l'+c)\log._\varepsilon\frac{l+c}{l'+c}-\frac{a}{b}Al+\frac{a}{b}Al'$$

And if we add to this the amount of work done before expansion, we shall get the whole work during one stroke of the engine.

But the work done before expansion commences $=p\,A\,l'$ $\therefore$ the whole work done during one stroke

$$=\left(\frac{a}{b}+p\right)A(l'+c)\log._\varepsilon\frac{l+c}{l'+c}-\frac{a}{b}Al+\left(\frac{a}{b}+p\right)Al'$$

$$=\left(\frac{a}{b}+p\right)A\left(\overline{l'+c}\log.\frac{l+c}{l'+c}+l'\right)-\frac{a}{b}Al$$

$$=\left(\frac{a}{b}+p\right)A(l'+c)\left(\log._\varepsilon\frac{l+c}{l'+c}+\frac{l'}{l'+c}\right)-\frac{a}{b}Al$$

For the sake of conciseness write C for $\log._\varepsilon\frac{l+c}{l'+c}+\frac{l'}{l'+c}$

Then the work done in one stroke

$$=\left(\frac{a}{b}+p\right)A(l'+c)C-\frac{a}{b}Al$$

Again, since the mean resistance to the motion is the same as in the former case, viz. $(\overline{1+\delta}R+p_1+f)A$,

$$\therefore\quad (\overline{1+\delta}R+p_1+f)Al=\left(\frac{a}{b}+p\right)A(l'+c)C-\frac{a}{b}Al$$

It is evident that engines will do more work at some velocities than they will at others; for, to take extreme cases, we may so increase the load that the speed of the engine becomes reduced till it can scarcely, if at all, turn its centres, in which case the product of the load moved, multiplied into the velocity, is very small; and again, if we go to the other extreme, we may increase the speed of the engine by diminishing the load, till the engine can do little more than overcome its own resistance, in which case the useful effect is scarcely any thing; there is therefore some intermediate speed at which the engine will move to enable it to produce the *greatest* useful effect. Now De

---

Now, to avoid the use of the quantity p, we must call to mind that the space $A(l'+c)$ is filled with steam of pressure p at each stroke.

If ∴ the evaporation be S, and the number of strokes n, we shall have

$$n.\frac{A(l'+c)}{S}=\frac{1}{a+bp}$$

But $n=\frac{v}{l}$ if v be the velocity in feet per minute.

$$\therefore \quad \frac{v}{l}.A.\frac{l'+c}{S}=\frac{1}{a+bp} \quad \ldots\ldots\ldots \text{(II.)}$$

$$\therefore \quad (a+bp)A(l+c)=\frac{lS}{v}$$

∴ substituting this in the equation, we have

$$\left\{R(1+\delta)+p_1+f\right\}Al=\frac{lS}{bv}.C-\frac{a}{b}Al$$

$$\therefore \quad A(R\overline{1+\delta}+p_1+f)=\frac{SC}{bv}-\frac{a}{b}A$$

$$AR(1+\delta)=\frac{SC}{bv}-\left(\frac{a}{b}+p_1+f\right)A$$

Hence $$ARv(1+\delta)=\frac{SC}{b}-\left(\frac{a}{b}+p_1+f\right)Av$$

and $$ARv=\frac{1}{1+\delta}(SC-(\frac{a}{b}+p_1+f)Av)$$

$$=\frac{1}{b(1+\delta)}\left\{(SC-(a+bp_1+f)Av\right\}$$

Now $$\frac{1}{b(1+\delta)}=[6{\cdot}531475]$$

Pambour shows that this will be accomplished by making the engine go as slow as it can to consume all the steam the boiler generates, in which case the pressure of the steam in the cylinder *approaches* to that in the boiler. It is manifest that they can never be practically equal; but the more nearly we arrive at this point the better. If the engine were to go slower than this, there would be a loss of steam at the safety-valve. The engineer, on this account, likes to see the steam just making itself visible at the safety-valve, well knowing that he gets then the most he can expect from it. In the marine engine the resistance and velocity of a given engine are always connected together, from the circumstance that the resistance of a given surface varies as the square of the velocity; so that the only way of reducing the speed is by increasing the resist-

---

and the log. of C or $\frac{l'}{l'+c} + \log._{\varepsilon} \frac{l+c}{l'+c}$ corresponding to the given degree of expansion $\frac{l'}{l}$ is given in column 3, Table E (Appendix).

Hence $$\text{H. P.} = \frac{[6{\cdot}531475]\ \text{S.C} - [2{\cdot}747750]\ d^2\, v}{33000} \quad . \quad . \quad . \quad \text{(B)}$$

from which we deduce Rule I. Case II. p. 282.

To determine the Velocity of maximum useful effect.

It has been said above, that when the velocity of the engine is such as to give the maximum effect, the pressure of the steam in the cylinder approximates to that in the boiler. But if p be the pressure in the cylinder, we know by equation (I.) that

$$\frac{\text{A}v(l+c)}{\text{S}l} = \frac{1}{a+bp}$$ when the engine is not working expansively; and that by (II.) $\frac{v\text{A}(l'+c)}{l\text{S}} = \frac{1}{a+bp}$ when working at the grade of expansion represented by $\frac{l'}{l}$. Hence if we consider p to represent the pressure of the steam in the *boiler*, these expressions will give us the velocity corresponding to the maximum useful effect.

ing surface of the floats; and the engine may be considered to be at its best speed when the floats are of such a size that the steam in the boiler is on the point of blowing off. De Pambour's investigation, founded on this fundamental principle, is given below; the practical rule depending on it is as follows:

RULE II.

To find the Velocity of an Engine corresponding to the maximum useful effect.

CASE I.—*When not working expansively.*—To logarithm of pressure (per square inch) in the boiler add the con-

---

Equation (I.) gives $v=\frac{S}{A}\cdot\frac{l}{l+c}\cdot\frac{1}{a+bp}$ . . . . (C)

and (II.) $v=\frac{Sl}{A(l+c)}\frac{1}{a+bp}$ . . . . (D)

Taking equation (C), $v=\frac{S}{A}\cdot\frac{l}{l+c}\cdot\frac{1}{a+bp}$

$$=\frac{S}{A}\frac{l}{l+c}\frac{100000}{(4{\cdot}227+[0{\cdot}569982]\,p)}$$

$$=\frac{Sl}{d^2\times{\cdot}7854\times(l+c)}\times\frac{100000}{(4{\cdot}227+[0{\cdot}569982]p)}$$

also $\frac{l}{{\cdot}7854\times(l+c)}\times100000=[5{\cdot}083720]$

Hence $v=\frac{S\,[5{\cdot}083720]}{d^2(4{\cdot}227+[0{\cdot}569982].p)}$

From which formula we get Rule II. Case I., given above.

Again, taking equation (D), $v=\frac{S}{A}\frac{l}{l'+c}\cdot\frac{1}{a+bp}$

$$=\frac{Sl}{d^2.(l'+c)}\frac{\frac{100000}{{\cdot}7854}}{(4{\cdot}227+[0{\cdot}569982]\,p)}$$

$$=\frac{Sl}{d^2.(l'+c)}\frac{[5{\cdot}104909]}{(4{\cdot}227+[0{\cdot}569982]\,p)}$$

Now the log. of $\frac{l}{l'+c}$ to the given degree of expansion $\frac{l'}{l}$ is given in column 2, Table E (Appendix).

stant logarithm 0·569982; take out the natural number corresponding, and add to it the number 4·227. To the log. of this sum add twice the logarithm of the diameter of the piston in feet. Call the result log. A.

Again, to logarithm of evaporation (in cubic feet per minute) add constant logarithm 5·083720, and from this sum subtract log. A: the result will be the logarithm of the velocity of maximum useful effect.

CASE II. *When working expansively.*—First find log. A, as before; then to log. evaporation in cubic feet per minute add constant log. 5·104909, and the number from Table E (Appendix), col. 2 corresponding to the amount of expansion as tabulated in the column on the left hand, and from their sum subtract log. A, and the result will be the

---

Hence we get Rule II. Case II., given above.

Again, since by equation (A)

$$\text{H.P.} = \frac{[6{\cdot}510286]\,\text{S} - [2{\cdot}747750]\,d^2v}{33000}$$

$$\therefore \quad 33000 \times \text{H.P.} = [6{\cdot}510286]\,\text{S} - [2{\cdot}747750]\,d^2v$$

$$\text{or} \quad [6{\cdot}510286]\,\text{S} = 33000 \times \text{H.P.} + [2{\cdot}747750]\,d^2v$$

$$\therefore \quad \text{S} = \frac{[2{\cdot}747750]\,d^2v + 33000 + \text{H.P.}}{[6{\cdot}510286]}$$

Hence we get Rule III. Case I., given in p. 289.

Similarly, from equation (D) we get

$$p = \frac{1}{[0{\cdot}569982]}\left(\frac{[5{\cdot}104909]\,\frac{l}{l'+c}.\text{S}}{d^2v} - 4{\cdot}227\right)$$

whence Rule IV. Case II. p. 291.

Again, to find the diameter of the cylinder.

Since, from equation (A),

$$\text{H.P.} = \frac{[6{\cdot}510286]\,\text{S} - [2{\cdot}747750]\,d^2v}{33000}$$

$$\therefore \quad [2{\cdot}747750]\,d^2v = [6{\cdot}510286]\,\text{S} - 33000\,\text{H.P.}$$

$$d^2 = \frac{[6{\cdot}510286]\,\text{S} - 33000\,\text{H.P.}}{[2{\cdot}747750]\,.\,v}$$

$$d = \sqrt{\left(\frac{[6{\cdot}510286]\,\text{S} - 33000\,\text{H.P.}}{[2{\cdot}747750]\,v}\right)}$$

which gives Rule V. Case I. p. 292.

log. of the velocity corresponding to the maximum useful effect.

Example 2.—Find the velocity of maximum useful effect of the engine mentioned in Example 1; the pressure of the steam being 10 lbs. above that of the atmosphere.

Here $p = 25$ lbs.

log. p	$= 1{\cdot}397940$	log. S	$= {\cdot}675136$
constant log.	$= 0{\cdot}569982$	constant log.	$= 5{\cdot}083720$
log. 92·88	$= 1{\cdot}967922$		$5{\cdot}758856$
	$4{\cdot}227$	log. A	$= 3{\cdot}634198$
log. 97·107	$= 1{\cdot}987250$	log. 133	$= 2{\cdot}124658$
log. diam.	$= {\cdot}823865$		
"	$= {\cdot}823865$		

log. A $= 3{\cdot}634198$

∴ velocity of maximum useful effect = 133 feet.

Also, if the engine be working expansively, we have from equation (B)

$$\text{H. P.} = \frac{[6{\cdot}531475]\ \text{S. C} - [2{\cdot}747750]\ d^2 v}{33000}$$

$$\therefore \quad 33000 \times \text{H. P.} = [6{\cdot}531475]\ \text{S C} - [2{\cdot}747750]\ d^2 v$$

$$\therefore \quad [2{\cdot}747750]\ d^2 v = [6{\cdot}531475]\ \text{S C} - 33000 \times \text{H. P.}$$

$$\text{and} \quad d^2 = \frac{[6{\cdot}531475]\ \text{S C} - 33000 \times \text{H. P.}}{[2{\cdot}747750]\ .\ v}$$

$$d = \sqrt{\left(\frac{[6{\cdot}531475]\ \text{S C} - 33000 \times \text{H.P.}}{[2{\cdot}747750]\ .\ v}\right.}$$

from whence we deduce Rule V. Case II., given in p. 292.

Again, from equation (I.),

$$\frac{\text{A}\, v\, (l + \text{C})}{\text{S}\,.\, l} = \frac{1}{a + b p}$$

$$\therefore \quad \text{S} = \frac{\text{A}\, v\, (l + c)}{l \dfrac{1}{a + b p}}$$

But $\dfrac{1}{a + b p}$ is the relative volume of the steam under the pressure p, and is given in Table A (Appendix).

RULE III.

To find the effective evaporation of a condensing Engine of given dimensions and horse-power, the Piston moving with a given velocity.

CASE I. *Where the Engine does not work expansively.*— To the constant logarithm 2·747750 add twice the logarithm of the diameter in feet, and logarithm of velocity of piston in feet; take the natural number of the result, and add to it the useful effect (or the horse-power of the engine × 33000). From the logarithm of the sum subtract the constant logarithm 6·510286; the result will be the evaporation in cubic feet per minute.

Let this $= r$

$$\therefore \quad S = \frac{A\, v\, (l + c)}{l \,.\, r} = \frac{\frac{21}{20} \times {\cdot}7854 \times d^2 v}{r}$$

$$= \frac{d^2 v}{[0{\cdot}83720]\, r}$$

whence we obtain Rule VI. Case I., given in p. 295.

Again, from equation (B),

$$\text{H. P.} = \frac{[6{\cdot}531475]\, S \,.\, C - [2{\cdot}747750]\, d^2 v}{33000}$$

$$\therefore \quad [6{\cdot}531475]\, S \,.\, C = [2{\cdot}747750]\, d^2 v + 33000 \times \text{H. P.}$$

$$\text{or} \quad S = \frac{[2{\cdot}747750[\, d^2 v + 33000 \times \text{H. P.}}{[6{\cdot}531475] \,.\, C}$$

from which we get Rule III. Case II. p. 290.

Again, by equation (C),

$$v = \frac{S}{A} \frac{l}{l + c} \frac{1}{a + bp}$$

which was subsequently reduced to

$$v = \frac{S\, [5{\cdot}083720]}{d^2 (4{\cdot}227 + [0{\cdot}569982]\, p)}$$

$$\text{whence} \quad 4{\cdot}227 + [0{\cdot}569982]\, p = \frac{S\, [5{\cdot}083720]}{d^2 v}$$

$$\text{and} \quad [0{\cdot}569982]\, p = \frac{S\, [5{\cdot}083720]}{d^2 v} - 4{\cdot}227$$

CASE II. *When working expansively.*—To the constant logarithm 6·531475 add the logarithm of the number corresponding to the degree of expansion, as given in col. 3, Table E (Appendix), and use this logarithm instead of the logarithm 6·510286 in the preceding case. The result will be, as before, the logarithm of the evaporation in cubic feet per minute.

Example.—Given the diameter of the piston of an engine of 200 H.P. 60 inches, velocity of piston 210 feet; find the effective evaporation when not working expansively.

Here diameter = 60 inches = 5 feet
horse-power = 200 ∴ useful effect = 6600000
velocity of piston = 210 feet.

Then, by Case I.

constant log. = 2·747750
log. diameter = ·698970

$$\therefore \qquad p = \frac{1}{[0{\cdot}569982]}\left(\frac{[5{\cdot}083720]\,.\,S}{d^2 v} - 4{\cdot}227\right)$$

from which we get Rule IV. Case I. p. 291.

Again, if the engine work expansively, the space $l' + c$ is filled with steam at each stroke, and the formula becomes

$$\frac{A\,v\,(l'+c)}{S\,l} = \frac{1}{a + b\,p}$$

$$\therefore \qquad S = \frac{A\,v\,(l'+c)}{l\dfrac{1}{a+b\,p}}$$

$$= \frac{A\,v\,(l'+c)}{l\,.\,r}$$

$$= \frac{{\cdot}7854\,d^2 v\,.\,(l'+c)}{l\,.\,r}$$

$$= \frac{d^2 v\,.\,(l'+c)}{[0{\cdot}104909]\,l\,.\,r}$$

$$= \frac{d^2 v}{[0{\cdot}104909]\,\dfrac{l}{l'+c}\,.\,r}$$

Now $\dfrac{l}{l'+c}$ is given in column 2, Table E (Appendix); and r is to be obtained, as before, in Table A. Hence we get Rule VI. Case II. p. 296.

log. diameter = ·698970
log. velocity = 2·322219

log. 2937000 = 6·467909
usual effect = 6600000

log. 9537000 = 6·979412
constant log. = 6·510286

log. 2·945 = ·469126
∴ the effective evaporation = 2·945 cubic feet.

RULE IV.

To find the Pressure of Steam in the Cylinder, knowing the effective evaporation.

CASE I. *Not working expansively.*—To logarithm of the evaporation add the constant logarithm 5·083720; call the result log. A.

Also to twice logarithm of the diameter in feed add logarithm velocity of piston, and subtract their sum from log. A.

Find the natural number of the resulting log., from which subtract the number 4·227.

From the logarithm of the difference subtract the constant logarithm 0·569982, and find the natural number of the result, which will be the pressure of steam in the cylinder per square inch.

CASE II. *When working expansively, we have the following modification of Case I.*—To log. of evaporation add the constant log. 5·104909, and the number in column 2, Table E (Appendix), corresponding to the proper degree of expansion, the result will be log. A; then proceed as before.

Example.—Find the pressure of steam in the cylinder of the engine investigated in the last problem.

log. evaporation = ·469126
constant log. = 5·083720

log. A = 5·552846

log. diameter = ·698970
" = ·698970
log. velocity = 2·322219

3·720159

log. 68·02 = 1·832687
4·227

log. 63·793 = 1.804753
constant log. = ·569982

log. 17·17 = 1·234771
∴ pressure = 17·17 lbs. per square inch.

RULE V.

To find the Diameter of a Cylinder to work at a certain speed, knowing the evaporating power of the Boiler.

CASE I. *When not working expansively.*—To logarithm of the evaporation add the constant logarithm 6·510286. Take the natural number of the resulting logarithm, from which subtract the useful effect, or H.P × 33000. Find the logarithm of the difference, which call log. A.

Again, to logarithm of velocity of piston in feet add the constant logarithm 2·747750. Call the sum log. B.

From log. A subtract log. B, and divide by 2; the result will be the logarithm of the diameter in feet.

CASE II. *When working expansively, we have the following modification of the preceding case.*—To logarithm of the evaporation in feet add the constant logarithm 6·531475, and the number taken from column 3, Table E (Appendix), corresponding to the proper degree of expansion. Take the natural number of the resulting logarithm, from which subtract useful effect (or H.P. × 33000); find the logarithm of the difference, which call log. A; then proceed as before.

Example.—What must be the diameter of the cylinder of a 100 H.P. engine, connected with a boiler evaporating 1·5 cubic feet a minute, the speed of the piston being 180 feet?

log. 1·5 = ·176091
constant log. = 6·510286

log. 4857000 = 6·686377
3300000 = useful effect

log. 1557000 = 6·192289 = log. A.

Again, log. 180 = 2·255272
constant log. = 2·747750

5·003022 = log. B.

6·192289
5·003022

2)1·189267

log. 3·932 = ·594633

∴ the diameter = 3·932 feet, or 47·184 inches.

As an example on expansive working, let us proceed to find the diameter, that the engine may have the same power, and evaporate $\frac{9}{10}$ of a cubic foot per minute, the steam being cut off at $\frac{1}{2}$ the stroke.

Here log. 0·9 = $\bar{1}$·954242
constant log. = 6·531475
from Table E. = ·191730

log. 4758254 = 6·677447
3300000 = useful effect

log. 1458254 = 6·163757 = log. A.
as before 5·003022 = log. B.

2)1·160735

log. 3·805 = ·580368

∴ the diameter = 3·805 feet = 45·660 inches.

To find the pressure of the Steam in the Cylinder in the two cases just investigated.

Case I.

log. 1·5	=	0·176091
constant log.	=	5·083720
log. A	=	5·259811
log. *d*	=	0·594633
"	=	0·594633
log. velocity	=	2·255272
		3·444538
log. 65·351	=	1·815273
4·227		
log. 61·124	=	1·786211
constant log.	=	0·569982
log. 16.45	=	1·216229

∴ pressure of steam = 16.45 lbs.

Case II.

log. 0·9	=	1·954242
constant log.	=	5·104909
from Table E	=	0·259594
log. A.	=	5·318745
log. *d*	=	0·580368
"	=	0·580368
log. velocity	=	2·255272
		3·416008
log. A.	=	5·318745

log. 79·993 = 1·902737
4·227

log. 75·766 = 1·879531
constant log. = 0·569982

log. 20·39 = 1·309549

∴ pressure = 20·39

These two cases are remarkable for their results, and deserve especial consideration. The two engines have the same power, they have also the same speed, and, therefore, as far as effects are concerned, they are identically the same; but the evaporation of the one is 1·5 cubic feet a minute, and that of the other ·9, or, in other words, we may say the consumption of fuel in the two engines is as 15 to 9. Now this arises from the fact that the one engine uses the steam at uniform pressure throughout the stroke (viz. 16·45 lbs.), and the other, commencing with steam of 20·37 lbs., works expansively. It is also to be noticed that any advantage arising from the difference in the areas of the cylinders is in favor of the one of greater consumption.

RULE VI.

To find the Evaporation of Water in the Boiler of an Engine, knowing the velocity and diameter of the Piston, together with the Pressure of Steam in the Cylinder.

CASE I. *When not working expansively.*—To twice the logarithm of the diameter in feet, add the logarithm of the velocity in feet; call the result log. A. Again, to log. of the relative volume of steam in Table A (Appendix), corresponding to the pressure of steam in the cylinder, add the constant log. ·083720, and call the result log. B. Take log. B from log. A, and find the natural number of the difference, which will be the evaporation of the boiler.

CASE II. *When working expansively.*—Find log. A as before; then to log. of relative volume corresponding to the pressure of steam in the boiler, as given in Table A (Appendix), add the logarithm of number given in column 1, Table E (Appendix), corresponding to the given degree of expansion, and to this add the constant logarithm ·104909; call the sum log. B; take this from log. A, and find the natural number of the result for the evaporation.

Example 1.—The diameter of the Bee's cylinder is 20 inches; the number of revolutions when working with the highest grade of expansion ($\frac{1}{8}$ of the stroke) is 30, the length of stroke 2 feet; find the effective evaporation: the pressure of steam in the cylinder is 10 lbs. above the atmosphere.

Here, relative volume corresponding to pressure 25 lbs. = 1044; and log. 1044 = 3·018700.

Again, log. from tables for $\frac{l'}{l}(=\frac{1}{8})$ = ·602060.

Hence	log. d	= ·221675
	"	= ·221675
	g. v	= 2·079181
	log. A	= 2·522531
Again,	log. 1044	= 3·018700
	from table	= ·602060
	constant log.	= ·104909
	log. B	= 3·725669
	log. S	= $\bar{2}$·796862

∴ S = ·0627.

Example 2.—Find the horse-power of the Bee's engine, at the foregoing degree of expansion.

log. S	= $\bar{2}$·796862	constant log.	= 2·747750
constant log.	= 6·531475	log. velocity	= 2·079181
from tables	= ·349277	log. diameter	= ·221675
		"	= ·221675
log. 476500	= 5·677614	186300	= 5·270281

A = 476500
B = 186300

useful effect = 290200
H.P. = 8·8

Example 3.—To find the effective evaporation in the boiler of the foregoing engine, the steam being cut off by the slide, and the horse-power the same as that in the result of the last question.

Note.—The slide of the Bee cuts off the steam at two-thirds of the stroke.

Now, by Rule III. Case II.

constant log. = 6·531475
log. from tables = ·120903
6·652378

const. log. = 2·747750
log. diam. = ·221675
" = ·221675
log. velocity = 2·079181

log. 186300 = 5·270281
290200 = useful effect

log. 476500 = 5·678063
constant log. = 6·652378

log. ·1061 = $\bar{1}$·025685

Example 4.—The steam being cut off by the slide as in the last example, and the horse-power and cylinder as before, to find the pressure of steam in the cylinder.

log. S = $\bar{1}$·025685
constant log. = 5·104909
log. from tables = ·148911
4·279505
2·52253

log. velocity = 2·079181
log. diameter = ·221675
" = ·221675
2·522531

log. 57·14 = 1·756974
4·23

log. 52·91 = 1·723538
const. log. = ·569982

log. 14·24 = 1·153556

∴ the pressure of steam is 14·24 lbs.

These examples, when analyzed, will be found very profitable. Examples 1 and 2 correspond to the expansive working of the engine, and Examples 3 and 4 to the throttle-valve; for in the latter cases the steam must be throttled to produce the same revolutions as when working expansively. Now the cases are these:

(1.) By expansive working, the pressure of the steam before expansion is 25 lbs. per inch, and the effective evaporation is ·0627 cubic feet a minute; and (2) when the steam is throttled, the velocity and horse-power are precisely the same, but the pressure of steam in the cylinder is only 14·24 lbs., and the effective evaporation is ·1061; we obtain therefore an economical result by using steam at the higher pressure, and expanding it, over what we should get by the throttle-valve under similar circumstances, in the ratio of 627 to 1061 in this particular instance.

327. *On the Screws of Steam-vessels.*

(Continued from page 145.)

We have before stated that the surface of a screw may be conceived to be produced by supposing a line to travel along the line T′Q′ at the same time that it revolves around it. Let T′Q′OP be the surface so generated: then this surface is called the *blade* of a screw; T′Q′ is called the *length;* the angle POH is called the *angle;* and what T′Q′ would become if OH were continued through a whole revolution, is called the *pitch* of the screw; and OP is called the thread. Now since the angle POH is constant, if the triangle POH were unfolded on paper, it would form a *plane* triangle, of which PH (the length of the screw) would form the perpendicular, and OH (the

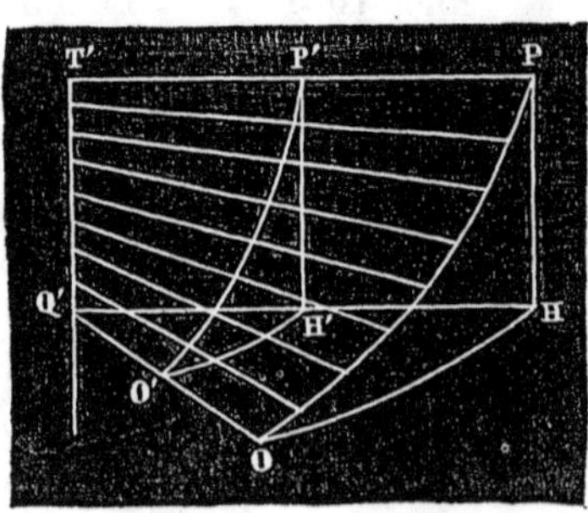

portion of the circumference described) would be the base, and O P the hypothenuse. Also, if P′O′H′ be another cylindrical surface surrounding T′Q′, it may similarly be formed into a triangle, whose perpendicular P′H′ is also the length of the screw, but having a smaller base O′H′, and therefore a larger angle P′O′H′: hence we see that screws may have the same pitch but different angles, if their diameters differ.

328. *To find approximately the Area of a Screw-blade* T′Q′O P.

If we trace a series of curves such as P′O′ on the surface, we may obtain approximately the area of the surface by the following means.

Let all the lines P O . . . . P′O′ . . . . T′Q′ be added together, and divide the result by the number of lines so added to get a mean breadth of the surface. Then, if this be multiplied by Q′O (the radius of the blade), it will give the area sufficiently near for all practical purposes.

The only thing we have, therefore, to do is, to explain the method of getting the lengths of O P, O′P′, etc. To do this, let us bear in mind what was before said in explanation of the principle of the screw. Thus, it was said that every portion of O P had the same inclination to the base; hence it follows that P O H is a right-angled triangle wrapped round a cylinder, and it may evidently be unfolded on paper.

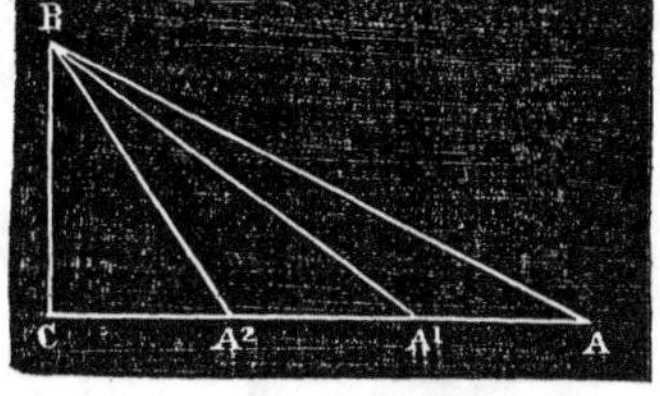

Let B A C, therefore, be the right-angled triangle, having B C = P H or T′Q′ (the length of the screw) and A B = O P; and therefore A C = H O. Now by examining O′P′H′ in the curve surface, we see, as was stated, that it also will unfold into a right-angled triangle, having the *same perpendicular*, but a *less base*, and therefore a *greater angle* at the base; and hence B C will serve also for the perpendicular of *this* triangle and some length A_1C will serve for the base, and consequently A_1B will serve for the line O′P′. Now our object in drawing the lines O′P′, etc., being merely to get a sufficient number of means between O P and T′Q′, we shall effect the same object by dividing A C into *any* number of equal parts, and drawing the straight lines B A_1 B A_2. Generally speaking, two means, as in the figure, or even one, will be amply sufficient, and the surface of the blade will be

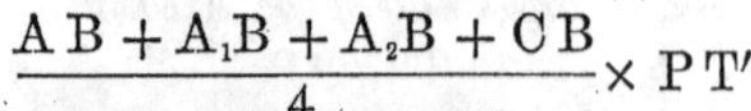

$$\frac{AB + A_1B + A_2B + CB}{4} \times PT'$$

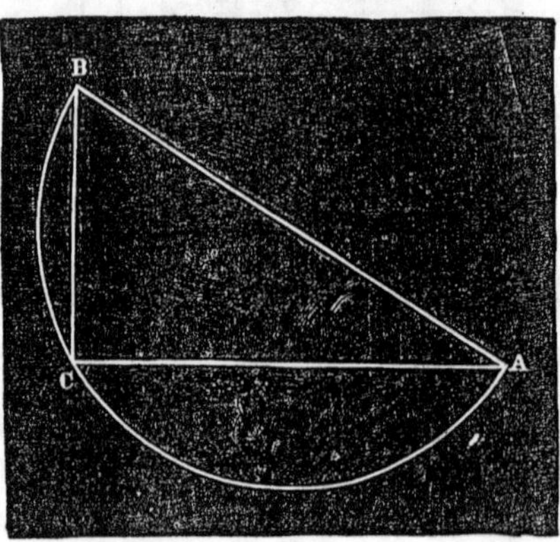

Let the outer edge of the propeller be accurately measured and laid down upon paper according to some scale; and let A B represent this edge. On A B describe a semicircle A C B. Measure the *length* of the propeller; and, on the same scale as before, let B C be the length drawn from the point B within the semicircle. Join A C; then A C B will represent the triangle P O H.

329. *To find the Angle of a Helix or Thread of a Screw-propeller.*

The angle of a helix is the angle (at the circumference) between the outer edge, or thread, and the plane perpendicular to the axis. Hence it is the angle B A C above.

Construct, therefore, the same diagram as before, viz., by drawing a line A B to represent the outer edge of the propeller, and after describing on it a semicircle A C B, within this semicircle let the line B C be drawn equal in length to the *length* of the propeller (as measured along the axis); then join A C, and the angle B A C at the base is the angle of the propeller. This angle may be measured by the aid of *mathematical instruments*, or its value may be calculated: thus let A B or O P $= a$, and B C $= l$; then sin. B A C $= \frac{l}{a}$, whence the angle may be found by logarithmic tables.

330. *To find the Pitch of a Screw-propeller.*

Knowing the diameter of the propeller, find the circumference of a circle of this diameter; and if a right triangle be constructed, having the angle at the base equal to the angle of the propeller, as found in last article, the perpendicular will be the pitch required. This is clear from what was stated in p. 298.

$$\frac{\text{pitch}}{\text{base}} = \text{tan. B A C}$$

$$\text{and pitch} = \text{base} \times \text{tan. B A C.}$$
$$= 3{\cdot}14159 \times \text{diameter} \times \text{tan. B A C.}$$

Table I. has been calculated from this formula, for propellers of 1 foot diameter; and consequently if the number given there be multiplied by the diameter of the propeller, the result will give the pitch.

331. *What must be the Pitch of a Screw to advance a given number of Knots (a) per hour, when making a given number of revolutions (n) per minute.*

Let $x =$ the pitch of the propeller, in feet

$nx =$ space advanced per minute, ditto

$60\,nx =$ space advanced per hour, ditto

$\frac{60\,nx}{6080} =$ space advanced per hour in knots

$$\therefore \quad \frac{60\,nx}{6080} = a$$

$$\text{or } x = \frac{6080}{60} \cdot \frac{a}{n} = \frac{304}{3} \cdot \frac{a}{n}$$

$$= 101 \frac{a}{n} \text{ nearly.}$$

332. *Given the speed of a ship and the slip per cent. of the Screw, and the number of revolutions of the Propeller, to find the Pitch of the Screw.*

Let a be the speed of the screw in knots;
b be the speed of the ship in knots;
$m =$ the slip per cent.

Then, preserving the same notation as in the last problem.

$$\frac{60\,nx}{6080} = a$$

But
$$\frac{a - b}{a} = \frac{m}{100}$$

$$\therefore \quad 100\,a - 100\,b = ma$$

$$(100 - m)\,a = 100\,b$$

$$a = \frac{100}{100 - m}\,b$$

$$\frac{60\,nx}{6080} = \frac{100\,b}{100 - m}$$

$$\therefore\ x = \frac{60800}{6\,n} \times \frac{b}{100 - m}$$

333. *To find accurately the Surface of a Screw-blade.*

Let $O'\,P'$ * $= s$; $H\,Q'\,O = \beta$; $Q\,T = l$;
$P\,O\,H = \alpha$; $Q'\,H = a$.

$\therefore\ O\,H = a.\ \beta$; $P\,H = a\,\beta \tan.\ \alpha = b\,\beta$ (suppose)

Let $P'\,O'\,H' = \theta$, and $Q'\,H' = r$.

Hence, since $P'\,H' = O'\,H' \tan.\ \theta$

$= r\,\beta \tan.\ \theta$

$P\,H = O\,H \tan.\ \alpha$

---

* See diagram p. 298.

$$= a\,\beta \tan. \alpha$$

$$\therefore \quad r \tan. \theta = a \tan. \alpha = b$$

$$\therefore \quad \tan. \theta = \frac{b}{r}$$

Now $$s = \mathrm{O'\,P'} = \mathrm{O'\,H'} \sec. \theta$$

$$= r\,\beta . \sqrt{1 + \tan.^2 \theta}$$

$$= r\,\beta \sqrt{1 + \frac{b^2}{r^2}} = \beta \sqrt{r^2 + b^2}$$

And the surface

$$= \int s\,d\,r$$

$$= \beta \int \sqrt{r^2 + b^2}\;d\,r$$

$$= \frac{\beta}{2} \left\{ b^2 \log._\varepsilon \left(r + \sqrt{b^2 + r^2}\right) + r \sqrt{r^2 + b^2} \right\} + \text{Cor.}$$

$$\left.\begin{matrix} r=o \\ =a \end{matrix}\right\} = \frac{\beta}{2} \left\{ b^2 \log._\varepsilon \left(\frac{a + \sqrt{b^2 + a^2}}{b}\right) + a \sqrt{a^2 + b^2} \right\}$$

$$= \frac{\beta}{2} \left\{ a^2 \tan.^2 \alpha \log._\varepsilon \left(\frac{1 + \sqrt{1 + \tan.^2 \alpha}}{\tan. \alpha}\right) + a^2 \sec. \alpha \right\}$$

$$= \frac{a^2 \beta}{2} \left\{ \tan.^2 \alpha \,.\, \log._\varepsilon \left(\frac{1 + \cos. \alpha}{\sin. \alpha}\right) + \sec. \alpha \right\}$$

$$= \frac{a^2 \beta}{2} (\tan.^2 \alpha \log._\varepsilon \cot. \frac{\alpha}{2} + \sec. \alpha)$$

$$= \frac{a\,a\,\beta \tan. \alpha}{2} (\tan. \alpha \log._\varepsilon \cot. \frac{\alpha}{2} + \operatorname{cosec.} \alpha)$$

or, if expressed in terms of the length,

$$= \frac{a\,l}{2} \tan. \alpha \log._\varepsilon \cot. \frac{\alpha}{2} + \operatorname{cosec.} \alpha)$$

334. *Investigation of the Power exerted by a Screw.*

Let n = the number of revolutions per minute of the screw.

$\therefore 2\,\pi\,.\,n$ = the angle described in a minute.

And hence the velocity of a particle of the screw M about the axis T′ Q′ is $2\,\pi\,.\,n.\,r$.

Now, using the same notation as before, $\angle$ P′ O′ H′ $= \theta$, therefore the motion of the screw makes the same angle θ with its surface, at the point M.

If now this velocity be resolved in direction perpendicular to O′ P′, the resolved velocity in this direction $= 2\pi n r$ sin. θ.

Again, if $u =$ velocity of ship in direction Q′ T′, the velocity in direction perpendicular to O′ P′ $= u$ cos. θ.

Hence the difference between these two velocities

$$= 2\pi n r \sin.\theta - u \cos.\theta.$$

But the pressure of the fluid varies as the square of the normal velocity;

$$\therefore \text{force at distance } r \propto (2\pi n r \sin.\theta - u \cos.\theta)^2$$

$$\therefore \text{force at distance } r = k(2\pi n r \sin.\theta - u \cos.\theta)^2$$

where $k =$ pressure on unit of surface moving with velocity unity.

Resolving this force in direction parallel and perpendicular to screw-shaft, we have (1) in direction of shaft

$$\text{force} = k(2\pi n r \sin.\theta - u \cos.\theta)^2 \cos.\theta$$

and (2) in a plane perpendicular to shaft,

$$\text{force} = k(2\pi n r \sin.\theta - u \cos.\theta)^2 \sin.\theta$$

and the resolved pressures on the strip $s\,d\,r$ in these two directions are respectively

$$k(2\pi n r \sin.\theta - u \cos.\theta)^2 \cos.\theta\, s\,d\,r$$

and $$k(2\pi n r \sin.\theta - u \cos.\theta)^2 \sin.\theta\, s\,d\,r$$

Let now P = pressure on the piston

V = velocity of ditto

$$\therefore \quad \text{P V} = k\int 2\pi n r(2\pi n r \sin.\theta - u \cos.\theta)^2 \sin.\theta\, s\,d\,r$$

Let $2\pi n = \omega$; and since $\tan.\theta = \frac{b}{r}$

$$\sin.\theta = \frac{b}{\sqrt{r^2 + b^2}}$$

$$\cos.\theta = \frac{r}{\sqrt{r^2 + b^2}}$$

$$s = \beta\sqrt{r^2 + b^2}$$

$$\therefore \text{PV} = k\omega\int r\left(\omega\frac{r\,b}{\sqrt{r^2+b^2}} - \frac{u\,r}{\sqrt{r^2+b^2}}\right)^2 \frac{b}{\sqrt{r^2+b^2}}\,\beta\sqrt{r^2+b^2}\,d\,r$$

$$= k\,\omega\,\beta\int\frac{r^3}{(r^2+b^2)}\cdot(\omega\,b - u)^2\,b\,d\,r$$

$$= k\,\omega\, b\,\beta\,(\omega\, b - u)^2 \int \frac{r^3}{r^2 + b^2}\, dr$$

$$\begin{matrix} r = o \\ = a \end{matrix} \quad = k\,\omega\, b\,\beta\,(\omega\, b - u)^2\ \text{A (suppose).}$$

Again, if u be the velocity of the ship, and H the effective area of the midship section,

the pressure against the bows $= k\,\text{H}\,u^2$

But pressure of water on the strip of the screw $s\,d\,r$ in direction of the keel

$$= k\,(2\,\pi\,n\,r\sin.\,\theta - u\cos.\,\theta)^2\cos.\,\theta\, s\, d\,r$$

$$= k\left(\omega\frac{r\,b}{\sqrt{r^2+b^2}} - u\frac{r}{\sqrt{r^2+b^2}}\right)^2 \cdot \frac{r}{\sqrt{r^2+b^2}}\,\beta\sqrt{r^2+b^2}\,d\,r$$

$$= k\,\beta\,(\omega\, b - u)^2 \cdot \frac{r^3}{r^2+b^2}\cdot d\,r$$

$$\therefore \text{ whole pressure} = k\,\beta\,(\omega\, b - u)^2 \int \frac{r^3}{r^2+b^2}\, d\,r$$

from $r = o$
to $r = a$

$$= k\,\beta\,(\omega\, b - u)^2\,\text{A}$$

Hence $\quad k\,\text{H}\,u^2 = k\,\beta\,(\omega\, b - u)^2\,\text{A}$

$\therefore \quad \text{H}\,u^2 = \beta\,\text{A}\,(\omega\, b - u)^2$

or $\quad \sqrt{\text{H}}\,u = \sqrt{\beta\,\text{A}}\,(\omega\, b - u)$

But $\omega\, b$ = velocity of screw in advance; that is to say, in the direction of the keel $= v$ (suppose).

$\therefore \quad \sqrt{\text{H}}\,u = \sqrt{\beta\,\text{A}}\,(v - u)$

or $\quad (\sqrt{\text{H}} + \sqrt{\beta\,\text{A}})\,u = \sqrt{\beta\,\text{A}}\,.\,v$

Let $\quad \dfrac{v - u}{v} = \text{S}$ (the slip of the screw)

$$\therefore\ \text{S} = 1 - \frac{u}{v} = 1 - \frac{\sqrt{\beta\,\text{A}}}{\sqrt{\text{H}} + \sqrt{\beta\,\text{A}}} = \frac{\sqrt{\text{H}}}{\sqrt{\text{H}} + \sqrt{\beta\,\text{A}}}$$

And $\text{P V} = k\,\omega\, b\,(\omega\, b - u)^2\,\text{A}$
$\quad = k\,v\,\beta\,(v - u)^2\,\text{A}$
$\quad = k\,v\,\beta\,(v\,\text{S})^2\,\text{A}$
$\quad = k\,\beta\,\text{S}^2\,v^3\,\text{A}$

Hence, so long as the same screw is made use of in the same ship, the Indicator horse-power varies as v^3, or varies as the cube of the speed of the ship.

Again, since $\quad H u^2 = \beta A (v - u)^2$

$= \beta A v^2 S^2$

$\therefore \quad P V = k H u^2 v$

If, therefore, the screw be changed in the same ship, the horse-power no longer varies as the cube of the speed of the ship, but as the square of the speed of the ship multiplied by the speed of the screw. Hence the Indicator horse-power will in all cases be found to be proportional to the continued product of the square of the speed of the ship, the number of revolutions of the screw, and the pitch.

335. *To find how far the Slip of a Screw depends on its form and Dimensions.*

$$S = \frac{v - u}{v} = \frac{\sqrt{H}}{\sqrt{H} + \sqrt{\beta A}}$$

But $A = \int \frac{r^3}{(r^2 + b^2)} d r$

$$= \tfrac{1}{2} (r^2 + b^2 \log._\varepsilon \overline{r^2 + b^2}) + \text{Cor}$$

$$\begin{matrix} r = o \\ = a \end{matrix} \quad = \tfrac{1}{2} \left(a^2 + b^2 \log._\varepsilon \frac{b^2}{a^2 + b^2}\right)$$

$$= \frac{a^2}{2} \left(1 + \tan.^2 \alpha \log._\varepsilon \frac{\tan.^2 \alpha}{1 + \tan.^2 \alpha}\right)$$

$$= \frac{a^2}{2} (1 + \tan.^2 \alpha \log._\varepsilon \sin.^2 \alpha)$$

$$= \frac{a}{2} (1 + \tan.^2 \alpha \log._\varepsilon \overline{1 - \cos.^2 \alpha})$$

$$= \frac{a^2}{2} \left\{1 - \tan.^2 \alpha \left(\cos.^2 \alpha + \frac{\cos.^4 \alpha}{2} + \frac{\cos.^6 \alpha}{3} + \cdots\right)\right\}$$

$$= \frac{a^2}{2} \left(1 - \sin.^2 \alpha - \sin.^2 \alpha \overline{\frac{\cos.^2 \alpha}{2} + \frac{\cos.^4 \alpha}{3} +} \cdots\right)$$

$$= \frac{a^2}{2} \left(\cos.^2 \alpha - \sin.^2 \alpha \overline{\frac{\cos.^2 \alpha}{2} + \frac{\cos.^4 \alpha}{3} +} \cdots\right)$$

$$= \frac{a^2 \cos.^2 \alpha}{2} \left(1 - \sin.^2 \alpha . \tfrac{1}{2} + \overline{\frac{\cos.^2 \alpha}{3} +} \cdots\cdots\right)$$

$$= \frac{a^2 \cos.^2 \alpha}{2} \left\{1 - \overline{1 - \cos.^2 \alpha} \left(\tfrac{1}{2} + \tfrac{1}{3} \cos.^2 \alpha + \tfrac{1}{4} \cos.^4 \alpha + \ldots\right)\right\}$$

$$= \frac{a^2 \cos.^2 \alpha}{2} \left\{ 1 - \tfrac{1}{2} - \tfrac{1}{3} \cos.^2 \alpha - \tfrac{1}{4} \cos.^4 \alpha - \ldots \right.$$

$$\left. + \tfrac{1}{2} \cos.^2 \alpha + \tfrac{1}{3} \cos.^4 \alpha + \ldots \right\}$$

$$= \frac{a^2 \cos.^2 \alpha}{4} (\tfrac{1}{2} + \tfrac{1}{6} \cos.^2 \alpha + \tfrac{1}{12} \cos.^4 \alpha + \ldots\ldots$$

$$= \frac{a^2 \cos.^2 \alpha}{2} (1 + \tfrac{1}{3} \cos.^2 \alpha + \tfrac{1}{6} \cos.^4 \alpha + \ldots\ldots)$$

Consequently β A increases as a increases, and it diminishes as α increases; also it increases as β A increases.

But the slip $= \dfrac{\sqrt{H}}{\sqrt{H} + \sqrt{\beta A}}$, $\therefore$ the slip increases as β A decreases, and *vice versâ.*

Hence, as a general rule, we shall find, cæteris paribus, *that*—

(1.) *The slip is diminished by decreasing the angle of the screw.*

(2.) *The slip is diminished by increasing the diameter of the screw.*

(3.) *The slip is diminished by increasing the length of the screw.*

This investigation does not enter into the practical question of the effect of the friction of the water on the blades of a screw, which increases rapidly with the surface, and affects the result obtained in (3).

336. *On the most advantageous Speed for Vessels steaming up a River, or in a Tide-way.*

Let v = velocity of opposing current;
x = velocity of the ship through the water;
$x - v$ = space passed over in a unit of time.

Now the horse-power of the ship, or the consumption of fuel in a unit of time $\propto x^3$ and $= a\,x^3$ (suppose) $\therefore \dfrac{a\,x^3}{x - v}$ = consumption of fuel for every unit of space moved over.

Hence $\dfrac{a\,x^3}{x - v}$ = a minimum.

$\therefore \quad 3\,x^2\,(x - v) - x^3 = 0$ (by differential calculus)

$\therefore \quad 3\,x - 3\,v - x = 0$

$$2\,x = 3\,v$$

$$x = \frac{3}{2} v$$

In plain words, the rule is, *that the ship should steam half as fast again as the opposing current.* If v be taken as the speed of another ship which we are desirous of overtaking, a similar investigation will show that the same result will obtain in that case also; viz., that the rate should be half as fast again as that of the ship to be overtaken, when economy is alone considered. See *Economy of Fuel,* by Captain A. Ryder, R.N.

337. *On the Motion of Paddle-Steamers in still Water.*

Def.—The slip of a paddle is the difference between the rate of the wheel and the rate of the ship, divided by the rate of the wheel.

(The investigations connected with what follows are given below.)*

---

* Let R = pressure of the fluid against the bows of the vessel when moving with the velocity V.

R′ = the mean pressure of the floats against the water, the floats moving with velocity U.

Then it is evident, if the motion be uniform, R = R′. Now R depends on the form of the bows and the square of the speed, ∴ $R = A^2V^2$, where A^2 is constant for the same vessel so long as the immersion remains the same. Again, $R' = B^2(U - V)^2$, where B^2 is some constant depending on the immersion and size of the floats.

$$\therefore \quad A^2V^2 = B^2(U-V)^2$$

$$\text{or} \quad AV = B(U-V)$$

$$\text{and} \quad \overline{A+B}\,V = BU$$

$$\text{or} \quad U = \left(1 + \frac{A}{B}\right)V \quad . \quad . \quad . \quad . \quad . \quad . \quad (1)$$

Again, let P = effective pressure on the surface of the piston, and V_1 its velocity; then, since the motion of the engine is uniform,

$$\begin{aligned} PV_1 &= RU \\ &= B^2(U-V)^2U \\ &= A^2V^2U \\ &= A^2V^2\left(1+\frac{A}{B}\right)V \\ &= \frac{A^2}{B}(A+B)V^3 \end{aligned}$$

Now PV_1 = effective force of the engine, and this, when divided by 33000, gives the horse-power, and consequently the horse-power

Slip.—So long as the immersion of a ship and the paddles remains unaltered, the speed of the ship is proportional to the speed of the wheel, and therefore the slip is constant for all speeds. See equation (1).

338. *Consumption of Fuel in a given time.*

The *horse-power* of a paddle-steamer is proportional to the cube of the speed; or, in other words, the *consumption of fuel in a given time*, such as a day, or an hour, or a week, *varies as the cube of the speed of the vessel.* See equation (2). Hence if a ship be at a great distance from port, and the fuel begin to fail, it would be bad policy to urge the vessel, with the idea of reaching her destination. On the contrary, unless she meets with opposing winds or tides, the slower the engines can move, subject to the condition that no

---

$$\propto \frac{A^2}{B}(A+B)V^3$$

$$\propto V^3 \quad . \quad . \quad . \quad . \quad . \quad . \quad . \quad . \quad . \quad . \quad (2)$$

Also, since $PV_1 = pA_1v_1$, where p = pressure of steam per square inch, and A_1 = the area of the piston, and A_1v_1 = volume of steam used in a unit of time at the pressure p: hence PV_1 is a measure of the steam used in a unit of time whatever that unit be, and therefore measures the consumption of fuel in any given time. Consequently the consumption of fuel *in a given time* varies as the cube of the velocity of the engine or ship.

Let C_1 = consumption of fuel in one hour

and N = the number of hours of a voyage between two places whose distance is a.

$\therefore$ C_1N = whole consumption;

and $C_1N \propto V^3 \times N \propto V^2 \times VN.$

But $a = VN$

$$\therefore \quad C_1N \propto V^2a. \quad . \quad . \quad . \quad . \quad . \quad . \quad . \quad . \quad . \quad (3)$$

or the consumption of fuel between two places whose distance is a varies as V^2a, where V is the velocity of the vessel.

Let $U = rV_1$, where r is the ratio between the velocity of the wheel and the velocity of the piston, and therefore depends on the nature of the machine, so that r will be reduced by reefing the wheels, or by interposing any multiple gearing between the piston and wheel (as is the case in some towing vessels) to increase the velocity of the piston in proportion to that of the wheel.

steam is escaping from the safety-valve, the more economically she will proceed; and this will be the effect without any consideration of the advantages to be gained by expansive working, which will be so much additional. If, however, she meet with opposition from wind or tide, it is evident no economy will result from letting her lose ground, or even by consuming fuel in merely keeping her place; but she should go at a rate half as great again as that at

---

Now since $P\,V_1 = B^2(U - V)^2 U$

$$= A^2 V^2 U$$

$$= A^2 V^2 \times r\,V_1$$

$$\therefore \quad P = r.A^2 V^2$$

$$\text{or} \quad V = \sqrt{\frac{P}{r\,A^2}} \quad \ldots\ldots \quad (4)$$

$$\text{and by (I)} \quad U = \left(1 + \frac{A}{B}\right) V$$

$$\therefore \quad U = \left(1 + \frac{A}{B}\right) \sqrt{\frac{P}{r\,A^2}} = \frac{A+B}{A\,B} \sqrt{\frac{P}{r}} \quad \ldots \quad (5)$$

Also, since $P = r\,A^2 V^2$

$$= r\,A^2 \frac{U^2}{\left(1 + \frac{A}{B}\right)^2} = r\,A^2. \frac{r^2 V_1^2}{\left(1 + \frac{A}{B}\right)^2}$$

$$\therefore \quad P = \frac{r^3 A^2 B^2}{(A+B)^2}. V_1^2$$

$$\text{or} \quad V_1 = \frac{A+B}{A\,B}. \sqrt{\frac{P}{r^3}} \quad \ldots\ldots \quad (6)$$

Let now r be altered to r', and consequently V be altered to V' V_1 to V_2; the other quantities remaining the same as before.

$$\text{Then} \quad V = \sqrt{\frac{P}{A^2 r}} \text{ and } V' = \sqrt{\frac{P}{A^2 r'}}$$

$$\therefore \quad \frac{V}{V'} = \sqrt{\frac{r'}{r}}.$$

$$\text{also} \quad V_1 = \frac{A+B}{A\,B} \sqrt{\frac{P}{r^3}}$$

$$\text{and} \quad V_2 = \frac{A+B}{A\,B} \sqrt{\frac{P}{r'^3}}$$

$$\therefore \quad \frac{V_1}{V_2} = \sqrt{\frac{r'^3}{r^3}} = \frac{V^3}{V'^3} \quad \ldots\ldots \quad (7)$$

which the wind or tide would drive her from the port she desires to reach. Thus if she would drift at the rate of 4 knots, the engines should force her through the water at the rate of 6 knots, to make good 2. If at the rate of 6 knots, the engines should drive her 9, and so on.

339. *On the Consumption of Fuel in a Passage between any two places.*

By equation (3) we see that the consumption of fuel varies as the product of the square of the speed multiplied by the distance to be steamed over. Hence, if the consumption of fuel be C when the speed is V, and distance in miles a; and the consumpion be C_1 when the speed is V_1, and distance in miles a_1, we shall have

$$C : C_1 :: V^2 \times a : V_1^2 \times a_1.$$

340. *On reefing Paddle-Wheels, to obtain greater speed.*

The rate at which the wheel revolves depends on the surface of the paddle-boards; but, provided all the steam be used that the boiler can generate, the speed of the ship is independent of their size. And therefore, whenever we are able to make use of all the steam the engine requires, no gain will be effected by diminishing the surface of the floats. The only effect would be to increase the slip and the consumption of fuel, without obtaining a proportionate increase of speed. But, on the other hand, if the wheel revolves so slowly that a portion of the steam escapes by the safety-valve, then we see by equation (4) and (6) that (by diminishing r, that is) by reefing the wheels, the speed of the ship is to a small extent increased, on account of the great increase of speed of the piston (since the former depends on the effective diameter of the wheels, and the latter on the cube of the diameter). So that, the wheels being reefed, the effective diameter of the wheels is altered, and the piston moves fast enough to enable the engines to consume all the steam generated by the boilers, which then acts effectively on the ship.

In reefing the wheels, however, there would be no practical gain in the speed of the vessel if the upper edge of the lowest board were allowed to come above the surface of the water; for that would have the result of effectually diminishing the surface of the float, and therefore would increase the speed of the engine without producing any effect on the speed of the ship.

If by means of multiple gearing, or reefing, or otherwise, the speed of the ship and engine be increased, it will be found (see 7) that the speed of the engine varies as the cube of the speed of the ship.

341. *Measure of the Locomotive Performance of Marine Steam-Engines.*

Let A be the effective resisting midship section of a steamship, and v its speed,

Then the amount of resistance $\propto Av^2$

and the work to be performed $\propto Av^3$.

Again, since the expenditure of fuel may be approximately estimated by the Indicator horse-power, the work to be overcome by a unit of fuel is $\frac{Av^3}{I}$ (where I is the Indicator horse-power).

But if D be the displacement and l the length of the ship, we shall have for similar ships,

$$D \propto l^3 \therefore l \propto D^{\frac{1}{3}}$$

and $$A \propto l^2 \text{ and } l \propto A^{\frac{1}{2}}$$

Hence $$A^{\frac{1}{2}} \propto D^{\frac{1}{3}}, \text{ or } A \propto D^{\frac{2}{3}}$$

$\therefore$ the measure required is $\frac{D^{\frac{2}{3}}v^3}{I}$

It must, however, be observed, that this formula does not strictly apply to ships of different build, or in comparing different screws in the same ship, or with different grades of expansion.

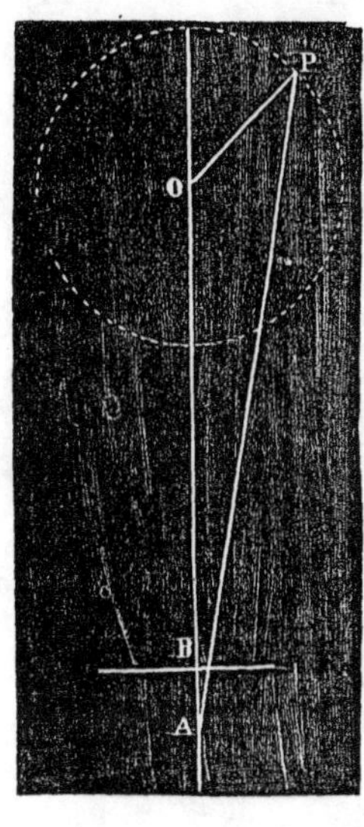

342. *To find the Angle the Crank has moved through when the Piston is at a given distance from the top of the Stroke.*

Let O P be the position of the crank; P A the connecting-rod at the distance B A from its highest point B;

and let $OP = a$; $PA = c$

$BA = x$; $\angle POA = \theta$

Then $OB = c - a$

And by Trigonometry,

$$\text{Cos.}\ \frac{\theta}{2} = \sqrt{\frac{(OP + OA + PA)(OP + OA - AP)}{4 \cdot OP \cdot OA}}$$

$$= \sqrt{\frac{(a + c - a + x + c)(a + c - a + x - c)}{4 \cdot a \cdot (c - a + x)}}$$

$$= \sqrt{\frac{(2c + x) \cdot x}{4a(c - a + x)}}$$

Hence, having given c, a, and x, we may find $\frac{\theta}{2}$ and therefore θ.

343. *To find the amount of Work developed by a Crank in half a complete Revolution, if a constant pressure act vertically at the lower end of the Connecting-rod.*

Let the crank O P (in any position) make an angle P O A $= \theta$ with the vertical line, and P A O $= \phi$

$$OP = a,\ PA = c.$$

Then if P be the upward pressure at A, let R be the force in the direction of the connecting-rod;

$\therefore$ resolving R horizontally and vertically, we have

$$R\cos.\phi = P \qquad (1)$$

and the moment of the force to turn the crank $= Ra\sin.\overline{\theta+\phi}$

$$\therefore = Pa\frac{\sin.\overline{\theta+\phi}}{\cos.\phi}$$

and the amount of work while moving through an angle $d\theta$

$$= Pa\frac{\sin.\overline{\theta+\phi}}{\cos.\phi}d\theta$$

$\therefore$ the work performed while the piston is ascending

$$= Pa\int\frac{\sin.\overline{\theta+\phi}}{\cos.\phi}d\theta$$

taken between the limits $\theta = 0$ and $\theta = \pi$;

$$\therefore W = Pa\int\frac{\sin.\theta\cos.\phi + \cos.\theta\sin.\phi}{\cos.\phi}d\theta$$

$$Pa\int(\sin.\theta + \frac{\sin.\phi}{\cos.\phi}\cos.\theta)\,d\theta$$

But $\sin.\phi = \frac{a}{c}\sin.\theta$;

$$\therefore W = Pa\int\left(\sin.\theta + \frac{\frac{a}{c}\sin.\theta\cos.\theta}{\sqrt{1-\frac{a^2}{c^2}\sin.^2\theta}}\right)d\theta$$

$$= Pa\left(-\cos.\theta - \frac{c}{a}\sqrt{1-\frac{a^2}{c^2}\sin.^2\theta}\right) + \text{cor.}$$

$$\begin{matrix}\theta = 0 \\ = \pi\end{matrix} \qquad = P.2a$$

which is the same as would have been obtained if the power had acted through the vertical diameter without the intervention of a crank. It is evident that this result might have been arrived at immediately by the principle of virtual velocities; but since it is frequently imagined power is lost by the use of a crank, it has been thought advisable to give an independent investigation.

344. *To find the length of the Radius-bar in a side-lever Engine.*

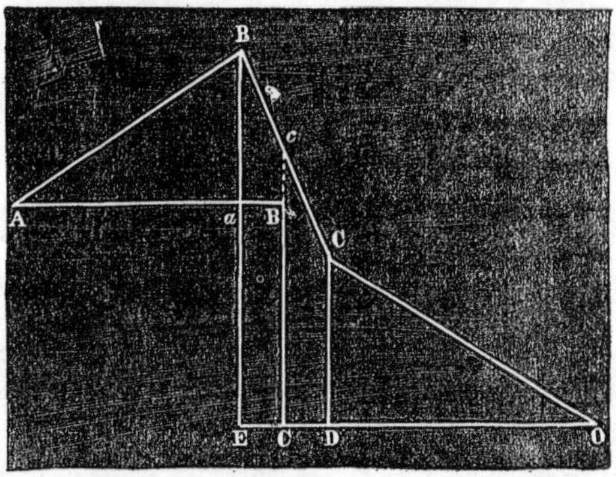

Let A B be the radius-bar; B C the parallel-motion side-rod; C O that portion of the side-lever between O (the main centre) and B C.

Let A B $= x$; $B'c = a$; $C'c = b$; C O $= y$; $\angle$ B' A B $= \theta$; $\angle$ C c C' $= \psi$; C' O C $= \phi$.

Now we have $x \cos. \theta + a \sin. \psi = x$ (1)

also $y \cos. \phi + b \sin. \psi = y$ (2)

and $x \sin. \theta + (a + b) = (a + b) \cos. \psi + y \sin. \phi$ (3)

And (1) let θ, ψ, and ϕ be small angles, which is the case where the radius-bar is long.

Then from these equations we get

$$x\left(1 - \frac{\theta^2}{2}\right) + a\psi = x\,; \text{ or } a\psi = \frac{x}{2}\theta^2$$

also $$y\left(1 - \frac{\phi^2}{2}\right) + b\psi = y\,; \text{ or } b\psi = \frac{y}{2}\phi^2$$

and $$x\theta + (a + b) = (a + b) + y\phi\,; \text{ or } x\theta = y\phi.$$

Hence $$\frac{a}{b} = \frac{x}{y} \cdot \frac{\theta^2}{\phi^2}$$

and $$\frac{\theta}{\phi} = \frac{y}{x}$$

$$\therefore \quad \frac{a}{b} = \frac{x}{y} \cdot \frac{y}{x} = \frac{y}{x}\,; \text{ or A B}' : \text{C}' \text{O} :: \text{C}' c : c \text{B}'.$$

(2.) Let θ be large, and ψ and ϕ small; which is the case where the radius-bar is short.

Then, as before, $x \cos. \theta + a\psi = x$

also $$y\left(1 - \frac{\phi^2}{2}\right) + b\psi = y$$

and $$x \sin. \theta + (a + b) = (a + b) + y\phi$$

$$\therefore \qquad x \cos.\, \theta = x - a\psi$$

also
$$b\psi = \frac{y\phi^2}{2}$$

and
$$x \sin.\, \theta = y\phi$$

$$\therefore \qquad x \cos.\, \theta = x - \frac{a}{b}y\frac{\phi^2}{2}$$

$$\therefore \quad x^2 (\sin.^2 \theta + \cos.^2 \theta) = x^2 - \frac{a}{b}x y\phi^2 + \frac{a^2}{b^2}y^2\frac{\phi^4}{4} + y^2\phi^2$$

Hence
$$\frac{a}{b}\cdot\frac{x}{y} = 1 + \frac{a^2}{b^2}\cdot\frac{\phi}{4}$$

$$\frac{x}{y} = \frac{b}{a} + \frac{a}{b}\cdot\frac{\phi^2}{4}$$

But the angle described by the side-lever is usually about 20°.

Hence
$$\phi = \frac{\pi}{9} \text{ and } \frac{\phi^2}{4} = \frac{\pi^2}{324} = \cdot 0304$$

and $\therefore$
$$\frac{x}{y} = \frac{b}{a} + \cdot 0304\frac{a}{b}$$

the correction to the first approximation being $\cdot 0304\frac{a}{b}$.

345. *To find the amount of Work done in the up and down stroke of an Air-pump (neglecting friction, etc.)*

(1.) Suppose the pump fitted with an air-tight delivery-valve, and that there is a vacuum above and below the air-pump bucket.

Let B = the area of the bucket.
h = the length of stroke.
b = distance from surface of water in the bucket to the cover of the air-pump.
$h - b$ = height of water in the bucket.
σ = specific gravity of ditto.
w = weight of water to be lifted $= \sigma (h - b)$ B.

This will be raised through a space b, when the delivery-valve will open.

Let the top of the air-pump be at a depth l below the surface of the water, and k the height of water due to the atmospheric pressure.

$\therefore$ the mean pressure on the bucket after the delivery-valve opens is $\sigma B\left(l+k+\frac{h-b}{2}\right)$, and the space to be passed over is $h-b$.

$\therefore$ the whole work is $\sigma(h-b)Bb+\sigma B\left(l+k+\frac{h-b}{2}\right)$ $(h-b)$

$$=\sigma(h-b)B\left(l+k+\frac{h-b}{2}+b\right)$$

$$=w\left(l+k+\frac{h+b}{2}\right)$$

and there is no work in the down-stroke.

2. Suppose the air-pump not to have a delivery-valve, then the mean pressure in the up-stroke is $\sigma B\left(l+k+\frac{h}{2}\right)$; and the space passed over is h.

$\therefore$ the work in the up-stroke is $\sigma B\left(l+k+\frac{h}{2}\right)h$.

Again, in the down-stroke, the mean pressure is $\sigma B\left(l+k+\frac{b}{2}\right)$, and the space passed through till the water is reached by the bucket is b;

$\therefore$ the *negative* work in the down-stroke is $\sigma B\left(l+k+\frac{b}{2}\right)b$.

Hence the whole work in the up and down stroke is

$$\sigma B\left(l+k+\frac{h}{2}\right)h-\sigma B\left(l+k+\frac{b}{2}\right)b=\sigma B(h-b)(l+k)+\sigma B\frac{h^2-b^2}{2}$$

$$=\sigma B(h-b)\left(l+k+\frac{h+b}{2}\right)=w\left(l+k+\frac{h+b}{2}\right),$$

precisely the same as in the former case.

346. *To determine the amount of Fuel lost by the process of Blowing-out.*

Let $x=$ the number of gallons blown-out in a given time.

$y=$ " of water evaporated.

$\therefore$ $x+y=$ quantity entering as feed.

Let $t=$ temperature of feed-water.

$T=$ " of water in boiler.

$\therefore$ $(1212-t)y=$ quantity of heat expended in the formation of steam.

$(T - t)\,x =$ quantity expended in heating water to be blown-out.

$\therefore\ (1212 - t)\,y + (T - t)\,x =$ whole quantity of fuel expended.

If, therefore, Q be the amount of fuel lost per cent in blowing-out,

$$\frac{Q}{100} = \frac{(T - t)\,x}{(1212 - t)\,y + (T - t)\,x}$$

from which formula the last column in Table D may be calculated.

347. *To determine the best Temperature for the Condenser of a Steam-Engine.*

The best temperature is evidently that in which the residue of work done (after making allowance for the duty of the air-pump) by the heat requisite to raise the water from the temperature of the condenser to that of the boiler may be a maximum.

Let therefore $t^\circ =$ temperature of injection-water.
$a^\circ =$ amount of heat in a unit of steam (1212°).
$x^\circ =$ the temperature of condensation.
$P =$ mean pressure on piston.
$p =$ pressure of uncondensed steam.
$\therefore\ P - p =$ effective pressure.
Again, let $A =$ area of piston.
$l =$ length of stroke.
$n\,l =$ height to which the air pump has to raise the water.
$w =$ weight of cylinderful of steam.
$X =$ weight of injection-water admitted to condense it.

$\therefore\ (P - p)\,l\,A =$ work done by steam in one stroke.
$(w + X)\,n\,l =$ work expended by air-pump.
$w\,(a^\circ - x^\circ) =$ amount of heat expended.

$$\therefore\ \frac{(P - p)\,l\,A - (w + X)\,n\,l}{w\,(a - x)} = \text{a max.}$$

or

$$\frac{(P - p)\,A - (w + X)\,n}{a - x} = \text{a max.}$$

Now

$$x = \frac{a\,w + X\,t}{w + X} \quad . \quad . \quad . \quad . \quad . \quad . \quad (\text{p. } 32)$$

$$\therefore \qquad X = \frac{w(a-x)}{x-t}$$

$$\text{and} \therefore \qquad \frac{(P-p)A - \frac{w(a-t)}{x-t}.n}{a-x} = \text{a max.}$$

Hence, differentiating, we get

$$\left\{-\frac{dp}{dx}.A + nw\frac{a-t}{(x-t)^2}\right\}\overline{a-x} + \overline{P-p}\,A - \frac{nw(a-t)}{x-t} = 0$$

$$\therefore \quad \frac{dp}{dx}A(a-x) - \overline{P-p}\,A = \frac{nw(a-t)}{x-t}\left(\frac{a-x}{x-t} - 1\right)$$

$$\text{and} \quad \frac{dp}{dx}A(a-x) - \overline{P-p}\,A = \frac{nw(a-t)(a-x)}{(x-t)^2}\text{ nearly.}$$

But by Tredgold's formula,

$$p = \frac{1}{2}\left(\frac{100+x}{177}\right)^6$$

$$\therefore \qquad \frac{dp}{dx} = \frac{3}{177}\left(\frac{100+x}{177}\right)^5 = \frac{1}{59}\left(\frac{100+x}{177}\right)^5$$

$$\text{Hence } \frac{1}{59}\left(\frac{100+x}{177}\right)^5\overline{a-x} - \overline{P-p} = \frac{nw}{A}\,\frac{(a-t)\cdot(a-x)}{(x-t)^2}$$

$$\therefore \left(\frac{100+x}{177}\right)^5(a-x) - 59(P-p) = \frac{59\,nw}{A}\,\frac{(a-t)(a-x)}{(x-t)^2}$$

$$\left(\frac{100+x}{177}\right)^5 - \frac{59(P-p)}{a} = \frac{59\,nw(a-t)}{A(x-t)^2}$$

$$\therefore \quad (x-t)^2 = \frac{\frac{59\,nw(a-t)}{A}}{\left(\frac{100+x}{177}\right)^5 - \frac{59(P-p)}{a-x}} \quad . \quad . \quad . \quad . \qquad (1)$$

From which equation we must determine x approximately. To do this, we must first substitute for x on the right-hand side of the equation whatever we consider to be the most probable value; and solving the equation on this supposition, we shall get a corresponding value of x on the left-hand side. Now, from the form of the equation, we see, that if we substitute too high a value at first, we shall get too low a result, and *vice versâ:* hence the true value must be somewhere between the two. Let, therefore, a mean of the assumed and resulting value be taken, which substitute again as an assumed value, to get a closer approximation, and so on.

Now in (1) $w=$ the weight of a cylinderful of steam.

But the weight of a cylinderful of water $=\frac{62\cdot5}{144}l\,A$ in lbs. A being expressed in square inches.

Hence by M. de Pambour's formula,

$$w=\frac{62\cdot5}{144}l\,A\,(a+bp_1)$$

where $p_1=$ the pressure at the end of the stroke.

$$\text{Hence }(x-t)^2=\frac{\frac{62\cdot5\times59}{144}nl\,(a+bp_1)'\,(a-t)}{\left(\frac{100+x}{177}\right)^5-\frac{59\,(P-p)}{a-x}}$$

$$\text{or}\quad x=t+5\cdot061\sqrt{\frac{nl\,(a+bp_1)\,(a-t)}{\left(\frac{100+x}{177}\right)^5-\frac{59\,(P-p)}{a-x}}}$$

Again, $n\,l=$ height due to the pressure on the air-pump, $=30+h$ nearly, since the pressure of the atmosphere $=34$ feet, and we may reckon the deficiency of the vacuum in the condenser at 4 feet; also h is the height from the bottom of the air-pump to the surface of the water outside the ship.

$$\therefore\quad x=t+5\cdot061\sqrt{\frac{(30+h)\,(a+bp_1)\,(a-t)}{\left(\frac{100+x}{177}\right)^5-\frac{59\,(P-p)}{a-x}}}$$

The most suitable temperature, therefore, depends on h, p_1, and t, as we stated in our general principles, art. 239.

As an example, let $t=60^\circ$
$h=4$
$p_1=14$
and $x=100^\circ$
We get as a result $x=83\cdot25$
and $\therefore$ taking the mean,

$$\begin{array}{r} 83\cdot25 \\ 100\cdot00 \\ \hline 2)183\cdot25 \\ \hline 91\cdot62 \end{array}$$

Again, substituting this value, we get $x = 86{\cdot}59$;
and taking the mean,

$$\begin{array}{r} 91{\cdot}62 \\ 86{\cdot}59 \\ \hline 2)178{\cdot}21 \\ \hline x = 89{\cdot}10 \end{array}$$

348. *On the Qualities of Fuel.*

The following remarks on the subject of fuel are extracted from the result of some researches undertaken by the direction and at the cost of the Admiralty, at the Museum of Practical Geology, by Sir Henry de la Beche and Dr. Lyon Playfair. The nature of our present work requires little more than the mere result of the investigations; and those who want fuller information must refer to "Reports on the Coals suited to the Steam Navy, by Sir Henry de la Beche and Dr. Lyon Playfair."

Experiments necessary to ascertain the true practical value of coal involve a large series of observations, extended over a considerable period, and directed to special objects of inqury. The qualities for which particular kinds of fuel are pre-eminent being so varied, it is impossible to deduce general results from a limited series of observations. Even in the one economical application of coals, their evaporative value, or their power of forming steam, one variety of coal, which may be admirably adapted, from its quick action for raising steam in a short period, may be far exceeded by another variety, inferior in this respect, but capable of converting a much larger quantity of water into steam, and therefore more valuable in the production of force. A coal uniting these two qualities in a high degree might still be useless for naval purposes on account of its mechanical structure. If the cohesion of its particles be small, the effect of transport, or the attrition of one coal against another by the motion of a vessel, might so far pulverize it as materially to reduce its value. Even supposing the three qualities united, rapidity and duration of action with considerable resistance to breakage, there are many other properties which should receive attention in the selection of a fuel, without the combination of which it might be valueless for our steam-navy.

349. *Weight of Coal when used as Fuel.*

There is an important difference existing between varieties of coals in the bulk or space occupied by a certain weight. For the purposes of stowage-room this cannot be ascertained by specific gravity alone, because the mechanical formation of the coal may enable one of less density to take up a smaller space than that occupied by another of a higher gravity. This is far from an imaginary difference, being sometimes as great as 60 per cent., and not unfrequently 40 per cent. The mere theoretical determination of the density of coals would therefore give results useless for practice. The space occupied between two varieties of coals, often equally good as regards their evaporative value, differs occasionally 20 per cent.; that is, where 80 tons of one coal could be stowed, 100 tons of another of equal evaporative value might be placed, by selecting it according to its mechanical structure. These facts are mentioned merely to show that a hasty generalization should not be made, and to account for drawing attention to these various points as a means of preventing the selection of a fuel from any one quality.

350. *Patent Fuels.*

Various compositions, under the name of Patent, or Artificial Fuels, have been experimented on, and the results entered in the accompanying Tables. Patent fuels are usually made up in the form of bricks, and would therefore be very convenient for stowage, if sufficient time could be spared for packing them when they are received on board This, however, is rarely the case either in vessels of war or packets, except perhaps on leaving a home port. Owing then, to their low specific gravity, they occupy, on ordi nary occasions, a greater space per ton than any species of coal. They are usually composed of a mixture of coal-dust and tarry or bituminous matter; water, and occasionally other ingredients, being used for cementing the compound.

Warlich's fuel is composed of one ton of Graigola or Resolven coal-dust, containing on an average 16 gallons of water, intimately mixed with 16 gallons of coal-tar.

Holland and Green's fuel is of the following composition:

Lime	100	parts
Gypsum	17	"
Alum	17	"
Common salt	17	"
Aluminous clay	28	"
Screenings of Newcastle coal	2240	"

Mixed with about 20 gallons of pure water.

But fuel containing much foreign matter in its composition generally produces a large amount of clinker and ash. The evaporating powers of the other five patent fuels rank high as compared with that of the coals experimented on. In general, however, they do not light readily; they emit great quantities of black smoke, and produce much soot.

To remedy these defects, and as it has been repeatedly stated by eminent engineers that the value of fuel for steam purposes depends on the quantity of fixed carbon it contains, experiments were made at the suggestion of the late First Lord of the Admiralty to ascertain how far mixtures of anthracite with more bituminous coals were likely to prove advantageous in the manufacture of artificial fuel. The experiments were undertaken at Swansea, the proprietors of Warlich's Patent Fuel Works having allowed the use of their apparatus for the purpose. It was found, however, that the advantages of these additions were not such as to recommend their adoption. The cementing-tar, though partially carbonized by the heat of the coking-ovens, in which the prepared fuels are heated, was so much more combustible than the dense and slowly igniting anthracite, that the latter remained after the combustion of the former; and therefore either accumulated on the bars, obstructing the draught, or, falling through the grate, escaped combustion. If thrown again on the fire, it choked the air-way, and impeded the proper action of the fuel. The evaporative power of the fuels thus prepared was certainly found to increase in proportion to the addition of fixed carbon; but this would appear to arise from the fuel then assuming more of the characters of the anthracite, or coke, from which it was made. The results of the experiments pointed to the necessity of keeping a uniform character in the fuels manufactured.

351. *Effects of Stowage upon Coals.*

It is of much importance in an economical inquiry on coals, to obtain exact information as to the effect likely to be produced upon them by stowage and continued exposure to high temperature, not only as regards their deterioration, but also as to the emission of dangerous gases by their progressive changes. The retention of coal in iron bunkers, if these are likely to be influenced by moisture, and especially when by any accident wetted with sea-water, will cause a speedy corrosion of the iron, with a rapidity proportionate to its more or less efficient protection from corroding influences. This corrosion seems due to the action of carbon or coal forming with the iron a voltaic couple, and thus promoting oxidation. The action is similar to that of the tubercular concretions which appear on the inside of iron water-pipes, when a piece of carbon, not chemically combined with the metal, and in contact with saline water, produces a speedy corrosion. Where the "make" of iron shows it to be liable to be thus corroded, a mechanical protection is generally found sufficient. This is sometimes given by Roman cement, by a lining of wood, or by a drying oil driven into the pores of the iron under great pressure.

Recent researches on the gases evolved from coal prove

that carbonic acid and nitrogen are constantly mixed with the inflammable portion, showing that the coal must still be uniting with the oxygen of the atmosphere, and entering into further decay.

352. *Decay of Coals.*

Decay is merely a combustion proceeding without flame, and is always attended with the production of heat. The gas evolved during the progress of decay, in free air, consists principally of carbonic acid, a gas very injurious to animal life. It is well known that this change in coal proceeds more rapidly at an elevated temperature, and therefore is liable to take place in hot climates. Dryness is unfavorable to the change, while moisture causes it to proceed with rapidity. When sulphur or iron pyrites (a compound of sulphur and iron) is present in considerable quantity in a coal still changing under the action of the atmosphere, a second powerful heating-cause is introduced, and both acting together may produce what is termed *spontaneous combustion.* The latter cause is in itself sufficient, if there be an unusual proportion of sulphur or iron pyrites present. The best method of prevention in all such cases is to insure perfect dryness in the coals when they are stowed away, and to select a variety of fuel not liable to the progressive decomposition to which allusion has been made.

353. *Qualities of Coals suited to Steam-Navigation.*

The various qualities of coal on which its value, as far as steam-navigation is concerned, depends, are thus summed up:

1. The fuel should burn so that steam may be raised in a short period, if this be required; in other words, it should be capable of a quick action.

2. It should possess high evaporative power; that is be capable of converting much water into steam with a small consumption of fuel.

3. It should not be bituminous, lest so much smoke be generated as to betray the position of ships-of-war, when it is desirable that this should be concealed.

4. It should possess considerable cohesion of its particles, so that it may not be broken into too small fragments by the constant attrition which it may experience in the vessel.

5. It should combine a considerable density with such mechanical structure that it may easily be stowed away in small space; a condition which, in coals of equal evaporative values, often involves a difference of more than 20 per cent.

6. It should be free from any considerable quantity of sulphur, and should not progressively decay; both of which circumstances render it liable to spontaneous combustion.

It never happens that all these conditions are united in one coal. To take an instance, anthracite has very high evaporative power; but not being easily ignited, is not suited for quick action: it has great cohesion in its particles, and is not easily broken up by attrition; but it is not a caking coal, and therefore would not cohere in the furnace when the ship rolled in a gale of wind: it emits no smoke; but from the intensity of its combustion causes the iron of the bars and boilers to oxidate or waste rapidly away. Thus, then, with some pre-eminent advantages, it has disadvantages which, under ordinary circumstances, preclude its use.

The following abstract of the working Tables will give a general view of the relative value of the coals experimented upon. It must not, however, be taken as the exact expression of their values without a reference to the detailed description of each experiment as given in the "Report" from which these extracts are made.

TABLE I. *Power and Duty, etc., of various Coals.*

Locality or Name of Coal.	Pounds of Water evaporated from 212° by 1 lb. of Coal.	Weight of 1 cubic foot as used for Fuel.	Weight of 1 cubic foot calculated from density.	Space occupied by 1 ton in cubic feet (as used for Fuel.)	Comparative cohesive power.	Rate of Evaporation. lbs. of Water evaporated per hour.	lbs. of Clinker per ton of Coals.
WELSH.	A.	B.	C.	D.	E.	F.	G.
Aberaman Merthyr	10·75	48·9	81·91	45·80	...	...	13·3
Ebbw Vale	10·21	53·3	78·81	42·26	45·0	460·22	...
Thomas's Merthyr	10·16	53·0	82·29	42·26	57·5	520·8	3·9
Duffryn	10·14	53·22	82·72	42·09	56·2	409·32	...
Nixon's Merthyr	9·96	51·7	82·29	43·32	64·5	511·4	5·7
Binea	9·94	57·08	81·357	39·24	51·2	486·95	...
Bedwas	9·79	50·5	82·6	44·32	54·0	476·96	...
Hill's Plymouth Work	9·75	51·2	84·78	43·74	64·0	531·6	7·5
Aberdare Co.'s Merthyr	9·73	49·3	81·73	45·43	74·5	489·5	9·8
Gadly Nine-feet Seam	9·56	54·8	83·16	40·87	76·0	517·3	6·0
Resolven	9·53	58·66	82·354	38·19	35·0	390·25	...
Mynydd Newydd	9·52	56·33	81·73	39·76	53·7	470·69	...
Abercarn	9·47	50·3	83·22	44·53	54·5	480·00	20·0
Anthracite, Jones and Co	9·46	58·25	85·786	38·45	68·5	409·37	...
Ward's Fiery Vein	9·40	57·433	83·85	39·00	46·5	529·90	...
Neath Abbey	9·38	59·3	83·57	37·77	50·0	546.1	19·2
Graigola	9·35	60·166	81·107	37·23	49·3	441·48	...
Gadly Four-feet Seam	9·29	51·6	82·79	43·41	68·5	400·0	11·6
Machen Rock Vein	9·23	48·1	80·91	46·56	52·5	488·75	12·4
Birch Grove, Graigola	9·22	51·0	84·85	43·92	59·0	507·50	28·6
Llynvi	9·19	53·3	80·35	42·02	...	399·50	36·0
Cadoxton	8·97	58·1	85·97	38·55	...	344·16	34.7
Oldcastle Fiery Vein	8·94	50·916	80·42	43·99	57·7	464·30	...
Vivian and Sons' Mirfa	8·92	47·9	81·04	46·76	54·0	421·25	18·0
Llangennech	8·86	56·93	81·85	39·34	53·5	373·22	...
Three-quarter Rock Vein	8·84	56·388	83·60	39·72	52·7	486·86	...
Pentrepoth	8·72	57·72	81·73	38·80	46·5	381·50	...
Cwm Frood Rock Vein	8·70	55·277	78·299	40·52	72·5	379·80	...
Cwm Nanty Gros	8·42	56·0	79·859	40·00	55·7	404·16	...
Brymbo Main	8·36	47·0	81·10	47·65	...	435·83	10·7
Vivian and Sons' Rock Vawr	8·08	48·9	81·16	45·80	70·5	492·50	30·1
Coleshill	8·0	53·0	80·483	42·26	62·0	406·41	...
Byrmbo Two-yard	7·85	47·9	80·04	46·76	79·5	441·66	19·5
Rock Vawr	7·68	55·0	80·21	40·72	65·5	397·5	38·0
Porth-mawr	7·53	53·3	86·722	42·02	62·0	347·44	...
Pontypool	7·47	55·7	83·35	40·216	57·5	250·40	...
Pentrefelen	6·36	66·166	84·726	33·85	52·7	247·24	...
NEWCASTLE.							
Willington	9·95	53·2	79·87	42·10	43·00	...	7·0
Andrews House Tanfield	9·39	52.1	78·86	42·99	...	351·2	3·2
Bowden Close	9·38	50.6	79·87	44·26	38·5	...	6·6
Haswell Wallsend	8·87	47·4	80·23	47·25	73·0	411·66	3·5
Newcastle Hartley	8·23	50·5	80·27	44·35	78·5	308·0	17·0
Hedley's Hartley	8·16	52·0	81·79	43·07	85·5	300·8	14·4
Bates' West Hartley	8·04	50·8	78·17	44·10	69·5	406·8	1·4
West Hartley Main	7·87	48·9	78·86	45·80	79·0	457·50	2·8
Buddle's West Hartley	7·82	50·6	77·11	44·09	80·0	413·3	5·9
Hastings' Hartley	7·77	48·5	78·04	46·18	75·5	404·5	1·7
Carr's Hartley	7·71	47·8	78·23	46·86	77·5	344·3	5·0
Davison's West Hartley	7·61	47·7	78·36	46·96	76·5	402·9	2·1
North Percy Hartley	7·57	49·1	78·29	45·62	60·0	423·5	7·8
Haswell Coal Co.'s Steamboat Wallsend	7·48	49·5	79·36	45·25	79·5	291·8	9·8
Derwentwater Hartley	7·42	50·4	78·79	44·44	63·5	451·1	28·3
Broomhill	7·3	52·5	77·988	42.67	65·7	397·78	...
Original Hartley	6·82	49·1	77·98	45·62	80·0	428·4	10·1
Cowpen and Sidney's Hartley	6·79	47·9	78·67	46·76	74·0	350·4	3·7

TABLE I. (*continued.*)

Locality or Name of Coal.	Pounds of Water evaporated from 212° by 1 lb. of Coal.	Weight of 1 cubic foot as used for Fuel.	Weight of 1 cubic foot calculated from density.	Space occupied by 1 ton in cubic feet (as used for Fuel.)	Comparative cohesive power.	Rate of Evaporation. lbs. of Water evaporated per hour.	lbs. of Clinker per ton of Coals.
	A.	B.	C.	D.	E.	F.	G.
DERBYSHIRE.							
Earl Fitzwilliam's Elsecar	8·52	47·2	80·85	47·45	77·0	412·70	6·6
Hoyland and Co.'s Elsecar	8·07	48·2	82·16	46·47	82·5	372·91	1·7
Earl Fitzwilliam's Park Gate	7·92	47·0	81·79	47·65	78·0	393·75	none
Butterly Co.'s Portland	7·92	47·1	81·16	47·55	89·0	487·08	10·3
Butterly Co.'s Langley	7·80	47·8	78·86	46·86	84·5	398·69	10·0
Stavely	7·26	49·9	79·79	44·88	88·5	466·2	12·6
Loscoe Soft	6·88	44·8	80·17	50·00	62·0	499·06	8·4
Loscoe Hard	6·32	5·9	79·60	48·80	86·0	431·42	8·5
LANCASHIRE.							
Ince Hall Co.'s Arley	9·47	47·6	79·36	47·05	73·5	487·29	10·7
Hoydock Little Delf	9·13	44·9	78·42	49·88	66·5	532·91	9.6
Balcarres Arley	8·83	50·5	78·17	44·35	76·0	454·1	11·0
Blackley Hurst	8·81	48·0	78·90	46·66	65·0	500·8	12·2
Ince Hall Pemberton Yard	8·78	48·0	84·10	46·66	75·5	461·25	10·8
Haydock Rushy Park	8·74	49·3	82·54	45·43	77·0	461·66	7.8
Moss Hall Pemberton Four-feet.	8·52	47·3	78·48	47·35	71·5	480·00	7·1
Haydock Higher Florida	8·39	49·5	75·99	45·25	74·0	467·50	13.2
Ince Hall Pemberton Four-feet	8·34	51·8	79·60	43·24	74·5	497·39	2.1
Blackbrook Little Delf	8·29	51·0	78·16	43·92	61·5	440·4	none
King	8·17	50·8	81·10	44·09	78·5	395·41	47·1
Rushy Park Mine	8·08	47·0	80·04	47·65	67·0	419·1	2·7
Blackbrook Rushy Park	8·02	55·3	80·15	40·50	80·5	481·2	·1
Johnson & Wirthington's Rushy Park	8·01	50·0	80·10	44·80	69·0	454·5	8·6
Laffak Rushby Park	7·98	52·6	84·07	42·58	75·5	435·0	5·1
Balcarres Haigh Yard	7·90	50·8	80·10	44·13	80·0	398·3	26·4
Haydock Florida Main	7·83	48·0	79·04	46·66	81·5	422·50	9·0
Wigan Four-feet	7·77	53·4	75·49	41·94	75·0	414·79	37·6
Ince Hall Pemberton Five-feet	7·72	51·8	79·17	43·24	71·5	495·20	20·4
Cannel (Wigan)	7·70	48·3	76·80	46·37	95·0	381·1	21·1
Ince Hall Co.'s Furnace Vein	7·47	49·3	81·98	45·43	71·5	435·21	25·3
Balcarres Lindsay	7·44	51·1	78·61	43·83	70·0	431·5	22·3
Caldwell & Thompson's Rushby Park	7·34	47·5	76·29	47·15	76·0	449·79	5.1
Balcarres Five-feet	7·21	49·0	79·11	45·71	44·5	489·5	21·8
Moss Hall Pemberton Five-feet	7·13	48·3	80·04	46·37	78·5	417·18	31·9
Moss Hall Co.'s New Mine	7·04	48·4	79·75	46·28	76·5	422·08	34·2
Caldwell and Thompson's Higher Delf	6·85	48·4	79·48	46·28	77·0	484·28	38·6
Johnson and Wirthington's Sir John	6·32	51·6	81·73	43·41	82·0	360·7	34·4
SCOTCH.							
Wallsend Elgin	8·46	54·6	78·611	41·02	64·0	435·77	...
Wellewood	8·24	52·6	79·78	42·58	80·0	438·5	28·5
Dalkeith Coronation Seam	7·71	51·66	78·611	43·36	88·2	370·08	...
Kilmarnock Skerrington	7·66	44·7	77·42	50·11	63·5	470·83	6·4
Fordel Splint	7·56	55·0	78·611	40·72	63·0	464·98	...
Grangemouth	7·40	54.25	80·48	40·13	69.7	380·4	...
Eglinton	7·37	52·0	79·84	43·07	79·5	406·2	8.2
Dalkeith Jewel Seam	7·08	49·8	79·672	44·98	85·7	355·18	...
IRISH.							
Slievardagh Irish Anthracite	9·85	62·8	99·57	35·66	74·0	473·18	...
VARIOUS.							
Coleshill Co.'s Bagilt Main	8·33	49·6	79·17	45·16	79·0	461.25	5·7
Ewloe	7.02	50·4	79·54	44·44	84·0	363·95	4·4
Ibstock	6·91	47·3	80·54	47·35	62·0	454·16	14·1
Lydney (Forest of Dean)	8·52	54·44	80·046	41·14	55·0	487·19	...
Conception Bay, Chili	5·72	...	80·54	...	...	425·0	44·5

TABLE I. (*continued.*)

Locality or Name of Coal.	Pounds of Water evaporated from 212° by 1 lb. of Coal.	Weight of 1 cubic foot as used for Fuel.	Weight of 1 cubic foot calculated from density.	Space occupied by 1 ton in cubic feet (as used for Fuel.)	Comparative cohesive power.	Rate of Evaporation. lbs. of Water evaporated per hour.	lbs. of Clinker per ton of Coals.
PATENT FUELS.	A.	B.	C.	D.	E.	F.	G.
Warlich's Patent Fuel	10·36	69·05	72·248	32·44	...	457·84	...
Livingstone's Steam Fuel	10·03	65·6	73·86	34·14	...	483·95	28·2
Lyon's Patent Fuel	9·58	61·1	74·73	36·66	...	409·1	38·7
Wylam's	8·92	65·08	68·629	34·41	...	418·89	...
Bell's	8·53	65·3	71·124	34·30	...	549·11	...
Holland and Green's	7·59	64·8	81·23	34·56	...	470·0	87·6

TABLE II. *Mean Composition of average Samples of various Coals.*

Locality or Name of Coal.	Specific Gravity of Coal.	Carbon.	Hydrogen.	Nitrogen.	Sulphur.	Oxygen.	Ash.	Percentage of Coke left by each Coal.
WELSH.	A.	B.	C.	D.	E.	F.	G.	H.
Aberaman Merthyr	1·305	90·94	4·28	1·21	1·18	0·94	1·45	85·0
Ebbw Vale	1·275	89·78	5·15	2·16	1·02	0·39	1·50	77·5
Thomas's Merthyr	1·30	90·12	4·33	1·00	0·85	2·02	1·68	86·53
Duffryn	1·326	88·26	4·66	1·45	1·77	0·60	3·26	84·3
Nixon's Merthyr	1·31	90·27	4·12	0·63	1·20	2·53	1·25	79·11
Binea	1·304	88·66	4·63	1·43	0·33	1·03	3·96	88·10
Bedwas	1·32	80·61	6·01	1·44	3·50	1·50	6·94	71·7
Hill's Plymouth Work	1·35	88·49	4·00	0·46	0·84	3·82	2·39	82·25
Aberdare Co.'s Merthyr	1·31	88·28	4·24	1.66	0·91	1·65	3·26	85·83
Gadly Nine-feet Seam	1·33	86·18	4·31	1·09	0·87	2·21	5·34	86·54
Resolven	1·32	79·33	4·75	1·38	5·07	Included in Ash.	9·41	83·9
Mynydd Newydd	1·31	84·71	5·76	1·56	1·21	3·52	3·24	74 98
Abercarn	1·334	81·26	6·31	·77	1·86	9·76	2·04	68·4
Anthracite, Jones & Co	1·375	91·44	3·46	0·21	0·79	2·58	1·52	92·9
Ward's Fiery Vein	1·349	87·87	3·93	2·02	0·83	Included in Ash.	7·04	...
Neath Abbey	1·31	89·04	5·05	1·07	1·60	...	3·55	61·42
Graigola	1·30	84·87	3·84	0·41	0·45	7·19	3·24	85·5
Gadly Four-feet Seam	1·32	88·56	4·79	0·88	1·21	...	4·88	88·23
Machen Rock Vein	1·297	71·08	4·88	·95	1·37	17·87	3·85	65·2
Birch Grove, Graigola	1·360	84·25	4·15	·73	·86	5·58	4·43	85·1
Llynvi	1·28	87·18	5·06	0·86	1·33	2·53	3·04	72·94
Cadoxton	1·378	87·71	4·34	1·05	1·75	1·58	3·57	82·0
Oldcastle Fiery Vein	1·289	87·68	4·89	1·31	0·09	3·39	2·64	79·8
Vivian and Sons' Merthyr	1·299	82·75	5·31	1·04	·95	4·64	5·31	67·1
Llangennech	1·312	85·46	4·20	1·07	0·29	2·44	6·54	83·69
Three-quarter Rock Vein	1·34	75·15	4·93	1.07	2·85	5·04	10·96	62·5
Pentrepoth	1·31	88·72	4·50	0·18	...	3·24	3·36	82·5
Cwm Frood Rock Vein	1·255	82·25	5·84	1·11	1·22	3·58	6·00	68·8
Cwm Nanty Gros	1·28	78·36	5·59	1·86	3·01	5·58	5·60	65·6
Byrmbo Main	1·300	77·87	5·09	·57	2·73	9.52	4·22	55·4
Vivian and Sons' Rock Vawr	1·301	79·09	5·20	·66	2·41	8·34	4·30	58·6
Coleshill	1·29	73·84	5·14	1·47	2·34	8·29	8·92	56·0
Byrmbo Two-yard	1·283	78·13	5·53	.54	1·88	8·02	5·90	56·2
Rock Vawr	1·29	77·98	4·39	0·57	0·96	8·55	7·55	62·50
Porth-mawr	1·39	74·70	4·79	1·28	0·91	3·60	14·72	63·1
Pontypool	1·32	80·70	5·66	1·35	2·39	4·38	5·52	64·8
Pentrefelin	1·358	85·52	3·72	Trace	0·12	4·55	6·09	85·0

TABLE II. (*continued*).

Locality or Name of Coal.	Specific Gravity of Coal.	Carbon.	Hydrogen.	Nitrogen.	Sulphur.	Oxygen.	Ash.	Percentage of Coke left by each Coal.
NEWCASTLE.	A.	B.	C.	D.	E.	F.	G.	H.
Willington	...	86·81	4·96	1·05	0·88	5·22	1·08	72·19
Andrews House, Tanfield	1·26	85·58	5·31	1·26	1.32	4·39	2·14	65·13
Bowden Close	...	84·92	4·53	0·96	0·65	6·66	2·28	69·69
Haswell Wallsend	1·286	83·47	6·68	1·42	·06	8·17	0·20	62·70
Newcastle Hartley	1·29	81·81	5·50	1·28	1·69	2·58	7·14	64·61
Hedley's Hartley	1·31	80·26	5·28	1·16	1·78	2·40	9·12	72.31
Bates' West Hartley	1·25	80·61	5·26	1·52	1·85	6·51	4·25	...
West Hartley Main	1·264	81·85	5·29	1·69	1·13	7·53	2·51	53·20
Buddle's West Hartley	1·23	80·75	5·04	1·46	1·04	7·86	3·85	...
Hastings' Hartley	1·25	82·24	5·42	1·61	1·35	6·44	2·94	35·60
Carr's Hartley	1·25	79·83	5·11	1·17	0·82	7·86	5·21	60·63
Davison's West Hartley	1·25	83·26	5·31	1·72	1·38	2·50	5·84	59·49
North Percy Hartley	1·25	80·03	5·08	0·98	0·78	9·91	3·22	57·18
Haswell Coal Co.'s Steam-boat Wallsend	1·27	83·71	5·30	1·06	1·21	2·79	5·93	61·38
Derwentwater Hartley	1·26	78·01	4·74	1·84	1·37	10·31	3·73	54·83
Broomhill	1·25	81·70	6·17	1·84	2·85	4·37	3·07	59·20
Original Hartley	1·25	81·18	5·56	0·72	1·44	8·03	3·07	58·22
Cowpen and Sidney's Hartley	1·26	82·20	5·10	1·69	0·71	7·97	2·33	58·59
DERBYSHIRE.								
Earl Fitzwilliam's Elsecar	1·296	81·93	4·85	1·27	·91	8·58	2·46	61.6
Hoyland and Co.'s Elsecar	1·317	80·05	4·93	1·24	1·06	8·99	3·73	62·5
Earl Fitzwilliam's Park Gate	1·311	80·07	4.92	2·15	1·11	9·95	1·80	61·7
Butterly Co.'s Portland	1·301	80.41	4·65	1.58	·86	11·26	1·23	60·9
Butterly Co.'s Langley	1·264	77·97	5·58	.80	1·14	9·86	4·65	54·9
Stavely	1·27	79·85	4·84	1·25	0·72	10·96	2·40	57·86
Loscoe Soft	1·285	77·49	4·86	1·64	1·30	12·41	2·30	52·8
LANCASHIRE.								
Ince Hall Co.'s Arley	1·272	82·61	5·86	1·76	·80	7·44	1·53	64·0
Haydock Little Delf	1.257	79·71	5·16	·54	·52	10·65	3·42	58·1.
Balcarres Arley	1·26	83·54	5·24	·98	·05	5·87	3·32	62·89
Blackley Hurst	1·26	82·01	5·55	1·68	1·43	5·28	4·05	57·84
Ince Hall Pemberton Yard	1·348	80·78	6·23	1·30	1·82	7·53	2·34	60·6
Haydock Rushy Park	1·323	77·65	5·53	2·50	1·73	10·91	3·68	59·4
Moss Hall Pemberton Four-feet.	1·258	75·53	4·82	2·05	3·04	7·98	6·58	55·7
Haydock Higher Florida	1·218	77·33	5·56	1·01	1·03	12·02	3·05	51·1
Ince Hall Pemberton Four-feet.	1·276	77·01	3·93	1·40	1·05	5·52	1·09	57·1
Blackbrook Little Delf	1·26	82·70	5·55	1·48	1·07	4·89	4·31	58·48
King	1·300	73·66	5·30	1·68	1·58	9·06	8·72	62·4
Rushy Park Mine	1·28	77·76	5·23	1·32	1·01	8·99	1·69	56·66
Blackbrook Rushy Park	1·27	81·16	5·99	1·35	1·62	7·20	2·68	58·10
Johnson & Wirthington's Rushy Park	1·28	79·50	5·15	1·21	2·71	9·24	2·19	57·52
Laffak Rushy Park	1·35	80·47	5·72	1·27	1·39	8·33	2·82	56·26
Balcarres Haigh Yard	1·28	82·26	5·47	1·25	1·48	5·64	3·90	66·09
Haydock Florida Main	1·267	77·49	5·50	1·27	·88	12·84	2·02	54·4
Wigan Four-feet	1·209	78·86	5·29	·86	1·19	9·57	4·23	60·0
Ince Hall Pemberton Five-feet	1·269	68·72	4.76	2·20	1.35	18·63	14·34	56·5
Cannel (Wigan)	1·23	79·23	6·08	1·13	1·43	7·24	4·84	60·33
Ince Hall Co.'s Furnace Vein	1·314	74·74	5·71	1·58	·96	13·52	4·04	58·4
Balcarres Lindsay	1·26	83·90	5·66	1·40	1·51	5·53	2·00	57·84
Caldwell and Thompson's Rushy Park	1·271	76·17	5·46	1·09	·91	14·87	1·50	58·7
Balcarres Five-feet	1·26	74·21	5·03	·77	2·09	8·69	9·21	55·90
Moss Hall Pemberton Five-feet	1·283	76·16	5·35	1·29	1·05	10·13	6·02	56·1
Moss Hall Co.'s New Mine	1·278	77·50	4·84	·98	1·36	12·16	3·16	57·7
Caldwell and Thompson's Higher Delf	1·274	75·40	4·83	1·41	2·43	19·98	5·95	54·2
Johnson and Wirthington's Sir John	1·31	72·86	4·98	1·07	1·54	8·15	11·40	56·15

TABLE II. (*continued.*)

Locality or Name of Coal.	Specific Gravity of Coal.	Carbon.	Hydrogen.	Nitrogen.	Sulphur.	Oxygen.	Ash.	Percentage of Coke left by each Coal.
SCOTCH.	A.	B.	C.	D.	E.	F.	G.	H.
Wallsend Elgin	1·20	76·09	5.22	1·41	1·53	5·05	10·70	58·45
Wellewood	1·27	81·36	6·28	1·53	1·57	6·37	2·89	59·15
Dalkeith Coronation Seam	1·316	76·94	5·20	Trace.	0·38	14·37	3·10	53·5
Kilmarnock Skerrington	1·241	79·82	5·82	·94	·86	11·31	1·25	49·3
Fordel Splint	1·23	79·58	5·50	1·13	1·46	8·33	4·00	52·03
Grangemouth	1·29	79·85	5·28	1·35	1·42	8·58	3·52	56·6
Eglinton	1·25	80·03	6·50	1·55	1·38	8·05	2·44	54·94
Dalkeith Jewel Seam	1·277	74·55	5·14	0·10	0·33	15·51	4·37	49·8
IRISH.								
Slieverdagh Irish Anthracite	1·59	80·03	2·30	0·23	6·76	Included in Ash.	10·80	90·1
VARIOUS.								
Coleshill Co.'s Bagilt Main	1·269	88·48	5·62	2·02	1·36	0·86	1·62	55·8
Ewloe	1·275	80·97	4·96	1·10	1·40	8·20	3·37	54·5
Ibstock	1·291	74·97	4·83	·88	1·45	11·88	5·99	50·8
PATENT FUELS.								
Warlich's Patent Fuel	1·15	90·02	5·56	Trace.	1·62	Included in Ash.	2·91	85·1
Livingstone's Steam Fuel	1·184	86·07	4·13	1·80	1·45	2·03	4·52	...
Lyon's Patent Fuel	1·13	86·36	4·56	1·06	1·29	2·07	4·66	...
Wylam's	1·10	79·91	5·69	1·68	1·25	6·63	4·84	65·8
Bell's	1·14	87·88	5·22	0·81	0·71	0·42	4·96	71·7
Holland and Green's	1·302	70·14	4·65	1·15	...	...	13·73	...
VAN DIEMAN'S LAND.								
South Cape	...	63·40	2·89	1·27	0·98	1·01	30·45	...
Mount Nicholas Break o' Day	...	57·37	3·91	1·15	0·90	9·10	27·55	...
Tingal	...	57·21	3·38	1·20	1·32	7·80	29·09	...
Jerusalem	...	68·18	3·99	1·62	1·12	5·89	19·20	...
Douglas River, East Coast	...	70·44	4·20	1·11	0·70	9·27	14·38	...
Tasman's Peninsula	...	65·54	3·36	1·91	1·03	1·75	26·41	...
Schonten Island	...	64·01	3·55	0·94	0·85	3·38	27·17	...
Whale's Head, South Cape	...	65·86	3·18	1·12	1·14	7·20	21·50	...
Adventure Bay	...	80·22	3·05	1·36	1·90	4·80	8·67	...
Sydney, New South Wales	...	82·39	5·32	1·23	0·70	8·32	2·04	...
Borneo (Labuan kind)	1·28	64·52	4·74	0·80	1·45	20·75	7·74	...
" Three-feet Seam	1·37	54·31	5·03	0·98	1·14	24·22	14·32	...
" Eleven-feet Seam	1·21	70·33	5·41	0·67	1·17	19·19	3·23	...
Formosa Island	1·24	78.26	5·70	0·64	0·49	10·95	3·96	...
Vancouver's Island	...	66·93	5·32	1·02	2·20	8·70	15·83	...
Lignite, Trinidad	...	65·20	4·25	1·33	0·69	21·69	6·84	...
CHILI.								
Conception Bay	1·29	70·55	5·76	0·95	1·98	13·24	7·52	...
Port Famine	...	64·18	5·33	0·50	1·03	22·75	6·21	...
Chirique	...	38·98	4·01	0·58	6·14	13·38	36·91	...
Laredo Bay	...	58·67	5·52	0·71	1·14	17·33	16·63	...
Talcahnano Bay	...	70·71	6·44	1·08	0·94	13·95	6·92	...
Colcurra Bay	...	78·30	5·50	1·09	1·06	8·37	5·68	...
PATAGONIA.								
Sandy Bay, No. 1	...	62·25	5.05	0·63	1·13	17·54	13·40	...
" No. 2	...	59·63	5·68	0·64	0·96	17·45	15·64	...

TABLE III. *Average Value of Coals from different Localities.*

LOCALITY.	Evaporating power or number of lbs. of water evaporated from 212° by 1 lb. of Coal.	Rate of evaporation, or number of lbs. evaporated per hour.	Weight in lbs. of 1 cubic foot of Coal as used for Fuel.	Space occupied by 1 ton in cubic feet.	Results obtained in experiments on cohesive power of Coals (percentage of large Coals).	Percentage amount of Sulphur contained in Coals.
	A.	B.	C.	D.	E.	F.
Average of 37 samples from Wales.........	9·05	448·2	53·1	42.71	60·9	1·42
" 17 " Newcastle...........	8·37	411·1	49·8	45·3	67·5	0·94
" 28 " Lancashire..........	7·94	447·6	49·7	45·15	73·5	1·42
" 8 " Scotland.............	7·70	431·4	50·0	49·99	73·4	1·45
" 8 " Derbyshire	7·58	432·7	47·2	47·45	80·9	1·01

TABLE IV. *Average Composition of Coals from different Localities*

LOCALITY.	Specific Gravity of Coal.	Carbon.	Hydrogen.	Nitrogen.	Sulphur.	Oxygen.	Ash.	Percentage of Coke left by each Coal.
	A.	B.	C.	D.	E.	F.	G.	H.
Average of 36 samples from Wales	1·315	83·78	4·79	0·98	1·43	4·15	4·91	72.60
" 18 " Newcastle.........	1·256	82·12	5·31	1·35	1·24	5·69	3·77	60·67
" 28 " Lancashire	1·273	77·90	5·32	1·30	1·44	9·53	4·88	60·22
" 8 " Scotland	1·259	78·53	5·61	1·00	1·11	9·69	4·03	54·22
" 7 " Derbyshire.	1·292	79·68	4·94	1·41	1·01	10·28	2·65	59·32

APPENDIX.

USEFUL RULES IN MENSURATION.

354. *To find the Circumference of a Circle the Diameter being given, and* vice versâ.

1. Multiply the diameter by 3·1416, and the result will be the circumference.

2. Divide the circumference by 3·1416, and the result wil be the diameter.

355. *To find the Area of a Circle, having given the Diameter, and* vice versâ.

1. Multiply the square of the diameter by ·7854, and the result will be the area.

2. Divide the area by ·7854, and take the square root of the quotient, which will give the diameter.

356. *To find the Surface of a Cylinder, having given the Diameter and Length.*

Multiply the diameter by 3·1416 to get the circumference of the section, and again multiply this product by the length of the cylinder.

357. *To find the Volume of a Cylinder, having given the Diameter and Length.*

Multiply the square of the diameter by ·7854 to get the area of the section, and then multiply this area by the length.

358. *To find the Surface of a Sphere.*

Multiply the diameter of the sphere by its circumference, and the product will be the surface.

359. *To find the Volume of a Sphere.*

Multiply the cube of the diameter by ·5236, and the product will be the volume required.

360. *To find the Volume of a Cone.*

Proceed exactly as in art. 357, and divide the result by 3.

361. *Circular Inch; Comparison of Circular Inch and Square Inch.*

A circular inch is a *circle* whose diameter is an inch; and consequently its area is less than a square inch, being the circle inscribed within the square inch. Since the area of a circle is found by multiplying the square of its diameter by ·7854, therefore the area of a circular inch $= \cdot 7854 \times 1^2 = \cdot 7854$; and hence the number of square inches in any surface being given, divide that number by ·7854, and the result will be the number of circular inches; and, on the contrary, the number of circular inches in any surface being given, multiply by ·7854, and the result will be the number of square inches.

362. *To find the Area of an Ellipse.*

Multiply the greatest and least diameters together, and that product by ·7854, and the result will be the area.

363. *To find the Circumference of an Ellipse.*

Multiply half the sum of the two diameters by 3·1416, and the result will give the circumference sufficiently accurate for practice.

364. *Definition.*

The frustrum of a cone is the part that is left after the top or end is cut off by a plane parallel to the base.

365. *To find the Volume of the Frustum of a Cone.*

Multiply the areas of the two ends together; to the square root thereof add the two areas; that sum multiplied by one-third the height gives the solid content.

366. *To find the Weight of a known Substance of given Dimensions.*

Having found the volume, if the result be in cubic feet, multiply the weight of a cubic foot, as given in Table G,

p. 355; but if the volume be in cubic inches, divide the product so obtained by 1728.

367. *Useful Rules to be observed when Coaling.*

1. Before purchasing coal, it is advisable to inspect the "bill of lading," which, by giving the name or locality of the mine, will enable the officer to ascertain its quality by reference to the Tables given in the miscellaneous Chapter; it will also give the quantity of the coal, and may rectify mistakes of false weighing when purchasing coals on foreign stations.

2. If there be a choice of fuel, care should be taken, generally speaking, to select the best; for although dearer at first, it will be found most economical in the end. It is a common occurrence for a steam-vessel to consume 30 or 40 per cent. more coal when of an inferior quality than she would otherwise do; while the price per ton is not more than two or three shillings cheaper than that of a better kind. In addition to which, the speed of the ship will probably not be so great; while the labor of the stokers will be increased.

3. The coals selected should be dry, and the officer should satisfy himself that they have not been exposed for any length of time in the open air to the influence of the sun's rays, especially in a tropical climate; for under such circumstances coals rapidly deteriorate from a species of slow combustion (p. 337). In case, as may sometimes happen, no other coals can be procured, he should take especial care *not to receive those which have formed the exposed surface.*

4. Coal having a brassy appearance, thus indicating the presence of iron pyrites, should be avoided; or, if received, it should be borne in mind that such coal has a tendency to spontaneous combustion, which is much increased by wet or moisture: and it should be remembered that wet coals have a very injurious effect on the coal-bunkers, especially when wetted with salt-water (p. 324).

TABLE A.

Pressures of Steam, and the corresponding Temperatures and relative Volumes.

Pressure in lbs. per square inch.	Temperature by Fahrenheit.	Relative volume.	Pressure in lbs. per square inch.	Temperature by Fahrenheit.	Relative volume.	Pressure in lbs. per square inch.	Temperature by Fahrenheit.	Relative volume.
1	103·0	20911	25	240·9	1043	49	281·4	564
2	126·0	10890	26	243·2	1006	50	282·7	554
3	141·0	7446	27	245·3	972	51	284·0	543
4	152·2	5690	28	247·4	939	52	285·2	533
5	161·4	4620	29	249·4	910	53	286·4	525
6	169·2	3899	30	251·4	882	54	287·6	516
7	175·9	3378	31	253·3	856	55	288·8	507
8	182·0	2984	32	255·2	832	56	290·0	499
9	187·4	2675	33	257·1	809	57	291·2	492
10	192·4	2426	34	258·9	787	58	292·4	484
11	197·0	2222	35	260·6	766	59	293·6	476
12	201·3	2050	36	262·3	747	60	294·8	468
13	205·3	1903	37	264·0	728	61	295·9	462
14	209·0	1777	38	265·6	711	62	297·0	455
15	212·9	1669	39	267·2	694	63	298·1	448
16	216·3	1573	40	268·8	678	64	299·2	442
17	219·6	1488	41	270·2	663	65	300·2	436
18	222·7	1411	42	271·7	649	66	301·2	430
19	225·6	1343	43	273·2	635	67	302·3	424
20	228·4	1281	44	274·6	622	68	303·3	418
21	231·1	1225	45	276·0	609	69	304·3	413
22	233·8	1173	46	277·4	597	70	305·3	407
23	236·3	1126	47	278·8	585			
24	238·6	1083	48	280·1	574			

TABLE B.

General Effects of Heat according to certain Temperatures.

	Fahrenheit.
Extremity of Wedgwood's scale	32277°
Cast iron thoroughly melted	20577
Cast iron begins to melt	17977
Welding heat of iron (greatest)	13427
" " (least)	12777
Fine gold melts	5237
Fine silver melts	4717
Swedish copper melts	4587
Brass melts	3807
Red-heat fully visible in daylight	1077
Iron red-hot in twilight	884
Heat of a common fire	790
Iron bright red in the dark	752
Zinc melts	700
Quicksilver boils	660
Linseed-oil boils	600
Lead melts	594
Polished steel acquires a deep-blue color	580
Oil of turpentine boils	560
Bismuth melts	476
Polished steel acquires a pale straw-color	460
Tin melts	442
Tin and bismuth (equal parts) melt	283
Sulphur melts	226
A saturated solution of salt boils	218
Water boils	212
Five parts bismuth, three of tin, and two of lead melt	212
Eight of bismuth, three of tin, and five of lead melt	210
Alcohol boils	174
Beeswax melts	142
Spermaceti melts	112

	Fahrenheit.
Vital heat	96°
Tallow melts	92
Olive-oil begins to solidify	36
Fresh water freezes	32
Sea-water freezes	28
Strong wines freeze	20
Oil of turpentine solidifies	14
Alcohol one part, water three parts	7
Proof spirits	0
Alcohol one part, water one part	—7
Freezing-point of quicksilver	—39
Alcohol becomes oily	—132

TABLE C.

Of the linear Expansion of Solid Bodies by Heat.

Dimensions which a bar takes at 212°, whose length at 32° is 1·000000.

Substance	Dimension	Substance	Dimension
Cast iron	1·00111111	Cast brass	1·0018750
Steel (rod)	1·00114470	Silver	1·0018900
Steel, not tempered	1·00107875	Tin	1·0028400
Ditto, tempered yellow	1·00136900	Lead	1·00284836
Ditto, at a higher rate	1·00123956	Zinc	1·00294200
Iron	1·00118203	Glass from 32° to 212°	1·00086130
Soft iron, forged	1·00122045	Glass from 212° to 392°	1·00091827
Gold	1·00150000	Glass from 392° to 572°	1·00101114
Copper	1·00191000		

Expansion of Fluids by Heat.

Mercury from	32° to 212°	0·018099
Ditto	212° to 392°	0·018184
Ditto	392° to 572°	0·018870
Water from	39° to 212°	0·043320
Alcohol (to its boiling-point)		0·1100
Fixed oils		0·0800

TABLE D.

To keep the satura-tion at	Ratio of feed and quantity blown out to the evaporation.			Boiling-point in air at that degree of saturation.	Boiling-point in a boiler loaded to 10 lbs.	Loss of Fuel per cent., the feed being supplied at 100° F.
	Evapora-tion.	Blown out.	Feed.			
$\frac{2}{33}$	1	1	2	214·4	242·4	11·35
$\frac{3}{33}$	1	$\frac{1}{2}$	$\frac{3}{2}$	215·5	243·5	6·06
$\frac{4}{33}$	1	$\frac{1}{3}$	$\frac{4}{3}$	216·6	244·6	4·15
$\frac{5}{33}$	1	$\frac{1}{4}$	$\frac{5}{4}$	217·9	245·9	3·18

TABLE E.

Portion of stroke performed before expansion, or $\frac{l'}{l}$	Logarithm of $\frac{l}{l'+c}$	Logarithm of $\frac{l'}{l'+c}$ + log. $\frac{l+c}{l'+c}$	Portion of stroke performed before expansion, or $\frac{l'}{l}$	Logarithm of $\frac{l}{l'+c}$	Logarithm of $\frac{l'}{l'+c}$ + log. $\frac{l+c}{l'+c}$
·10	0·823930	0·417139	·25	0·522835	0·319106
·11	0·795880	0·409764	·26	0·508664	0·313656
·12	0·769525	0·402433	·27	0·494850	0·307924
·13	0·744762	0·395326	·28	0·481443	0·302331
·14	0·721233	0·388456	·29	0·461495	0·296665
·15	0·698970	0·381656	·30	0·455910	0·291147
·16	0·677789	0·374932	·31	0·443732	0·285782
·17	0·657629	0·368473	·32	0·431846	0·280578
·18	0·638289	0.361917	·33	0·420286	0·275081
·19	0·619823	0·355643	·34	0·408918	0·269980
·20	0·602060	0·349277	·35	0·397940	0·264818
·21	0·585009	0·343014	·36	0·387212	0·259594
·22	0·568671	0·337060	·37	0·376759	0·254548
·23	0·552790	0·330819	·38	0·366610	0·249443
·24	0.537567	0·325105	·39	0·356599	0·244277

Portion of stroke performed before expansion, or $\frac{l'}{l}$	Logarithm of $\frac{l}{l'+c}$	Logarithm of $\frac{l'}{l'+c}$ + log. $\frac{l+c}{l'+c}$	Portion of stroke performed before expansion, or $\frac{l'}{l}$	Logarithm of $\frac{l}{l'+c}$	Logarithm of $\frac{l'}{l'+c}$ + log. $\frac{l+c}{l'+c}$
·40	0·346744	0·239550	·65	0·155032	0·125156
·41	0·337259	0·234517	·66	0·148911	0·120903
·42	0·327972	0·229682	·67	0·142702	0·116608
·43	0·318689	0·224792	·68	0·136721	0·112270
·44	0·309843	0·220108	·69	0·130655	0·107888
·45	0·301030	0·215373	·70	0·124820	0·103462
·46	0·292478	0·210586	·71	0·119256	0·099335
·47	0·283979	0·205745	·72	0·113609	0·093422
·48	0·275772	0·201124	·73	0·107888	0·090963
·49	0·267641	0·196452	·74	0·102434	0·086716
·50	0·259594	0·191730	·75	0·096910	0·082785
·51	0·251881	0·187239	·76	0·091667	0·078094
·52	0·244277	0·182700	·77	0·086360	0·074085
·53	0·236537	0·178113	·78	0·080987	0·070030
·54	0.229170	0·173478	·79	0·075912	0·065953
·55	0·221936	0·169086	·80	0·070776	0·061452
·56	0·214579	0·164650	·81	0·065580	0·057286
·57	0·207634	0·159868	·82	0·060320	0·053463
·58	0·200577	0·155640	·83	0·055378	0·048830
·59	0·193959	0·151370	·84	0·050380	0·044931
·60	0·187239	0·146748	·85	0·045714	0·040998
·61	0·180413	0·142389	·86	0·040998	0·036629
·62	0·174060	0·137987	·87	0·036229	0·032619
·63	0·167613	0·133858	·88	0·031408	0·028164
·64	0·161068	0·129368	·89	0·026942	0·024075
			·90	0·022428	0·019947

TABLE F.

Of Capacities of Bodies for Heat referred to Water as the Standard.

Water	1·0000	Hardened steel	·1230
Ice	·9000	Steel softened by fire..	·1200
Olive-oil	·7100	Soft bar-iron	·1190
Alcohol	·7000	Brass	·1160
Linseed-oil	·5280	Copper	·1140
Oil of turpentine	·4720	Zinc	·1000
Pit-coal	·2777	Ashes of charcoal	·0909
Chalk	·2700	Silver	·0820
Sea-salt	·2300	Tin	·0704
Sulphur	·1900	White-lead	·0670
Ashes of cinders	·1855	Gold	·0500
Black-lead	·1830	Lead	·0420
Ashes of elm-wood	.1402	Mercury	·0330
Iron	·1300		

TABLE G.

Mechanical Properties of Materials.

Names of materials.	Specific gravity.	Weight of 1 cubic foot in lbs.	Tenacity per square inch in lbs.
Air (atmospheric)	·001228	0·0768	
Ash	·690 to	43·12 to	
	·845	53·81	17207
Beech	·854 to	53·37 to	15784 to
	·690	43·12	17850
Birch (common)	·792	49·50	15000
Ditto (American)	·648	40·50	—
Bismuth (cast)	9·810	613·87	3250
Box (dry)	·960	60·00	19891
Brass (cast)	8·399	525·00	17968
Ditto (wire-drawn)	8·544	534·00	—

Names of materials.	Specific gravity.	Weight of 1 cubic foot in lbs.	Tenacity per square inch in lbs.
Cedar (Canadian, fresh)......	0·909	56·81	11400
Ditto (seasoned)...............	0·753	47·06	
Chalk	2·784 to 1·869	174·00 to 116·81	
Chestnut	0·657	41·06	
Clay (common)	1·919	119·93	
Coal (Welsh furnace).........	1·337	83·56	
Ditto (Coke)	1·000	62·50	
Ditto (Alfreton)................	1·235	77·18	
Ditto (Butterly)	1·264	79·00	
Ditto (Coke).....................	1·000	68·75	
Ditto (Welsh stone)..........	1·368	85·50	
Ditto (Coke).....................	1·390	86·87	
Ditto (Welsh Slaty)..........	1·409	88·06	
Ditto (Derbyshire Cannel)...	1·278	79·87	
Ditto (Kilkenny)	1·602	100·12	
Ditto (Coke).....................	1·657	103·56	
Ditto (Slaty).....................	1·443	90·18	
Ditto (Bonlavoomeen)	1·436	89·75	
Ditto (Coke).....................	1·596	99·75	
Ditto (Corgee)	1·403	87·68	
Ditto (Coke)	1·656	103·50	
Ditto (Staffordshire)..........	1·240	78·12	
Ditto (Swansea)...............	1·357	84·81	
Ditto (Wigan)..................	1·268	79·25	
Ditto (Glasgow)........	1·290	80·62	
Ditto (Newcastle)	1·257	78·56	
Ditto (common Cannel)......	1·232	77·00	
Ditto (slaty Cannel)	1·426	89·12	
Copper (cast)..................	8·607	537·93	19072
Ditto (sheet)....................	8·785	549·06	
Ditto (wire-drawn)............	8·878	560·00	61228
Ditto (in bolts)................	......	......	48000
Deal (Christiana middle)	0·698	43·62	12400
Ditto (Memel middle)........	0·590	36·87	
Ditto (Norway Spruce)......	0·340	21·25	17600
Ditto (English)................	0·470	29·37	7000
Elm (seasoned)................	0·588	36·75	13489
Fir (New England)	0·553	34·56	
Ditto (Riga)....................	0·753	47·06	11549 to 12857

Names of materials.	Specific gravity.	Weight of 1 cubic foot in lbs.	Tenacity per square inch in lbs.
Iron (wrought English)......	7·700	481·20	25½ tons.
Ditto (in bars)..................	7·600 to 7·800	475·50 487·00	25½ tons.
Ditto (hammered)............	....	....	30 tons.
Ditto Russian (in bars)	....	....	27 tons.
Ditto Swedish (in bars)	....	....	32 tons.
Ditto English (in wire, $\frac{1}{10}$ inch in diameter)............	....	....	36 to 43 tons.
Ditto Russian (in wire, $\frac{1}{20}$ to $\frac{1}{30}$ inch in diameter)........	....	....	60 to 91 tons.
Ditto (rolled in sheets, and cut lengthwise).............	....	....	14 tons.
Ditto (cut crosswise).........	....	....	18 tons.
Ditto (in chains, oval links, 6 inch clear, iron ½ in. diameter)	....	....	21½ tons.
Ditto (Brunton, with stay across links)................	....	....	25 tons.
Ditto, cast (Carron, No. 2, cold blast)	7·066	441·62	16683
Ditto (hot blast)	7·046	440·37	13505
Ditto, cast (Carron, No. 3, cold blast)....................	7·094	443·37	14200
Ditto (hot blast)...............	7·056	441·00	17755
Ditto (Devon, No. 3, cold blast)	7·295	455·93	
Ditto (hot blast)...............	7·229	451·81	21907
Ditto (Buffery, No. 1, cold blast)	7·079	442·43	17466
Ditto (hot blast)...............	6·998	437·37	13434
Ditto (Coed Talon, No. 2, cold blast)	6·955	434·06	18855
Ditto (hot blast)...............	6·968	435·50	16676
Ditto (Coed Talon, No. 3, cold blast)....................	7·194	449·62	
Ditto (hot blast)...............	6·970	435·62	
Ditto (Elsicar, No. 1, cold blast)	7·030	439·37	
Ditto (Milton, No. 1, hot blast)	6·976	436·00	
Ditto (Muirkirk, No. 1, cold blast)	7·113	444·56	
Ditto (hot blast)	6·953	434·56	

Names of materials.	Specific gravity.	Weight of 1 cubic foot in lbs.	Tenacity per square inch in lbs.
Lead (cast English)	11·446	717·45	1824
Ditto (milled sheet)...........	11·407	712·93	3328
Ditto (wire)......................	11·317	705·12	2581
Lignum Vitæ	1·220	76·25	11800
Mahogany (Spanish)	0·800	50·00	16500
Mercury at 32°	13·619	851·18	
Ditto at 60°....................	13·580	848·75	
Oak (English)..................	0·934	58·37	17300
Ditto (Canadian)	0·872	54·50	10253
Ditto (Dantzic)	0·756	47·24	12780
Ditto (Adriatic)...............	0·993	62·06	
Ditto (African middle)	0·972	60·75	
Pine (pitch).....................	0·660	41·25	7818
Ditto (red)	0·657	41·06	
Ditto (American yellow)....	0·461	28·81	
Silver (Standard).............	10·312	644·50	40902
Slate (Welsh)	2·888	180·50	12800
Steel (soft)	7·780	486·25	120000
Ditto (razor tempered)	7·840	490·00	150000
Teak (dry).......................	0·657	41·06	15000
Tin (cast)	7·291	455·68	5322
Water (sea)......................	1·027	64·18	
Ditto (rain)	1·000	62·50	
Walnut............................	0·671	41·93	8130
Zinc	7·028	439·25	

TABLE H.

Circumferences and Areas of Circles of given Diameters.

DIAM.	CIRCUM.	AREA.	DIAM.	CIRCUM.	AREA.
			5 in.	15·7080	19·6350
⅛	·3927	·0122	⅛	16·1007	20·6290
¼	·7854	·0490	¼	16·4934	21·6475
⅜	1·1781	·1104	⅜	16·8861	22·6907
½	1·5748	·1963	½	17·2788	23·7583
⅝	1·9635	·3068	⅝	17·6715	24·8505
¾	2·3562	·4417	¾	18·0642	25·9672
⅞	2·7489	·6013	⅞	18·4569	27·1085
1 in.	3·1416	·7854	6 in.	18·8496	28·2743
⅛	3·5343	·9940	⅛	19·2423	29·4647
¼	3·9270	1·2272	¼	19·6350	30·6796
⅜	4·3197	1·4848	⅜	20·0277	31·9192
½	4·7124	1·7671	½	20·4204	33·1831
⅝	5·1051	2·0739	⅝	20·8131	34·4717
¾	5·4978	2·4053	¾	21·2058	35·7847
⅞	5·8905	2·7611	⅞	21·5985	37·1224
2 in.	6·2832	3·1416	7 in.	21·9911	38·4846
⅛	6·6759	3 5465	⅛	22·3838	39·8713
¼	7·0686	3·9761	¼	22·7765	41·2825
⅜	7·4613	4·4302	⅜	23·1692	42·7184
½	7·8540	4·9087	½	23·5619	44·1786
⅝	8·2467	5·4119	⅝	23·9546	45·6636
¾	8·6394	5·9396	¾	24·3473	47·1730
⅞	9·0321	6·4918	⅞	24·7400	48·7070
3 in.	9·4248	7·0686	8 in.	25·1327	50·2655
⅛	9·8175	7·6699	⅛	25·5254	51·8486
¼	10·2102	8·2957	¼	25·9181	53·4562
⅜	10·6029	8·9462	⅜	26·3108	55·0885
½	10·9956	9·6211	½	26·7035	56·7450
⅝	11·3883	10·3206	⅝	27·0962	58·4263
¾	11·7810	11·0447	¾	27·4889	60·1320
⅞	12·1737	11·7932	⅞	27·8816	61·8624
4 in.	12·5664	12·5664	9 in.	28·2743	63·6173
⅛	12·9591	13·3640	⅛	28·6670	65·3967
¼	13·3518	14·1863	¼	29·0597	67·2006
⅜	13·7445	15·0331	⅜	29·4524	69·0292
½	14·1372	15·9043	½	29·8451	70·8822
⅝	14·5299	16·8001	⅝	30·2378	72·7598
¾	14·9226	17·7205	¾	30·6305	74·6619
⅞	15·3153	18·6655	⅞	31·0232	76·5886

DIAM.	CIRCUM.	AREA.	DIAM.	CIRCUM.	AREA.
10 in.	31·4159	78·5398	16 in.	50·2655	201·0619
$\frac{1}{8}$	31·8086	80·5156	$\frac{1}{8}$	60·6582	204·2158
$\frac{1}{4}$	32·2013	82·5159	$\frac{1}{4}$	51·0509	207·3942
$\frac{3}{8}$	32·5940	84·5407	$\frac{3}{8}$	51·4436	210·5971
$\frac{1}{2}$	32·9867	86·5901	$\frac{1}{2}$	51·8363	213·8246
$\frac{5}{8}$	33·3794	88·6642	$\frac{5}{8}$	52·2290	217·0767
$\frac{3}{4}$	33·7721	90·7626	$\frac{3}{4}$	52·6217	220·3533
$\frac{7}{8}$	34·1648	92·8858	$\frac{7}{8}$	53·0144	223·6544
11 in.	34·5575	95·0332	17 in.	53·4071	226·9801
$\frac{1}{8}$	34·9502	97·2054	$\frac{1}{8}$	53·7998	230·3303
$\frac{1}{4}$	35·3429	99·4020	$\frac{1}{4}$	54·1925	233·7050
$\frac{3}{8}$	35·7356	101·6233	$\frac{3}{8}$	54·5852	237·1044
$\frac{1}{2}$	36·1283	103·8689	$\frac{1}{2}$	54·9779	240·5282
$\frac{5}{8}$	36·5210	106·1392	$\frac{5}{8}$	55·3706	243·9766
$\frac{3}{4}$	36·9137	108·4340	$\frac{3}{4}$	55·7633	247·4495
$\frac{7}{8}$	37·3064	110·7534	$\frac{7}{8}$	56·1560	250·9470
12 in.	37·6991	113·0973	18 in.	56·5487	254·4690
$\frac{1}{8}$	38·0918	115·4658	$\frac{1}{8}$	56·9414	258·0156
$\frac{1}{4}$	38·4845	117·8589	$\frac{1}{4}$	57·3341	261·5867
$\frac{3}{8}$	38·8772	120·2764	$\frac{3}{8}$	57·7268	265·1824
$\frac{1}{2}$	39·2699	122·7185	$\frac{1}{2}$	58·1195	268·8025
$\frac{5}{8}$	39·6626	125·1852	$\frac{5}{8}$	58·5122	272·3473
$\frac{3}{4}$	40·0553	127·6763	$\frac{3}{4}$	58·9049	276·1165
$\frac{7}{8}$	40·4480	130·1921	$\frac{7}{8}$	59·2976	279·8104
13 in.	40·8407	132·7323	19 in.	59·6903	283·5287
$\frac{1}{8}$	41·2334	135·2972	$\frac{1}{8}$	60·0830	287·2717
$\frac{1}{4}$	41·6261	137·8865	$\frac{1}{4}$	60·4757	291·0391
$\frac{3}{8}$	42·0188	140·5005	$\frac{3}{8}$	60·8684	294·8305
$\frac{1}{2}$	42·4115	143·1388	$\frac{1}{2}$	61·2611	298·6477
$\frac{5}{8}$	42·8042	145·8018	$\frac{5}{8}$	61·6538	302·4888
$\frac{3}{4}$	43·1969	148·4893	$\frac{3}{4}$	62·0465	306·3544
$\frac{7}{8}$	43·5896	151·2014	$\frac{7}{8}$	62·4392	310·2446
14 in.	43·9823	153·9380	20 in.	62·8319	314·1593
$\frac{1}{8}$	44·3750	156·6992	$\frac{1}{8}$	63·2246	318·0985
$\frac{1}{4}$	44·7677	159·4849	$\frac{1}{4}$	63·6173	322·0623
$\frac{3}{8}$	45·1604	162·2953	$\frac{3}{8}$	64·0100	326·0507
$\frac{1}{2}$	45·5531	165·1299	$\frac{1}{2}$	64·4026	330·0636
$\frac{5}{8}$	45·9458	167·9893	$\frac{5}{8}$	64·7953	334·1011
$\frac{3}{4}$	46·3385	170·8732	$\frac{3}{4}$	65·1880	338·1630
$\frac{7}{8}$	46·7312	173·7817	$\frac{7}{8}$	65·5807	342·2496
15 in.	47·1239	176·7146	21 in.	65·9734	346·3606
$\frac{1}{8}$	47·5166	179·6722	$\frac{1}{8}$	66·3661	350·4962
$\frac{1}{4}$	47·9093	182·6542	$\frac{1}{4}$	66·7588	354·6564
$\frac{3}{8}$	48·3020	185·6609	$\frac{3}{8}$	67·1515	358·8412
$\frac{1}{2}$	48·6947	188·6919	$\frac{1}{2}$	67·5442	363·0503
$\frac{5}{8}$	49·0874	191·7477	$\frac{5}{8}$	67·9369	367·2842
$\frac{3}{4}$	49·4801	194·8278	$\frac{3}{4}$	68·3296	371·5424
$\frac{7}{8}$	49·8728	197·9326	$\frac{7}{8}$	68·7223	375·8253

DIAM.	CIRCUM.	AREA.	DIAM.	CIRCUM.	AREA.
22 in.	69·1150	380·1327	28 in.	87·9646	615·7522
⅛	69·5077	384·4646	⅛	88·3573	621·2623
¼	69·9004	388·8212	¼	88·7500	626·7968
⅜	70·2931	393·2023	⅜	89·1427	632·3561
½	70·6858	397·6078	½	89·5354	637·9397
⅝	71·0785	402·0379	⅝	89·9281	643·5480
¾	71·4712	406·4926	¾	90·3208	649·1807
⅞	71·8639	410·9719	⅞	90·7135	654·8381
23 in.	72·2566	415·4756	29 in.	91·1062	660·5199
⅛	72·6493	420·0039	⅛	91·4989	666·2264
¼	73·0420	424·5568	¼	91·8916	671·9572
⅜	73·4347	429·1343	⅜	92·2843	677·7128
½	73·8274	433·7361	½	92·6770	683·4928
⅝	74·2201	438·3626	⅝	93·0697	689·2974
¾	74·6128	443·0137	¾	93·4624	695·1265
⅞	75·0055	447·6892	⅞	93·8551	700·9802
24 in.	75·3982	452·3893	30 in.	94·2478	706·8583
⅛	75·7909	457·1140	⅛	94·6405	712·7611
¼	76·1836	461·8632	¼	95·0332	718·6884
⅜	76·5763	466·6370	⅜	95·4259	724·6403
½	76·9690	471·4352	½	95·8186	730·6167
⅝	77·3617	476·2581	⅝	96·2113	736·6176
¾	77·7544	481·1055	¾	96·6040	742·6430
⅞	78·1471	485·9775	⅞	96·9967	748·6932
25 in.	78·5398	490·8739	31 in.	97·3894	754·7676
⅛	78·9325	495·7949	⅛	97.7821	760·8668
¼	79·3252	500·7404	¼	98·1748	766·9904
⅜	79·7179	505·7106	⅜	98.5675	773·1387
½	80·1106	510·7052	½	98·9602	779·3113
⅝	80·5033	515·7244	⅝	99·3529	785·5086
¾	80·8960	520·7681	¾	99·7456	791·7304
⅞	81·2887	525·8364	⅞	100·1383	797·9768
26 in.	81·6814	530·9292	32 in.	100.5310	804·2477
⅛	82·0741	536·0465	⅛	100·9237	810·5432
¼	82·4668	541·1884	¼	101·3164	816·8632
⅜	82·8595	546·3549	⅜	101·7091	823·2078
½	83·2522	551·5459	½	102·1018	829·5768
⅝	83·6449	556·7615	⅝	102·4945	835·9705
¾	84·0376	562·0015	¾	102·8872	842·3886
⅞	84·4303	567·2662	⅞	103·2799	848·8314
27 in.	84·8230	572·5553	33 in.	103·6726	855·2986
⅛	85·2157	577·8690	⅛	104·0653	861·7904
¼	85·6084	583·2072	¼	104·4580	868·3068
⅜	86·0011	588·5701	⅜	104·8507	874·8477
½	86·3938	593·9574	½	105·2434	881·4139
⅝	86·7865	599·3693	⅝	105·6361	888·0030
¾	87·1792	604·8057	¾	106·0288	894·6176
⅞	87·5719	610·2667	⅞	106·4215	901·2567

DIAM.	CIRCUM.	AREA.	DIAM.	CIRCUM.	AREA.
34 in.	106·8142	907·9203	40 in.	125·6640	1256·6370
⅛	107·2069	914·6084	⅛	126·0567	1264·5032
¼	107·5995	921·3211	¼	126·4494	1272·3941
⅜	107·9922	928·0584	⅜	126·8421	1280·3094
½	108·3849	934·8202	½	127·2348	1288·2493
⅝	108·7779	941·6066	⅝	127·6275	1296·2138
¾	109·1703	948·4174	¾	128·0202	1304·2027
⅞	109·5630	955·2529	⅞	128·4129	1312·2163
35 in.	109·9557	962·1127	41 in.	128·8053	1320·2543
⅛	110·3484	968·9973	⅛	129·1983	1328·3170
¼	110·7411	975·9063	¼	129·5910	1336·4041
⅜	111·1338	982·8400	⅜	129·9837	1344·5159
½	111·5265	989·7980	½	130·3764	1352·6520
⅝	111·9192	996·7807	⅝	130·7691	1360·8129
¾	112·3119	1003·7879	¾	131·1618	1368·9981
⅞	112·7046	1010·8197	⅞	131·5545	1377·2080
36 in.	113·0974	1017·8760	42 in.	131·9472	1385·4424
⅛	113·4901	1024·9568	⅛	132·3399	1393·7013
¼	113·8826	1032·0622	¼	132·7326	1401·9848
⅜	114·2757	1039·1922	⅜	133·1253	1410·2929
½	114·6680	1046·3467	½	133·5180	1418·6254
⅝	115·0611	1053·5257	⅝	133·9107	1426·9826
¾	115·4535	1060·7293	¾	134·3034	1435·3642
⅞	115·8465	1067·9575	⅞	134·6961	1443·7705
37 in.	116·2389	1075·2101	43 in.	135·0888	1452·2012
⅛	116·6316	1082·4873	⅛	135·4815	1460·6565
¼	117·0242	1089·7890	¼	135·8742	1469·1364
⅜	117·4179	1097·1154	⅜	136·2669	1477·6310
½	117·8096	1104·4662	½	136·6596	1486·1697
⅝	118·2027	1111·8416	⅝	137·0523	1494·7234
¾	118·5951	1119·2415	¾	137·4450	1503·3012
⅞	118·9881	1126·6660	⅞	137·8377	1511·9038
38 in.	119·3805	1134·1149	44 in.	138·2304	1520·5308
⅛	119·7735	1141·5885	⅛	138·6231	1529·1825
¼	120·1659	1149·0866	¼	139·0158	1537·8587
⅜	120·5589	1156·6083	⅜	139·4085	1546·5475
½	120·9516	1164·1564	½	139·8012	1555·2847
⅝	121·3443	1171·7282	⅝	140·1939	1564·0346
¾	121·7370	1179·3244	¾	140·5866	1572·8089
⅞	122·1297	1186·9453	⅞	140·9793	1581·6079
39 in.	122·5224	1194·5906	45 in.	141·3717	1590·4313
⅛	122·9151	1202·2605	⅛	141·7647	1599·2777
¼	123·3078	1209·9550	¼	142·1574	1608·1518
⅜	123·7005	1217·6740	⅜	142·5505	1617·0390
½	124·0932	1225·4175	½	142·9428	1625·9705
⅝	124·4859	1233·1856	⅝	143·3355	1634·9267
¾	124·8786	1240·9782	¾	143·7282	1643·8874
⅞	125·2713	1248·7954	⅞	144·1209	1652·8827

DIAM.	CIRCUM.	AREA.	DIAM.	CIRCUM.	AREA.
46 in.	144·5133	1661·9025	52 in.	163·3628	2123·7166
⅛	144·9060	1670·9469	⅛	163·7555	2133·9390
¼	145·2987	1680·0158	¼	164·1482	2144·1861
⅜	145·6914	1689·0993	⅜	164·5409	2154·4576
½	146·0841	1698·2272	½	164·9336	2164·7537
⅝	146·4768	1707·3698	⅝	165·3263	2175·0744
¾	146·8695	1716·5368	¾	165·7190	2185·4195
⅞	147·2622	1725·7284	⅞	166·1117	2195·7893
47 in.	147·6549	1734·9445	53 in.	166·5044	2206·1834
⅛	148·0476	1744·1852	⅛	166·8971	2216·6022
¼	148·4403	1753·4505	¼	167·2898	2227·0456
⅜	148·8330	1762·7304	⅜	167·6825	2237·5132
½	149·2257	1772·0546	½	168·0752	2248·0059
⅝	149·6184	1781·3936	⅝	168·4679	2258·5229
¾	150·0111	1790·7569	¾	168·8606	2269·0644
⅞	150·4038	1800·1450	⅞	169·2533	2279·6305
48 in.	150·7964	1809·5574	54 in.	169·6460	2290·2210
⅛	151·1891	1818·9944	⅛	170·0387	2300·8362
¼	151·5818	1828·4560	¼	170·4314	2311·4759
⅜	151·9745	1837·9322	⅜	170·8241	2322·1392
½	152·3672	1847·4528	½	171·2168	2332·8289
⅝	152·7599	1856·9881	⅝	171·6095	2343·5423
¾	153·1526	1866·5478	¾	172·0022	2354·2801
⅞	153·5453	1876·1322	⅞	172·3949	2365·0426
49 in.	153·9380	1885·7410	55 in.	172·7876	2375·8294
⅛	154·3307	1895·3744	⅛	173·1803	2386·6411
¼	154·7234	1905·0323	¼	173·5730	2397·4770
⅜	155·1161	1914·7150	⅜	173·9657	2408·3377
½	155·5088	1924·4218	½	174·3584	2419·2227
⅝	155·9015	1934·1534	⅝	174·7511	2430·1775
¾	156·2942	1943·9095	¾	175·1438	2441·0666
⅞	156·6869	1953·6902	⅞	175·5365	2452·0254
50 in.	157·0796	1963·4954	56 in.	175·9292	2463·0086
⅛	157·4723	1973·3251	⅛	176·3219	2474·0145
¼	157·8650	1983·1794	¼	176·7146	2485·0489
⅜	158·2577	1993·0583	⅜	177·1073	2496·1059
½	158·6504	2002·9617	½	177·5000	2507·1873
⅝	159·0431	2012·8897	⅝	177·8927	2518·2934
¾	159·4358	2022·8421	¾	178·2854	2529·4239
⅞	159·8285	2032·8172	⅞	178·6781	2540·5781
51 in.	160·2212	2042·8206	57 in.	179·0708	2551·7586
⅛	160·6139	2052·8467	⅛	179·4635	2562·9629
¼	161·0066	2062·8974	¼	179·8562	2574·1916
⅜	161·3993	2072·9727	⅜	180·2449	2585·4450
½	161·7920	2083·0723	½	180·6416	2596·7227
⅝	162.1847	2093·1966	⅝	181·0343	2608·0251
¾	162·5774	2103·3554	¾	181·4270	2619·3520
⅞	162·9701	2113·5188	⅞	181·8237	2630·7035

DIAM.	CIRCUM.	AREA.	DIAM.	CIRCUM.	AREA.
58 in.	182·2124	2642·0794	64 in.	201·0620	3216·9909
⅛	182·6051	2653·4800	⅛	201·4547	3229·5695
¼	182·9978	2664·9051	¼	201·8474	3242·1707
⅜	183·3905	2676·3549	⅜	202·2401	3254·8005
½	183·7832	2687·8289	½	202·6328	3267·4527
⅝	184·1759	2699·3277	⅝	203·0255	3280·1296
¾	184·5686	2710·8508	¾	203.4182	3292·8309
⅞	184·9613	2722·3988	⅞	203·8109	3305·5566
59 in.	185·3540	2733·9710	65 in.	204·2035	3318·3072
⅛	185·7467	2745·5681	⅛	204·5962	3331·0822
¼	186·1394	2757·1893	¼	204·9889	3343·8818
⅜	186·5321	2768·8355	⅜	205·3816	3356·7059
½	186·9248	2780·5059	½	205·7743	3369·5545
⅝	187·3175	2792·2010	⅝	206·1670	3382·4277
¾	187·7102	2803·9205	¾	206·5597	3395·3253
⅞	188·1029	2815·6647	⅞	206·9524	3408·2476
60 in.	188·4956	2827·4334	66 in.	207·3451	3421·1944
⅛	188·8883	2839·2266	⅛	207·7378	3434·1657
¼	189·2810	2851·0444	¼	208·1305	3447·1616
⅜	189·6737	2862·8868	⅜	208·5232	3460·1820
½	190·0664	2874·7536	½	208·9159	3473·2270
⅝	190·4591	2886·6450	⅝	209·3086	3486·3966
¾	190·8518	2898·5610	¾	209·7013	3499·3906
⅞	191·2445	2910·5016	⅞	210·0940	3512·5093
61 in.	191·6372	2922·4666	67 in.	210·4867	3525·6524
⅛	192·0299	2934·4562	⅛	210·8794	3538·8201
¼	192·4226	2946·4703	¼	211·2721	3552·0123
⅜	192·8153	2958·5091	⅜	211·6648	3565·2292
½	193·2080	2970·5722	½	212·0575	3578·4704
⅝	193·6007	2982·6600	⅝	212·4502	3591·7363
¾	193·9934	2994·7723	¾	212·8429	3605·0267
⅞	194·3861	3006·9092	⅞	213·2356	3618·3417
62 in.	194·7788	3019·0705	68 in.	213·6283	3631·6811
⅛	195·1715	3031·2560	⅛	214·0210	3645·0451
¼	195·5642	3043·4670	¼	214·4137	3658·4337
⅜	195·9569	3055·7021	⅜	214·8064	3671·8469
½	196·3396	3067·9616	½	215·1991	3685·2845
⅝	196·7423	3080·2458	⅝	215·5918	3698·7468
¾	197·1350	3092·5544	¾	215·9845	3712·2335
⅞	197·5277	3104·8877	⅞	216·3772	3725·7450
63 in.	197·9204	3117·2453	69 in.	216·7699	3739·2807
⅛	198·3131	3129·6273	⅛	217·1626	3752·8411
¼	198·7058	3142·0344	¼	217·5553	3766·4260
⅜	199·0985	3154·4659	⅜	217·9480	3780·0356
½	199·4912	3166·9217	½	218·3407	3793·6695
⅝	199·8839	3179·4022	⅝	218·7334	3807·3281
¾	200·2766	3191·9072	¾	219·1261	3821·0112
⅞	200·6693	3204·4368	⅞	219·5189	3834·7189

DIAM.	CIRCUM.	AREA.	DIAM.	CIRCUM.	AREA.
70 in.	219·9115	3848·4510	76 in.	238·5611	4536·4598
1/8	220·3042	3862·2077	1/8	239·1538	4551·3946
1/4	220·6969	3875·9890	1/4	239·5464	4566·3540
3/8	221·0896	3889·7948	3/8	239·9392	4581·3379
1/2	221·4823	3903·6252	1/2	240·3319	4596·3464
5/8	221·8750	3917·4802	5/8	240·7246	4611·3895
3/4	222·2677	3931·3596	3/4	241·1173	4626·4370
7/8	222·6604	3945·2636	7/8	241·5100	4641·5192
71 in.	223·0531	3959·1921	77 in.	241·9047	4656·6257
1/8	223·4458	3973·1452	1/8	242·2954	4671·7569
1/4	223·8385	3987·1229	1/4	242·6861	4686·9126
3/8	224·2312	4001·1252	3/8	243·0808	4702·0929
1/2	224·6239	4015·1518	1/2	243·4735	4717·2977
5/8	225·0166	4029·2031	5/8	243·8662	4732·5271
3/4	225·4093	4043·2788	3/4	244·2589	4747·7810
7/8	225·8020	4057·3884	7/8	244·6516	4763·0595
72 in.	226·1947	4071·5041	78 in.	245·0443	4778·3624
1/8	226·5874	4085·6532	1/8	245·4370	4793·6890
1/4	226·9801	4099·8275	1/4	245·8297	4809·0420
3/8	227·3728	4114·0260	3/8	246·2224	4824·4187
1/2	227·7655	4128·2490	1/2	246·6151	4839·8198
5/8	228·1582	4142·4967	5/8	247·0078	4855·2455
3/4	228·5509	4156·7689	3/4	247·4005	4870·7958
7/8	228·9436	4171·0656	7/8	247·7932	4886·1707
73 in.	229·3363	4185·3868	79 in.	248·1859	4901·6669
1/8	229·7290	4199·7326	1/8	248·5786	4917·1938
1/4	230·1217	4214·1029	1/4	248·6713	4932·7423
3/8	230·5144	4228·4979	3/8	249·3640	4948·3154
1/2	230·9071	4242·9171	1/2	249·7567	4963·9127
5/8	231·2998	4257·3611	5/8	250·1494	4979·5310
3/4	231·6925	4271·8296	3/4	250·5421	4995·1814
7/8	232·0852	4286·3227	7/8	250·9348	5010·8526
74 in.	232·4779	4300·8404	80 in.	251·3275	5026·5482
1/8	232·8706	4315·3826	1/8	251·7202	5042·2785
1/4	233·2633	4329·9492	1/4	252·1129	5058·0133
3/8	233·6560	4344·5405	3/8	252·5056	5073·7826
1/2	234·0487	4359·1563	1/2	252·8983	5089·5764
5/8	234·4414	4373·7967	5/8	253·2910	5105·3948
3/4	234·8341	4388·4613	3/4	253·6837	5121·2378
7/8	235·2268	4403·1508	7/8	254·0764	5137·1054
75 in.	235·6195	4417·8647	81 in.	254·4691	5152·9978
1/8	236·0122	4432·6032	1/8	254·8618	5168·9140
1/4	236·4049	4447·3662	1/4	255·2545	5184·8551
3/8	236·7976	4462·1539	3/8	255·6472	5200·8208
1/2	237·1903	4476·9659	1/2	256·0399	5216·8109
5/8	237·5830	4491·8026	5/8	256·4326	5232·8258
3/4	237·9757	4506·6637	3/4	256·8252	5248·8650
7/8	238·3684	4521·5495	7/8	257·2180	5264.9289

DIAM.	CIRCUM.	AREA.	DIAM.	CIRCUM.	AREA.
82 in.	257·6106	5281·0172	88 in.	276·4602	6082·1234
⅛	258·0033	5297·1302	⅛	276·8529	6099·4145
¼	258.3960	5313·2677	¼	277·2456	5116·7300
⅜	258·7887	5329·4297	⅜	277·6383	6134·0702
½	259·1814	5345·6162	½	278·0310	6151·4349
⅝	259·5741	5361·8273	⅝	278·4237	6168·8240
¾	259·9668	5378·0630	¾	278·8164	6186·2377
⅞	260·3595	5394·3233	⅞	279·2091	6203·6751
83 in.	260·7522	5410·6079	89 in.	279·6018	6221·1389
⅛	261·1449	5426·9172	⅛	279·9945	6238·6263
¼	261·5376	5443·2511	¼	280·3872	6256·1382
⅜	261·9303	5459·6096	⅜	280·7799	6273·6746
½	262·3230	5475·9923	½	281·1726	6291·2356
⅝	262·7157	5492·3998	⅝	281·5653	6308·8212
¾	263·1084	5508·8318	¾	281·9580	6326·4313
⅞	263·5011	5525·2884	⅞	282·1507	6344·0660
84 in.	263·8938	5541·7694	90 in.	282·7434	6361·7251
⅛	264·2865	5558·2751	⅛	283·1361	6379·4069
¼	264·6792	5574·8053	¼	283·5288	6397·1171
⅜	265·0719	5591·3600	⅜	283·9215	6414·8499
½	265·4646	5607·9392	½	284·3142	6432·6073
⅝	265·8572	5624·5430	⅝	284·7069	6450·3893
¾	266·2500	5641·1714	¾	285·0996	6468·1954
⅞	266·6427	5657·8236	⅞	285·4923	6486·0265
85 in.	267·0354	5674·5017	91 in.	285·8850	6503·8821
⅛	267·4281	5691·2037	⅛	286·2777	6521·7622
¼	267·8208	5707·9302	¼	286·6704	6539·6669
⅜	268·2135	5724·6814	⅜	287·0631	6557·5962
½	268·6062	5741·4569	½	287·4558	6575·5498
⅝	268·9989	5758·2631	⅝	287·8485	6593·5281
¾	269·3916	5775·0818	¾	288·2412	6611·5308
⅞	269·7843	5791·9311	⅞	288·6339	6629·5582
86 in.	270·1770	5808·8048	92 in.	289·0266	6647·6100
⅛	270·5696	5825·7032	⅛	289·4193	6665·6865
¼	270·9624	5842·6260	¼	289·8120	6683·7875
⅜	271·3551	5859·5735	⅜	290·2047	6701·9131
½	271·7478	5876·5454	½	290·5974	6720·0630
⅝	272·1405	5893·5420	⅝	290·9901	6738·2377
¾	272·5332	5910·5630	¾	291·3828	6756·4368
⅞	272·9259	5927·6087	⅞	291·7755	6774·6605
87 in.	273·3186	5944·6787	93 in.	292·1682	6792·9087
⅛	273·7113	5961·7734	⅛	292·5609	6811·1814
¼	274·1040	5978·8926	¼	292·9536	6829·4788
⅜	274·4967	5996·0365	⅜	293·3463	6847·8007
½	274·8894	6013·2047	½	293·7390	6866·1471
⅝	275·2821	6030·3975	⅝	294·1317	6884·5182
¾	275·6748	6047·6149	¾	294·5244	6902·9135
⅞	276·0675	6064·8569	⅞	294·9171	6921·3336

DIAM.	CIRCUM.	AREA.	DIAM.	CIRCUM.	AREA.
94 in.	295·3097	6939·7782	97 in.	304·7345	7389·8113
$\frac{1}{8}$	295·7024	6958·2474	$\frac{1}{8}$	305·1272	7408·8695
$\frac{1}{4}$	296·0951	6976·7410	$\frac{1}{4}$	305·5299	7427·9522
$\frac{3}{8}$	296·4878	6995·2593	$\frac{3}{8}$	305·9126	7447·0595
$\frac{1}{2}$	296·8805	7013·8019	$\frac{1}{2}$	306·3033	7466·1913
$\frac{5}{8}$	297·2732	7032·3693	$\frac{5}{8}$	306·6980	7485·3478
$\frac{3}{4}$	297·6659	7050·9612	$\frac{3}{4}$	307·0907	7504·5285
$\frac{7}{8}$	298·0586	7069·5777	$\frac{7}{8}$	307·4834	7523·7340
95 in.	298·4513	7088·2184	98 in.	307·8761	7542·9640
$\frac{1}{8}$	298·8440	7106·8839	$\frac{1}{8}$	308·2688	7562·2186
$\frac{1}{4}$	299·2367	7125·5799	$\frac{1}{4}$	308·6615	7581·4976
$\frac{3}{8}$	299·6294	7144·2886	$\frac{3}{8}$	309·0542	7600·8012
$\frac{1}{2}$	300·0221	7163·0276	$\frac{1}{2}$	309·4469	7620·1293
$\frac{5}{8}$	300·4148	7181·7914	$\frac{5}{8}$	309·8396	7639·4810
$\frac{3}{4}$	300·8075	7200·5794	$\frac{3}{4}$	310·2323	7658·8593
$\frac{7}{8}$	301·2002	7219·3921	$\frac{7}{8}$	310·6250	7678·2610
96 in.	301·5929	7238·2295	99 in.	311·0177	7697·6874
$\frac{1}{8}$	301·9856	7257·0914	$\frac{1}{8}$	311·4104	7717·1383
$\frac{1}{4}$	302·3783	7275·9777	$\frac{1}{4}$	311·8031	7736·6137
$\frac{3}{8}$	302·7710	7294·8886	$\frac{3}{8}$	312·1958	7756·1137
$\frac{1}{2}$	303·1637	7313·8240	$\frac{1}{2}$	312·5885	7775·6382
$\frac{5}{8}$	303·5564	7332·7841	$\frac{5}{8}$	312·9812	7795·1873
$\frac{3}{4}$	303·9491	7351·7686	$\frac{3}{4}$	313·3739	7814·7608
$\frac{7}{8}$	304·3418	7370·7777	$\frac{7}{8}$	313·7666	7834·3590
			100 in.	314·1593	7853·9816

NOTE.—This Table has been calculated by the following process:

1. *To find the Circumferences.*—Add ·392699 to any of those previously found, and it will give the next in succession.

2. *To find the Areas.*—Having calculated two in succession to eight places of decimals, take their difference, to which add ·02454369, and add the result to the last found area, and cut off the last four figures, and it will give the next; and so on.

TABLE I.

To find the Pitch of a Screw from the Angle and Diameter.

[Multiply the number in this Table corresponding to the degrees and minutes of the angle by the diameter, and the result will be the pitch.]

	14°	15°	16°	17°	18°	19°	20°	21°	22°	23°	24°	25°	26°	27°	28°	29°	30°
0′	·7833	·8418	·9008	·9605	1·0207	1·0817	1·1434	1·2059	1·2693	1·3335	1·3987	1·4649	1·5322	1·6006	1·6704	1·7414	1·8138
1′	·7842	·8428	·9018	·9615	1·0218	1·0827	1·1445	1·2070	1·2703	1·3346	1·3998	1·4661	1·5334	1·6018	1·6716	1·7426	1·8150
2′	·7852	·8438	·9028	·9625	1·0228	1·0837	1·1456	1·2080	1·2714	1·3357	1·4009	1·4672	1·5345	1·6030	1·6728	1·7438	1·8162
3′	·7862	·8448	·9038	·9635	1·0238	1·0848	1·1465	1·2091	1·2724	1·3367	1·4020	1·4683	1·5356	1·6042	1·6739	1·7450	1·8174
4′	·7871	·8458	·9048	·9645	1·0248	1·0858	1·1476	1·2101	1·2735	1·3378	1·4031	1·4694	1·5368	1·6053	1·6751	1·7462	1·8186
5′	·7881	·8467	·9058	·9655	1·0258	1·0868	1·1486	1·2112	1·2746	1·3389	1·4042	1·4705	1·5379	1·6065	1·6762	1·7474	1·8199
6′	·7891	·8477	·9068	·9665	1·0268	1·0879	1·1497	1·2122	1·2756	1·3400	1·4053	1·4716	1·5390	1·6076	1·6774	1·7486	1·8211
7′	·7900	·8487	·9078	·9675	1·0278	1·0889	1·1507	1·2133	1·2767	1·3410	1·4064	1·4727	1·5402	1·6088	1·6786	1·7498	1·8223
8′	·7910	·8497	·9087	·9685	1·0288	1·0899	1·1517	1·2143	1·2778	1·3421	1·4075	1·4738	1·5413	1·6099	1·6798	1·7510	1·8235
9′	·7920	·8507	·9097	·9695	1·0298	1·0909	1·1528	2·2154	1·2788	1·3432	1·4086	1·4749	1·5425	1·6111	1·6810	1·7522	1·8248
10′	·7930	·8516	·9107	·9705	1·0309	1·0920	1·1538	1·2164	1·2799	1·3443	1·4097	1·4761	1·5436	1·6123	1·6821	1·7534	1·8260
11′	·7940	·8526	·9117	·9715	1·0319	1·0930	1·1548	1·2175	1·2810	1·3454	1·4108	1·4772	1·5447	1·6134	1·6833	1·7546	1·8272
12′	·7949	·8536	·9127	·9725	1·0329	1·0940	1·1559	1·2185	1·2820	1·3465	1·4119	1·4783	1·5458	1·6146	1·6845	1·7558	1·8284
13′	·7959	·8546	·9137	·9735	1·0339	1·0950	1·1569	1·2196	1·2831	1·3475	1·4130	1·4794	1·5470	1·6157	1·6856	1·7570	1·8297
14′	·7969	·8556	·9147	·9745	1·0349	1·0960	1·1579	1·2206	1·2842	1·3486	1·4141	1·4806	1·5481	1·6169	1·6868	1·7582	1·8309
15′	·7979	·8565	·9157	·9755	1·0359	1·0971	1·1590	1·2217	1·2852	1·3497	1·4152	1·4817	1·5492	1·6180	1·6880	1·7594	1·8321
16′	·7989	·8575	·9167	·9765	1·0369	1·0981	1·1600	1·2227	1·2863	1·3508	1·4163	1·4828	1·5503	1·6192	1·6892	1·7606	1·8333
17′	·7998	·8585	·9177	·9775	1·0379	1·0991	1·1611	1·2238	1·2874	1·3519	1·4174	1·4839	1·5514	1·6203	1·6904	1·7618	1·8345
18′	·8008	·8595	·9187	·9785	1·0389	1·1001	1·1621	1·2248	1·2884	1·3530	1·4185	1·4850	1·5526	1·6215	1·6916	1·7630	1·8358
19′	·8018	·8605	·9197	·9795	1·0399	1·1012	1·1631	1·2259	1·2895	1·3541	1·4196	1·4861	1·5537	1·6226	1·6927	1·7642	1·8370
20′	·8028	·8614	·9207	·9805	1·0410	1·1022	1·1642	1·2269	1·2906	1·3551	1·4207	1·4872	1·5549	1·6238	1·6939	1·7654	1·8383
21′	·8037	·8624	·9216	·9815	1·0420	1·1032	1·1652	1·2280	1·2916	1·3562	1·4218	1·4884	1·5560	1·6250	1·6951	1·7666	1·8395
22′	·8047	·8634	·9226	·9825	1·0430	1·1042	1·1663	1·2290	1·2927	1·3573	1·4229	1·4895	1·5572	1·6261	1·6962	1·7678	1·8407
23′	·8057	·8644	·9236	·9835	1·0440	1·1053	1·1673	1·2301	1·2938	1·3584	1·4240	1·4906	1·5583	1·6273	1·6974	1·7690	1·8419
24′	·8067	·8654	·9246	·9845	1·0450	1·1063	1·1683	1·2312	1·2948	1·3595	1·4251	1·4917	1·5595	1·6284	1·6986	1·7702	1·8432
25′	·8076	·8663	·9256	·9855	1·0460	1·1073	1·1694	1·2322	1·2959	1·3606	1·4262	1·4928	1·5606	1·5296	1·6998	1·7714	1·8444
26′	·8086	·8673	·9266	·9865	1·0471	1·1084	1·1704	1·2333	1·2970	1·3616	1·4273	1·4939	1·5618	1·6307	1·7010	1·7726	1·8456
27′	·8096	·8683	·9276	·9875	1·0481	1·1094	1·1715	1·2343	1·2981	1·3627	1·4284	1·4951	1·5629	1·6319	1·7022	1·7738	1·8468
28′	·8105	·8693	·9286	·9885	1·0491	1·1104	1·1725	1·2354	1·2991	1·3638	1·4295	1·4962	1·5641	1·6331	1·7034	1·7750	1·8481

29′	·8115	·8703	·9296	·9895	1·0501	1·1114	1·1735	1·2364	1·3002	1·3649	1·4306	1·4973	1·5653	1·6342	1·7045	1·7762	1.8493
30′	·8125	·8712	·9306	·9905	1·0512	1·1125	1.1746	1·2375	1·3013	1·3660	1·4317	1·4984	1·5664	1·6354	1·7057	1·7774	1·8505
31′	·8134	·8722	·9316	·9915	1·0522	1·1135	1·1756	1·2385	1·3023	1·3671	1·4328	1·4996	1·5675	1·6366	1·7069	1·7786	1·8517
32′	·8144	·8732	·0326	·9925	1·0532	1·1145	1·1767	1·2396	1·3034	1·3682	1·4339	1·5007	1·5686	1·6377	1·7081	1·7798	1·8530
33′	·8154	·8742	·9335	·9935	1·0542	1·1156	1·1777	1·2406	1·3045	1·3693	1·4350	1·5018	1·5698	1·6389	1·7093	1·7810	1·8542
34′	·8164	·8752	·9345	·9945	1·0552	1·1166	1·1787	1·2417	1·3055	1·3704	1·4361	1·5029	1·5709	1·6400	1·7105	1·7822	1·8554
35′	·8173	·8761	·9355	·9955	1·0562	1·1176	1·1798	1·2427	1·3066	1·3714	1·4372	1·5040	1·5720	1·6412	1·7117	1·7834	1·8567
36′	·8183	·8771	·9365	·9965	1·0572	1·1187	1·1808	1·2437	1·3077	1·3725	1·4383	1·5052	1·5732	1·6424	1·7129	1·7846	1·8579
37′	·8193	·8781	·9375	·9975	1·0582	1·1197	1·1819	1·2448	1·3088	1·3736	1·4394	1·5063	1·5743	1·6435	1·7141	1·7859	1·8591
38′	·8203	·8791	·9385	·9985	1·0592	1·1207	1·1829	1·2458	1·3099	1·3747	1·4405	1·5074	1·5755	1·6447	1·7152	1·7871	1·8604
39′	·8212	·8801	·9395	·9995	1·0602	1·1218	1·1839	1·2469	1·3109	1·3758	1·4416	1·5085	1·5766	1·6459	1·7164	1·7883	1·8616
40′	·8222	·8811	·9405	1·0006	1·0613	1·1228	1·1850	1·2479	1·3120	1·3769	1·4427	1·5097	1·5777	1·6470	1·7176	1·7895	1·8628
41′	·8232	·8821	·9415	1·0016	1·0623	1·1238	1·1860	1·2490	1·3131	1·3780	1·4438	1·5108	1·5789	1·6482	1·7188	1·7907	1·8641
42′	·8242	·8831	·9425	1·0026	1·0633	1·1249	1·1871	1·2500	1·3141	1·3791	1·4450	1·5119	1·5801	1·6493	1·7200	1·7919	1·8653
43′	·8252	·8840	·9435	1·0036	1·0643	1·1259	1·1881	1·2511	1·3152	1·3801	1·4461	1·5130	1·5812	1·6505	1·7212	1·7931	1·8665
44′	·8261	·8850	·9445	1·0046	1·0653	1·1269	1·1891	1·2521	1·3163	1·3812	1·4472	1·5142	1·5824	1·6517	1·7224	1·7944	1·8678
45′	·8271	·8860	·9455	1·0056	1·0663	1·1280	1·1902	1·2532	1·3174	1·3823	1·4483	1·5153	1·5835	1·6528	1·7235	1·7956	1·8690
46′	·8281	·8870	·9465	1·0066	1·0673	1·1290	1·1912	1·2542	1·3185	1·3834	1·4494	1·5164	1·5846	1·6540	1·7247	1·7968	1·8703
47′	·8291	·8880	·9475	1·0076	1·0683	1·1300	1·1923	1·2553	1·3195	1·3845	1·4505	1·5176	1·5858	1·6552	1·7259	1·7980	1·8715
48′	·8301	·8890	·9485	1·0086	1·0694	1·1310	1·1933	1·2564	1·3206	1·3856	1·4516	1·5187	1·5869	1·6563	1·7271	1·7992	1·8727
49′	·8310	·8900	·9495	1·0096	1·0704	1·1321	1·1943	1·2574	1·3217	1·3867	1·4527	1·5198	1·5881	1·6575	1·7283	1·8004	1·8740
50′	·8320	·8909	·9505	1·0106	1·0714	1·1331	1·1954	1·2585	1·3228	1·3878	1·4538	1·5209	1·5892	1·6587	1·7295	1·8016	1·8752
51′	·8330	·8919	·9515	1·0116	1·0725	1·1342	1·1964	1·2596	1·3238	1·3889	1·4549	1·5220	1·5903	1·6599	1·7307	1·8028	1·8765
52′	·8340	·8929	·9525	1·0126	1·0735	1·1352	1·1975	1·2607	1·3249	1·3900	1·4560	1·5232	1·5915	1·6611	1·7319	1·8041	1·8777
53′	·8350	·8939	·9535	1·0136	1·0745	1·1362	1·1985	1·2618	1·3260	1·3911	1·4571	1·5243	1·5926	1·6622	1·7331	1·8053	1·8789
54′	·8359	·8949	·9545	1·0147	1·0755	1·1373	1·1995	1·2629	1·3270	1·3922	1·4582	1·5255	1·5938	1·6634	1·7343	1·8065	1·8802
55′	·8369	·8959	·9555	1·0157	1·0765	1·1383	1·2006	1·2639	1·3281	1·3933	1·4594	1·5266	1·5949	1·6645	1·7355	1·8077	1·8814
56′	·8379	·8969	·9565	1·0167	1·0776	1·1393	1·2016	1·2650	1·3292	1·3944	1·4605	1·5277	1·5961	1·6657	1·7366	1·8089	1·8827
57′	·8389	·8978	·9575	1·0177	1·0786	1·1404	1·2027	1·2661	1·3303	1·3955	1·4616	1·5288	1·5972	1·6669	1·7378	1·8101	1·8839
58′	·8399	·8988	·9585	1·0187	1·0796	1·1414	1·2037	1·2671	1·3314	1·3966	1·4627	1·5299	1·5984	1·6681	1·7390	1·8114	1·8852
59′	·8408	·8998	·9595	1·0197	1·0806	1·1424	1·2047	1·2682	1·3324	1·3977	1·4638	1·5311	1·5996	1·6692	1·7402	1·8126	1·8864

TABLE K.

Knot-Table.

The minutes and seconds of time in which a vessel passes over the measured knot being known, look for the corresponding number in this Table, which will be the rate of the vessel in knots.

Sec.	3m	4m	5m	6m	7m	8m	9m	10m	11m	12m	13m	14m
0	20·000	15·000	12·000	10·000	8·571	7·500	6·666	6·000	5·454	5·000	4·615	4·285
1	19·890	14·938	11·960	9·972	8·551	7·484	6·654	5·990	5·446	4·993	4·609	4·280
2	19·780	14·876	11·920	9·944	8·530	7·468	6·642	5·980	5·438	4·986	4·603	4·275
3	19·672	14·815	11·880	9·917	8·510	7·453	6·629	5·970	5·429	4·979	4·597	4·270
4	19·564	14·754	11·841	9·890	8·490	7·438	6·617	5·960	5·421	4·972	4·591	4·265
5	19·460	14·694	11·803	9·863	8·470	7·422	6·605	5·950	5·413	4·965	4·585	4·260
6	19·355	14·634	11·764	9·830	8·450	7·407	6·593	5·940	5·405	4·958	4·580	4·255
7	19·251	14·575	11·726	9·809	8·459	7·392	6·581	5·930	5·397	4·951	4·574	4·250
8	19·150	14·516	11·688	9·783	8·413	7·377	6·569	5 921	5·389	4·945	4·568	4·245
9	19·047	14·457	11·650	9·756	8·391	7·362	6·557	5·911	5·381	4·938	4·562	4·240
10	18·947	14·400	11·613	9·729	8·372	7·346	6·545	5·901	5·373	4·931	4·556	4·235
11	18·848	14·342	11·575	9·703	8·352	7·331	6·533	5·891	5·365	4·924	4·551	4·230
12	18·750	14·285	11·538	9·677	8·333	7·317	6·521	5·882	5·357	4·918	4·545	4·225
13	18·652	14·220	11·501	9·651	8·314	7.302	6·509	5·872	5·349	4·911	4·539	4·220
14	18·556	14·173	11·465	9·625	8·295	7·287	6·498	5·863	5·341	4·904	4·534	4·215
15	18·461	14·118	11·428	9·600	8·275	7·272	6·486	5·853	5·333	4·897	4·528	4·210
16	18·367	14·063	11·392	9·574	8·256	7·258	6·474	5·844	5·325	4·891	4·522	4·206
17	18·274	14·008	11·356	9·549	8·238	7·243	6·463	5·834	5·317	4·884	4·516	4·201
18	18·181	13·953	11·323	9·524	8·219	7·229	6·451	5·825	5·309	4·878	4·511	4·196
19	18·090	13·900	11·285	9·490	8·200	7.214	6·440	5·815	5·301	4·871	4·505	4·191
20	18·000	13·846	11·250	9·473	8·181	7·200	6·428	5·806	5·294	4·864	4·500	4·186
21	17·910	13·793	11·214	9·448	8·163	7·185	6·417	5·797	5·286	4.858	4·494	4·181
22	17.823	13·740	11·180	9·424	8·144	7·171	6·405	5·787	5·278	4·851	4·488	4·176
23	17·734	13·688	11·145	9·399	8·127	7.157	6·394	5·778	5·270	4·845	4·483	4·171
24	17·647	13·636	11·111	9·375	8·108	7·142	6·383	5·769	5·263	4·838	4·477	4·166
25	17·560	13·584	11·077	9·350	8·090	7·128	6·371	5·760	5·255	4·832	4·472	4·161
26	17·475	13·533	11·043	9·326	8·071	7·114	6·360	5·750	5·247	4 825	4·466	4·157
27	17·391	13·483	11·009	9·302	8·053	7·100	6·349	5·741	5·240	4·819	4·460	4·152
28	17·307	13·432	10·975	9·278	8·035	7·086	6·338	5·732	5·232	4·812	4·455	4·147
29	17·225	13·383	10·942	9·254	8·017	7·072	6·327	5·723	5·224	4·806	4·449	4·142
30	17·143	13 333	10·909	9·230	8·000	7·059	6 315	5·714	5·217	4·800	4.444	4·137
31	17·061	13·284	10·876	9·207	7·982	7·045	6·304	5·705	5·210	4·793	4·438	4·133
32	16·981	13·235	10·843	9·183	7·964	7·031	6·283	5·696	5·202	4·787	4.433	4·128
33	16·901	13·186	10·810	9·160	7·947	7·017	6·282	5·687	5·195	4·780	4·428	4·123
34	16·822	13·138	10·778	9·137	7·929	7·004	6·271	5·678	5·187	4·774	4·422	4·118
35	16·744	13·092	10·764	9·113	7·912	6·990	6·260	5·669	5·179	4·768	4·417	4·114
36	16·667	13·043	10·714	9·090	7·895	6·977	6·250	5·666	5·172	4·761	4·411	4·110
37	16·590	12·996	10·682	9·068	7·877	6·963	6·239	5·651	5·164	4·755	4·406	4·105
38	16·514	12·950	10·651	9·044	7·860	6·950	6·228	5·642	5·157	4·749	4·400	4·100
39	16·438	12·903	10·619	9·022	7·843	6·936	6·217	5·633	5·150	4·743	4·395	4·095
40	16·363	12·857	10·588	9·000	7·826	6·923	6·007	5·625	5·142	4·738	4·390	4·090
41	16·289	12·811	10·557	8·977	7·809	6·909	6·196	5·616	5·135	4·730	4·384.	4·086
42	16·216	12·766	10·526	8·955	7·792	6·896	6·185	5·607	5·128	4·724	4·379	4·081
43	16·143	12·711	10·495	8·933	7·775	6·883	6·174	5·598	5·121	4·718	4·374	4·077
44	16·071	12·676	10·465	8·911	7·758	6·870	6·164	5·590	5·114	4·712	4·368	4·072
45	16·000	12·631	10·434	8·889	7·741	6·857	6·153	5·581	5·106	4·706	4·363	4·067
46	15·929	12·587	10·404	8·867	7·725	6·844	6·143	5·572	5·099	4·700	4·358	4·063
47	15·859	12·543	10·375	8·845	7·708	6·831	6·132	5·564	5·091	4·693	4 353	4·058
48	15·789	12·500	10·345	8·823	7·692	6·818	6·122	5·555	5·084	4·687	4·347	4·054
49	15·721	12·456	10·315	8·801	7·675	6·805	6·112	5·547	5·077	4·681	4·342	4·049
50	15·652	12·413	10·286	8·780	7·659	6·792	6·101	5·538	5·070	4·675	4·337	4·044
51	15·584	12·371	10·256	8·759	7·643	6·779	6·091	5·530	5·063	4·669	4·332	4·040
52	15·517	12·329	10·227	8·737	7·627	6·766	6.081	5·521	5·056	4·663	4·326	4·035
53	15·450	12·287	10·198	8·716	7·611	6·754	6·071	5·513	5·049	4·657	4·321	4·031
54	15·384	12·245	10·169	8·695	7·595	6·741	6·060	5·504	5·042	4·651	4·316	4·026
55	15·319	12·203	10·140	8·675	7·579	6·729	6·050	5·496	5·035	4·645	4·311	4·022
56	15·254	12·162	10·112	8·654	7·563	6·716	6·040	5·487	5·028	4·639	4·306	4·017
57	15·190	12·121	10·084	8·633	7·547	6·704	6·030	5·479	5·020	4·633	4·301	4·013
58	15·125	12·080	10·055	8 612	7·531	6·691	6·020	5·471	5·013	4·627	4·295	4·008
59	15·062	12·040	10·027	8·591	7.515	6·679	6·010	5·463	5·006	4·621	4·290	4·004

List of Screw Steamers in her Majesty's Navy.

Name of Ship.	Horse-power.	Maker of Engines.	Diameter of Cylinder.	Length of Stroke.	Revolutions per minute.	Screw. Pitch.	Screw. Diameter.	Remarks.
			in.	ft. in.		ft. in.	ft. in.	
Aboukir	400	Penn and Son.	58	3 3	60	18 0	17 0	NOTE.—In cases where engines are fitted with trunks, the number of inches in the diameter of the cylinder expresses the equivalent, and not the actual diameters.
Adventure......	400	Fawcett.	45	3 0	...	22 7½	17 2¼	
Ætna	200	....	...	...	...	......	......	
Agamemnon ...	600	Penn and Son.	70¾	3 6	60	20 6	18 0	
Ajax	450	Maudslay and Field.	55	2 0	48	18 0	16 0	
Alacrity.........	200	Ravenhill and Salkeld.	45	2 0	86	16 0	11 0	
Alert..............	100	Ditto.	32	2 0	75	12 0	10 0	
Algerine.........	80	....	...	...	...	......	......	
Algiers	600	Maudslay and Field.	76	3 6	45	25 6	18 0	
Amphion	300	Ravenhill and Salkeld.	48	3 0	45	21 0	15 0	
Anson	800	Maudslay and Field.	82	4 0	45	27 6	19 0	
Archer	202	Ravenhill and Salkeld.	54	3 0	41	7 3	9 0	
Ariadne	800	Maudslay and Field.	82	3 8	50	27 6	20 0	
Ariel	60	Ravenhill and Salkeld.	25½	1 9	81	10 9	9 0	
Arrogant.........	360	Penn and Son.	55	3 0	61	15 2	15 6	
Arrow............	160	Humphrey & Tennant.	42	1 9	93	14 0	11 0	
Assistance	400	Fawcett.	45	3 0	...	22 7½	17 2¼	
Assurance.......	200	Ravenhill and Salkeld.	45	2 0	87	16 0	11 0	
Atlas..............	800	Maudslay and Field.	82	4 0	45	27 6	19 0	
Aurora	400	Ditto.	64	3 0	50	22 6	17 0	
Bacchante.......	600	Ditto.	76	3 6	45	25 6 to 28 6	19 4	
Barrosa	400	....	...	...	...	......	......	
Beagle	160	Humphrey & Tennant.	42	1 9	86	14 0	11 0	
Bee	10	Maudslay and Field.	20	2 0	40	5 0	4 0	Fitted with screw and paddle.
Black Prince...	1250	Penn and Son.	104¼	4 0	54	24 6	......	
Blenheim........	450	Seaward.	52	3 0	43	20 0	16 0	
Brisk..............	250	Scott and Sinclair.	152	3 6	34	12 0	12 0	
Brunswick	400	Ravenhill and Salkeld.	64	3 0	53 5	20 7	17 0	
Buffalo	80	....	...	...	...	......	......	
Bulwark	......	....	...	...	...	......	......	
Cæsar.............	400	Penn and Son.	58	3 3	60	18 10	17 0	
Cadmus	400	Ditto.	58	3 3	58	23 6	16 0	
Cameleon........	200	Maudslay and Field.	45	2 0	75	15 0	12 4	
Centurion	400	Ravenhill and Salkeld.	64	3 0	54	21 0	17 1	
Challenger......	400	Penn and Son.	58	3 3	67	23 6	16 0	
Charybdis.......	400	Ravenhill and Salkeld.	64	3 0	40	26 0	16 0	
Chasseur	70	....	...	...	...	......	......	Floating factory.
Chesapeake.....	400	Maudslay and Field.	64	3 0	50	22 6	17 0	
Clio................	400	Ravenhill and Salkeld.	64	3 0	50	26 0	16 0	
Colossus	400	Penn and Son.	58	3 3	60	18 6	17 1	
Conflict..........	400	Seaward.	46¼	2 0	64	20 0	13 7	
Conqueror	800	Penn and Son.	82	4 0	55	26 0	19 0	
Coquette.........	200	Ravenhill and Salkeld.	45	2 0	82¼	16 0	11 0	
Cordelia..........	150	....	...	...	...	......	......	
Cormorant......	200	Napier.	45	2 0	86	16 0	11 0	
Cornwallis......	200	Penn and Son.	30¼	2 6	103	9 6	12 0	High pressure.
Cossack	250	Maudslay and Field.	51	2 3	64	16 7	12 1	
Cressy............	400	Ditto.	64	3 0	55	21 0	17 0	
Cruiser	60	Rennie.	28	2 0	53	6 9	9 0	
Curacoa..........	350	Maudslay and Field.	57½	2 9	64	20 1	14 2	
Curlew	60	Ditto.	27	2 0	53	8 1	9 0	
Cygnet	80	Napier.	32	1 6	106	11 4	9 0	
Dart	80	Ditto.	32	1 6	106	11 4	9 0	
Dauntless	580	Ditto.	84	4 0	31	16 4	14 9	Multiple 2·3 to 1.
Defiance.........	800	Maudslay and Field.	82	4 0	45	27 6	19 0	
Desperate	400	Ditto.	55	2 6	34¼	14 0	13 0	
Diadem...........	800	Ditto.	82	4 0	54	31 to 33	18 0	
Donegal..........	800	Penn and Son.	82	4 0	52	28 6	19 0	
Doris	800	Ditto.	82	4 0	53	30 0	20 0	

Name of Ship.	Horse-power.	Maker of Engines.	Diameter of Cylinder.	Length of Stroke.	Revolutions per minute.	Screw. Pitch.	Screw. Diameter.	Remarks.
			in.	ft. in		ft. in.	ft. in.	
Duke of Wellington	700	Napier.	93⅝	4 6	30	16 3	18 0	
Duncan	800	Penn and Son.	82	4 0	55	26 0	19 0	
Eclipse	200	Napier.	45	2 0	86	15 6	11 0	
Edgar	600	Maudslay and Field.	76	3 6	45	26 0	18 0	
Edinburgh	450	Ditto.	55	2 6	54	18 9	16 0	
Emerald	600	Ravenhill and Salkeld.	76	3 6	45	28 0	18 0	
Encounter	360	Penn and Son.	55	2 3	82	16 9	12 0	
Erebus	200	Napier.	32	2 2	...	13 6	8 0	High pressure.
Esk	250	Scott Russell.	50	2 9	68	17 1	12 2½	
Espoir	80	....	...	...	...	......	......	
Eurotas	200	Penn and Son.	30¼	2 6	100	12 0	10 0	High pressure.
Euryalus	400	Ditto.	58	3 3	57	21 0	17 0	
Exmouth	400	Maudslay and Field.	64	3 0	53	21 0	17 0	
Fairy	128	Penn and Son.	42	3 0	40	8 0	6 6	Multiple 5 to 1.
Falcon	100	Ravenhill and Salkeld.	32	2 0	80	11 9	10 0	
Fawn	100	Ditto.	32	2 0	75	12 0	10 0	
Flying-fish	350	Maudslay and Field.	53	2 3	82	20 6	11 0	
Forth	200	Penn and Son.	30¼	2 6	110	10 0	12 0	High pressure.
Fox	200	Ravenhill and Salkeld.	45	2 0	75	11 10	12 1	
Foxhound	200	Humphrey & Tennant.	42¼	1 9	93	14 3	11 0	
Frederick William	500	Maudslay and Field.	66	3 6	50	21 0	18 0	
Galatea	800	Penn and Son.	82	3 8	58	28 6	20 0	
Gannett	150	Ravenhill and Salkeld.	39	2 0	75	14 6	10 0	
Gibraltar	800	Maudslay and Field.	82	4 0	45	27 6	19 0	
Glasgow	600	Ravenhill and Salkeld.	76	3 6	45	26 0	18 0	
Glatton	150	Ditto.	25½	2 0	127	14 0	6 3	High pressure.
Goliath	400	Penn and Son.	58	3 3	65	18 6	17 0	
Grayhound	200	Ravenhill and Salkeld.	45	2 0	75	14 6	12 0	
Griffon	80	Napier.	32	1 6	106	11 4	9 0	Multiple not known.
Hannibal	450	Scott and Sinclair.	71¼	4 0	27·5	12 6	17 0	
Harrier	100	Humphrey & Tennant.	34	1 9	93	10 0	10 0	
Hastings	200	Maudslay and Field.	30	2 6	78	12 3	12 0	
Hawke	200	Penn and Son.	30	2 6	80	9 6	12 0	
Hero	600	Maudslay and Field.	76	3 6	45	26 6	19 0	
Hesper	120	....	...	...	...	......	......	
Highflyer	250	Maudslay and Field.	55¼	2 6	50½	9 8	13 0	
Himalaya	700	Penn and Son.	77¾	3 6	...	......	......	
Hogue	450	Seaward.	55½	3 0	47	21 1	16 1	
Hood	600	Maudslay and Field.	76	3 6	...	......	......	
Horatio	250	Seaward.	54	3 0	41¼	13 0	14 0	
Hornet	100	Boulton and Watt.	38	2 0	71	13 6	10 0	
Howe	1000	Penn and Son.	92½	4 0	54	28 0	20 0	
Icarus	150	Humphrey & Tennant.	...	...	...	......	......	
Immortalite ...	600	Maudslay and Field.	76	3 6	45	25 6 to 29 6	19 5	Fitted with a screw of an increasing pitch.
Imperieuse	360	Penn and Son.	55	3 0	68	16 0	16 0	
Industry	80	....	...	...	...	......	......	
Intrepid	350	Maudslay and Field.	58¼	2 3	77	21 3	11 0	
Irresistible	400	Penn and Son.	58	3 3	66	17 0	17 0	
James Watt	600	Boulton and Watt.	52	3 0	54	24 4	17 0	
Jason	80	Ravenhill and Salkeld.	64	3 0	50	26 0	16 0	
Jasper	80	Maudslay and Field.	18	1 6	...	8 0	6 6	
Landrail	80	Humphrey & Tennant.	32	1 4	...	9 6	9 0	Not tried.
Lapwing	200	Ravenhill and Salkeld.	45	2 0	35	15 7	11 0	
Lee	80	Napier.	32	1 6	106	11 4	9 0	
Leven	80	....	...	...	...	......	......	
Liffey	600	Penn and Son.	70¼	3 6	57	25 6	18 0	
Lilly	80	Napier.	45	2 0	86	16 6	11 0	
Lion	400	Penn and Son.	58	3 3	43	18 0	17 0	
Liverpool	600	Humphrey & Tennant.	76	3 3	...	22 6	18 0	
London	500	Penn and Son.	71	3 0	50	20 0	18 0	
Lynx	80	Ditto.	35¼	1 8	113	9 8½	11 0	
Lyra	60	Ravenhill and Salkeld.	25½	1 9	80	11 0	9 0	
Majestic	400	Maudslay and Field.	64	3 0	50	21 0	17 0	

Name of Ship.	Horse-power.	Maker of Engines.	Diameter of Cylinder.	Length of Stroke.	Revolutions per minute.	Screw. Pitch.	Screw. Diameter.	Remarks.
			in.	ft. in		ft. in.	ft in.	
Malacca..........	200	Penn and Son.	28⅜	2 6	37½	11 0	13 6	High pressure.
Marlborough...	800	Maudslay and Field.	82	4 0	50	26 9	19 1	
Mars..............	400	Ditto.	64	3 0	58	21 0	17 0	
Meeanee.........	400	Penn and Son.	58	3 3	62	19 0	17 0	
Megæra	350	Rennie.	49½	2 0	74	16 0	14 6	
Melpomene.....	600	Penn and Son.	70¼	3 6	59	25 6	18 0	
Mersey	1000	Maudslay and Field.	92	4 0	45	31 6	20 0	
Meteor	150	Ditto.	26⅛	2 0	139	12 6	6 0	High pressure.
Minx	10	Seaward.	9⅛	0 9	196	8 7	4 1	Multiple not known.
Miranda	250	Napier.	56¾	3 9	28·5	11 6	12 0	
Mohawk.........	200	Humphrey & Tennant.	42¼	2 2	91	14 3	11 0	
Mullett..........	80	Napier.	32	1 6	106	11 4	9 0	
Mutine	200	Maudslay and Field.	45	2 0	82	15 0	12 4	
Narcissus	400	Ravenhill and Salkeld.	64	3 0	50	21 0	17 0	
Nelson	500	Ditto.	71	3 0	50	22 6	18 0	
Neptune..........	500	Ditto.	71	3 0	50	19 9	18 0	
Newcastle.......	600	Ditto.	76	3 6	45	26 0	18 0	
Niger	400	Maudslay and Field.	42¼	1 10	70	17 5	12 6	
Nile	500	Seaward.	47⅝	3 6	26	16 0	17 6	
Nimrod...........	175	Maudslay and Field.	58⅛	2 3	70	20 6	11 0	
Octavia..........	500	Ditto.	66	3 6	50	......	......	
Orestes...........	400	....	...	...	...	......	......	
Orion	600	Penn and Son.	70¼	3 6	63	23 0	18 0	
Orlando..........	1000	Ditto.	92½	4 0	52	32 6	20 0	
Orpheus..........	400	Humphrey & Tennant.	400	2 8	64	20 0	16 0	
Osprey...........	200	Maudslay and Field.	45	2 0	75	16 0	11 0	
Pantaloon.......	150	....	...	...	...	......	......	
Pearl..............	400	Penn and Son.	58⅛	3 3	50	23 6	16 0	
Pelican	200	Ravenhill and Salkeld.	45	2 0	75	14 6	12 0	
Pelorus...........	400	Ditto.	64	3 0	50	26 0	16 0	
Pembroke	200	Maudslay and Field.	30	2 6	82	12 0	12 0	High pressure.
Penguin	80	Napier.	32	1 6	106	11 4	9 0	
Perseverance...	360	Penn and Son.	55	3 0	61	......	......	
Phaeton	400	Boulton and Watt.	...	...	...	......	......	
Phœbe............	500	Napier.	65	3 0	60	22 0	18 0	
Phœnix	260	Penn and Son.	62¼	4 6	22	9 10	11 0	Multiple not known.
Philomel	80	Napier.	32	1 6	106	11 4	9 0	
Pioneer...........	350	Ravenhill and Salkeld.	55	2 6	82	20 6	11 0	
Plover............	80	Napier.	32	1 6	106	11 4	9 0	
Plumper.........	60	Ditto.	27	2 0	43½	6 0	6 8½	Multiple not known.
Prince of Wales	800	Penn and Son.	82	4 0	50	26 0	19 0	
Princess Royal	400	Ditto.	64	3 0	58¼	24 6	17 1	
Plyades	350	Ditto.	55	3 0	62	20 0	15 9	
Queen	500	Maudslay and Field.	66	3 6	66	18 6 to 23 6	18 0	
Racer	150	Humphrey & Tennant.	40	1 8	99	13 6	10 0	
Racehorse.......	200	Napier.	45	2 0	86	16 0	11 0	
Racoon...........	400	Ravenhill and Salkeld.	64	3 0	58½	26 0	16 0	
Ranger	80	Rennie.	...	...	...	......	......	
Renown	800	Penn and Son.	82	4 0	54½	28 0	19 0	
Repulse..........	......	....	...	...	...	......	......	
Revenge.........	800	Maudslay and Field.	82	4 0	45	27 6	19 0	
Reynard.........	200	Humphrey & Tennant.	42¼	1 9	94	14 3	11 0	
Rifleman	100	Ravenhill and Salkeld.	34	2 9	35½	8 5	9 0	Multiple not known.
Rinaldo	200	Humphrey & Tennant.	42¼	2 2	....	14 0	12 0	Not tried.
Ringdove	200	Ravenhill and Salkeld.	45	2 0	84	15 9	11 0	
Rodney...........	500	Maudslay and Field.	66	3 6	50	21 0	18 0	
Roebuck.........	175	Ravenhill and Salkeld.	55	2 6	70	20 5	11 0	
Rosario	......	....	...	...	...	......	......	
Royal Albert...	500	Penn and Son.	64¼	3 4	60	19 2	17 0	
Royal George..	400	Ditto.	58	3 3	62	17 to 18	17 0	Fitted with a screw of an increasing pitch.
Royal Sovereign	800	Maudslay and Field.	82	4 0	45	26 to 28	19 0	
Royal William	500	Napier	65	3 0	60	22 0	18 0	
Russell	200	Penn and Son.	30	2 6	91½	9 6	12 0	

Name of Ship.	Horse-power.	Maker of Engines.	Diameter of Cylinder.	Length of Stroke.	Revolutions per minute.	Screw. Pitch.	Screw. Diameter.	Remarks.
			in.	ft. in.		ft. in.	ft. in.	
Sanspariel	400	Boulton and Watt.	43½	3 0	50	16 0	16 0	
Satellite	400	Penn and Son.	58	3 3	63	23 6	16 0	
Scout	400	Ditto.	58	3 3	63	23 6	16 0	
Scylla	400	Ditto.	58	3 3	63	23 6	16 0	
Seahorse	200	Ditto.	30¼	2 6	112	10 0	12 0	High pressure.
Serpent	200	Napier.	45	2 0	86	16 4	11 0	
Severn............	500	Maudslay and Field.	66	3 6	50	21 0	18 0	
Shannon.........	600	Penn and Son.	70¾	3 6	56	25 3	18 1	
Sharpshooter...	202	Ravenhill and Salkeld.	46	3 6	38	9 11	8 10	Multiple not known.
Simoom	400	Portsmouth Yard.	62½	2 6	55	20 7	16 0	
Slaney	80	Maudslay and Field.	18	1 6	...	8 0	6 6	
Snake	160	Penn and Son.	35¼	1 8	112	10 0	11 0	
Snipe	80	Napier.	32	1 6	106	11 4	9 0	
Sparrow	80	Ditto.	32	1 6	106	11 4	9 0	
Sparrowhawk .	200	Humphrey & Tennant.	42¼	2 2	92	14 3	11 0	
Star..............	200	Napier.	45	2 0	86	16 6	11 0	
Steady............	80	Ditto.	32	1 6	106	11 4	9 0	
St. George.......	500	Ravenhill and Salkeld.	71	3 0	50	20 0	18 0	
St. Jean d'Arc.	600	Penn and Son.	70¼	3 6	61	21 8	18 0	
Supply	80	....	...	...	...	......	......	
Surprise.........	200	Ravenhill and Salkeld.	45	2 0	88	16 0	11 0	
Sutlej.............	500	Maudslay and Field.	66	3 6	50	21 0	18 0	
Swallow.........	60	Ravenhill and Salkeld.	25½	1 9	80	10 10	9 0	
Tarter............	250	Maudslay and Field.	51	2 3	65	16 6	12 0	
Tarte	400	Ditto.	64	3 0	50	22 6	17 0	
Teazer	40	Penn and Son.	27	2 6	51	7 0	5 0	Multiple 3·73 to 1.
Termagant	310	Portsmouth Factory.	62½	3 6	55	20 0	16 0	
Terror............	200	Napier.	...	...	...	......	......	High pressure.
Thunder.........	150	Ravenhill and Salkeld.	25½	2 0	138	14 0	6 2½	Ditto.
Thunderbolt ...	200	Ditto.	32	2 0	108	12 0	8 0	Ditto.
Topaze	600	Maudslay and Field.	76	3 6	45	25 to 28 6	19 4	
Torch	80	Napier.	32	1 6	106	11 4	9 0	
Trafalgar	500	Maudslay and Field.	66	3 6	50	21 0	18 0	
Tribune..........	300	Ditto.	55	2 6	67	17 7	14 1	
Trusty	'150	Ravenhill and Salkeld.	25½	2 0	108	14 0	6 0	High pressure.
Undaunted......	600	Ditto.	76	3 6	45	26 0	18 0	
Urgent	400	Maudslay and Field.	64	3 0	59	22 4	17 0	
Victor............	350	Ravenhill and Salkeld.	55	2 6	82	20 6	11 0	
Victor Emmanuel	600	Maudslay and Field.	76	3 6	55½	26 2	18 2	
Victoria	1000	Ditto.	92	4 0	45	25 to 30 0	20 0	Fitted with a screw of an increasing pitch.
Vigilant	200	Ditto.	45	2 0	84	16 0	11 0	
Viper	80	Ditto.	40½	2 0	87	14 11	11 0	
Vulcan	400	Ditto.	64	3 0	50	22 6	17 0	
Wanderer	200	Ditto.	45	2 0	83	16 0	11 0	
Warrior..........	1250	Penn and Son.	104¼	4 0	54	......	24 6	
Wasp	100	Ravenhill and Salkeld.	34	2 9	53	13 6	11 0	
Waterloo.........	500	Ditto.	71	3 0	50	28 0	18 0	
Windsor Castle	500	Penn and Son.	64⅜	3 4	18½	18 6	17 0	
Wolverine	......	....	...	...	...	......	......	
Wrangler........	160	Maudslay and Field.	40¼	2 0	83	15 0	11 0	
Wye	100	....	...	...	...	......	......	
Zealous	......	....	...	...	...	......	......	
Zebra	200	Humphrey & Tennant.	42¼	2 2	...	12 0	14 0	Not tried.

With one or two exceptions, the engines are "horizontal," and coupled direct to the shaft.

The length of the screw employed in the Royal Navy is generally about $\frac{1}{6}$ of the pitch, and the angle varying from 20° to 30°.

The steam-pressure in boilers is 20 lbs., with the exception of some few of the early screw ships, in which it is something less.

List of Paddle Steamers in her Majesty's Navy.

Name of Ship.	Horse-power.	Maker of Engine.	Diameter of Cylinder.	Length of Stroke.	Revolutions per minute.	Diameter of Wheel.
			in.	ft. in.		ft. in.
Adder	100	Boulton and Watt.	39½	3 6	29	14 0
Advice	100	Ditto.	39½	3 6	27	14 0
African	90	Maudslay and Field.	35½	3 6	27	14 0
Alban	100	Boulton and Watt.	39½	3 6	28	14 0
Alecto	200	Seaward and Capel.	53⅛	4 6	14	21 11
Antelope	260	Penn and Son.	64	4 6	26	20 0
Ardent	200	Seaward and Capel.	53	4 6	18½	20 9
Argus	300	Penn and Son.	64	6 0	16	23 5
Asp	50	Boulton and Watt.	......	2 6	33	10 0
Avon	160	Ditto.	48½	4 6	16	......
Bann	80	......	......	......	...	......
Banshee	350	Penn and Son.	72¼	5 0	...	......
Barracouta	300	......	......	......	...	......
Basilisk	400	Ravenhill.	74	6 0	...	......
Bee*	10	Maudslay and Field.	20	2 0	40	8 4
Black Eagle	260	Penn and Son.	......	......	...	......
Bloodhound	150	Napier.	......	......	...	......
Brune	80	......	......	......	...	......
Bulldog	500	Rennie.	......	5 6	16	......
Bustler	100	......	......	......	...	......
Buzzard	300	......	64	6 0	...	......
Caradoc	350	Seaward and Capel.	75	4 4	24	......
Centaur	540	Boulton and Watt.	85½	6 0	18	28 0
Comet	80	Ditto.	35½	3 6	28	13 6
Confiance	100	Maudslay and Field.	40	4 0	23	14 0
Coromandel	150	......	......	......	...	......
Cuckoo	100	Boulton and Watt.	39½	3 6	27	14 6
Cyclops	320	Seaward and Capel.	64	5 6	16	26 0
Dasher	100	Ditto.	40½	3 4	28	16 0
Dee	220	Maudslay and Field.	54	5 0	18	20 0
Devastation	400	Ditto	54	6 0	18	......
Dover	90	Fawcett.	38	3 0	28	13 6
Dragon	560	Fairbairn.	88	5 9	17	27 6
Driver	280	Seaward and Capel.	62	5 4	19	26 6
Echo	140	Maudslay and Field.	44½	4 6	18	18 6
Elfin	40	Rennie.	27	2 6	...	11 4
Fearless	76	Boulton and Watt.	35½	3 2	32	12 0
Firebrand	410	Seaward and Capel.	75½	5 9	18	26 6
Firefly	220	Maudslay and Field.	55½	5 0	21	20 0
Fire Queen	120	Napier.	60	3 9	31	16 3
Furious	400	Ravenhill.	72	7 0	16	27 4
Fury	515	Rigby.	84	5 9	21	25 6
Geyser	280	Seaward.	63	5 3	18	26 6
Gladiator	430	Ravenhill.	78¾	5 9	22	26 0
Gorgon	320	Seaward.	64	5 6	18	26 0
Harpy	200	Napier.	49	4 0	23	16 0
Hearty	100	......	......	......	...	......
Hecate	240	Scott and Sinclair.	60	5 9	16	25 0
Hecla	240	Ditto.	60	5 9	18	24 0
Hermes	220	Maudslay and Field.	40	4 6	19	19 0
Hydra	220	Boulton and Watt.	56	5 0	17	24 0
Inflexible	378	Fawcett.	72	5 9	...	......
Jackal	150	Napier.	48	4 0	21	18 0
Kite	170	......	47½	4 3	22	18 0
Leopard	560	Seaward and Capel.	91½	6 8	17	32 0
Lightning	100	Maudslay and Field.	40	4 0	25	17 9
Lizard	150	Napier.	48	4 0	22	15 4
Locust	100	Maudslay and Field.	40	3 6	27	16 0
Lucifer	180	Ditto.	48	4 6	...	......
Magicienne	400	Penn and Son.	72	7 0	...	27 4
Medea	350	Maudslay and Field.	50	5 3	...	......

* Paddle and Screw.

Name of Ship.	Horse-power.	Maker of Engine.	Diameter of Cylinder.	Length of Stroke.	Revolutions per minute.	Diameter of Wheel.
			in.	ft. in.		ft. in.
Medina	312	Fawcett.	64	6 0	19	24 6
Medusa	312	Ditto.	64	6 0	19	24 6
Merlin	312	Ditto.	64	6 0	19	24 6
Monkey	130	Boulton and Watt.	35½	3 6	27	14 0
Myrmidon	150	Ditto.	48	2 6	24	17 0
Myrtle	50	Ditto.	30	4 0	34	19 9
Oberon	260	Rennie.	61	5 0	21	21 0
Odin	560	Fairbairn.	88½	5 9	18	27 6
Osborne	430	Maudslay and Field.	54	6 0	19	32 0
Otter	120	Boulton and Watt.	44¼	3 6	28	14 0
Penelope	650	Seaward and Capel.	91½	6 8	16	32 0
Pigmy	100	Fawcett.	35	3 6	27	......
Pike	50	......	30½	2 6	32	10 0
Pluto	100	Boulton and Watt.	39½	3 6	27	14 0
Porcupine	132	Maudslay and Field.	46¼	4 0	...	15 6
Princess Alice	120	Ditto.	......	......	...	......
Prometheus	200	Seaward.	53	4 6	...	22 6
Prospero	144	......	46	4 0	...	14 9
Recruit	160	......	......	......	...	......
Redpole	160	......	......	......	...	......
Retribution	400	Penn and Son.	72	7 0	...	25 0
Rhadamanthus	220	Maudslay and Field.	55½	5 0	18	20 0
Rosamond	280	Ravenhill.	65¼	5 0	17	23 4
Salamander	220	Maudslay and Field.	55½	5 0	18	21 0
Sampson	467	Rennie.	81	5 8	18	27 6
Scourge	420	Maudslay and Field.	54	6 0	18	28 0
Sidon	560	Seaward.	86½	6 0	16	27 6
Sphynx	500	Penn and Son.	82½	6 0	17	28 0
Spiteful	280	Scott and Sinclair.	62	6 0	16	26 0
Spitfire	140	Butterly Company.	44¼	4 6	24	17 6
Sprightly	100	Boulton and Watt.	39½	3 6	27	14 6
Stromboli	280	Napier.	63	6 0	16	25 0
Styx	280	Seaward.	63	5 3	16	24 0
Tartarus	136	Boulton and Watt.	46	3 6	28	15 6
Terrible	800	Maudslay and Field.	72	8 0	14	34 0
Thalis	80	......	......	......	...	......
Torch	150	Seaward and Capel.	49	3 9	24	......
Trident	350	Ditto.	71	5 0	24	17 0
Triton	260	Boulton and Watt.	64	4 6	...	......
Valorous	400	Penn and Son.	72	7 0	...	......
Vesuvius	280	Napier.	63	6 0	...	25 0
Victoria and Albert	600	Penn and Son.	......	7 0	24	......
Virago	300	Boulton and Watt.	66½	5 0	17	24 9
Vivid	160	Penn and Son.	49½	4 0	...	......
Vixen	280	Seaward and Capel.	63	5 3	18	26 6
Volcano	140	Ditto.	45	4 4	21	19 0
Vulture	470	Fairbairn.	80⅝	5 9	19	25 0
Wallace	100	......	......	......	...	......
Weser	160	......	......	......	...	......
Widgeon	90	......	38	3 2	26	13 9
Wildfire	76	......	35½	3 0	27	12 0
Zephyr	100	Boulton and Watt.	39½	3 6	27	14 0

The steam-pressure in the paddle steam-ship's boilers varies from 8 lbs. to 16 lbs.; some few are working at 20 lbs.

Most of the paddle-steamers have common paddle-wheels. Her Majesty's yacht "Victoria and Albert," and a few other vessels, have the "feathering wheel,"—that known as "Morgan's wheel.'

*List of Steam Gun-boats (High Pressure) in the Royal Navy.**

	Horse-power.		Horse-power.
Albacore	60	Dapper	60
Amelia	60	Delight	60
Angler	20	Decoy	20
Ant	20	Dove	60
Badger	60	Drake	40
Banterer	60	Dwarf	20
Beaver	60	Earnest	60
Beacon	60	Erne	60
Biter	60	Escort	60
Blazer	60	Fancy	60
Blossom	20	Fenella	40
Bouncer	60	Fervent	60
Boxer	60	Fidget	20
Brave	60	Firm	60
Brazen	60	Flamer	60
Bullfinch	60	Flirt	20
Bullfrog	60	Fly	60
Bustard	60	Foam	60
Camel	60	Forester	60
Carnation	60	Forward	60
Caroline	60	Gadfly	20
Charger	60	Garland	20
Charon	60	Garnet	40
Cheerful	20	Gleaner	60
Cherokee	60	Gnat	20
Chub	20	Goldfinch	60
Clinker	60	Goshawk	60
Clown	40	Grappler	60
Cochin	60	Grasshopper	60
Cockchafer	60	Grinder	60
Confounder	60	Griper	60
Cracker	60	Growler	60
Crocus	60	Handy	40
Daisy	20	Hardy	60

* Most of the gun-boats are fitted by Maudslay and Penn with engines of the locomotive and trunk kind coupled direct to the screw-shaft.

Diameter of cylinder	(60 horse power)	15⅜ in. . .	Maudslay.
" "	(60 ")	21 in. Trunk 11 in.	Penn
" "	(40 ")	21 in. . .	"
" "	(20 ")	15 in. . .	"

	Horse-power.
Hasty	60
Haughty	60
Havock	60
Herring	60
Highlander	60
Hind	60
Hunter	40
Hyæna	60
Insolent	60
Jackdaw	60
Janus	40
Julia	60
Kestrel	40
Lark	60
Leveret	60
Lively	60
Louisa	60
Mackerel	60
Magnet	60
Magpie	60
Manly	60
Mastiff	60
Mayflower	60
Midge	20
Mistletoe	60
Nettle	20
Nightingale	60
Onyx	20
Opossum	60
Parthian	60
Partridge	60
Peacock	60
Pelter	60
Pest	20
Pet	20
Pheasant	60
Pickle	60
Pincher	60
Plover	60
Porpoise	60
Primrose	60
Procris	60
Prompt	60
Quail	60
Rainbow	60
Rambler	20
Raven	60
Ready	40
Redbreast	60
Redwing	60
Ripple	60
Rocket	60
Rose	60
Ruby	60
Sandfly	60
Savage	60
Seagull	60
Sepoy	60
Shamrock	60
Sheldrake	60
Shipjack	60
Skylark	60
Snap	60
Snapper	60
Spanker	60
Spey	60
Spider	60
Starling	60
Staunch	60
Stork	60
Surly	60
Swan	60
Swinger	60
Thistle	60
Thrasher	60
Thrush	60
Tickler	60
Tilbury	60
Tiny	60
Traveller	60
Violet	60
Watchful	40
Wave	60
Weazel	60
Whiting	60
Wolf	60
Woodcock	40

ALPHABETICAL INDEX.

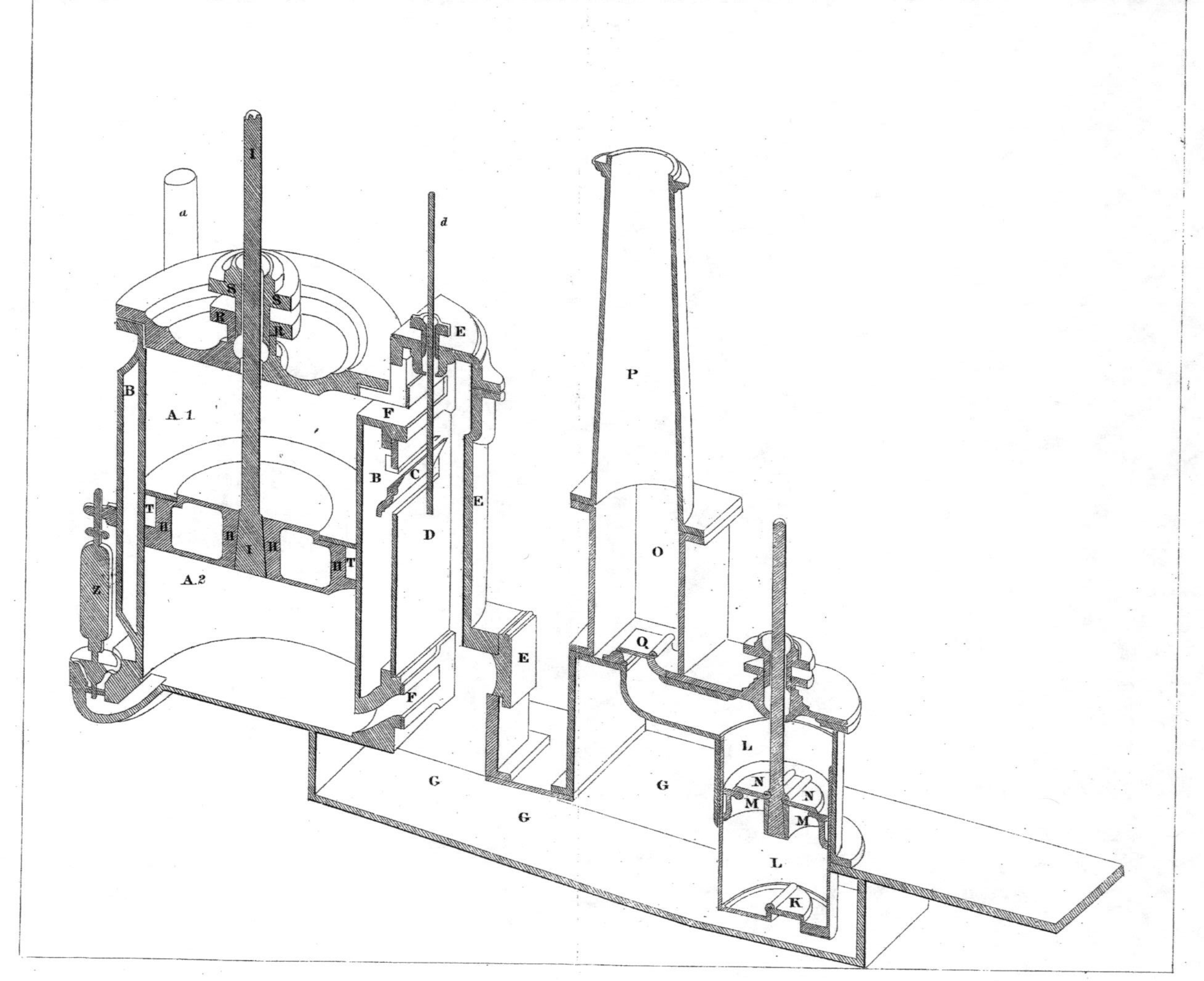

A.1
A.2
B
C
D
E
F
G
H
I
K
L
M
N
O
P
Q
R
S
T
Z
a
d

PLATE II

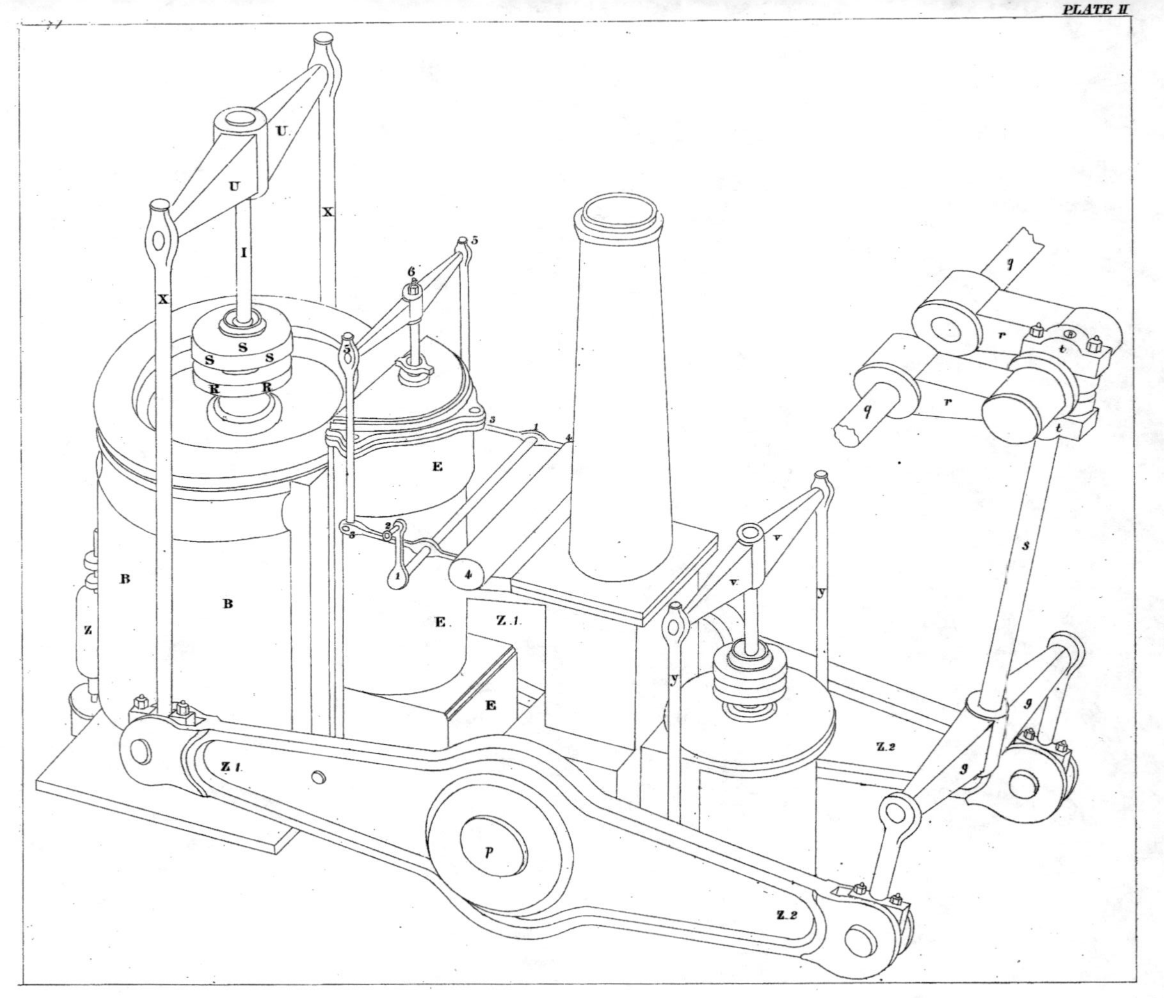

PRACTICAL
AND
SCIENTIFIC BOOKS,

PUBLISHED BY

HENRY CAREY BAIRD,

INDUSTRIAL PUBLISHER,

No. 406 WALNUT STREET,

PHILADELPHIA.

☞ **Any of the following Books will be sent by mail, free of postage, at the publication price. Catalogues furnished on application.**

American Miller and Millwright's Assistant:

A new and thoroughly revised Edition, with additional Engravings. By William Carter Hughes. In one Volume, 12mo. $1.50

Armengaud, Amoroux, and Johnson.

THE PRACTICAL DRAUGHTSMAN'S BOOK OF INDUSTRIAL DESIGN, and Machinist's and Engineer's Drawing Companion; forming a complete course of Mechanical Engineering and Architectural Drawing. From the French of M. Armengaud the elder, Prof. of Design in the Conservatoire of Arts and Industry, Paris, and MM. Armengaud the younger, and Amoroux, Civil Engineers. Rewritten and arranged with additional matter and plates, selections from and examples of the most useful and generally employed mechanism of the day. By William Johnson, Assoc. Inst. C. E., Editor of "The Practical Mechanic's Journal." Illustrated by fifty folio steel plates and fifty wood-cuts. A new edition, 4to $10.00

Among the contents are:—*Linear Drawing, Definitions and Problems*, Plate I. Applications, Designs for inlaid Pavements, Ceilings, and Balconies, Plate II. Sweeps, Sections, and Mouldings, Plate III. Elementary

Gothic Forms and Rosettes, Plate IV. Ovals, Ellipses, Parabolas, and Volutes, Plate V. Rules and Practical Data. *Study of Projections*, Elementary Principles, Plate VI. Of Prisms and other Solids, Plate VII Rules and Practical Data. *On Coloring Sections, with Applications*—Conventional Colors, Composition or Mixture of Colors, Plate X. *Continuation of the Study of Projections*—Use of sections—details of machinery, Plate XI Simple applications—spindles, shafts, couplings, wooden patterns, Plate XII Method of constructing a wooden model or pattern of a coupling, Elementary applications—rails and chairs for railways, Plate XIII. *Rules and Practical Data*—Strength of material, Resistance to compression or crushing force, Tensional Resistance, Resistance to flexure, Resistance to torsion Friction of surfaces in contact.

THE INTERSECTION AND DEVELOPMENT OF SURFACES WITH APPLICATIONS.—*The Intersection of Cylinders and Cones*, Plate XIV. *The Delineation and Development of Helices, Screws, and Serpentines*, Plate XV. Application of the helix—the construction of a staircase, Plate XVI. The Intersection of surfaces—applications to stopcocks, Plate XVII. *Rules and Practical Data*—Steam, Unity of heat, Heating surface, Calculation of the dimensions of boilers, Dimensions of fire grates, Chimneys, Safety valves.

THE STUDY AND CONSTRUCTION OF TOOTHED GEAR.—Involute, cycloid, and epicycloid, Plates XVIII. and XIX. Involute, Fig. 1, Plate XVIII. Cycloid, Fig. 2, Plate XVIII. External epicycloid, described by a circle rolling about a fixed circle inside it, Fig. 3, Plate XIX. Internal epicycloid, Fig. 2, Plate XIX. Delineation of a rack and pinion in gear, Fig. 4, Plate XVIII. Gearing of a worm with a worm-wheel, Figs. 5 and 6, Plate XVIII. *Cylindrical or Spur Gearing*, Plate XIX. Practical delineation of a couple of Spur-wheels, Plate XX. *The Delineation and Construction of Wooden Patterns for Toothed Wheels*, Plate XXI. *Rules and Practical Data*—Toothed gearing, Angular and circumferential velocity of wheels, Dimensions of gearing, Thickness of the teeth, Pitch of the teeth, Dimensions of the web, Number and dimensions of the arms, wooden patterns.

CONTINUATION OF THE STUDY OF TOOTHED GEAR.—Design for a pair of bevel-wheels in gear, Plate XXII. Construction of wooden patterns for a pair of bevel-wheels, Plate XXIII. *Involute and Helical Teeth*, Plate XXIV. *Contrivances for obtaining Differential Movements*—The delineation of eccentrics and cams, Plate XXV. *Rules and Practical Data*—Mechanical work of effect, The simple machines, Centre of gravity, On estimating the power of prime movers, Calculation for the brake, The fall of bodies, Momentum, Central forces.

ELEMENTARY PRINCIPLES OF SHADOWS.—*Shadows of Prisms, Pyramids and Cylinders*, Plate XXVI. *Principles of Shading*, Plate XXVII. *Continuation of the Study of Shadows*, Plate XXVIII. *Tuscan Order*, Plate XXIX. *Rules and Practical Data*—Pumps, Hydrostatic principles, Forcing pumps, Lifting and forcing pumps, The Hydrostatic press, Hydrostatical calculations and data—discharge of water through different orifices, Gauging of a water-course of uniform section and fall, Velocity of the bottom of water-courses, Calculations of the discharge of water through rectangular orifices of narrow edges, Calculation of the discharge of water through overshot outlets, To determine the width of an overshot outlet, To determine the depth of the outlet, Outlet with a spout or duct.

APPLICATION OF SHADOWS TO TOOTHED GEAR, Plate XXX. *Application of Shadows to Screws*, Plate XXXI. *Application of Shadows to a Boiler and its Furnace*, Plate XXXII. *Shading in Black—Shading in Colors*, Plate XXXIII.

THE CUTTING AND SHAPING OF MASONRY, Plate XXXIV. *Rules and Practical Data*—Hydraulic motors, Undershot water-wheels, with plane floats and a circular channel, Width, Diameter, Velocity, Number, and capacity of the buckets, Useful effect of the water-wheel, Overshot water-wheels, Water-wheels with radical floats, Water-wheel with curved buckets, Turbines. *Remarks on Machine Tools.*

THE STUDY OF MACHINERY AND SKETCHING.—Various applications and combinations: *The Sketching of Machinery*, Plates XXXV. and XXXVI. *Drilling Machines; Motive Machines;* Water-wheels, Construction and setting up of water-wheels, Delineation of water-wheels, Design of a water-wheel, Sketch of a water-wheel; *Overshot Water-wheels, Water Pumps*, Plate XXXVII. *Steam Motors;* High-pressure expansive steam-engine, Plates XXXVIII., XXXIX., and XL. *Details of Construction; Movements of the Distribution and Expansion Valves; Rules and Practical Data*—Steam-engines: Low-pressure condensing engines without expansion valve, Diameter of piston, Velocities, Steam pipes and passages, Air-pump and condenser, Cold-water and feed-pumps, High-pressure expansive engines, Medium pressure condensing and expansive steam-engine, Conical pendulum or centrifugal governor.

OBLIQUE PROJECTIONS.—Application of rules to the delineation of an oscillating cylinder, Plate XLI.

PARALLEL PERSPECTIVE.—Principles and applications, Plate XLII.

TRUE PERSPECTIVE.—Elementary principles, Plate XLIII. Applications—flour mill driven by belts, Plates XLIV. and XLV. Description of the mill, Representation of the mill in perspective, Notes of recent improvements in flour mills, Schiele's mill, Mullin's "ring millstone," Barnett's millstone, Hastie's arrangement for driving mills, Currie's improvements in millstones. *Rules and Practical Data*—Work performed by various machines, Flour mills, Saw-mills, Veneer sawing machines, Circular saws.

EXAMPLES OF FINISHED DRAWINGS OF MACHINERY.—Plate A, Balance water-meter; Plate B, Engineer's shaping machine; Plates C, D, E, Express locomotive engine; Plate F, Wood planing machine; Plate G, Washing machine for piece goods; Plate H, power-loom; Plate I, Duplex steam boiler; Plate J, Direct-acting marine engines.

DRAWING INSTRUMENTS.

Arrowsmith. Paper-Hanger's Companion:

By James Arrowsmith. 12mo., cloth................$1.25

Baird. The American Cotton Spinner, and Manager's and Carder's Guide:

A Practical Treatise on Cotton Spinning; giving the Dimensions and Speed of Machinery, Draught and Twist Calculations, etc.; with notices of recent Improvements: together with Rules and Examples for making changes in the sizes and numbers of Roving and Yarn. Compiled from the papers of the late Robert H. Baird. 12mo..............$1.50

CONTENTS.—Introduction; On the Plan of a Factory Building; On the Main Gearing; On Water-wheels; Calculations of Horse-Power for Propelling Cotton Spinning Machinery; Willie or Picking Machine; On Wileying Cotton; Spreading Machine; On Spreading Cotton; Carding; Cards and Carding; Covering Emery Rollers and Emeries; The Drawing-frame; Roving; General Remarks on Drawing and Roving; Throstles; Remarks on Throstles; Mule Spinning; General Observations on Mule Spinning; Weaving; Belting; Miscellaneous matters.

Beans. A Treatise on Railroad Curves and the Location of Railroads:

By E. W. Beans, C. E. 12mo. (In press.)

Bishop. A History of American Manufactures:

From 1608 to 1866: exhibiting the Origin and Growth of the Principal Mechanic Arts and Manufactures, from the Earliest Colonial Period to the Present Time; with a Notice of the Important Inventions, Tariffs, and the Results of each Decennial Census. By J. Leander Bishop, M. D.; to which is added Notes on the Principal Manufacturing Centres and Remarkable Manufactories. By Edward Young and Edwin T. Freedley. In three vols., 8vo......................$8.00

Blinn. A Practical Workshop Companion for Tin, Sheet-Iron, and Copper-Plate Workers:

Containing Rules for describing various kinds of Patterns used by Tin, Sheet-Iron, and Copper-Plate Workers; Practical Geometry; Mensuration of Surfaces and Solids; Tables of the Weights of Metals, Lead Pipe, etc.; Tables of Areas and Circumferences of Circles; Japan, Varnishes, Lackers, Cements, Compositions, etc., etc. By Leroy J. Blinn, Master Mechanic. With over One Hundred Illustrations. 12mo. $2.50

CONTENTS.—*Rules for Describing Patterns.*—An Envelope for a Cone, A Frustrum of a Cone, A Can top or Deck flange; A Pattern for, or an Envelope for a Frustrum of a Cone, A Tapering Oval Article to be in four Sections, A Tapering Oval Article to be in two Sections, A Tapering Oval Article, A Tapering Oval and Oblong Article, the sides to be Straight, with Quarter Circle corners, to be in two Sections, A Tapering Oval or Oblong Article, the sides to be Straight, one end to be a Semicircle, the other end to be Straight, with Quarter Circle corners, to be in two Sections, A Tapering Oval or Oblong Article, the sides to be Straight, with Semicircle ends, to be in two Sections, Covering of Circular Roofs, Two different Principles, To cover a Dome by the first Method, To cover a Dome by the second Method, To ascertain the Outline of a Course of covering to a Dome, without reference to a Section of the Dome, To describe a Pattern for a Tapering Square Article, A Square Tapering Article to be in two Sections, A Tapering Article, the Base to be Square, and the Top a Circle, in two Sections, A Tapering Article, the Base to be a Rectangle, and the Top Square, in two Sections, A Tapering Article, the Base to be a Rectangle, and the Top a Circle, in two Sections, A Tapering Article, the Top and Base to be a Rectangle, in two Sections, Tapering Octagon Top or Cover, A Miter Joint at Right Angles for a Semicircle Gutter, A Miter Joint at any Angle for a Semicircle Gutter, A Miter Joint for an O G Gutter at Right Angles, A Miter Joint for an O G Cornice at Right Angles, also an Offset, An Octagon O G Lamp Top or Cover, A T Pipe at Right Angles, A T Pipe at any Angle, A T Pipe, the Collar to be smaller than the Main Pipe, A T Pipe at any Angle, the Collar to set on one side of the Main Pipe, A Pipe to fit a flat Surface at any Angle, as the Side of a Roof of a Building, A Pipe to fit two flat Surfaces, as the Roof of a Building, An Elbow at Right Angles, An Elbow Pattern at any Angle, An Elbow in three Sections, An Elbow in four Sections, An Elbow in five Sections, A Tapering Elbow, An Oval Boiler Cover, A Flange for a Pipe that goes on the Roof of a Building, Octagon or Square Top or Cover, Steamer Cover, An Ellipse or Oval, having two Diameters given, An Ellipse with the Rule and Compasses, the Transverse and Conjugate Diameters being given, that is, the Length and Width, To find the Centre and the two Arcs of an Ellipse, To find the Radius and Versed Sine for a given Frustrum of a Cone, Practical Geometry, Decimal Equivalents to Fractional Parts of Lineal Measurement, Definitions of Arithmetical Signs, Mensuration of Surfaces, Mensuration of Solids and Capacities of Bodies, Tables of Weights of Iron, Copper, and Lead, Tables of the Circumferences and Areas of Circles, Sizes and capacity of Tinware in form of Frustrum of a Cone, such as Pans, Dish Kettles, Pails, Coffee-pots, Wash Bowls, Dippers, Measures, Druggists' and Liquor Dealers' Measures, American Lap Welded Iron Boiler Flues, Table of Effects upon Bodies by Heat, Weight of Water, Effects produced by Water in an Aeriform State, Practical Properties of Water, Effects produced by Water in its Natural State, Effects of Heat at certain Temperatures, Tempering, Effects produced by Air in its Natural and in a Rarefied State, Table of the Expansion of Atmospheric Air by Heat, Size, Length, Breadth, and Weight of Tin Plates, Crystallized Tin Plate, List of Calibre and Weights of Lead Pipe, Calibre and Weights of Fountain or Aqueduct Pipes, To ascertain the Weights of Pipes of various Metals, and any Diameter required, Weight of a Square Foot of Sheet Iron, Copper, and Brass, as per Birmingham Wire Gauge, Recapitulation of

Weights of Various Substances. *Practical Receipts.*—Japanning and Varnishing, Varnishes—Miscellaneous, Lackers, Cements, Miscellaneous Receipts, Britannia, Solders, etc., Strength of Materials.

Booth and Morfit. The Encyclopedia of Chemistry, Practical and Theoretical:

Embracing its application to the Arts, Metallurgy, Mineralogy, Geology, Medicine, and Pharmacy. By James C. Booth, Melter and Refiner in the United States Mint, Professor of Applied Chemistry in the Franklin Institute, etc., assisted by Campbell Morfit, author of "Chemical Manipulations," etc. 7th edition. Complete in one volume, royal 8vo. 978 pages, with numerous wood-cuts and other illustrations $5.00

Brewer; (The Complete Practical.)

Or Plain, Concise, and Accurate Instructions in the Art of Brewing Beer, Ale, Porter, etc., etc., and the Process of making all the Small Beers. By M. Lafayette Byrn, M. D. With Illustrations. 12mo..........................$1.25

Buckmaster. The Elements of Mechanical Physics.

By J. C. Buckmaster, late Student in the Goverment School of Mines; Certified Teacher of Science by the Department of Science and Art; Examiner in Chemistry and Physics in the Royal College of Preceptors; and late Lecturer in Chemistry and Physics of the Royal Polytechnic Institute. Illustrated with numerous engravings. In one volume, 12mo. $2.00

CONTENTS.—*The Elements of Mechanical Physics*—CHAP. I.—Statics and Dynamics; Force; Gravitation and Weight; On Matter—its Mass, Density, and Volume. II.—Centre of Gravity; Stable and Unstable Equilibrium; To find the Centre of Gravity of a Material Straight Line of Uniform Density; To find the Centre of Gravity of two heavy Points joined by a rigid bar without Weight; To find the Centre of Gravity of a number of heavy points; To find the Centre of Gravity of a Material Plain Triangle. III.—Levers; Levers are of three kinds; Virtual Velocity; Balances; The Safety Valve; Mechanical Combinations and their Advantages. IV.—The Wheel and Axle; The Compound Wheel and Axle. V.—The Pulley; Wheels and Pinions; Cranks and Fly-Wheel. VI.—The Inclined Plane; The Wedge; The Screw. VII.—Composition and Resolution of Forces. VIII.—Falling Bodies; Ascent of Bodies; Projection of Bodies Horizontally. IX.—Momentum. X.—Sound; The Pendulum.

Elements of Hydrostatics.—CHAP. I.—Hydrostatics; Bramah Hydrostatic Press. II.—Specific Gravity; Table of Specific Gravities. III.—Elastic Fluids; The Air Pump and its Operation; The Construction of the Condenser and its Operation; The Barometer; The Action of the Siphon; How to Graduate a common Thermometer; To Reduce the Degrees of a Thermometer in Fahrenheit's scale to a centigrade and the converse; The Construction of a Siphon gauge; The Construction of a common Pump and its Operation; The Construction and Operation of a Force Pump; The Operation of a Fire Engine; The Operation of a Lifting Pump; The Hydraulic Ram; The Archimedian Screw; The Chain Pump; Mercurial Steam Gauge; Examination Papers.

APPENDIX.—Examples; Answers to Examples.

Bullock. The Rudiments of Architecture and Building:

For the use of Architects, Builders, Draughtsmen, Machinists, Engineers and Mechanics. Edited by John Bullock, author of "The American Cottage Builder." Illustrated by Two Hundred and Fifty Engravings. In one volume, 8vo..$3.50

Burgh. The Slide Valve Practically Considered.

By N. P. Burgh, Engineer. Completely Illus. 12mo...$2.00

Burgh. Practical Rules for the Proportion of Modern Engines and Boilers for Land and Marine Purposes.

By N. P. Burgh, Engineer. 12mo..................$2.00

CONTENTS.—High Pressure Engines; Beam Engines (condensing); Marine Screw Engines; Oscillating Engines; Valves, etc.; Land and Marine Boilers. *Miscellaneous.*—Coal Bunkers. Marine; Decimals, etc.; Eccentric, Position of, for Land Engines; Eccentric, Position of. for Marine Screw Engines; Fire Bars; Keys and Cotters; Link for Land Engine, Radius of; Levers; Link for Oscillating Engine, Radius of; Link for Marine Screw Engine, Radius of; Proportion of Connecting Rods having Strap Ends; Paddle Wheels, Centres of Radius Rods; Plummer Blocks; Proportions of Steam Cocks with Plugs secured by Nuts and Screws; Proportion of Marine Cocks; Proportions of Bolts, Nuts, etc.; Proportions of Pins, Studs, Flanges, etc.; Proportions of Copper Pipes; Proportions of Engines; Sliding Quadrant; Toothed Wheels (Gearing). *Proportions of Engines Produced by the Rules:* Proportions of an Engine 20 HP nominal; Proportions of a Condensing Beam Engine 150 HP nominal; Proportions of a Pair of Marine Engines of 200 HP Collectively; Proportions of a Pair of Oscillating Engines of 400 HP Collectively; Proportions of Boilers.

Byrne. Pocket Book for Railroad and Civil Engineers.

Containing New, Exact, and Concise Methods for Laying out Railroad Curves, Switches, Frog Angles and Crossings; the Staking out of Work; Leveling; the Calculation of Cuttings, Embankments, Earth-work, etc. By Oliver Byrne. Illustrated, 18mo..................................$1.25

Byrne. The Practical Metal-Worker's Assistant.

Comprising Metallurgic Chemistry; the Arts of Working all Metals and Alloys; Forging of Iron and Steel; Hardening and Tempering; Melting and Mixing; Casting and Founding; Works in Sheet Metal; the Process dependent on the Ductility of the Metals; Soldering; and the most Improved Processes and Tools employed by Metal-Workers. With the Application of the Art of Electro-Metallurgy to Manufacturing Processes: collected from Original Sources, and from the Works of Holtzapffel, Bergeron, Leupold, Plumier, Napier, and others. By Oliver Byrne. A New, Revised, and Improved Edition, with additions by John Scoffern, M. B., William Clay, William Fairbairn, F. R. S., and James Napier. With Five Hundred and Ninety-two Engravings, illustrating every Branch of the Subject. In one volume, 8vo. 652 pages $7.00

CONTENTS.—On Metallurgic Chemistry; Special Metallurgic Operations; Recently Patented Refining Processes; Refining and Working of Iron; Manufacture of Steel; Forging Iron and Steel; On Wrought-Iron in Large Masses; General Examples of Welding, Hardening and Tempering; Hardening Cast and Wrought-Iron; On the Application of Iron to Ship-Building; The Metals and Alloys most commonly used; Remarks on the Character of the Metals and Alloys; Melting and Mixing the Metals; Casting and Founding; Works in Sheet Metal made by Joining; Works in Sheet Metal made by raising and flattening of thin Plates of Metal; Processes dependent on Ductility; Soldering; Shears; Punches; Drills; Screw-cutting Tools; Electro-Metallurgy.

Byrne. The Handbook for the Artisan, Mechanic, and Engineer.

By Oliver Byrne. Illustrated by 11 large plates and 185 wood engravings. 8vo..............................$5.00

CONTENTS.—Grinding Cutting Tools on the Ordinary Grindstone; Sharpening Cutting Tools on the Oilstone; Setting Razors; Sharpening Cutting Tools with Artificial Grinders; Production of Plane Surfaces by Abrasion: Production of Cylindrical Surfaces by Abrasion; Production of Conical Surfaces by Abrasion; Production of Spherical Surfaces by Abrasion; Glass Cutting; Lapidary Work; Setting, Cutting, and Polishing Flat and Rounded Works; Cutting Faucets; Lapidary Apparatus for Amateurs; Gem and Glass Engraving; Seal and Gem Engraving; Cameo Cutting; Glass Engraving, Varnishing, and Lackering; General Remarks upon Abrasive Processes; Dictionary of Apparatus; Materials and Processes for Grinding and Polishing, commonly employed in the Mechanical and Useful Arts.

Byrne. The Practical Model Calculator:

For the Engineer, Mechanic, Manufacturer of Engine Work, Naval Architect, Miner, and Millwright. By Oliver Byrne. 1 vol. 8vo., nearly 600 pages $4.50

The principal objects of this work are: to establish model calculations to guide practical men and students; to illustrate every practical rule and principle by numerical calculations, systematically arranged; to give information and data indispensable to those for whom it is intended, thus surpassing in value any other book of its character; to economize the labor of the practical man, and to render his every-day calculations easy and comprehensive. It will be found to be one of the most complete and valuable practical books ever published.

Cabinet-maker's and Upholsterer's Companion.

Comprising the Rudiments and Principles of Cabinet-making and Upholstery, with Familiar Instructions, illustrated by Examples for attaining a proficiency in the Art of Drawing, as applicable to Cabinet-work; the processes of Veneering, Inlaying, and Buhl-work; the Art of Dyeing and Staining Wood, Bone, Tortoise Shell, etc. Directions for Lackering,

Japanning, and Varnishing; to make French Polish; to prepare the best Glues, Cements and Compositions, and a number of Receipts particularly useful for workmen generally. By J. Stokes. In one vol., 12mo. With Illustrations...$1.25

Calvert. On Improvements and Progress in Dyeing and Calico Printing since 1851.

Illustrated with Numerous Specimens of Printed and Dyed Fabrics. By Dr. F. Grace Calvert, F. R. S., F. C. S. A Lecture delivered before the Society of Arts. Revised and enlarged by the author. (*Nearly Ready.*)

Carey. The Works of Henry C. Carey:

CONTRACTION OR EXPANSION? REPUDIATION OR RESUMPTION? Letters to Hon. Hugh McCulloch. 8vo.....38

FINANCIAL CRISES, their Causes and Effects. 8vo. paper.....25

FRENCH AND AMERICAN TARIFFS: Compared in a Series of Letters addressed to Mons. M. Chevalier. 8vo. paper.....50

HARMONY OF INTERESTS: Agricultural, Manufacturing, and Commercial. 8vo., paper.....$1.00
Do. do. cloth..... 1.50

LETTERS TO THE PRESIDENT OF THE UNITED STATES. Paper.....75

MANUAL OF SOCIAL SCIENCE. Condensed from Carey's "Principles of Social Science." By Kate McKean. 1 vol., 12mo.....$2.25

The Text-Book of the Universities of Berlin (Prussia), Pennsylvania, and Michigan, and of the College of New Jersey, Princeton.

MISCELLANEOUS WORKS: comprising "Harmony of Interests," "Money," "Letters to the President," "French and American Tariffs," "Financial Crises," "The Way to Outdo England without Fighting Her," "Resources of the Union," "The Public Debt," "Contraction or Expansion?" etc., etc. 1 vol. 8vo., cloth.....$3.50

MONEY: A LECTURE before the N. Y. Geographical and Statistical Society. 8vo., paper.....25

PAST, PRESENT, AND FUTURE 8vo.....$2.50

PRINCIPLES OF SOCIAL SCIENCE. 3 volumes. 8vo., cloth.....$10.00

CONTENTS.—Volume I: Of Science and its Methods; Of Man, the Subject of Social Science; Of Increase in the Numbers of Mankind; Of the Occupation of the Earth; Of Value; Of Wealth; Of the Formation of Society;

Of Appropriation; Of Changes of Matter in Place; Of Mechanical and Chemical Changes in the Forms of Matter. Volume II: Of Vital Changes in the Form of Matter; Of the Instrument of Association. Volume III: Of Production and Consumption; Of Accumulation; Of Circulation; Of Distribution; Of Concentration and Centralization; Of Competition; Of Population; Of Food and Population; Of Colonization; Of the Malthusian Theory; Of Commerce; Of the Societary Organization; Of Social Science.

THE PUBLIC DEBT, LOCAL AND NATIONAL. How to provide for its discharge while lessening the burden of Taxation. Letter to David A. Wells, Esq., U. S. Revenue Commission. 8vo., paper .25

THE RESOURCES OF THE UNION. A Lecture read, Dec. 1865, before the American Geographical and Statistical Society, N. Y., and before the American Association for the Advancement of Social Science, Boston .25

THE SLAVE-TRADE, DOMESTIC AND FOREIGN: Why it Exists, and How it may be Extinguished. 12mo. cloth $1.50

THE WAY TO OUTDO ENGLAND WITHOUT FIGHTING HER. LETTERS TO THE HON. SCHUYLER COLFAX, Speaker of the House of Representatives United States, on "The Paper Question," "The Farmer's Question," "The Iron Question," "The Railroad Question," and the "Currency Question." 8vo., paper .75

Campin. A Practical Treatise on Mechanical Engineering:

Comprising Metallurgy, Moulding, Casting, Forging, Tools, Workshop Machinery, Mechanical Manipulation, Manufacture of Steam-engines, etc., etc. With an Appendix on the Analysis of Iron and Iron Ores. By Francis Campin, C. E. To which are added, Observations on the Construction of Steam Boilers and remarks upon Furnaces used for Smoke Prevention; with a Chapter on Explosions. By R. Armstrong, C. E., and John Bourne. Rules for Calculating the Change Wheels for Screws on a Turning Lathe, and for a Wheel-cutting Machine. By J. La Nicca. Management of Steel, including Forging, Hardening, Tempering, Annealing, Shrinking, and Expansion. And the Case-hardening of Iron. By G. Ede. 8vo. Illustrated with 29 plates and 100 wood engravings $6.00

CONTENTS.—Introduction—On Metallurgy; On Forging Iron; On Moulding and Casting; On Cutting Tools; On Workshop Machinery; On Manipulation; On the Physical Basis of the Steam-engine; On the Principles of Mechanical Construction; On the General Arrangement of the Steam-engine; On the General Principles of Steam Boilers; Preliminary considerations on the Applicability of various kinds of Steam-engines to various purposes; On the details of Steam-engines; On Pumps and Valves; On Steam Boilers; On Propellers; On various applications of Steam-power and Apparatus connected therewith; On Pumping Engines; On Rotative Engines; On Marine Engines; On Locomotive Engines; On Road Locomotives; On Steam Fire Engines; On Boilers generally, and a Radical Reform in those for Marine purposes suggested; Smoke Prevention and its fallacies; Remarks on Smoke-burning, by John Bourne; Explosions: an investigation into some of the causes producing them, and into the deterioration of Boilers generally; Rules for Calculating the Change Wheels for Screws on a Turning Lathe, and for a Wheel-cutting Machine; Explanation of the Methods of Calculating Screw Threads; The Management of Steel.

APPENDIX.—The Analysis of Iron and Iron Ores.

GLOSSARY.—INDEX.

Capron de Dole. Dussauce. Blues and Carmines of Indigo.

A Practical Treatise on the Fabrication of every Commercial Product derived from Indigo. By Felicien Capron de Dôle. Translated, with important additions, by Professor H. Dussauce. 12mo....................................$2.50

Clough. The Contractor's Manual and Builder's Price-Book:

Designed to elucidate the method of ascertaining, correctly, the Value and Quantity of every description of Work and Materials, used in the Art of Building, from their Prime Cost in any part of the United States, collected from extensive experience and observation in Building and Designing; to which are added a large variety of Tables, Memoranda, etc., indispensable to all engaged or concerned in erecting buildings of any kind. By A. B. Clough, Architect, 24mo., cloth...75

Colburn. The Locomotive Engine:

Including a Description of its Structure, Rules for Estimating its Capabilities, and Practical Observations on its Construction and Management. By Zerah Colburn. Illustrated. A new edition. 12mo........................$1.25

Daguerreotypist and Photographer's Companion.

12mo., cloth......................................$1.25

Distiller. (The Complete Practical).

By M. Lafayette Byrn, M. D. With Illust'ns. 12mo....$1.50

Duncan. Practical Surveyor's Guide.

By Andrew Duncan. Illustrated. 12mo., cloth......$1.25

Dussauce. Practical Treatise on the Fabrication of Matches, Gun Cotton, and Fulminating Powders.

By Professor H. Dussauce. 12mo. $3.00

CONTENTS.—*Phosphorus*—History of Phosphorus; Physical Properties; Chemical Properties; Natural State; Preparation of White Phosphorus; Amorphous Phosphorus, and Bonoxide of Lead. *Matches*—Preparation of

Wooden Matches; Matches inflammable by rubbing, without noise; Common Lucifer Matches; Matches without Phosphorus; Candle Matches; Matches with Amorphous Phosphorus; Matches and Rubbers without Phosphorus. *Gun Cotton*—Properties; Preparation; Paper Powder; use of Cotton and Paper Powders for Fulminating Primers, etc.; Preparation of Fulminating Primers, etc., etc.

Dussauce. A New and Complete Treatise on the Arts of Tanning, Currying, and Leather Dressing:

Comprising all the Discoveries and Improvements made in France, Great Britain, and the United States. Edited from Notes and Documents of Messrs. Sallerou, Grouvelle, Duval, Dessables, Labarraque, Payen, René, De Fontenelle, Malapeyre, etc., etc. By Prof. H. Dussauce, Chemist. Illustrated by 212 wood engravings. 8vo................$10.00

Dussauce. Treatise on the Coloring Matters Derived from Coal Tar:

Their Practical Application in Dyeing Cotton, Wool, and Silk; the Principles of the Art of Dyeing and of the Distillation of Coal Tar, with a Description of the most Important New Dyes now in use. By Professor H. Dussauce, Chemist. 12mo....................................$2.50

Dyer and Color-maker's Companion:

Containing upwards of two hundred Receipts for making Colors, on the most approved principles, for all the various styles and fabrics now in existence; with the Scouring Process, and plain Directions for Preparing, Washing-off, and Finishing the Goods. In one vol., 12mo.............$1.25

Easton. A Practical Treatise on Street or Horse-power Railways:

Their Location, Construction, and Management; with general Plans and Rules for their Organization and Operation; together with Examinations as to their Comparative Advantages over the Omnibus System, and Inquiries as to their Value for Investment; including Copies of Municipal Ordinances relating thereto. By Alexander Easton, C. E. Illustrated by 23 plates. 8vo. cloth..................$2.00

Engineer's Handy-Book:

Containing a Series of Useful Calculations for Engineers, Tool-makers, Millwrights, Draughtsmen, Foremen, and Mechanics generally. (*In Press.*)

Erni. Coal Oil and Petroleum:

Their Origin, History, Geology, and Chemistry; with a view of their importance in their bearing on National Industry.

By Dr. Henri Erni, Chief Chemist, Department of Agriculture. 12mo.................. ....$2.50

Erni. The Theoretical and Practical Chemistry of Fermentation:

Comprising the Chemistry of Wine, Beer, Distilling of Liquors; with the practical methods of their Chemical examination, preservation, and improvement—such as Gallizing of Wines. With an Appendix, containing well-tested Practical Rules and Receipts for the manufacture, etc., of all kinds of Alcoholic Liquors. By Henri Erni, Chief Chemist, Department of Agriculture. (*In Press.*)

Fairbairn. On Machinery of Transmission.

By William Fairbairn, C. E., LL.D., etc. Illustrated by numerous engravings. (*In Press.*)

CONTENTS.—On Wheels and Pullies; Wrapping Connectors; Toothed Wheels; Spur Gearing; Pitch of Wheels; Teeth of Wheels; Bevel Wheels; Skew Bevels; The Worm and Wheel; Strength of the Teeth of Wheels; ON THE STRENGTH AND PROPORTIONS OF SHAFTS; Material of which Shafting is Constructed; Transverse Strain; Torsion; Velocity of Shafts; On Journals; Friction; Lubrication; ON COUPLINGS FOR SHAFTS AND ENGAGING AND DISENGAGING GEAR; Couplings; Disengaging and Re-engaging Gear; Hangers; Plummer Blocks, etc., for carrying Shafting; Main Shafts.

Fairbairn. Useful Information for Engineers.

By William Fairbairn. (*In Press.*)

Kobell. Erni. Mineralogy Simplified:

A short method of Determining and Classifying Minerals, by means of simple Chemical Experiments in the Wet Way. Translated from the last German edition of F. Von Kobell, with additions, by Henri Erni, M. D., Chief Chemist, Depart-partment of Agriculture, author of "Coal Oil and Petroleum." In one volume, 12mo.......................$2.50

Fisher's Photogenic Manipulation.

16mo., cloth 62

French Dyer, (The):

Comprising the Art of Dyeing in Woollen, Silk, Cotton, etc., etc. By M. M. Riffault, Vernaud, De Fontenelle, Thillaye, and Mallepeyre. (*In Press.*)

Gilbart. A Practical Treatise on Banking.

By James William Gilbart, F. R. S. A new enlarged and improved edition. Edited by J. Smith Homans, editor of "Banker's Magazine." To which is added "Money," by H. C. Carey. 8vo..................................$3.50

Gregory's Mathematics for Practical Men;

Adapted to the Pursuits of Surveyors, Architects, Mechanics, and Civil Engineers. 8vo., plates, cloth..........$2.50

Gas and Ventilation.

A Practical Treatise on Gas and Ventilation. By E. E. Perkins. 12mo., cloth $1.25

Griswold. Railroad Engineer's Pocket Companion for the Field.

By W. Griswold. 12mo., tucks $1.25

Hartmann. The Practical Iron Manufacturer's Vade-mecum.

From the German of Dr. Carl Hartmann. Illustrated. (*In Press.*)

Hay. The Interior Decorator:

The Laws of Harmonious Coloring adapted to Interior Decorations: with a Practical Treatise on House-Painting. By D. R. Hay, House-Painter and Decorater. Illustrated by a Diagram of the Primary, Secondary, and Tertiary Colors. 12mo. (*In Press.*)

Inventor's Guide:

Patent Office and Patent Laws; or, a Guide to Inventors, and a Book of Reference for Judges, Lawyers, Magistrates, and others. By J. G. Moore. 12mo., cloth..........$1.25

Jervis. Railway Property.

A Treatise on the Construction and Management of Railways; designed to afford useful knowledge, in the popular style, to the holders of this class of property; as well as Railway Managers, Officers, and Agents. By John B. Jervis, late Chief Engineer of the Hudson River Railroad, Croton Aqueduct, etc. One volume, 12mo., cloth $2.00

CONTENTS.—Preface—Introduction. *Construction.*—Introductory: Land and Land Damages; Location of Line; Method of Business; Grading; Bridges and Culverts; Road Crossings; Ballasting Track; Cross Sleepers; Chairs and Spikes; Rails; Station Buildings; Locomotives, Coaches and Cars. *Operating.*—Introductory: Freight; Passengers; Engine Drivers Repairs to Track; Repairs of Machinery; Civil Engineer; Superintendent; Supplies of Material; Receipts; Disbursements; Statistics; Running Trains; Competition; Financial Management; General Remarks.

Johnson. A Report to the Navy Department of the United States on American Coals,

Applicable to Steam Navigation, and to other purposes. By Walter R. Johnson. With numerous illustrations. 607 pp. 8vo., half morocco $6.00

Johnson. The Coal Trade of British America:

With Researches on the Characters and Practical Values of American and Foreign Coals. By Walter R. Johnson, Civil and Mining Engineer and Chemist. 8vo. $2.00

☞ These important volumes of Prof. Johnson, now becoming scarse, contain the results of the experiments made for the Navy Department, upon which their Coal contracts are at present based.

Johnston. Instructions for the Analysis of Soils, Limestones, and Manures.

By J. F. W. Johnston. 12mo. 38

Keene. A Hand-book of Practical Gauging,

For the Use of Beginners: tc which is added a Chapter on Distillation, describing the process in operation at the Custom-House for ascertaining the strength of Wines. By James B. Keene, of H. M. Customs. (*In Press.*)

Kentish. A Treatise on a Box of Instruments,

And the Slide Rule; with the Theory of Trigonometry and Logarithms, including Practical Geometry, Surveying, Measuring of Timber, Cask and Malt Gauging, Heights and Distances. By Thomas Kentish. In one volume, 12mo...$1.25

Larkin. The Practical Brass and Iron Founder's Guide:

A Concise Treatise on Brass Founding, Moulding, the Metals and their Alloys, etc.: to which are added Recent Improvements in the Manufacture of Iron, Steel by the Bessemer Process, etc., etc. By James Larkin, late Conductor of the Brass Foundry Department in Reaney, Neafie & Co.'s Penn Works, Philadelphia. Fifth edition, revised, with Extensive Additions. In one volume, 12mo....................$2.25

Lieber. Assayer's Guide;

Or, Practical Directions to Assayers, Miners, and Smelters. By Oscar M. Lieber. 12mo., cloth..................$1.25

Love. The Art of Dyeing, Cleaning, Scouring, and Finishing,

On the Most Approved English and French Methods: being Practical Instructions in Dyeing Silks, Woollens, and Cottons, Feathers, Chips, Straw, etc.; Scouring and Cleaning Bed and Window Curtains, Carpets, Rugs, etc.; French and English Cleaning, any Color or Fabric of Silk, Satin, or Damask. By Thomas Love, a working Dyer and Scourer. In 1 vol., 12mo..$3.00

Lowig. Principles of Organic and Physiological Chemistry.

By Dr. Carl Löwig. Translated by Daniel Breed, M. D. 8vo., sheep...$3.50

Main and Brown. The Marine Steam-engine.

By Thomas J. Main, Professor of Mathematics, Royal Naval College, and Thomas Brown, Chief Engineer, R. N. Illustrated by engravings and wood-cuts. 8vo., cloth $5.00

☞ THE TEXT BOOK OF THE UNITED STATES NAVAL ACADEMY.

CONTENTS.—Introductory Chapter—The Boiler; The Engine; Getting up the Steam; Duties to Machinery when under Steam; Duties to Machinery during an Action or after an Accident; Duties to Engine, etc., on arriving in Harbor. Miscellaneous. Appendix.

Main and Brown. Questions on Subjects Connected with the Marine Steam-engine,

And Examination Papers; with hints for their Solution. By Thomas J. Main, Professor of Mathematics, Royal Naval College, and Thomas Brown, Chief Engineer, R. N. 12mo., cloth...$1.50

Main and Brown. The Indicator and Dynamometer,

With their Practical Applications to the Steam-engine By Thomas J. Main and Thomas Brown. With Illustrations...$1.50

Makins. A Manual of Metallurgy,

More particularly of the Precious Metals, including the Methods of Assaying them. Illustrated by upwards of 50 engravings. By George Hogarth Makins, M. R. C. S., F. C. S., one of the Assayers to the Bank of England; Assayer to the Anglo-Mexican Mints; and Lecturer upon Metallurgy at the Dental Hospital, London. In one vol., 12mo...$3.50

CONTENTS.—General Properties of the Metals; General View of the Combining Properties of the Metals; Combination of Metals with the Non-Metallic Elements; Of Metallic Salts; Of Heating Apparatus, Furnaces, etc.; Of Fuels Applicable to Metallurgic Operations; Metals of the First Class; Metals of the Second Class; The Principles of Electro-Metallurgy.

Marble Worker's Manual:

Containing Practical Information respecting Marbles in general, their Cutting, Working, and Polishing; Veneering, etc., etc. 12mo., cloth.............................$1.50

Molesworth. Pocket-book of Useful Formulæ and Memoranda for Civil and Mechanical Engineers.

By Guilford L. Molesworth, Member of the Institution of Civil Engineers, Chief Resident Engineer of the Ceylon Railway. From the Tenth London edition $2.00

CONTENTS.—*Civil Engineering*—Surveying, Levelling, Setting Out, etc.; Earthwork, Brickwork, Masonry, Arches, etc.; Beams, Girders, Bridges, etc.; Roofs, Floors, Columns, Walls, etc.; Railways, Roads, Canals, Rivers, Docks, etc.; Water-works, Sewers, Gas-works, Drainage, etc.; Warming, Ventilation, Light, Sound, Heat, etc.

Mechanical Engineering.—Gravity, Mechanical Centres and Powers; Mill-work, Teeth of Wheels, Shafting, Belting, etc.; Alloys, Solders, and Workshop Recipes; Steam Boilers, and Steam-engines; Water-wheels, Turbines, etc., and Windmills; Paddle and Screw Steamers; Miscellaneous Machinery.

Weights and Measures, English and Foreign; Logarithms of Numbers; Triangles, Trigonometry, and Tables of Sines, etc.; Properties of Ellipse, Parabola, Circle, etc.; Mensuration of Surfaces and Solids; Tables of Areas, and Circumferences of Circles; Weights and Properties of Materials; Squares, Cubes, Powers, Roots, and Reciprocals of Numbers; Engineering Memoranda and Tables; Supplement by J. T. Hurst, C. E., containing Additional Engineering Memoranda and Tables; Tables by Lewis Olrick, C. E.

Miles. A Plain Treatise on Horse-shoeing.

With illustrations. By William Miles, author of the "Horse's Foot"...$1.00

Morfit. A Treatise on Chemistry,

Applied to the Manufacture of Soap and Candles: being a Thorough Exposition in all their Minutiæ of the Principles and Practice of the Trade, based upon the most recent Discoveries in Science and Art. By Campbell Morfit, Professor of Analytical and Applied Chemistry in the University of Maryland. A new and improved edition. Illustrated with 260 engravings on wood. Complete in 1 volume, large 8vo...$20.00

Mortimer. The Pyrotechnist's Companion:

By G. W. Mortimer. Illustrated. 12mo., cloth......$1.25

Napier. Manual of Electro-Metallurgy:

Including the Application of the Art to Manufacturing Processes. By James Napier. From the second London edition, revised and enlarged. Illustrated by engravings. In one volume, 12mo..............................$1.50

Napier. Chemistry Applied to Dyeing.

By James Napier, F. C. S. Illustrated. 12mo $3.00

Nicholson. Bookbinding: A Manual of the Art of Bookbinding:

Containing full Instructions in the different Branches of Forwarding, Gilding, and Finishing. Also, the Art of Marbling Book-edges and Paper. By James B. Nicholson. Illustrated. 12mo., cloth $2.25

CONTENTS.—Sketch of the Progress of Bookbinding, Sheet-work, Forwarding the Edges, Marbling, Gilding the Edges, Covering, Half Binding, Blank Binding, Boarding, Cloth-work, Ornamental Art, Finishing, Taste and Design, Styles, Gilding, Illuminated Binding, Blind Tooling, Antique, Coloring, Marbling, Uniform Colors, Gold Marbling, Landscapes, etc.; Inlaid Ornaments, Harmony of Colors, Pasting Down, etc.; Stamp or Press-work, Restoring the Bindings of Old Books, Supplying imperfections in Old Books, Hints to Book Collectors, Technical Lessons.

Norris. A Hand-book for Locomotive Engineers and Machinists.

By Septimus Norris, C. E. New edition, illustrated, 12mo., cloth $2.00

Nystrom. On Technological Education and the Construction of Ships and Screw Propellers for Naval and Marine Engineers.

By John W. Nystrom, late Acting Chief Engineer U. S. N. Second edition, revised with additional matter. Illustrated by 7 engravings. 12mo. $2.50

CONTENTS.—On Technological Education; The knowledge of Steam Engineering behind the knowledge of Science; Failure of Steamers for a want of Applied Science; Fresh water Condensers, and combustion of Fuel; Knowledge of Steamship Performance; Expansion experiments made by the Navy Department; Natural effect of Steam or maximum work per unit of Heat; Natural effect of Steam-engines; Nystrom's Pocket-book; Reform wanted in Scientific Books; America has taken the lead in Popular Education; Technological Institutions wanted; The National Academy of Sciences; Object of Technological Institutions; Steam-engineering and Ship-building; Necessity of complete Drawings before the building of Steamers is commenced; America has taken the lead in the new Naval Tactics; The Naval Academy, at Annapolis, not proper for a School of Steam-engineering; Want of applied Science in our Workshops; Locomotive Engineering; Communication to the Secretary of the Navy on the Science of Ship-building; Ship-builders consider their Art a Craft; Ship-builders' jealousy; Ship-building developed to the condition of a Science; Memorandum; Chief Engineer Isherwood does not approve the Parabolic Construction of Ships; On the Parabolic Construction of Ships; Application of the Parabolic Construction of Ships; Recording Formulas; Recording Tables; The labor of calculating the Ship-building Tables; Mr. W. L. Hanscom, Naval Constructor, on the Parabolic Method; Mr. J. Vaughan Merrick on the Parabolic Construction; Resignation, by the Author, as Acting Chief Engineer in the Navy; Memorandum; The Science of Dynamics in a confused condition; Illustrations required in Dynamics; Mr. Isherwood declines having the subject of Dynamics cleared up; The subject of Dynamics submitted to the National Academy of Sciences; On the elements of Dynamics; *force*, *power*, and *work*, defined; *Work*, a trinity of Physical Elements; Discussion with Naval Engineers on the subject of Dynamics; Questions in Dynamics submitted to the Academy of Sciences; Vis-viva; Unit for Power; Unit for Work; Navy Departmen attempting to reorganize the Corps of Engineers; Washington Navy Yard; Engineers in the Navy Department; Captain Fox on Engineering and the Construction of Ships; Secrecy respecting Ships' Drawings; Steam Boiler Explosions; Review of Screw Propellers; To Construct a Plain Screw; Propeller with a Compound Expanding Pitch; Propeller as Constructed by Chief Engineer Isherwood; Propeller as Constructed from Mr. Isherwood's Drawings; Centripetal Propeller; Centripetal Propeller with Compound Expanding Pitch; The Office of the Coast Survey an example of what the Bureau of Steam-engineering should be; The Engineer-in-Chief of the Navy a Grand Admiral; Constructions ought not to be made in the Navy Department; The office of the Coast Survey and the Light-house Board naturally belong to the Navy.

O'Neill. Chemistry of Calico Printing, Dyeing, and Bleaching:

Including Silken, Woollen, and Mixed Goods; Practical and Theoretical. By Charles O'Neill. (*In Press.*)

O'Neill. A Dictionary of Calico Printing and Dyeing.

By Charles O'Neill. (*In Press.*)

Painter, Gilder, and Varnisher's Companion.

Containing Rules and Regulations in every thing relating to the Arts of Painting, Gilding, Varnishing, and Glass Staining; numerous useful and valuable Receipts; Tests for the detection of Adulterations in Oils, Colors, etc.; and a statement of the Diseases and Accidents to which Painters, Gilders and Varnishers are peculiarly liable, with the simplest and best methods of Prevention and Remedy; with directions for Graining, Marbling, Sign Writing and Gilding on Glass. Tenth edition. To which are added complete Instructions for Coach Painting and Varnishing. 12mo, cloth.....$1.50

Pallett. The Miller's, Millwright's, and Engineer's Guide.

By Henry Pallett. Illustrated. In 1 vol., 12mo.......$3.00

CONTENTS.—Explanation of Characters used; Definitions of Words used in this Work; United States Weights and Measures; Decimal Fractions; On the Selection of Mill-stones; On the Dressing of New Mill-stones—making their Faces Straight, and ready for putting in the Furrows; Furrows: the manner of Laying them out: their Draft, and cutting them in; Directions for laying off and cutting the Holes for the Balance Ryne and Driver; Directions for putting in the Balance Ryne and the Boxes for the Driver, and making them fast; Of Setting the Bed Stone, and fastening the Bush therein; Directions how to Bridge or Tram the Spindle; Instructions for Grinding off the Lumps of New Stones, Turning the Back of the Running Stone, Rounding the Eye and Balancing the Stone; Directions for Dressing and Sharpening Mill-stones when they become dull; Respecting the Irons of the Mill; Description of Plate 4, Showing the Principle upon which the Mill-stones work; How to Fit a New Back on a Stone that has been Running; Of the Elevator, Conveyor, and Hopper Boy; Of Bolting Reels and Cloths, with Directions for Bolting and Inspecting Flour; Directions for Cleaning Wheat; Instructions for Grinding Wheat; Directions for Grinding Wheat with Garlic amongst it, and for Dressing the Stones suitable thereto; Directions how to put the Stones in Order for Grinding Wheat that has Garlic amongst it; Directions for Grinding Middlings, and how to Prevent the Stones from Choking, so as to make the most of them; Reels for Bolting the Middlings; Instructions for a small Mill, Grinding different kinds of Grain; Of the Manner of Packing Flour; Table Showing the number of Pounds which constitute a Bushel, as established by Law in the States therein named; The Duty of the Miller; Pearl Barley or Pot Barley; The Art of Distillation; Of the Importance of Draughting and Planning Mills: Cogs: the best time for Seasoning and Cutting them; The Framing of Mill-work; Windmills; A Table of the Velocity of Wind; Instructions for Baking; Receipt for making Babbitt Metal, etc.; Cement; Solders; Table Showing the Product of a Bushel of Wheat of different Weights and Qualities, as ascertained from Experiments in Grinding Parcels; Of Saw-mills and their Management; The Circular Saw; Rules for Calculating the Speed the Stones and other pieces or parts of the Machinery run at: To find the Quantity, in Bushels, a Hopper will Contain; Table of Dry Measure; Spouts; the Necessity of making them Large; To lay off any required Angle: Of Masonry; of Artificer's Work; Bricklayer's Work; Bricks and Lathes—Dimensions; Timber Measure; Table—Diameters in inches of Saw Logs reduced to inch board measure; Of the Wedge; Of Pumps; The Screw; Table showing the power of Man or Horse as applied to Machinery; Measure of Solidity; Rules for calculating Liquids; A Table showing the Capacity of Cisterns, Wells, etc., in Ale Gallons and Hogsheads, in proportion to their Diameters and Depths; Steel—Of the various degrees of Heat required in the Manufacture of Steel; Composition for Welding Cast Steel; Directions for Making and Sharpening Mill Picks; A Composition for Tempering Cast Steel Mill Picks; Governors for Flouring Mills; The Governor or Regulator; The Pulley; Of the Velocity of Wheels, Pulleys, Drums, etc.; On Friction; Belting Friction; Of the Strength of different Bodies; Falling Bodies; Of the different Gearings for propelling Machinery; The Crown or Face Gearing; On matching Wheels to make the Cogs wear even; On Steam and the Steam-engine; Of Engines—their Management, etc.; Prevention of Incrustation in Steam Boilers; Double Engines; The Fly-wheel; Table of Circumferences and Areas of Circles, in Feet, suitable for Fly-wheels, etc.; To calculate the effects of a Lever and Weight upon the Safety-valve of a Steam Boiler, etc.; Of the Slide Valve; Boilers; Chimneys; Explosion of Boilers; On the Construction of Mill-dams; Rock Dam; Frame Dams; Brush or Log Dam; Gates; Description of Water-wheels; Of Non-elasticity and Fluidity in Impinging Bodies; Motion of Overshot Wheels; The Breast Wheel; Overshot or Breast Wheels; Table of the number of inches of water necessary to drive one run of Stones, with all the requisite Machinery for Grist and Saw-mills, under heads of water from four to thirty feet; Table containing the weight of columns of water, each one foot in length, and of various diameters; The Undershot Wheel; Tub Wheels; The Flutter Wheel; The Laws of Motion and Rest; Power of Gravity, Percussion, or Impulse, with the Reaction Attachment; Table of the velocities of the Combination Reaction Water-wheel per minute, from heads of from four to thirty feet; Tables to reckon the Price of Wheat from Thirty Cents to Two Dollars per Bushel.

Pradal, Malepeyre and Dussauce. A Complete Treatise on Perfumery:

Containing Notices of the Raw Material used in the Art, and the best Formulæ. According to the most approved methods followed in France, England, and the United States. By M. P. Pradal, Perfumer Chemist, and M. F. Malepeyre. Translated from the French, with extensive additions, by Professor H. Dussauce. 8vo. $7.50

CONTENTS.—Nature of the Trade of the Perfumer; Raw Material; Pomades; Almond Oils; Perfumed Oils, called Huile Antique; Powders Cosmetic Preparation for the Lips and Skin; Almond Pastes; Cosmetic Gloves Paints; Dentifrices; Volatile Oils; Aromatic Waters; Spirituous

Odors; Colors; Infusions; Tinctures; Spirits; Aromatic Alcohols; Fuming Pastils; Cloves; Sachets; Cosmetics; Cassolettes; Toilet Vinegars; Pharmaceutical Preparations made by the Perfumer; Toilet Soaps; Various Substances and Processes belonging to the Perfumer's Trade.

Proteaux. Practical Guide for the Manufacture of Paper and Boards.

By A. Proteaux, Civil Engineer, Graduate of the School of Arts and Manufactures, and Director of Thiers' Paper-mill, Puy-de-Dôme. With additions, by L. S. Le Normand. Translated from the French with Notes, by Horatio Paine, A. B., M. D. To which is added a Chapter on the Manufacture of Paper from Wood in the United States, by Henry T. Brown, of the "American Artisan." Illustrated by six plates, containing Drawings of Raw Materials, Machinery, Plans of Paper-mills, etc., etc. 8vo. $5.00

CONTENTS.—Chapt. I. *A Glance at the History of Paper-making.* Chapt. II. *Raw Materials*—Rags. Chapt. III. *Manufacture*—Sorting and Cutting; Dusting; Washing and Boiling; Reduction to Half-stuff; Drainage; Bleaching; Composition of the Pulp; Refining or Beating; Sizing; Coloring Matters; The Work of the Paper-machine; Finishing. Chapt. IV. *Manufacture of Paper from the Vat, or by Hand*—Manufacture of Paper by hand; Sizing; Finishing; Manufacture of Bank-note Paper, and Water-mark Paper in General; Comparison between Machine and Hand-made Papers; Classification of Paper. Chapt. V. *Further Remarks on Sizing*—Of the Sizing-room; Method of Extracting Galatine; Operation of Sizing; Drying after Sizing: the Dutch method preferable to the French; Some important Observations upon Sizing; Appendix upon Sizing; Theories of Sizing; Sizing in the Pulp; M. Canson's method of Sizing in the Pulp; Comparison of the Two methods. Chapt. VI. *Different Substances Suitable for Making Paper*—Straw Paper; Wood Paper. Chapt. VII. *Chemical Analysis of Materials employed in Paper-making*—The Waters; Alkalimetrical Test; Examination of Limes; Chlorometric Tests; Examination of Manganese; Chlorometric Degrees of Samples of Manganese; Antichlorine; Alums; Kaolin; Starch; Coloring Materials; Fuel; Examination of Papers; Materials of a Laboratory. Chapt. VIII. *Working Stock of a Paper-mill*—Motive Power; Rag Cutters; Dusters; Washing Apparatus; Boiling Apparatus; Washing and Beating-engines; Apparatus for Bleaching and Draining the Pulp; Paper-machines; Finishing-machines; General Working Stock of a Paper-mill; General Remarks upon the Establishment of a Paper-mill; General Remarks in reference to Building; General Considerations. Chapt. IX. *The Manufacture of Paper from Wood in the United States.* Chapt. X. *Manufacture of Boards.* Chapt. XI. *Manufacture of Paper in China and Japan.*
DESCRIPTION OF THE PLATES.

Regnault. Elements of Chemistry.

By M. V. Regnault. Translated from the French, by T. Forrest Betton, M. D., and edited, with notes, by James C. Booth, Melter and Refiner U. S. Mint, and Wm. L. Faber, Metallurgist and Mining Engineer. Illustrated by nearly 700 wood engravings. Comprising nearly 1,500 pages. In two volumes, 8vo., cloth. $10.00

AMONG THE CONTENTS ARE—Volume I.: French and English Weights, etc. Introduction—Crystallography; Chemical Nomenclature; Metalloids; Oxygen; Hydrogen; Selenium; Tellurium; Chlorine; Bromine; Iodine; Fluorine; Phosphorus; Arsenic; Boren; Silicum; Carbon; On the Equivalents of Metalloids. *Metals*—Geology; Physical Properties of the Metals; Chemical

Properties of the Metals. On Salts. I. *Alkaline Metals*—Potassium; Sodium; Lithium; Ammonia. II. *Alkalino-Earthy Metals*—Barium; Strontium; Calcium; Magnesium. III. *Earthy Metals*—Aluminum; Glucinum; Zirconium; Thorinum; Yttrium; Erbium; Terbium; Cerium; Lanthanum; Didymium. *Chemical Arts Dependent on the Preceding Bodies*—Gunpowder; Lime and Mortar; Glass; Kinds of Glass; Imperfections and Alterations of Glass; Pottery, the Paste of which becomes Compact by Burning; Pottery, the Paste of which remains Porous after Burning; Ornaments and Painting; Chemical Analysis of Earthenware.

Volume II.: Preparation of Ores, Manganese, Iron; Reduction in the Blast Furnace; Chromium; Cobalt; Nickel; Zinc; Cadmium; Tin; Titanium; Columbium; Niobium; Pelopium; Ilmenium; Lead, Metallurgy of; Bismuth, Metallurgy of; Antimony, Metallurgy of; Uranium; Tungsten; Molybdenum; Vanadium; Copper, Metallurgy of; Mercury, Metallurgy of; Silver, Metallurgy of; Gold, Metallurgy of; Platinum; Osmium; Iridium; Palladium; Rhodium; Ruthenium. IV. *Organic Chemistry*—Introduction—Ultimate Analysis of Organic Substances; Construction of a Formula; Analysis of Gases; Essential Proximate Principles of Plants; Acids Existing in Plants; Organic Alkaloids; Neutral Substances in Plants; Nitrils; Essential Oils; Products of Dry Distillation; Fats; Organic Coloring Matters; Action of Plants on the Atmosphere; Animal Chemistry; Secretions; Excretions; Technical Organic Chemistry; Manufacture of Bread; Brewing; Cider and Perry; Wine-making; Beet Sugar; Cane Sugar; Sugar-refining; Manufacture of Bone Black; Soap-boiling; Principles of Dyeing; Mordants; Calico-printing; Tanning; Charring Wood and Coal; Manufacture of Illuminating Gas.

Sellers. The Color Mixer:

Containing nearly Four Hundred Receipts for Colors, Pastes, Acids, Pulps, Blue Vats, Liquors, etc., etc., for Cotton and Woollen Goods: including the celebrated Barrow Delaine Colors. By John Sellers, an experienced practical workman. In one volume, 12mo........................$2.50

Shunk. A Practical Treatise on Railway Curves and Location, for Young Engineers.

By Wm. F. Shunk, Civil Engineer. 12mo. $1.50

Smith. The Dyer's Instructor:

Comprising Practical Instructions in the Art of Dyeing Silk, Cotton, Wool and Worsted, and Woollen Goods: containing nearly 800 Receipts. To which is added a Treatise on the Art of Padding; and the Printing of Silk Warps, Skeins, and Handkerchiefs, and the various Mordants and Colors for the different styles of such work. By David Smith, Pattern Dyer. 12mo., cloth..............................$3.00

☞ This is by far the most valuable book of PRACTICAL RECEIPTS FOR DYERS ever published in this country—has been eminently popular, and the third edition is just now ready for delivery.

Strength and other Properties of Metals.

Reports of Experiments on the Strength and other Properties of Metals for Cannon. With a Description of the Machines for testing Metals, and of the Classification of

Cannon in service. By Officers of the Ordnance Department U. S. Army. By authority of the Secretary of War. Illustrated by 25 large steel plates. In 1 vol., quarto.....$10.00

☞ The best treatise on cast-iron extant.

Tables Showing the Weight of Round, Square, and Flat Bar Iron, Steel, etc.,

By Measurement. Cloth 63

Taylor. Statistics of Coal:

Including Mineral Bituminous Substances employed in Arts and Manufactures; with their Geographical, Geological, and Commercial Distribution and amount of Production and Consumption on the American Continent. With Incidental Statistics of the Iron Manufacture. By R. C. Taylor. Second edition, revised by S. S. Haldeman. Illustrated by five Maps and many Wood engravings. 8vo. cloth.............$6.00

Templeton. The Practical Examinator on Steam and the Steam-engine:

With Instructive References relative thereto, arranged for the use of Engineers, Students, and others. By Wm. Templeton, Engineer. 12mo...........................$1.25

This work was originally written for the author's private use. He was prevailed upon by various Engineers, who had seen the notes, to consent to its publication, from their eager expression of belief that it would be equally useful to them as it had been to himself.

Turnbull. The Electro-Magnetic Telegraph:

With an Historical Account of its Rise, Progress, and Present Condition. Also, Practical Suggestions in regard to Insulation and Protection from the Effects of Lightning. Together with an Appendix, containing several important Telegraphic Devices and Laws. By Lawrence Turnbull, M. D., Lecturer on Technical Chemistry at the Franklin Institute. Second edition. Revised and improved. Illustrated by numerous engravings. 8vo......................$2.50

Turner's (The) Companion:

Containing Instruction in Concentric, Elliptic, and Eccentric Turning; also, various Steel Plates of Chucks, Tools, and Instruments; and Directions for Using the Eccentric Cutter, Drill, Vertical Cutter and Rest; with Patterns and Instructions for working them. 12mo., cloth $1.50

Ulrich. Dussauce. A Complete Treatise on the Art of Dyeing Cotton and Wool,

As practiced in Paris, Rouen, Mulhausen, and Germany. From the French of M. Louis Ulrich, a Practical Dyer in the principal Manufactories of Paris, Rouen, Mulhausen, etc., etc.; to which are added the most important Receipts for Dyeing Wool, as practiced in the Manufacture Impériale des Gobelins, Paris. By Prof. H. Dussauce. 12mo...$3.00

Watson. Modern Practice of American Machinists and Engineers:

Including the Construction, Application and Use of Drills, Lathe Tools, Cutters for Boring Cylinders and Hollow Ware generally, with the most economical speed for the same; the results verified by Actual Practice at the Lathe, the Vice, and on the Floor. Together with Workshop Management, Economy of Manufactures, the Steam-engine, Boilers, Gears, Belting, etc., etc. By Egbert P. Watson, late editor of the "Scientific American." Illustrated with Eighty-six Engravings. In 1 volume, 12mo..........$2.50

CONTENTS.

Part 1.—The Drill and its Office.
Part 2.—Lathe Work.
Part 3.—Miscellaneous Tools and Processes.
Part 4.—Steam and Steam-engine.
Part 5.—Gears, Belting, and Miscellaneous Practical Information.

Watson. The Theory and Practice of the Art of Weaving by Hand and Power:

With Calculations and Tables for the use of those connected with the Trade. By John Watson, Manufacturer and Practical Machine Maker. Illustrated by large drawings of the best Power-Looms. 8vo..........................$5.00

Weatherly. Treatise on the Art of Boiling Sugar, Crystallizing, Lozenge-making, Comfits, Gum Goods,

And other processes for Confectionery, etc., in which are explained, in an easy and familiar manner, the various methods of manufacturing every description of raw and refined Sugar goods, as sold by Confectioners and others. 12mo..$2.00

Williams. On Heat and Steam:

Embracing New Views of Vaporization, Condensation, and Expansion. By Charles Wye Williams, author of a Treatise on the Cumbustion of Coal Chemically and Practically Considered. With Illustrations. 8vo..............$3.50

Bullock. The American Cottage Builder:

A Series of Designs, Plans, and Specifications, from $200 to $20,000, for Homes for the People; together with Warming, Ventilation, Drainage, Painting, and Landscape Gardening. By John Bullock, Architect, Civil Engineer, Mechanician, and Editor of "The Rudiments of Architecture and Building," etc., etc. Illustrated by 75 engravings. In one vol., 8vo. $3.50

Contents.—Chap. I.—*Generally*—Where to Build a Cottage; Bird Cottage; Objects Desired. II.—*The Various Parts*—Walls; Cob Walls; Mud Walls; Silverlocks' Hollow Walls; Dearnes' Hollow Brick Wall; Loudon's Hollow Brick Walls; Flint Built Walls; Walls of Framed Timber, Rubble, and Plaster; Walls of Hollow Bricks; Covering for External Walls; Inside Work; Floors; Lime-ash Floors; Concrete Floors; Plaster Floor; Asphalte; Floor of Hollow Pots; Tile Floor; Floors of Arched Brickwork in Mortar; Fire-proof Floor; Tile-trimmer; Girder Floor; Stairs formed of Tile; Roofs; Thatch; Tile for Roofing; Slate Roof; Cast-iron Roofing; Eaves-gutter; Chimney-shaft; Ventilation and Warming. III.—*Terra del Fuego Cottage.* IV.—*Prairie Cottage*—Cottage of Unburnt Brick—Plan; Cross Section; Side View; Manner of Laying the Brick and the Foundation; Chimney-cap, Perspective, and Top Views. V.—*The Farm Cottage*—Ground Floor; Attic Floor. VI.—*The Village Cottage.* VII.—*Italian Cottage.* VIII. *Thatched Cottage.* IX.—*Cottage of the Society for Improving the Condition of the Poor.* X.—*Warming and Ventilation*—Ventilation. XI.—*Model Cottage*—Hollow Brick Work. XII.—*Rural Cottage*—Basement Plan; Plan of the First Floor; Plan of the Second Floor. XIII.—*Octagon Cottage*—Plan of Basement; Plan of Principal Story. XIV.—*Drainage.* XV.—*Rural Homes*—Circumstances to be taken into consideration in the Choice of a Situation; Elevation; The character of the Surface on which to Build; Aspect; Soil and Subsoil; Water; Villa; Rural Home, No. 1; Views of a Suburban Residence in the English style; Rural Home, No. 2; Rural Home, No. 3; Rural Home, No. 4. XVI.—*Paint and Color.* XVII.—*Suburban Residences*—Gothic Suburban Cottage of C. Prescott, Esq., Troy, N. Y.; Basement; First Floor; Attic; Second Floor; Suburban Octagonal Cottage. XVIII.—*Landscape Gardening*—First steps in Forming a Landscape Garden; The Roads and Paths; Trees, Shrubs, and Planting; Hills and Mounds; Valleys and Low Grounds; Rock-work; Of Water, and its Appropriation or Adoption; Fountains; General Observations; Formal Gardening; Pleasure Grounds and Flower Gardens; The Flower Garden; The Greenhouse; The Conservatory. XIX.—*Cost*—The Terra del Fuegan Cottage; The Prairie Cottage; The Village Cottage; The Italian Cottage; The Thatched Cottage; The Cottage of the Society for Improving the Condition of the Poor; Prince Albert's Model Cottage; The Rural Cottage; Mr. Fowler's Octagonal Cottage; Rural Home, No. 1; Rural Home, No. 2; Rural Home, No. 3; The Suburban Residence; The Octagonal Suburban Residence designed by Wilcox; The Byzantine Cottage; The Gothic Suburban Residence designed by Mr. Davis. XX.—*Two Residences*—The Byzantine Cottage; Ground Plan; Plan of Second Story; The Gothic Suburban Residence of W. H. C. Waddell, Esq., N. Y.; First Floor; Second Floor. XXI.—*Artist's and Artisan's Calling.*

Smeaton. Builder's Pocket Companion:

Containing the Elements of Building, Surveying, and Architecture; with Practical Rules and Instructions connected with the subject. By A. C. Smeaton, Civil Engineer, etc. In one volume, 12mo $1.25

Contents.—The Builder, Carpenter, Joiner, Mason, Plasterer, Plumber, Painter, Smith, Practical Geometry, Surveyor, Cohesive Strength of Bodies, Architect.

www.ingramcontent.com/pod-product-compliance
Lightning Source LLC
LaVergne TN
LVHW020110110826
845151LV00001B/122

* 9 7 8 1 4 2 5 5 4 4 1 5 7 *